Longman

Get on Board

with the #1 Publisher in Developmental Reading.

New from

Longman

Developmental

Reading—

Innovative

resources

for you and

your students.

Reading Skills
(Grades 6-9)

Joining A Community of Readers, 2/e

Roberta Alexander
Jan Lombardi, *both of San Diego City College*
©2002 • 560 pages • Paper • ISBN 0-321-05099-1

Joining a Community of Readers offers a thematic approach to basic reading skills. Multiple readings on adult-oriented themes—popular culture, our changing families, work and the community—give students more exposure to a topic. The text maintains a constant focus on key skills while providing ample practice through pre-reading, active reading, and post-reading activities.

NEW TO THIS EDITION

◎ **Mastery Tests** at the end of each chapter give students additional readings and practice.

◎ **Chapter 2: Working with Words** helps students master strategies and skills for improving vocabulary. In addition, vocabulary practice is featured throughout the book.

◎ **Additional Readings and Exercises** at the end of the text provide further options.

◎ **Visit the Web** at the end of each chapter encourages students to continue reading, to research the themes covered in the chapter, and to visit the book's Website for more practice.

◎ **Putting it Together** charts in each chapter graphically summarize the essential reading skills.

CONTENTS

BOOK-SPECIFIC SUPPLEMENTS

Annotated Instructor's Edition
ISBN 0-321-05100-9

Instructor's Manual
ISBN 0-321-05101-7

Test Bank
ISBN 0-321-05102-5

Companion Website
www.ablongman.com/alexander

Also Available by Alexander/Lombardi
A Community of Readers, 2/e
©2000 • 528 pages • Paper • ISBN 0-321-04594-7
For the more advanced reading skills course (grades 9-12).

Essential Reading Skills

Kathleen T. McWhorter, *Niagara County Community College*

©2002 • 432 pages • Paper • ISBN 0-321-08965-0

Essential Reading Skills is a 4-color text designed to improve students' reading and thinking skills through concise skill instruction, extensive guided practice, skill application, assessment, and feedback. Intended for low-level reading courses (8th-grade level and below), particularly courses that are designed to help students prepare for an exit exam.

FEATURES

◎ **Emphasis on Essential Skills.** The text contains only the most important reading skills for college success.

◎ **Four-Color, Visually Appealing Design.** To promote visual learning, the text is designed in four-color and contains numerous photographs, graphics, charts, and diagrams.

◎ **Many Practice Exercises, Review Tests and Mastery Tests.** Practice tests provide students with measurable evidence that they are learning and improving their skills.

◎ **Additional Readings.** 10 additional readings at the end of the text provide instructors with maximum flexibility in creating assignments.

CONTENTS

BOOK-SPECIFIC SUPPLEMENTS

Annotated Instructor's Edition
ISBN 0-321-08962-6

Instructor's Manual
ISBN 0-321-08964-2

Test Bank
ISBN 0-321-08963-4

PowerPoint Presentations
available on the Companion Website

Companion Website
www.ablongman.com/mcwhorter

Other Reading Texts Available by Kathleen T. McWhorter

Guide to College Reading, 5/e
©2000 • 535 pages • Paper • ISBN 0-321-03793-6
For the first reading skills course.

Efficient and Flexible Reading, 6/e *(see page 6)*

Reading Across the Disciplines: College Reading and Beyond *(see page 7)*

Academic Reading, 4/e
©2001 • 544 pages • Paper • ISBN 0-321-05111-4
For the advanced reading skills course.

The Main Idea, 3/e

Myrna Bigman Skidell
Sidney Graves Becker, *both of Nassau Community College*
©2002 • 480 pages • Paper • ISBN 0-205-33981-6

Based on an interactive reading model, this 7th-9th grade level reading text emphasizes reading to learn. Students develop an increasingly complex understanding of the reading process through the application of a series of incremental strategies and "game plans." Readings are of varied length within the chapters, and a casebook of longer readings (all based on the theme of intergenerational relationships) is included at the end of the text.

NEW TO THIS EDITION

◎ A section on **Written Patterns of Organization** explains how writers organize information.
◎ A section on **Study Patterns of Organization** helps students streamline the organization of information for study purposes.
◎ Material on **Reading the Web** (Chapter 10) offers strategies for using Internet resources.
◎ **Reading Selections** sample a wide variety of disciplines.

CONTENTS

BOOK-SPECIFIC SUPPLEMENTS

Instructor's Manual
ISBN 0-321-09482-4

Breaking Through: College Reading, 6/e

Brenda D. Smith, *Emerita, Georgia State University*

©2002 • 544 pages • Paper • ISBN 0-321-05103-3

Breaking Through, 6/e provides instruction and practice on the reading and study skills necessary for successful independent college learning. The use of college textbook materials offers a realistic and immediate application of those skills.

NEW TO THIS EDITION

- ◎ **Four-color design!**
- ◎ **Everyday Reading Skills** gives tips and strategies for daily reading tasks: how to do research on the Internet and how to read newspapers, magazines, advertisements, reference materials, fiction and nonfiction, and workplace mail.
- ◎ **Collaborative Problem Solving** questions offer four different questions at the end of each chapter for students to brainstorm ideas, think critically, reflect on chapter instruction, and present responses to the class.
- ◎ **Explore the Net** exercises with each longer reading selection encourage Web research on topics related to the reading.
- ◎ **Reader's Tips** boxes condense advice for students into practical hints for quick reference. Many focus on effective techniques for reading in different disciplines.
- ◎ **15 new longer textbook selections** offer practice with comprehension exercises on actual textbook material.

CONTENTS

BOOK-SPECIFIC SUPPLEMENTS

Annotated Instructor's Edition
ISBN 0-321-05104-1

Instructor's Manual
ISBN 0-321-05105-X

Test Bank
ISBN 0-321-05106-8

Assessment Test Packet
ISBN 0-321-08178-1

Companion Website
www.ablongman.com/smith

Also Available by Brenda D. Smith

Bridging the Gap, 6/e

©2000 • 528 pages • Paper • ISBN 0-321-04590-4
For the mid-level reading skills course with an emphasis on textbook learning (grades 9-12).

The Lifelong Reader (with Laura Courtney Headley)

©2001 • 512 pages • Paper • ISBN 0-321-04781-8
For the mid-level reading skills course with an emphasis on reading across the curriculum (grades 9-12).

The Reader's Handbook: Reading Strategies for College and Everyday Life

©2001 • 448 pages • Comb • ISBN 0-321-04758-3
The first comprehensive handbook for readers.

Reading Skills
(Grades 9-12)

Efficient and Flexible Reading, 6/e

Kathleen T. McWhorter, *Niagara County Community College*

©2002 • 656 pages • Paper • ISBN 0-321-05107-6

Emphasizing reading flexibility, *Efficient and Flexible Reading* teaches students how to vary their approach to written texts based on the nature of the material and their purpose for reading.

NEW TO THIS EDITION

◎ **4-color Insert "Reading in the 21st Century"** demonstrates the importance of reading in the electronic age, provides an introduction to online literacy, and discusses new reading and thinking strategies necessary for reading electronic text.

◎ **Chapter 12, "Evaluating Internet Sources"** guides students in selecting reliable, trustworthy sources of information. Students learn how to evaluate a Website's purpose, content, accuracy, and structure.

◎ **Additional Vocabulary Coverage:** "Checking Your Vocabulary" exercises at the end of each reading selection emphasize importance of vocabulary and integrate vocabulary instruction throughout the text.

CONTENTS

PART 1. DEVELOPING A BASIS FOR READING AND LEARNING
1. Developing Your Efficiency and Flexibility
2. Active Reading and Learning
3. Strengthening Your Word Power

PART 2. IMPROVING YOUR COMPREHENSION
4. Main Ideas and Paragraph Structure
5. Patterns: Relationships Among Ideas
6. Reading Essays and Articles

PART 3. READING AND LEARNING FROM COLLEGE TEXTS
7. Graphic, Visual, and Electronic Literacy
8. Learning and Retention Strategies
9. Techniques for Learning Textbook Material

PART 4. READING CRITICALLY
10. Critical Analysis
11. Evaluating Arguments and Persuasive Writing
12. Evaluating Internet Sources

PART 5. INCREASING YOUR RATE AND FLEXIBILITY
13. Skimming and Scanning
14. Techniques for Reading Faster

PART 6. MULTIPLE CHOICE QUESTIONS FOR SELECTIONS EVEN-NUMBERED READING

APPENDIX
A. Words-Per-Minute Conversion Chart
B. Reading Progress Graph

BOOK-SPECIFIC SUPPLEMENTS

Annotated Instructor's Edition
ISBN 0-321-05108-4

Instructor's Manual
ISBN 0-321-05109-2

Test Bank
ISBN 0-321-05110-6

Companion Website:
www.ablongman.com/mcwhorter

PowerPoint Presentations
available on Companion Website

Other Reading Texts Available by Kathleen T. McWhorter

Guide to College Reading, 5/e

©2000 • 535 pages • Paper • ISBN 0-321-03793-6   *For the first reading skills course.*

Reading Across the Disciplines: College Reading and Beyond *(See page 7)*

Academic Reading, 4/e

©2001 • 544 pages • Paper • ISBN 0-321-05111-4
For the advanced reading skills course with an emphasis on reading across the disciplines.

Reading Across the Disciplines:
College Reading and Beyond

Kathleen T. McWhorter, *Niagara County Community College*

©2002 • 528 pp • Paper • ISBN 0-321-08969-3

This engaging new four-color reader offers brief skill instruction and extensive guided practice through 50 high-interest readings from across the college curriculum. By tying college texts to periodicals, popular magazines, newspapers, and Internet sources, *Reading Across the Disciplines* demonstrates the relevance of the academic disciplines to students' daily lives.

FEATURES

◎ **Part One, "A Handbook for Reading and Thinking in College,"** offers a brief handbook of reading skills, introducing students to essential vocabulary, comprehension, critical reading, and reading rate skills.

◎ **Part Two, "Readings From Academic Disciplines,"** offers readings in 12 disciplines, from the social sciences to computer-related fields. Within each discipline, the readings are arranged from least to most difficult, providing students with the opportunity to strengthen skills, experience success, and build positive attitudes toward reading.

◎ **Part Three, "Textbook Chapter Readings,"** contains two complete textbook chapters—Psychology and Allied Health—helping students practice their skills on longer pieces of writing.

CONTENTS

BOOK-SPECIFIC SUPPLEMENTS

Annotated Instructor's Edition
ISBN 0-321-08968-5

Instructor's Manual
ISBN 0-321-08967-7

Test Bank
ISBN 0-321-08966-9

Companion Website
www.ablongman.com/mcwhorter

PowerPoint Presentations
available on Companion Website

Other Reading Texts Available by Kathleen T. McWhorter

Essential Reading Skills *(see page 3)*

Guide to College Reading, 5/e

©2000 • 535 pages • Paper • ISBN 0-321-03793-6
For the first reading skills course.

Efficient and Flexible Reading, 6/e *(see page 6)*

Academic Reading, 4/e

©2001 • 544 pages • Paper • ISBN 0-321-05111-4
For the advanced reading skills course with an emphasis on reading across the disciplines.

Longman

New! The Longman Literature for College Reader Series

Longman is pleased to announce the publication of a new series of literature titles designed for developing college readers. High on content and pedagogy but low on price, these texts are designed specially for the needs of college reading students and instructors.

American 24-Karat Gold: 24 Classic American Short Stories

Yvonne Collioud Sisko, *Middlesex County College*

©2002 • 480 pages • Paper • ISBN 0-321-08330-X

American 24-Karat Gold is a unique collection of American short stories chosen for the developmental reader. The text includes classic American writers (Mark Twain, O. Henry, Kate Chopin) along with diverse modern writers (Maxine Hong Kingston, Roberta Fernandez, Alice Walker).

FEATURES

◎ **Sample Lesson** uses Kate Chopin's "Ripe Figs" to introduce reading skills, note-taking skills, and commonly used literary terms.

◎ **Pre-Reading Vocabulary Exercises** help students to define and learn words necessary for understanding the story.

◎ **Pre-Reading Questions** set up purpose of each story and make it more accessible to the reader.

◎ **Biographical Headnotes** provide context.

◎ **Journal Entry Worksheet** after each story encourages students to participate in the story by developing an MLA Works Cited entry, separating main from supporting characters, identifying setting, sequencing and summarizing events, identifying conflicts, and more.

◎ **Comprehension Quizzes** (3 per story) test students' understanding through multiple-choice, short answer, and essay questions.

◎ **Writing Prompts** for further writing assign both personal and research writing.

CONTENTS

BOOK-SPECIFIC SUPPLEMENTS

Instructor's Manual
ISBN 0-321-08331-8

A Brief Guide to the Novel

Susan Naomi Bernstein, *University of Houston-Downtown*

©2002 • 224 pages • Paper • ISBN 0-321-08165-X

A *Brief Guide to the Novel* guides developmental reading students step-by-step through the novel and nonfiction narratives. Part 1 includes eight brief chapters introducing key concepts, such as character, plot, setting, and cultural contexts. Part 2 includes ten discussion guides for novels and nonfiction narratives commonly taught in developmental reading and writing courses such Steinbeck's *The Pearl* and McBride's *The Color of Water*.

FEATURES

◎ **Making Connections** ask students to tie chapter concepts to the novel they are reading.

◎ **Glossary of Key Terms** helps students learn literary terminology.

◎ **Annotated Bibliography** provides additional information on all works discussed in Part 1.

◎ **Discussion Guides** in Part 2 include: about the book, an author biography, a bibliography of other works, useful Websites, study questions, and writing prompts for each novel discussed.

◎ **A Companion Website** written by the author features links, study questions, biographies, and more.

CONTENTS

BOOK-SPECIFIC SUPPLEMENTS

Instructor's Manual
ISBN 0-321-08164-1

Companion Website
www.ablongman.com/bernstein

Vocabulary

The Interactive Vocabulary Series

Active Vocabulary

Amy Olsen
Patti C. Biley, *both of Imperial Valley College*
©2002 • 208 pages • Paper • ISBN 0-321-05498-9

Academic Vocabulary

Amy Olsen, *Imperial Valley College*
©2002 • 208 pages • Paper • ISBN 0-321-05500-4

A*ctive Vocabulary* and *Academic Vocabulary* are supplementary vocabulary worktexts designed to accompany reading texts at the middle and high reading levels. The readings in *Active Vocabulary* cover both general and academic words; the readings in *Academic Vocabulary* cover a variety of academic subjects to prepare students for future college study.

In each text, chapters and exercises are "scaffolded" so that content is reinforced progressively as students move through the book. Exercises in different formats appeal to different learning styles. Self-tests and interactive exercises in each chapter offer multiple exposures for each vocabulary word.

FEATURES

◎ **Full Four-Color Visual Design.** Visual clues linked with words facilitate vocabulary acquisition and expansion.
◎ **Interactive Exercises.** Each chapter's exercises give students an opportunity to play with words and put them into personal contexts to facilitate learning.
◎ **Word Parts.** Each text features four complete chapters on prefixes, roots, and suffixes.
◎ **Flashcards.** Flashcards are located at the end of each book.
◎ **Active Vocabulary and Academic Vocabulary CD-ROMs** with exercises and audio pronunciation available free with each text.
◎ **Affordable.**

BOOK-SPECIFIC SUPPLEMENTS

Active Vocabulary Instructor's Manual & Test Bank ISBN 0-321-05499-7

Active Vocabulary CD-ROM
ISBN 0-321-08841-7

Companion Website
http://www.ablongman.com/vocabulary

Academic Vocabulary Instructor's Manual & Test Bank ISBN 0-321-05501-2

Academic Vocabulary CD-ROM
ISBN 0-321-08842-5

Companion Website
http://www.ablongman.com/vocabulary

Also available by Bemis, Biley, and Olsen:
Interactive Vocabulary: General Words

©2001 • 208 pages • Paper • ISBN 0-321-05496-2
For students reading below the 8th grade level.

Vocabulary Simplified: Strategies for Developing Your College Vocabulary

Kathleen T. McWhorter, *Niagara County Community College*

©2002 • 128 pages • Paper • ISBN 0-321-08726-7

This inexpensive, brief vocabulary building worktext contains concise instruction and extensive practice exercises.

FEATURES

◎ **High-Utility Word Lists** arranged by academic discipline expand students' vocabulary with ample practice exercises.

◎ **Integrating and Applying What You Have Learned** exercises integrate chapter content and demonstrate relevance to textbook reading.

◎ **Website Cross References** direct students to Websites for skill reinforcement and practice.

◎ **Vocabulary for the 21st Century** explores interesting features of language to expand students' word awareness.

◎ **Exploring Language** boxes stimulate student interest in language and introduce them to unique language features, such as neologisms, euphemisms, and eponyms.

◎ **Practice Exercises** for each topic in a variety of formats maintain student interest and motivation.

◎ **Affordable!**

BOOK-SPECIFIC SUPPLEMENTS

Annotated Instructor's Edition
ISBN 0-321-09292-9

Test Bank
ISBN 0-321-08725-9

Companion Website
http://www.ablongman.com/vocabulary

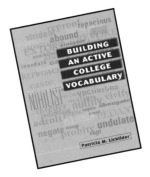

Building an Active College Vocabulary

Patricia M. Licklider, *John Jay College, CUNY*

©2002 • 464 pages • Paper • ISBN 0-321-08327-X

Building an Active College Vocabulary helps students acquire new words by introducing them in memorable contexts. The text shows students how to figure out the meaning of new words from contexts; how to use word parts; how to use a dictionary and a thesaurus efficiently and profitably; and how to improve their writing vocabulary for success in college.

FEATURES

◎ **Exercises** expose students to new words in memorable contexts, increasing the likelihood of recall.

◎ **Reading Selections from College-Level Texts** allow students to practice vocabulary-building skills on suitably challenging materials.

◎ **Brief Chapters** include Previews, Review Exercises, and Answers to Exercises, allowing students to work through the text on their own.

◎ **Emphasis on Mnemonics** offers helpful memorization strategies.

◎ **Post Tests** at the end of all units allow teachers and students to monitor progress.

◎ **Pronunciation Key** located on the inside cover and at the end of the text provides pronunciations of all words highlighted in text.

◎ **Glossaries** of words and word parts are included for handy reference.

BOOK-SPECIFIC SUPPLEMENTS

Instructor's Manual/Test Bank
ISBN 0-321-08328-8

Companion Website
http://www.ablongman.com/vocabulary

Innovative Resources from Longman

For Instructors

Electronic Test Bank for Developmental Reading CD-ROM

Offers more than 3,000 questions in all areas of reading, including vocabulary, main idea, supporting details, patterns of organization, critical thinking, analytical reasoning, inference, point of view, visual aids, and textbook reading. Instructors simply choose questions, then print out the completed test for distribution OR offer the test online.

FREE TO ADOPTERS ISBN 0-321-08179-X

Also available in a printed version ISBN 0-321-08596-5

Developmental English Electronic Newsletter

Twice a month during the spring and fall, subscribers receive a free copy of the Longman Developmental English Electronic Newsletter in their e-mailbox. Written by experienced classroom instructors, the newsletter offers teaching tips, classroom activities, book reviews and more. To subscribe, send us an email at: **BasicSkills@ablongman.com.**

For Students

The Longman Textbook Reader

Offers five complete chapters from our textbooks: computer science, biology, psychology, communications, and business. Each chapter includes additional comprehension quizzes, critical thinking questions, and group activities.

Available FREE when packaged with any Longman Basic Skills text.

With answers ISBN 0-321-04617-X

Without answers ISBN 0-321-07808-X

The Longman Reader's Journal
Kathleen T. McWhorter

The first journal for readers, *The Longman Reader's Journal* offers a place for students to record their reactions to and questions about any reading.

Available FREE when valuepacked.

ISBN 0-321-08843-3

The Longman Planner

Ideal for organizing a busy college life! Included are hour-by-hour schedules, monthly and weekly calendars, an address book, and an almanac of tips and useful information.

Available FREE valuepacked with any Longman Reading text.
ISBN 0-321-04573-4

10 Practices of Highly Effective Students

This study skills supplement includes topics such as time management, test-taking, reading critically, stress, and motivation.

Available FREE valuepacked with any Longman Reading text.
ISBN 0-205-30769-8

Newsweek Alliance
Newsweek Subscription card (12 weeks)

Newsweek gets students reading, writing, and thinking about what's going on in the world around them. The price of the subscription is added to the cost of the book. Instructors receive weekly lesson plans, quizzes, and curriculum guides as well as a complimentary *Newsweek* subscription.

Available with any Longman text. The price of the subscription is 57 cents per issue (a total of $6.84 for the subscription).
ISBN 0-321-04759-1

Interactive Guide to Newsweek

Available with the 12 week subscription to *Newsweek,* this free guide serves as a workbook for students who are using the magazine.

FREE when valuepacked with any Longman text.
ISBN 0-321-05528-4

Penguin Program

For instructors who like to use novels, a series of Penguin Putnam Inc. paperbacks is available at a significant discount when packaged with any Longman text. Some titles available are: Julia Alvarez's *How the Garcia Girls Lost Their Accents,* Mark Twain's *Huckleberry Finn,* John Steinbeck's *The Pearl,* James McBride's *The Color of Water,* and more. *For a complete list of titles or more information, contact your Longman sales consultant.*

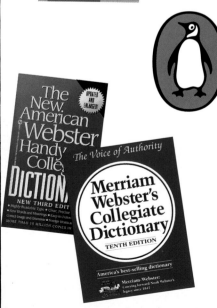

The Dictionary Deal
The New American Webster Handy College Dictionary

This paperback reference text is available at a significant discount when packaged with any Longman Reading text.

Merriam-Webster Collegiate Dictionary

This hardcover comprehensive dictionary is available at a significant discount when packaged with any Longman Reading text.

Reading Road Trip 2.0 Multimedia Software

Taking students on a tour of 15 cities and landmarks throughout the United States, each of the 15 modules corresponds to a reading or study skill (for example, finding the main idea, understanding patterns of organization, thinking critically). All modules contain a tour of the location, instruction and tutorial, exercises, interactive feedback, and mastery tests.

Available either in CD-ROM format, as a lab pack site license, or on the Web, FREE when valuepacked with any Longman Reading text.

CD ROM ISBN 0-321-07900-0

On the Web: www.ablongman.com/readingroadtrip (Web Version Access Pin Code: 0-321-09706-8)

The English Pages Web Site

http://www.ablongman.com/englishpages

Both students and instructors can visit this free, content-rich Website for additional reading selections and writing exercises. Visitors can conduct a simulated Web search, find additional reading and writing exercises, or browse a wide selection of links to various writing and research resources.

Florida Adopters

Thinking Through the Test: A Study Guide for the Florida College Basic Skills Exit Tests

by D.J. Henry

FOR FLORIDA ADOPTIONS ONLY. This workbook helps students strengthen their reading skills in preparation for the Florida College Basic Skills Exit Test. It features both diagnostic tests to help assess areas that may need improvement and exit tests to help tests skill mastery.

Available FREE valuepacked with any Longman Reading text.

ISBN 0-321-08066-1-with answers. ISBN 0-321-09988-5 -without answers.

Reading Skills Summary for the Florida State Exit Exam

by D.J. Henry

FOR FLORIDA ADOPTIONS ONLY. An excellent study tool for students preparing to take the Florida College Basic Skills Exit Test for Reading, this reading grid summarizes all the skills tested on the exam.

Available FREE valuepacked with any Longman Reading text.

ISBN 0-321-08478-0

Custom Solutions

The Longman Workshop:
Custom Resources in Reading, Writing, and Study Skills

The freedom to build the book you want—and your students need—is exactly what *The Longman Workshop* delivers. Create your own version of a text, or mix and match chapters from several texts. You may also include your own material or material from other publishers, and you may shrink-wrap your Longman Workshop custom book with any Longman or Pearson Custom Publishing text for a 10% discount off the package price!

The Longman Workshop gives you the following advantages—

- **Flexibility:** You can revise and update your book every term to suit your changing course needs.
- **Instructional Support:** You will receive desk copies of your Longman Workshop custom book and a custom answer key, and you'll have access to all supplements that accompany the traditional textbooks. A special instructor's manual will be available online in September 2001.
- **Cost Savings:** Your students pay only for material they use.
- **Quick Turnaround:** You can have your Longman Workshop custom book published in approximately 4-6 weeks from the time we receive your order from your bookstore.
- **Combine Your Custom Workbook or Text with a Custom Reader!** In addition to building your own Longman Workshop custom book, you can design your own custom reader using *The Mercury Reader*. You can then shrink-wrap your custom reader with your Longman Workshop text to take advantage of the 10% package discount!

PRICING INFORMATION

Each custom text is priced according to a $5.00 base charge plus $.08 per page. (Pricing is subject to change.) There is no minimum page length required. Please add $.10 per page for outside materials. If you choose to add copyrighted material, we will research permission costs and provide you with an estimate for inclusion. Minimum new order is 25 copies. Minimum reorder is 10 copies, with reprints available in 7-10 days. We will accept returns on up to 10% of the total order.

For more information on Longman Workshop, contact your Longman sales representative, or contact us directly at:

Project Editor - The Longman Workshop
Pearson Custom Publishing
75 Arlington Street, Suite 300
Boston, MA 02116
Phone: 1-800-877-6872 Ext. 2
FAX: 1-617-848-6366
Email: dbase.pub@pearsoncustom.com

Course Compass

Course Compass combines the strength of Longman content with state-of-the-art eLearning tools!

Course Compass is a nationally hosted, dynamic, interactive online course management system powered by Blackboard, leaders in the development of Internet-based learning tools. This easy-to-use and customizable program enables professors to tailor content and functionality to meet individual course needs! Every Course Compass course includes a range of pre-loaded content such as testing and assessment question tools, chapter-level objectives, chapter summaries, photos, illustrations, videos, animations, and Web activities-all designed to help students master core course objectives. For more information, or to see a demo, visit **www.coursecompass.com,** or contact your local Longman sales representative.

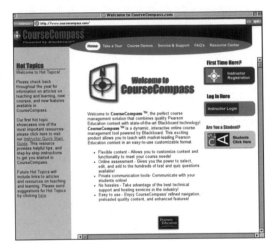

To order an examination copy of any of the texts in this brochure:

- ◎ Contact your local Allyn & Bacon/Longman sales representative
- ◎ Email your request to exam.copies@ablongman.com
- ◎ Phone us at (800) 852-8024
- ◎ Fax your request to (617) 848-7490
- ◎ Visit us on the Web at http://www.ablongman.com

www.ablongman.com/basicskills

ISBN: 0-321-10268-1

Essential
Reading Skills

Essential Reading Skills

Kathleen T. McWhorter

Niagara County Community College

New York • San Francisco • Boston
London • Toronto • Sydney • Tokyo • Singapore • Madrid
Mexico City • Munich • Paris • Cape Town • Hong Kong • Montreal

Vice President and Editor in Chief: Joseph Terry
Senior Acquisitions Editor: Steven Rigolosi
Associate Editor: Barbara Santoro
Development Manager: Janet Lanphier
Development Editor: Judy Voss
Marketing Manager: Melanie Craig
Supplements Editor: Donna Campion
Media Supplements Editor: Nancy Garcia
Production Manager: Joseph Vella
Project Coordination, Text Design, and Electronic Page Makeup:
      Thompson Steele, Inc.
Photo Research: Photosearch, Inc.
Cover Design Manager: John Callahan
Cover Designer: Kay Petronio
Cover Photos: Copyright © PhotoDisc, Inc.
Senior Manufacturing Buyer: Dennis J. Para
Printer and Binder: R.R. Donnelley & Sons, Inc.
Cover Printer: Coral Graphic Services

For permission to use copyrighted material, grateful acknowledgment is made to the copyright holders on pp. 419–422, which are hereby made part of this copyright page.

Library of Congress Cataloging-in-Publication Data
McWhorter, Kathleen T.
    Essential reading skills / Kathleen T. McWhorter.--1st ed.
      p.   cm.
    Includes bibliographical references and index.
    ISBN 0-321-08965-0 (alk. paper)--ISBN 0-321-08962-6 (AIE: alk. paper)
      1. Reading (Higher Education) 2. College readers. 3. Study skills. I. Title.

LB2395.3.M437   2002
428.4'071'1—dc21   2001038610

Please visit our website at http://www.ablongman.com

ISBN 0-321-08965-0   Student Edition
ISBN 0-321-08962-6   Annotated Instructor's Edition

1 2 3 4 5 6 7 8 9 10—DOC—04 03 02 01

Brief Contents

Detailed Contents

Chapter Reading Selections

Preface

Essential Reading Skills is designed to improve students' reading and thinking skills through concise skill instruction, extensive guided practice, assessment, and feedback. It was written to provide students at both two- and four-year colleges with a foundation of reading and thinking skills that will enable them to handle their college courses. The text offers brief strategies and extensive skill application for the reading skills essential to college success: active reading and thinking, vocabulary development, literal and critical comprehension, and organizing information.

Approach

This book is based on the premise that students learn by doing—that is, they improve their reading skills through guided practice and immediate, directed application of skills learned. The skills presentation in this text is kept to a minimum. Students are briefly introduced to a set of skills and then practice extensively in varied, increasingly longer and more difficult material.

The exercises, tests, and mastery tests in each chapter are designed to be objectively scored. A variety of question formats is used, including multiple-choice, true-false, matching, and fill-in-the-blank. Regardless of the format, students may score their own work, exchange papers with peers, or submit their work to their instructor for easy and convenient grading. Material on which the exercises and tests are based has been selected from college textbooks or related academic sources representative of the reading demands students will face in their courses. In order to demonstrate a particular feature, some passages have been adapted or specially prepared for this book.

This book also recognizes that students have varied learning styles and that many students are visual learners. Consequently, the skill instruction and exercise formats accommodate various learning styles; information is presented verbally, but, whenever possible, it is presented visually as well. For example, a drawing demonstrates the relationship between the main idea and supporting details within a paragraph; a diagram is used to describe how new words are formed by combining prefixes and roots; conceptual maps are used to display relationships within many passages and excerpts.

Content Overview

The text is organized into ten chapters, each focusing on a set of specific reading and thinking skills and each following a consistent format.

- **Chapter 1: Reading Actively.** Introduces students to active reading strategies and builds a positive attitude toward reading and learning in college. Students learn to build their concentration, preview before reading, and use guide questions to focus their reading.

- **Chapter 2: Building Vocabulary: Using Context Clues.** Shows students how to use four types of context clues to determine the meaning of unknown words.

- **Chapter 3: Building Vocabulary: Using Word Parts.** Demonstrates how to figure out the meaning of words using prefixes, roots, and suffixes.

- **Chapter 4: Locating Main Ideas.** Prepares students to identify main ideas within a paragraph by first explaining general versus specific ideas. The chapter also offers tips for finding the main idea and discusses placement of the topic sentence as well.

- **Chapter 5: Identifying Supporting Details.** Focuses on the use of details to support the main idea of a paragraph. Transitional words and phrases are also covered.

- **Chapter 6: Understanding Implied Main Ideas.** Explains the concept of implied ideas and offers practice in identifying implied main ideas in paragraphs. Although main ideas are often directly stated in topic sentences, sometimes they are not.

- **Chapter 7: Keeping Track of Information.** Identifies the five ways of organizing information: highlighting, marking, outlining, mapping, and summarizing.

- **Chapter 8: Recognizing the Basic Patterns of Organization.** Focuses on the five organizational patterns used in paragraphs and longer pieces of writing and the transitional words that signal them: example, definition, chronological order, process, and listing.

- **Chapter 9: Recognizing Comparison/Contrast and Cause/Effect Patterns.** Describes in detail the comparison/contrast and cause/effect organizational patterns along with the transitional words that signal them.

- **Chapter 10: Understanding Inference and the Writer's Purpose.** Provides an introduction to critical thinking skills and explores two essential critical reading skills: inference and author's purpose.

Chapter Format

Each chapter follows a regular format and sequence, giving students the benefit of a predictable, consistent structure.

Read Me First   The chapter opener begins with an engaging visual (a photograph, cartoon, or drawing) to elicit student response. This section immediately engages the students, sparks their interest, demonstrates the relevance of chapter content, and motivates them to progress through the chapter.

Concise Skill Instruction   Chapter skills are presented briefly and concisely, using frequent examples. This section tells students what they need to know in the simplest terms possible.

Practice Exercises   Interspersed within the concise skill instruction section are numerous exercises that provide students with ample opportunity to develop and apply skills. The exercises usually involve small steps, leading students through skills gradually and sequentially.

What Have You Learned?   This quiz reviews factual chapter content and enables students to determine whether they have understood and learned chapter concepts and ideas. Students may use this feature for review or as a self-test.

Using [name of skill] Tests   Three review tests at the end of every chapter encourage students to synthesize the skills they have learned. Often, these tests are based on slightly longer material.

Mastery Tests   Three mastery tests conclude each chapter. They may be used by students as additional practice or by the instructor as evaluative instruments. The first two tests require students to apply and integrate chapter-specific reading skills to paragraphs and short passages. The third mastery test, based on a full-length reading selection, includes general comprehension questions as well as questions on the specific skills taught within the chapter.

Special Features

The following features enhance the text's effectiveness and directly contribute to student success:

- **Emphasis on essential reading skills:** Because the instruction is brief and concise, students learn the most important college reading skills. The text does not contain extra material—often perceived by students as filler—that they have to pay for but do not use.

- **Visual elements:** Increasingly, college students have become visual learners as visual literacy has become critical to success in today's world. In addition, many students are more comfortable with images than with text. To facilitate visual learning and to accommodate students' visual learning preferences, this four-color book uses visual material to teach key concepts. Photographs, diagrams, and charts are used to clarify relationships, depict sequences, and demonstrate paragraph organization.

- **Consistent format:** Both students and instructors will benefit from the consistent format followed in each chapter. Students will learn the value of consistency, and instructors will find it easy to structure class time, plan assignments, and develop a grading system.

- **Extensive practice:** Numerous exercises enable students to successfully apply their learning. The chapter tests provide students with observable, measurable evidence that they are learning and improving their skills. Students may use these exercises as practice tests—as the "test before the test."

Book-Specific Ancillary Materials

- **Annotated Instructor's Edition:** This annotated edition (ISBN 0-321-08962-6) is identical to the student text, but includes all the answers printed directly on the pages where questions, exercises, or activities occur.

- **Instructor's Manual:** This manual (ISBN 0-321-08964-2), includes an answer key, and describes in detail the basic features of the text. This manual also offers suggestions for structuring the course, teaching non-traditional students, and approaching each chapter of the text.

- **Test Banks—Printed and Electronic:** This book-specific test bank (ISBN 0-321-08963-4) contains additional practice material and mastery tests for each chapter. It is printed in an 8½ by 11 inch format that allows for easy photocopying and distribution.

  The Longman Electronic Test Bank for Developmental Reading offers more than 3,000 questions in all areas of reading, including vocabulary, main idea, supporting details, patterns of organization, language, critical thinking, analytical reasoning, inference, point of view, visual aids, and textbook reading. With this easy-to-use CD-ROM, instructors simply choose questions from the electronic test bank, then print out the complete test for distribution. To order a copy of the electronic test bank, please contact your Longman sales consultant.

- **Book Website:** A complete Web site accompanies *Essential Reading Skills*—with additional quizzes, readings, and Web-based activities for each chapter of the text. Stop by for extra practice at **http://www. ablongman.com/mcwhorter.**

NEW! - **Reader's Journal:** Instructors may choose to shrinkwrap *Essential Reading Skills* with a free copy of *The Longman Reader's Journal*. This innovative journal provides students with a place to record their questions about, reactions to, and summaries of what they've read. Also included is a personal vocabulary log and additional pages for reflection. To preview the journal, contact your Longman sales consultant.

The Longman Developmental Reading Package

In addition to the book-specific ancillaries discussed above, Longman offers many other supplements to instructors and students. All of these supplements are available either free or at greatly reduced prices.

For Additional Reading and Reference

The Dictionary Deal   Two dictionaries can be shrinkwrapped with any Longman Reading title at a nominal fee. *The New American Webster Handy College Dictionary* is a paperback reference text with more than 100,000 entries. *Merriam Webster's Collegiate Dictionary*, Tenth Edition, is a hardback reference with a citation file of more than 14.5 million examples of English words drawn from actual use. For more details on ordering a dictionary with this text, contact your Longman sales representative.

Penguin Quality Paperback Titles A series of Penguin paperbacks is available at a significant discount when shrinkwrapped with any Longman title. The available titles include Toni Morrison's *Beloved*, Julia Alvarez's *How the Garcia Girls Lost Their Accents*, Mark Twain's *Huckleberry Finn*, Frederick Douglas's *Narrative of the Life of Frederick Douglas*, Harriet Beecher Stowe's *Uncle Tom's Cabin*, Dr. Martin Luther King Jr.'s *Why We Can't Wait*, as well as plays by Shakespeare, Miller, and Albee. For a complete list of titles or more information, contact your Longman sales consultant.

The Pocket Reader This inexpensive volume contains 80 brief readings (1 to 3 pages each) on a variety of themes: writers on writing, nature, women and men, customs and habits, politics, rights and obligations, and coming of age. Also included is an alternate rhetorical table of contents (0-321-07668-0).

The Longman Textbook Reader This supplement, for use in developmental reading courses, offers five complete chapters from Addison Wesley/Longman textbooks: computer science, biology, psychology, communications, and business. Each chapter includes additional comprehension quizzes, critical thinking questions, and group activities. For information on how to bundle the free *Longman Textbook Reader* with *Essential Reading Skills*, contact your Longman sales representative.

Newsweek **Alliance** Instructors may choose to shrinkwrap a 12-week subscription to *Newsweek* with any Longman text. The price of the subscription is 57 cents per issue (a total of $6.84 for the subscription). Available with the subscription is a free "Interactive Guide to *Newsweek*"—a workbook for students who are using the text. In addition, *Newsweek* provides a wide variety of instructor supplements free to teachers, including maps, skill builders, and weekly quizzes. For further information on the *Newsweek* Alliance, contact your Longman sales representative.

Florida Adopters: *Thinking Through the Test*, by D. J. Henry This special workbook, prepared specially for students in Florida, offers ample skill and practice exercises to help students prepare for the Florida State Exit Exam. It is available in two versions: with and without answers. To shrinkwrap this workbook free with your textbook, contact your Longman sales representative. Also available: Two laminated grids (one for reading, one for writing) that can serve as handy references for students preparing for the Florida State Exit Exam.

Electronic and Online Offerings

Reading Road Trip Multimedia Reading and Study Skills Software, Version 2.0 and Online Version   This innovative and exciting multimedia reading CD-ROM takes students on a tour of 15 cities and landmarks throughout the United States. Each of the 15 modules corresponds to a reading or study skill (for example, finding the main idea, understanding patterns of organization, and thinking critically). All modules contain a tour of the location, instruction and tutorial, exercises, interactive feedback, and mastery tests. To order the Reading Road Trip 2.0 CD-ROM with *Essential Reading Skills*, or to order passwords that grant access to the Reading Road Trip Website (**http://www.ablongman.com/readingroadtrip**), contact your Longman sales representative.

The Longman English Pages Website   Both students and instructors can visit our free content-rich Website for additional reading selections and writing exercises. From the Longman English pages, visitors can conduct a simulated Web search, learn how to write a resume and cover letter, or try their hand at poetry writing. Stop by and visit us at **http://www.ablongman. com/englishpages**.

The Longman Electronic Newsletter   Twice a month during the spring and fall, instructors who have subscribed receive a free copy of the Longman Developmental English E-Newsletter. Written by experienced classroom instructors, the newsletter offers teaching tips, classroom activities, book reviews, and more. To subscribe, visit the Longman Basic Skills Website at **http://www.ablongman.com/basicskills,** or send an e-mail to Basic Skills@ablongman.com.

Teaching Online: Internet Research, Conversation, and Composition, **Second Edition**   Ideal for instructors who have never surfed the Net, this easy-to-follow guide offers basic definitions, numerous examples, and step-by-step information about finding and using Internet sources. Free to adopters (0-321-01957-1).

Researching Online, **Fifth Edition**   A perfect companion for a new age, this indispensable supplement helps students navigate the Internet. Adapted from *Teaching Online,* the instructor's Internet guide, *Researching Online,* speaks directly to students, giving them detailed, step-by-step instructions for performing electronic searches. Available at no cost when shrinkwrapped with *Essential Reading Skills*. Contact your Longman sales consultant for information on how to order (0-321-09277-5).

For Instructors

CLAST Test Package, Fourth Edition   These two 40-item objective tests evaluate students' readiness for the CLAST exams. Strategies for teaching CLAST preparedness are included. Free with any Longman English title. Reproducible sheets: (0-321-01950-4). Computerized IBM version: (0-321-01982-2). Computerized Mac version: (0-321-01983-0).

TASP Test Package, Third Edition   These 12 practice pretests and posttests assess the same reading and writing skills covered in the TASP examination. Free with any Longman English title. Reproducible sheets: (0-321-01959-8). Computerized IBM version: (0-321-01985-7). Computerized Mac version: (0-321-01984-9).

Acknowledgments

I wish to express my gratitude to my reviewers for their excellent ideas, suggestions, and advice on the preparation of this text:

Richard D. Grossman, Tompkins Cortland Community College

Vonnye Rice-Gardner, Austin Community College

Maureen E. Hoffman, Central Community College

Paula Therrell, Holmes Community College

William McNeill, Robeson Community College

Given Parsons, Howard College

Carol G. Shier, Fullerton College

I also wish to thank Judy Voss, my developmental editor, for her creative vision of the project and for her assistance in preparing and organizing the manuscript. I am particularly indebted to Barbara Santoro, Associate Editor, for overseeing this project and attending to the many details to ready the book for production, and to Steven Rigolosi, Senior Acquisitions Editor, for his enthusiastic support, valuable advice, and expert guidance in the writing of this book.

Kathleen T. McWhorter

Essential
Reading Skills

Read Me First!

Look at the two photographs below, which show people watching a sporting event. How do the fans in each differ in their behavior? Which group seems interested and is actively participating in the game? Which group does not seem to be involved? These two photographs demonstrate the difference between active involvement and passive observation. The fans in only one photograph are responding and reacting—shouting, cheering, and interacting with the games they are watching. They feel and act as if it's their game, not just the players' game. In a similar way, active readers get involved with the material they are reading. They think, question, challenge, and criticize the author's ideas. They try to make the material *their* material. This chapter will give you some tips on how to become an active, successful reader.

Chapter 7

Reading Actively

Starting with a Positive Attitude

Just as active sports fans have a positive attitude about the games they watch, college students need to be positive about their courses and what they read. A positive attitude is a key to college success and to success on the job. Here are a few tips that will help you become a successful college student.

- **Be confident: Send yourself positive messages.** Tell yourself that college is something you want and can do. Negative thoughts such as "I might not be able to do this" or "What if I fail?" will only get in the way. Send yourself positive messages such as "I can do this" or "I've studied hard, and I'm going to pass this test."

- **Visualize success.** Close your eyes and imagine yourself completing a long or difficult assignment or doing well on an upcoming exam.

- **Set long-term goals for yourself.** You will feel more like working on assignments if you have specific objectives you are working toward. Goals such as "To get my own apartment," "To be able to quit my low-paying job," or "To become a registered nurse" will help you stick with daily tasks.

- **Plan on spending time reading.** Reading is not something you can rush through. The time you invest will pay off in better understanding and better grades.

- **Actively search for key ideas as you read.** Think of reading as a way of sifting and sorting out what you need to learn from the less important information.
- **Think of reading as a way of unlocking the writer's message to you, the reader.** Look for clues about the writer's personality, attitudes, opinions, and beliefs. This will put you in touch with the writer as a person and help you understand his or her message.
- **Stick with a reading assignment.** If an assignment is troublesome, experiment with different methods of completing it. Try highlighting important ideas or taking notes, for example. (Several methods are discussed in Chapter 7.)

Improve Your Surroundings

Make sure you create a workable study environment.

- **Choose a place with minimum distractions.**
- **Establish a study area** with a table or desk that is yours alone for study.
- **Control noise levels.** Determine how much background noise, if any, you require and choose a place best suited to you.
- **Eliminate distracting clutter.** Get rid of photos, stacks of bills, mementos, and so forth.
- **Have necessary supplies at your fingertips**—for example, dictionaries, pens, calculator, calendar, clock.

Pay Attention

Once your study area is set up, use the following ideas to help you pay attention to what you are reading or studying.

- **Establish goals and time limits for each assignment.** Deadlines will keep you motivated and create a sense of urgency in which you are less likely to daydream or become distracted.
- **Reward yourself.** Use rewards such as phoning a friend or ordering a pizza when you complete an evening of study.
- **Use writing to keep mentally and physically active.** Highlighting or taking notes will force you to keep your mind on the material you are reading.
- **Vary your activities.** Alternate between writing, reading, reviewing, and solving math problems.

- **Keep a distractions list.** As distracting thoughts enter your mind, jot them on a notepad. You may, for example, think of your mother's upcoming birthday as you're reading psychology. Writing it down will help you remember it and will eliminate the distraction.

Exercise 1–1

Directions: Rate each of the following statements from students as either helpful (H) or not helpful (NH) in building a positive attitude toward college and improving concentration. Then discuss how each of the statements marked NH could be changed to be more helpful.

___NH___ 1. This assignment is taking forever! My sister won't turn down her loud music, and I can't find my dictionary or notebook.

___NH___ 2. Whenever I imagine myself taking a test, I see myself getting nervous and my mind going blank.

___NH___ 3. If I do this reading assignment really fast, I'll get to watch my favorite TV show.

___H___ 4. This assignment is more difficult than I expected. I'll start over and try highlighting it.

___H___ 5. I plan to become an elementary school physical education teacher, so college is important to me.

___NH___ 6. This assignment is boring; I don't know why we have to read about World War I.

___H___ 7. I worked really hard and finished all of my assignments tonight. I think I'll celebrate by meeting Janie for Chinese food.

___H___ 8. This writer seems opposed to high-protein diets. I wonder if she'll give her reasons later in the reading.

___H___ 9. I read and reviewed the assignment twice, and I feel like I understand the material, so I should be able to pass the test on it.

___NH___ 10. I am attending college because my parents want me to.

Previewing Before You Read

You would not cross a city street without checking for traffic first. You would not pay to see a movie you had never heard of and knew nothing about. You would not buy a car without test-driving it or checking its mechanical condition.

Neither should you read an article or a textbook chapter without knowing what it is about or how it is organized. **Previewing** is a way of quickly familiarizing yourself with the organization and content of written material *before* beginning to read it. It is an easy method to use and will make a dramatic difference in how effectively you read.

How to Preview

When you preview, try to (1) find only the most important ideas in the material, and (2) note how they are organized. To do this, look only at the parts that state these important ideas and skip the rest. Previewing is a fairly rapid technique; it should take only a minute or two to preview any reading selection in this book. In fact, previewing is so fast that you should *not* take time to highlight or make notes. To preview an article or textbook chapter, look at the following parts.

- **Title and subtitle:** The title is a label that explains what the chapter is about. The subtitle, if there is one, suggests additional perspectives on the subject. For example, an article titled "Brazil" might be subtitled "The World's Next Superpower." In this instance, the subtitle tells which aspects of Brazil the article discusses.
- **First paragraph:** The first paragraph or introduction of a reading may provide an overview and offer clues about how a chapter or article will be organized.
- **Section headings:** Section headings, like titles, identify and separate important topics and ideas.
- **First sentence under each heading:** The first sentence following a heading often further explains the heading. It may also state the central thought of the section it begins.
- **Typographical aids:** Typographical aids are those features of a page that help to highlight and organize information. These include *italics*, **bold-faced type,** marginal notes, colored ink, <u>underlining</u>, and numbering.
- **Final paragraph or summary:** The final paragraph may summarize the reading or bring it to a close.

Demonstration of Previewing

The following excerpt, from a chapter of a communication textbook on nonverbal messages (messages that do not use words), discusses four major functions of eye communication. It has been included to help you understand previewing. Everything that you should look at or read has been highlighted. Preview this selection now, reading *only* the highlighted portions.

FUNCTIONS OF EYE COMMUNICATION

From Ben Jonson's poetic observation "Drink to me only with thine eyes, and I will pledge with mine" to the scientific observations of contemporary researchers, the eyes are regarded as the most important nonverbal message system. Researchers note four major functions of eye communication.

To Seek Feedback

You frequently use your eyes to seek feedback from others. In talking with someone, you look at her or him intently, as if to say, "well, what do you think?" As you might predict, listeners gaze at speakers more than speakers gaze at listeners. Research shows that the percentage of interaction time spent gazing while listening was between 62 and 75 percent. However, the percentage of time spent gazing while talking was between 38 and 41 percent.

Women make eye contact more and maintain it longer (both in speaking and in listening) than do men. This holds true whether the woman is interacting with other women or with men. This difference in eye behavior may result from women's tendency to display their emotions more than men; eye contact is one of the most effective ways of communicating emotions. Another possible explanation is that women have been conditioned more than men to seek positive feedback from others. Women may thus use eye contact in seeking this visual feedback.

To Regulate the Conversation

A second function of eye contact is to regulate the conversation and particularly to pass the speaking turn from one person to another. You use eye contact, for example, to tell the listener that you are finished with your thought and that you would now like to assume the role of listener and hear what the other person has to say. Or, by maintaining a steady eye contact while you plan your next sentence, you tell the other person that although you are now silent, you don't want to give up your speaking turn. You also see this in the college classroom when the instructor asks a question and then locks eyes with a student—without saying anything, the instructor clearly communicates the desire for that student to say something.

To Signal the Nature of the Relationship

Eye contact is also used to signal the nature of the relationship between two people—for example, a focused attentive glance indicates a positive relationship, but avoiding eye contact shows one of negative regard. You may also signal status relationships with your eyes. This is particularly interesting because the same movements of the eyes may signal either subordination or superiority. The superior individual, for example, may stare at the subordinate or may glance away. Similarly, the subordinate may look directly at the superior or perhaps at the floor.

Eye movements may also signal whether the relationship between two people is amorous, hostile, or indifferent. Because some of the eye movements expressing these different relationships are so similar, you often use information from other areas, particularly the rest of the face, to decode the message before making any final judgments.

To Make Up for Increased Physical Distance

Last, eye movements may make up for increased physical distance. By making eye contact you overcome psychologically the physical distance between you and the other individual. When you catch someone's eye at a party, for example, you become psychologically close even though separated by a large physical distance. Not surprisingly, eye contact and other expressions of psychological closeness, such as self-disclosure, are positively related; as one increases, so does the other.

—DeVito, *Human Communication*

Although you may not realize it, you have gained a substantial amount of information from the minute or so that you just spent previewing. You have become familiar with the key ideas in this selection.

**Exercise
1–2**

Directions: Read the following statements and mark each one true (T) or false (F) based on what you learned by previewing the selection above.

   T   1. The most important nonverbal message system involves the eyes.

   T   2. We can obtain feedback from others by using just our eyes.

   F   3. Eye movements cannot make up for physical distances.

   T   4. The relationship between two people can be signaled through eye contact.

   T   5. Eye contact regulates conversations.

This exercise tested your recall of some of the more important ideas in the article. Check your answers by referring back to the article. Did you get most or all of the above items correct? You can see, then, that previewing helps you learn the major ideas in a section before you read it.

Exercise 1–3

Directions: Carlos is taking a course in psychology and has been assigned to read an article from Psychology Today, *titled "Laughter: A Cure for What Ails You." He plans to preview the article before reading it. Circle the letter of the choice that best completes each of the following statements about this situation.*

1. The main reason that Carlos should preview his assignment is to
   a. memorize facts and details.
   b. evaluate the author's qualifications.
   c. identify the most important ideas in the material.
   d. decide how he feels about the topic.

2. Carlos can expect the subtitle, "A Cure for What Ails You," to
   a. indicate what aspect of laughter the article will discuss.
   b. reveal a personal story about the author.
   c. suggest that the author is going to list her reasons for liking or disliking laughter.
   d. explain how the author will organize her ideas.

3. The article contains five headings. Carlos can expect each heading to
   a. introduce a story or example.
   b. separate different kinds of research.
   c. continue with the same idea.
   d. introduce a new idea.

4. Several sentences in the article appear in boldfaced print. When previewing, Carlos should
   a. skip them.   c. copy them.
   b. read them.   d. read them aloud to a classmate.

5. Carlos should expect the last paragraph of the article to
   a. ask questions the reading leaves unanswered.
   b. suggest other uses of laughter.
   (c.) bring the article to a close.
   d. reveal the author's opinions on the topic.

Exercise 1–4

Directions: Match the previewing step listed in column A with the type of information it provides in column B. Use each item only once. Write the letter of your choice in the space provided.

Column A	Column B
__e__ 1. title	a. provides an overview
__a__ 2. first paragraph	b. summarizes the article
__c__ 3. section headings	c. identify and separate main topics
__d__ 4. typographical aids	d. indicate important information
__b__ 5. last paragraph	e. identifies the subject

Guide Questions

Did you ever read an entire page or more and not remember anything you read? Have you found yourself going from paragraph to paragraph without really thinking about what the writer is saying? Guide questions can help you overcome these problems. **Guide questions** are questions you expect to be able to answer while or after you read. Most students form them mentally, but you can jot them in the margin if you prefer.

The following tips can help you form questions to guide your reading. It is best to develop guide questions *after* you preview but *before* you read.

- **Turn each major heading into a series of questions.** The questions should ask something that you feel is important to know.
- **As you read a section, look for the answers to your questions.** Highlight the answers as you find them.
- **When you finish reading a section, stop and check to see whether you can recall the answers.** Place check marks by those you cannot recall. Then reread.

- **Avoid asking questions that have one-word answers, like** *yes* **or** *no.* Questions that begin with *what, why,* or *how* are more useful.

Here are a few textbook headings and some examples of questions you might ask:

Heading	Questions
Reducing Prejudice	How can prejudice be reduced? What type of prejudice is discussed?
The Deepening Recession	What is a recession? Why is it deepening?
Newton's First Law of Motion	Who was Newton? What is his First Law of Motion?

Exercise 1–5

Directions: Circle the letter of the guide question that would be most helpful in improving your understanding of the following textbook chapter sections that begin with these headings:

1. Defining Loneliness
   a. Is loneliness unusual?
   b. What does loneliness mean?
   c. Are adults lonelier than children?
   d. Can loneliness ever be positive?

2. The Four Basic Functions of Management
   a. How important is management?
   b. Are there other functions of management?
   c. What are management's four basic functions?
   d. Do poor managers cause serious problems?

3. Surface versus Depth Listening
   a. Is surface listening difficult?
   b. What is listening?
   c. How do surface and depth listening differ?
   d. Is depth listening important?

4. The Origins of the Cold War
   a. How did the Cold War start?
   b. Is the Cold War still going on?
   c. How did the United States deal with the Cold War?
   d. Did the Cold War end through compromise?

5. Some People Are More Powerful Than Others
   a. Does power affect relationships?
   b.) Why are some people more powerful than others?
   c. What is power?
   d. Can people learn to become more powerful?

Putting Your Positive Attitude to Work

Throughout this chapter you have picked up many tips for being an active reader. You know that a positive attitude is important as are a workable environment for studying and the ability to pay attention. You've also learned how to preview material before you read and how to ask guide questions from major headings. Now you can put your positive attitude and active reading skills to work throughout the remainder of the book.

What Have You Learned?

Directions: To check your understanding of the chapter and to review its major points, indicate whether each of the following statements is true (T) or false (F).

___F___   1. Worrying about failing a test can help you develop a positive attitude toward college.

___T___   2. Reading is not something you should rush through.

___F___   3. Where you study does not usually affect your concentration.

___T___   4. Setting goals and time limits for each assignment helps to keep you motivated.

___T___   5. Previewing is a quick way to become familiar with a chapter or article before you read it.

___F___   6. The best guide questions have one-word answers.

NAME _____ SECTION _____

DATE _____ SCORE _____

Directions: In the space provided, write the letter of the choice that best completes each of the following statements.

___b___ 1. Which of the following tips will *not* help you build a positive attitude toward college and reading?

    a. look for key ideas as you read.

    b. visualize the major problems you might encounter.

    c. establish long-term goals for yourself.

    d. send yourself positive messages.

___b___ 2. While studying and reading, you should

    a. speed up your reading whenever possible.

    b. stick with an assignment even if it is difficult.

    c. work on only one subject per week.

    d. set no time limits for yourself.

___c___ 3. To build your concentration, you should

    a. reward yourself after each hour of study.

    b. study in your bedroom.

    c. control the noise in your study environment.

    d. eliminate all time pressures.

___a___ 4. Previewing written material is a way to

    a. familiarize yourself with the material's important ideas.

    b. test your knowledge of the subject.

    c. draw conclusions from the material.

    d. determine the author's prejudices.

___d___ 5. When previewing a textbook chapter or article, you should read all of the following except

    a. the last paragraph.   c. the introductory paragraph.

    b. the section headings.   d. the references and footnotes.

___b___ 6. Developing guide questions is primarily intended to

    a. give you practice answering test questions.

    b. help you remember what you have read.

    c. force you to read out loud.

    d. eliminate distractions.

   d   7. The easiest way to form guide questions is to use the
               a. introduction.   c. summary.
               b. review questions.   d. headings.

   c   8. One way to pay attention as you read and study is to
               a. save your most difficult subject for last.
               b. call your classmates for advice.
               c. take notes to keep your mind on the material.
               d. study at different times during the day.

   b   9. The first paragraph of a chapter or reading usually provides
               a. review questions.
               b. an overview.
               c. the author's conclusion.
               d. a list of difficult vocabulary.

   b   10. Section headings are important because they usually
               a. identify the general subject.
               b. identify important topics and ideas.
               c. present summaries of the material.
               d. reveal the author's biases.

NAME _____ SECTION _____

DATE _____ SCORE _____

Directions: In the space provided, write the letter of the choice that best completes each of the following statements.

__b__   1. Guide questions should be asked
    a. before previewing.
    b. after previewing but before reading.
    c. after reading.
    d. during review.

__a__   2. Typographical aids include all of the following *except*
    a. introductions.   c. boldfaced type.
    b. colored ink.   d. underlining.

__c__   3. Which of the following guide questions would be the best to ask for a section in your history text on the Revolutionary War?
    a. When did it start?   c. Why did it start?
    b. Where did it start?   d. Did it last very long?

__d__   4. The main purpose of a distractions list is to
    a. keep your study area neat.
    b. organize your time after a study session.
    c. maintain your interest in a reading assignment.
    d. reduce the reminders that come to mind as you study.

__b__   5. The first sentence under a section heading usually
    a. gives the author's qualifications.
    b. further explains the heading.
    c. provides personal examples.
    d. announces the author's purpose for writing.

__d__   6. A useful type of guide question would probably begin with the word
    a. *who.*   c. *where.*
    b. *when.*   d. *why.*

_____b_____ 7. Building your concentration includes all of the following
except

a. eliminating distractions.

b. increasing your reading speed.

c. paying attention.

d. rewarding yourself.

_____d_____ 8. Maria has several reading assignments to complete in one
evening. Before she begins, it is important for her to

a. make a distractions list.

b. reward herself.

c. take some notes on the material.

d. organize her study area.

_____b_____ 9. Andrew has begun to preview an article called "Civil Rights
and Issues of Race." He can tell that this article will probably
discuss

a. feminism.   c. sexual harassment.

b. racial discrimination.   d. religious persecution.

_____d_____ 10. The best guide question for an article titled "U.S. Voter
Turnout: Among the Lowest in the World" would be

a. What country has the highest turnout rate?

b. What country has the lowest turnout rate?

c. How many Americans voted in the last presidential
election?

d. Why is voter turnout so low in the United States?

Directions: The following excerpt is from a business marketing textbook. Preview by reading **only** the highlighted sections of the reading, and then, in the space provided, write the letter of the choice that best completes the statements that follow. Do **not** read the section completely.

THE PHYSICAL ENVIRONMENT IN STORES AND RESTAURANTS

It's no secret that people's moods and behaviors are strongly influenced by their physical surroundings. Despite all their efforts to presell consumers through advertising, marketers know that the store environment influences many purchases. For example, consumers decide on about two out of every three supermarket product purchases in the aisles. Therefore, the messages they receive at the time and their feelings about being in the store are important influences on their decisions.

Factors That Influence Shoppers

Two dimensions, *arousal* and *pleasure*, determine if a shopper will react positively or negatively to a store environment. In other words, the person's surroundings can be either dull or exciting (arousing), and either pleasant or not. Just because the environment is arousing doesn't necessarily mean it will be pleasant—we've all been in crowded, hot stores that are anything but! Maintaining an upbeat feeling in a pleasant context is one factor behind the success of theme parks such as Disney World, which try to provide consistent doses of carefully calculated stimulation to patrons.

The Appeal of Themed Environments

The importance of these surroundings explains why many retailers are combining two favorite consumer activities, shopping and eating, into elaborate *themed environments*. According to a recent Roper Starch survey, eating out is the top form of out-of-home entertainment, and innovative firms are scrambling to offer customers a chance to eat, buy, and be entertained all at once. Planet Hollywood, for example, is crammed full of costumes and props, and the chain now grosses over $200 million a year around the world.

Visual and Audio Elements in Restaurants

A lot of the appeal of these themed environments is that there's plenty of interesting things to look at while wolfing down your burger. In addition to visual stimuli, though, other sensory cues can also influence consumers—that's why the Harley-Davidson Café features the roar of a "hog" engine as part of its décor. Sounds and music can affect eating behavior—one study found that diners who listened to loud, fast music ate more and faster than those who listened to classical. The researchers concluded that diners who choose soothing music at mealtimes can increase weight loss by at least five pounds a month!

Indeed, a growing recognition of the important role played by a store or restaurant's audio environment has created a new market niche, as some companies now are selling musical collections tailored to different activities. These include RCA Victor's "Classical Music for Home Improvements" and Sony Classics' "Cyber Classics" that are billed as music specifically for computer hackers to listen to while programming! Sony's "Extreme Classics," packaged just for bungee jumpers, is claimed to be the "loudest and most dangerous music ever written."

—Solomon and Stuart, *Marketing*, pp. 161–162

_____b_____ 1. The title suggests that the reading's general topic will be
   a. access for handicapped individuals.
   b. the physical surroundings within stores and restaurants.
   c. the personnel can influence business surroundings.
   d. how a store's surroundings can increase sales.

_____b_____ 2. All of the following previewing aids are found in the selection *except*
   a. an introductory paragraph.   c. typographical aids.
   b. a subtitle.   d. section headings.

_____d_____ 3. By reading the introductory paragraph as part of your preview, you would expect the reading to focus on
   a. the effects of advertising on shoppers.
   b. how supermarket products are sold.
   c. people's moods when they're not shopping.
   d. messages and feelings shoppers experience while in a store.

_____a_____ 4. The most helpful guide question to ask for the heading "Factors That Influence Shoppers" is
   a. What factors influence shoppers?
   b. Why do stores want to influence shoppers?
   c. Are shoppers easily influenced?
   d. What is influence?

_____b_____ 5. The two factors that are most likely to determine a shopper's response to a store's environment are
   a. convenience and location.
   b. arousal and pleasure.
   c. price and themes.
   d. crowds and arrangement of goods.

_____b_____ 6. The most helpful guide question to ask for the heading "The Appeal of Themed Environments" is
   a. Where are themed stores located?
   b. Why are themed stores popular?
   c. When did theme restaurants first open?
   d. What kinds of shoppers like themed stores?

_____d_____ 7. The two favorite consumer activities that themed stores combine are
   a. shopping and exercising.   c. shopping and socializing.
   b. shopping and relaxing.   d. shopping and eating.

_____c_____ 8. The third heading, "Visual and Audio Elements in Restaurants," tells you that
   a. store elements must be visual.
   b. restaurant personnel should be seen but not heard.
   c. what consumers see and hear is important.
   d. audio and visual equipment sells quickly.

_____b_____ 9. The sentence that follows the third heading, "Visual and Audio Elements in Restaurants," mentions only visual items. What other restaurant features would you expect to read about in this section?
   a. hours of operation   c. heating and cooling
   b. sound and music   d. service and friendliness

_____c_____ 10. The typographical aid that the writer uses to emphasize important terms is
   a. underlining.   c. italics.
   b. numbering.   d. marginal notes.

Scoring for Part A: Students should highlight each of the following parts of the reading.

title = 5 points

1st paragraph = 5 points

4 headings (4 × 5 = 20 points)

1st sentence under each heading (4 × 5 = 20 points)

<u>Total: 50 points</u>

A. *Directions:* Preview the following selection, which is from a study skills text. So that your instructor can see the parts you read, highlight each part you looked at. (Normally, it is too time consuming to highlight while previewing.)

CHANGING YOUR HABITS TO REDUCE STRESS

This section describes four strategies for reducing stress by changing your habits. Experiment to discover which strategies will work for you.

1 Control Your Own Time

Take charge of your time, do not permit friends, roommates, or neighbors to consume it. Make clear when study times are planned, and don't allow interruptions. If people call or visit during those times, be brief and firm; insist that you must get back to work. If friends call to invite you to a movie, explain that this is a study hour and suggest a time that is convenient for you. Stay in control of your time. Apply the same firmness to family members who want you to drive them somewhere or to parents who want you to run errands. Suggest an alternate time when you can fulfill their requests.

2 Give Yourself a Break

Constantly pushing yourself increases stress. Take a break; give yourself some down time or personal space in which you can just be you. During your break you are not a student, not an employee, not a parent, not the one who cooks dinner. Just be yourself. Think of something you enjoy—a special song, a favorite place, a friend whom you miss. Your break can be brief: Between one and five minutes is often enough to slow you down, provide relief from your routine, and reduce stress.

3 Help Someone Out

If you spend all your time thinking about yourself and the amount of work you have, your problems will grow out of proportion. Spend time helping someone else when you can afford the time. You might shop for an elderly relative, tutor a classmate, or volunteer at a soup kitchen or animal shelter. Once your mind is off yourself and you see others with problems, your problems will seem more manageable.

4 Get Some Exercise

Build an exercise routine into your weekly schedule. Exercise can reduce stress by helping your body release hormones, which will improve your aware-

One form of stress-reducing exercise.

ness and give you a sense of well-being. Fresh air is also helpful in reducing stress. It stimulates your mind and body and makes it easier for you to relax. Take a brisk walk outdoors when you feel stress mounting.

B. Directions: Write true (T) or false (F) before each of the following statements.

___T___ 1. The title gives you a good idea of what the selection is about.

___F___ 2. The last paragraph is a summary.

___T___ 3. A useful guide question for the first heading is "How can I control my time?"

___T___ 4. A useful guide question for the third heading is "Why should I help someone out?"

___F___ 5. A useful guide question for the fourth heading is "Who should exercise?"

NAME _____ SECTION _____

DATE _____ SCORE _____

Scoring for Part A: Students should highlight each of the following parts of the reading.

title = 5 points

1st paragraph = 10 points

5 headings (5 x 5 = 25 points)

1st sentence under each heading (5 x 5 = 25 points)

last paragraph = 10 points

Total: 75 points

A. Directions: Preview the following selection, which is from a communication text. Highlight each part that you have looked at so that your instructor can see what you have read. (Normally, it is too time consuming to highlight while previewing.)

TRY ACTIVE LISTENING

Active listening, an approach to listening developed by Thomas Gordon, is especially important in communicating with people. It's a method for encouraging the other person to explore his or her thoughts and talk about them.

Functions of Active Listening

Active listening serves several important functions. First of all, it helps you to check your understanding of what speakers mean. When you ask speakers about what they said, they can then confirm or deny your perceptions. Future messages will have a better chance of being meaningful.

Second, active listening enables you to say that you accept a speaker's feelings. Remember that a person's feelings—whether you see these as logical or illogical, reasonable or unreasonable—are extremely important to that person. A speaker needs to know that these feelings are accepted before he or she will talk about them.

Finally, and perhaps most important, active listening encourages the speaker to explore and express thoughts and feelings. For example, when you use active listening you provide Angela, who has expressed worry about getting fired, with the opportunity to explore these feelings in greater detail. You give Charlie, who hasn't had a date in four months, the opportunity to reflect openly on his feelings about dating and about his own loneliness. Active listening sets the stage for a dialogue of mutual understanding rather than one of attack and defense. In providing the speaker with the opportunity to talk feelings through, the active listener helps the speaker deal with them.

Techniques for Active Listening

Here are three techniques for effective active listening.

- **Paraphrase the speaker's thoughts.** When you paraphrase, you state in your own words what you think the speaker meant. This will help ensure understanding, since the speaker will be able to correct your restatement. It will show the speaker that you're interested in what is being said. The paraphrase also gives the speaker a chance to elaborate on or extend what was originally said. When you echo the speaker's thought, the speaker may then say more about his or her feelings. In your paraphrase, be especially careful that you do not lead the speaker in the direction you think he or she should go. Make your paraphrases as close to objective descriptions as you can.

- **Express understanding of the speaker's feelings.** In addition to para-phrasing the content, echo (repeat) the feelings you felt the speaker expressed or implied. ("I can imagine how you must have felt. You must have felt really horrible.") Just as the paraphrase enables you to check on your ideas about the content, the expression of feelings enables you to check on your ideas about the speaker's feelings. This expression of feel-ings will also help the speaker to see his or her feelings more objectively. It's especially helpful when the speaker feels angry, hurt, or depressed. We all need that objectivity; we need to see our feelings from a somewhat less impassioned perspective if we are to deal with them effectively.

- **Ask questions.** Ask questions to make sure that you understand the speaker's thoughts and feelings and to obtain additional information ("How did you feel when you saw that grade?"). The questions should be designed to provide just enough stimulation and support for the speaker to express the thoughts and feelings he or she wants to express. Questions should not pry into unrelated areas or challenge the speaker in any way. These questions will further confirm your interest and concern for the speaker.

If you follow these techniques, active listening will help you become a better communicator. Your relationships with friends, family members, and coworkers should improve.

—DeVito, *Messages*, p. 100

5 questions
(5 x 5 = 25 points)

B. Directions: The following guide questions are based on the headings in the selection. Read the entire selection, and then, in the space provided, write the letter of the choice that best answers each of the following questions.

_____d_____   1. What is the most important function of listening?

   a. It promotes acceptance of the speaker.

   b. It encourages understanding.

   c. It helps the listener clarify his or her thinking.

   d. It encourages the speaker to explore his or her feelings and ideas.

_____a_____ 2. What is active listening?

    a. a method of encouraging people to communicate

    b. a process of understanding difficult messages

    c. a means of prying into hidden emotions

    d. a procedure for requesting information

_____b_____ 3. What is paraphrasing?

    a. encouraging a speaker to explain an idea

    b. stating an idea in your own words

    c. correcting misinformation

    d. relying on visual cues

_____b_____ 4. How does a listener express understanding of a speaker's feelings?

    a. by paraphrasing the content

    b. by repeating (echoing) the speaker's feelings

    c. by being considerate

    d. by admitting that feelings are important

_____a_____ 5. Why is it useful to ask questions?

    a. to make sure you understand the speaker's thoughts and feelings

    b. to break up long explanations

    c. to help avoid arguments among friends

    d. to provide a format for a conversation

SURVIVAL OF THE FITTEST: HOW TO GET AND HOLD A JOB

DeVry Alumni Directions Newsletter

The DeVry Institute, a private, degree-granting, higher educational system, provides career-oriented programs in business and technology. This article appeared in a newsletter for its graduates.

Preview and then read this article, which outlines the skills workers will need to obtain and hold jobs in the changing workplace.

Vocabulary Preview

These are some of the difficult words in this essay. The definitions here will help you if you can't figure out the meanings from the sentence context or word parts.

evolution (par. 1) gradual change

capabilities (par. 1) general traits or abilities

facets (par. 2) aspects

expertise (par. 3) special skill or knowledge

mandatory (par. 4) required

asset (par. 7) resource or advantage

component (par. 10) part

cornerstones (par. 11) important elements or foundations

cutthroat (par. 12) ruthless, without principle

---

1   Let's face it. The days of graduating from school, beginning a one-company, lifelong career, and ticking off the years while waiting for the gold watch and retirement party are long gone. Today's workforce is dog-eat-dog, and to thrive in it takes the right combination of skills, attitude, and dedication. A recent DeVry survey of consumer and service goods companies as well as high-tech corporations shows a continuing evolution of what employers expect from recent graduates. It's no longer enough to simply present good grades and letters of recommendation and expect to receive on-the-job training. Today, new employees must enter the workforce "ready to run." Want to build a great career? Pay attention to the following list, which features the top ten capabilities corporations demand in new employees.

2 **Speak-Listen-Learn:** Excellent verbal and written skills are now key to career success. Special emphasis is placed on the ability to clearly communicate to project teammates and corporate leaders. It's also critical to listen to and understand information concerning all facets of the corporation.

3 **Can Do:** Prospects must demonstrate the hands-on ability to apply their classroom education. Those with expertise in theory alone are often not interviewed.

4 **Team Player:** Since most corporations now use project teams of professionals from different areas of expertise, it's mandatory for all employees to work well in groups of four to six people. This requires the ability to function effectively with those who may come from different ethnic and/or social backgrounds.

5 **Quick Change:** Because of rapid advances in technology and customer requirements, change is a constant factor in most work environments. Companies place great weight on the flexibility needed to comfortably adapt to and productively use new structures, programs, and procedures.

6 **Problematics:** Employees today must be able to recognize, define, and solve work-related problems. Critical-thinking skills combined with good communications capabilities are essential for success.

7 **Out of the Box:** No single answer is best for every situation. The ability to get "out of the box"—creatively go beyond currently accepted models and find breakthrough solutions—is considered a highly valuable asset. Individuals must have the confidence needed to try new or different ideas.

8 **Balancing Act:** Individuals who lead balanced lives, which include outside sports or social activities, are considered better at succeeding in today's high-stress world.

9 **Clock Control:** Success within a team requires the ability to effectively manage time and meet schedules. Dependable individuals generally advance quickly within an organization.

10 **Crash-Proof:** Breakthrough success requires professionals who are not afraid of failure. The ability to fail, learn from that failure, and then try again is a critical component in technical development.

11   **True Believer:** The ability to make a personal commitment to corporate or group goals adds a great deal to an individual's employability. These employees are seen as cornerstones to a company's long-range success.

12   No doubt Darwin wasn't referring to surviving in the modern workplace when he posed his famous theory of evolution, but with cutthroat competition among workers, the fittest—those who have what employers demand—will survive.

— ∙ —

Directions: In the space provided, write the letter of the choice that best completes each of the following statements.

CHECKING YOUR COMPREHENSION

___d___   1. The purpose of this selection is to
   a. suggest ten ways to keep a job.
   b. summarize facts about new employees in high-tech jobs.
   c. explain ten qualities college students will learn by the time they graduate.
   d. list the top qualities expected of an employee.

___b___   2. The DeVry survey included answers from employers in all of the following areas *except*
   a. consumer goods.   c. service goods.
   b. college teaching.   d. high-tech corporations.

___c___   3. "Can Do" employees are able to
   a. work very quickly.
   b. understand the business principles they learned in college.
   c. apply their classroom education to the job.
   d. come up with many new ideas.

___a___   4. According to the reading, being a "team player" means being able to
   a. work well with a small group of coworkers.
   b. talk with a person of a different social class.
   c. solve problems by dividing up tasks.
   d. balance work and home life.

_____d_____ 5. Being able to communicate well is important in

a. goal setting.

b. balancing priorities.

c. time management.

d. problem solving.

_____c_____ 6. A "crash-proof" employee is one who

a. experiences few, if any, difficulties.

b. never needs a vacation.

c. learns from failure.

d. has exciting ideas every week.

_____c_____ 7. All of the following employee qualities are important in today's job market *except*

a. excellent written skills.

b. the ability to adapt to changes.

c. the willingness to work weekends.

d. the ability to meet deadlines.

_____d_____ 8. All of the following previewing aids are found in the selection *except*

a. boldfaced headings.

b. introduction.

c. conclusion.

d. italics.

_____b_____ 9. The first part of the selection to tell you what the reading is about is the

a. introduction.

b. title and subtitle.

c. headings.

d. conclusion.

_____c_____ 10. The most useful guide question for the entire selection would be

a. Who said "the survival of the fittest"?

b. Why must employees stand out from their competition?

c. What are employers looking for?

d. Why do so many people change jobs in their lifetimes?

_d_ 11. The most useful guide question for the heading "Balancing Act" would be

    a. Why are people not balanced?

    b. Who should be balanced?

    c. When should balancing occur?

    d. What in a person's life must be balanced?

_a_ 12. The most useful guide question for the heading "True Believer" would be

    a. What does "true believer" mean?

    b. What if you disagree?

    c. Are true beliefs based on values?

    d. Should employees believe in themselves?

REVIEWING DIFFICULT VOCABULARY

Directions: Complete each of the following sentences by inserting a word from the Vocabulary Preview on page 23 in the space provided. A word should be used only once.

13. When Barbara applied for a sales job with an international company, she knew her knowledge of Spanish and French would be a(n) _____asset_____ .

14. The personnel director said foreign language skills were not _____mandatory_____ .

15. However, he was impressed with her _____expertise or capabilities_____ in both languages.

16. He went on to explain the various _____facets_____ of the company.

17. He also told Barbara the story of the company's _____evolution_____ from a small business to a giant corporation over the past fifty years.

18. Barbara asked if the sales department was considered an important

   _____component_____ of the company.

19. The personnel director emphasized the importance of the sales people,

   calling them the _____cornerstones_____ of the business.

20. In addition, he pointed out the high principles on which the

   company was based, making it clear to Barbara that

   _____cutthroat_____ activities were not allowed.

Chapter 1:   Reading Actively

RECORDING YOUR PROGRESS

Test	Number Right		Score
Practice Test 1-1	_____ × 10 =		_____%
Practice Test 1-2	_____ × 10 =		_____%
Practice Test 1-3	_____ × 10 =		_____%
Mastery Test 1-1	_____ × 10 =		_____%
Mastery Test 1-2	_____ × 10 =		_____%
Mastery Test 1-3	_____ × 5 =		_____%

EVALUATING YOUR PROGRESS

Based on your test performance, rate how well you have mastered the skills taught in this chapter by checking one of the boxes below or by writing your own evaluation.

☐ **Need More Improvement**

Tip: Try using the "Active Reading" Module on the Reading Road Trip CD-ROM or Website that accompanies this textbook to fine-tune the skills that you have learned in this chapter.

☐ **Need More Practice**

Tip: Try using the "Active Reading" Module on the Reading Road Trip CD-ROM that accompanies this textbook to brush up on the skills you have learned in this chapter, or visit this textbook's Website at **http://ablongman.com/mcwhorter** for extra practice.

☐ **Good**

Tip: To maintain your skills, do a quick review of this chapter by using the Website that accompanies this textbook by logging on to **http://ablongman.com/mcwhorter.**

☐ **Excellent**

YOUR EVALUATION: _____

_____

_____

_____

_____

Read Me First!

The photograph below is striking and humorous because you do not see what you expect. It is obvious that the man's head and body are missing. You can tell what is missing by looking at the rest of the photograph; the image of a man's hands clutching the coat suggests that a person is present. When reading a sentence or paragraph, if you find a word is missing from your vocabulary, you can often figure out its meaning by studying the sentence or paragraph in which it appears. The words surrounding an unknown word provide clues to its meaning, just as the details in the photograph provide clues about what is missing.

Chapter 2

Building Vocabulary: Using Context Clues

What Is Context?

Studying the details of the photograph on the opposite page helped you understand its meaning. Likewise, by studying closely the words in a sentence you can figure out the meaning of a particular word within the sentence. Read the following brief paragraph. Several words are missing. Try to figure out the missing words and write them in the blanks.

Sally has never been to Mexico, but she loves _____ food. Her favorite dish is _____, those delicious tortilla chips covered with cheese, beef, and beans. Just thinking about them makes Sally _____.

Did you insert the word *Mexican* in the first blank, *nachos* in the second blank, and *hungry* in the third blank? You were probably able to correctly identify all three missing words. You could tell from each sentence which word to put in. The words around each word—the sentence **context**—gave you clues as to which word would fit and make sense. Such clues are called **context clues.**

Even though you won't find missing words on a printed page, you will often find words that you do not know. Context clues can help you figure out the meanings of unfamiliar words.

EXAMPLE   Tony noticed that the **wallabies** at the zoo looked like kangaroos.

From the sentence, you can tell that *wallabies* are "animals that look like kangaroos."

EXAMPLE Many people have **phobias,** such as a fear of heights, a fear of water, or a fear of confined spaces.

You can figure out that *phobia* means "a fear of specific objects or situations."

Types of Context Clues

When you have trouble with a word, look for four types of context clues: (1) definition, (2) example, (3) contrast, and (4) inference.

Definition Clues

Writers often define a word right after they use it. They may give a brief definition or a **synonym** (a word that has the same meaning). They also use words and phrases such as *means*, *is*, *refers to*, and *are called*.

EXAMPLES *Broad, flat noodles that are served covered with sauce or butter* are called **fettuccine.**

Corona refers to *the outermost part of the sun's atmosphere.*

At other times, rather than formally define a word, a writer may provide a clue to its meaning.

EXAMPLE During the Christmas season, many people use decorative lights to **illuminate** their homes.

Here the word *lights* is a clue to the meaning of *illuminate*, which means to "light up."
 Sometimes a definition is only part of a sentence. In this kind of sentence, a writer may use three kinds of punctuation (commas, dashes, or parentheses) to separate the definition from the rest of the sentence.

EXAMPLES My Aunt Martha often serves **glog,** *a Swedish hot punch,* at her holiday parties.

The judge's **candor**—*his sharp, open frankness*—shocked the jury.

A leading cause of heart disease is a diet with too much **cholesterol** (*a fatty substance made of carbon, hydrogen, and oxygen*).

Textbook writers often use definition clues. As you read your texts, look for important words in **boldface type** or *italics*. These terms are usually right before or after a definition. Based on what you have just learned, what is the definition of **context** on page 31?

| **Exercise 2–1** | *Directions: Using the definition clues or synonyms in each sentence, circle the letter of the choice that best defines each boldfaced word.* |

1. The noise in the nursery school was **incessant;** the crying, yelling, and laughing never stopped.

   a. careless

   b. harmful

   c. bold

   (d.) continuous

2. There was a **consensus**—or unified opinion—among the students that the exam was difficult.

   a. requirement

   b. consequence

   c. disagreement

   (d.) agreement

3. Louie's **dossier** is a record of his credentials, including college transcripts and letters of recommendation.

   a. briefcase or valise

   b. checking account statement

   c. diploma

   (d.) collection of materials

4. Hearing, which is known as **audition**, begins when a sound wave reaches the outer ear.

   a. loud sound

   (b.) sense of hearing

   c. deafness

   d. the inner ear

5. When preparing job application letters, Serena develops one standard letter or **prototype.** Then she changes that letter to fit the specific jobs she is applying for.

   a. variation

   (b.) model

   c. detail

   d. introduction

6. The mayor worried that the town council was trying to **usurp** her power, but how could she prevent the council members from taking over?

   a. support

   (b.) take away

   c. improve

   d. allow

7. Joe was **hesitant** about asking Katy for a date because he wasn't sure if she liked him.
   a. definite
   (b.) uncertain
   c. casual
   d. heroic

8. The old man avoided his family; in fact, he **eschewed** the company of anyone who knew about his past.
   a. sought out
   b. enjoyed
   (c.) shunned
   d. welcomed

9. Rico is in favor of new drunk driving laws, but he does not **endorse** taking away drunk drivers' cars.
   a. stop
   b. regret
   c. start
   (d.) support

10. The teenager died from drinking a **lethal** amount of alcohol during a party.
    a. harmless
    b. moderate
    (c.) deadly
    d. excessive

Example Clues

Writers, especially textbook writers, often include examples to help explain or clarify a word. Suppose you do not know the meaning of the word *toxic*, and you find it used in a science text:

Toxic materials, such as arsenic, asbestos, pesticides, and lead, can cause bodily damage.

This sentence gives four examples of toxic materials, all of which are poisonous substances. You could conclude, then, that *toxic* means "poisonous." When writers put examples in a sentence, they often introduce them with the words *like*, *such as*, *for example*, or *including*.

EXAMPLES

In the past month, we have had almost every type of **precipitation**, including rain, snow, sleet, and hail.

Newsmagazines, like *Time* or *Newsweek*, are more detailed than newspapers.

Lena doesn't mind planting her favorite **annuals**—marigolds and zinnias—even though she has to do it every year.

By using the example clues, can you figure out that *precipitation* means "the forms in which water returns to earth" and that *newsmagazines* are "magazines that give in-depth coverage of news events"? Can you also tell that *annuals* are "plants that can't survive the winter"?

**Exercise
2-2**

Directions: Using the example clues in each sentence, circle the letter of the choice that best defines each boldfaced word.

1. Many **pharmaceuticals,** including morphine and penicillin, are not readily available in some countries.
   a. aspirin tablets
   b. pharmacists
   (c.) drugs
   d. substances

2. Jerry's child was **reticent** in every respect; she would not speak, refused to answer questions, and avoided looking at anyone.
   (a.) reserved
   b. noisy
   c. undisciplined
   d. rigorous

3. Most **condiments,** such as pepper, mustard, and catsup, are used to improve the flavor of foods.
   a. ingredients
   (b.) seasonings for food
   c. sauces
   d. appetizers

4. Dogs, cats, parakeets and other **sociable** pets can provide senior citizens with companionship.
   a. weak
   (b.) friendly
   c. dangerous
   d. unattractive

5. Paul's grandmother is a **sagacious** businesswoman; once she turned a small ice cream shop into a popular restaurant and sold it for a huge profit.
   a. old fashioned
   (b.) shrewd
   c. dishonest
   d. foolish

6. Rosie's dog was **submissive**—crouching, flattening its ears, and avoiding eye contact.
   a. friendly and excitable
   (b.) yielding to the control
      of another
   c. aggressive
   d. active

7. Many things about the library make it **conducive** to study, including good lighting and many reference books.
   a. unattractive
   b. uncomfortable
   c. helpful
   d. sociable

8. Clothing is available in a variety of **fabrics,** including cotton, wool, polyester, and linen.
   a. types of leather
   b. styles
   c. materials
   d. fashions

9. The raccoons were a **menace** to our backyard. They ate all of our tomato plants and dug holes in the grass.
   a. help
   b. barrier
   c. threat
   d. force

10. Murder, rape, and armed robbery are **reprehensible** crimes.
    a. reasonable
    b. unusual
    c. very bad
    d. rural

Contrast Clues

Sometimes you can determine the meaning of an unknown word from an **antonym**—a word or phrase that has an opposite meaning. Notice how the antonym *resisted* in the following sentence provides a clue to the meaning of the boldfaced term:

> One of the dinner guests **succumbed** to the temptation to have a second piece of cake, but the others resisted.

Since the others resisted a second dessert, you can tell that one guest gave in and had a piece. Thus, *succumbed* means the opposite of *resist*; that is, "to give in to." When writers use contrasting words or phrases, they often introduce them with words such as *but*, *though*, and *whereas*.

EXAMPLES

The professor **advocates** testing on animals, but many of her students are opposed to it.

Though Liz felt sad and depressed, most of the graduates were **elated.**

My Uncle Saul is quite **portly,** whereas his wife is very thin.

Can you tell from the contrast clues that *advocates* means "favors," *elated* means "happy," and *portly* means "heavy"?

Copyright © 2002 by Kathleen T. McWhorter

Exercise 2–3

Directions: Using the contrast clues or antonyms in each sentence, circle the letter of the choice that best defines each boldfaced word or phrase.

1. Freshmen are often **naive** about college at first, but by their second semester they are usually quite sophisticated in the ways of their new school.
   - (a.) innocent
   - b. sociable
   - c. annoyed
   - d. elated

2. Although most members of the class agreed with the instructor's evaluation of the film, several strongly **objected.**
   - a. agreed
   - b. debated
   - c. obliterated
   - (d.) disagreed

3. Little Jill hid shyly behind her mother when she met new people, yet her brother Matthew was very **gregarious.**
   - a. insulting
   - (b.) sociable
   - c. concerned
   - d. embarrassed

4. The child remained **demure** while the teacher scolded but became violently angry afterward.
   - (a.) quiet and reserved
   - b. boisterous
   - c. cowardly
   - d. upset and distraught

5. Some city dwellers are **affluent;** others live in or near poverty.
   - a. poor
   - b. arrogant
   - (c.) wealthy
   - d. agreeable

6. I am certain that the hotel will hold our reservation; however, if you are **dubious,** call to make sure.
   - a. confused
   - (b.) doubtful
   - c. sure
   - d. energetic

7. The speaker **denounced** certain legal changes while praising other reforms.
   - a. laughed at
   - b. cherished
   - (c.) spoke against
   - d. denied

8. The woman's parents **thwarted** her marriage plans though they liked her fiancé.
   - (a.) prevented
   - b. encouraged
   - c. idolized
   - d. organized

9. Extroverted people tend to be outgoing and talkative, while introverted people are more **reticent.**

    (a.) reserved   c. overbearing

    b. showy   d. helpless

10. Unlike other male-dominated species, Indian elephants live in a **matriarchal** society.

    a. aggressive   (c.) led by females

    b. nonthreatening   d. passive

Inference Clues

When you read, you often figure out the meaning of an unknown word through **inference**—a process that uses logic and reasoning skills. For instance, look at the following sentence:

Bob is quite **versatile:** he is a good student, a top athlete, an excellent car mechanic, and a gourmet cook.

Since Bob is successful at many different types of activities, you could infer that *versatile* means "capable of doing many things well."

EXAMPLES

When my friend tried to pay with Mexican **pesos,** the clerk explained that the store accepted only U.S. dollars.

On hot, humid summer afternoons, I often feel **languid.**

The vase must have been **jostled** in shipment because it arrived with several chips in it.

By using logic and your reasoning skills, can you figure out that *pesos* are a kind of "Mexican money"? Can you also tell that *languid* means "lacking energy" and *jostled* means "bumped"?

Exercise 2-4

Directions: Using logic and your own reasoning skills, circle the letter of the choice that best defines each boldfaced word.

1. To **compel** Clare to hand over her wallet, the mugger said he had a gun.

    a. discourage   (c.) force

    b. entice   d. imagine

2. Student journalists are taught how to be **concise** when writing in a limited space.

   a. peaceful
   b. clear and brief
   c. proper
   d. wordy

3. There should be more **drastic** penalties to stop people from littering.

   a. dirty
   b. suitable
   c. extreme
   d. dangerous

4. To **fortify** his diet while weightlifting, Monty took twelve vitamins a day.

   a. suggest
   b. strengthen
   c. avoid
   d. approve of

5. On our wedding anniversary, my husband and I **reminisced** about how we first met.

   a. sang
   b. remembered
   c. argued
   d. forgot

6. For their own safety, household pets should be **confined** to their own yard.

   a. led
   b. restricted
   c. shown
   d. used

7. The quarterback **sustained** numerous injuries: a fractured wrist, two broken ribs, and a hip injury.

   a. caused
   b. experienced
   c. displayed
   d. noticed

8. Sam's brother advised him to be **wary** of strangers he meets on the street.

   a. suspicious
   b. trusting
   c. congenial with
   d. generous toward

9. The lawyer tried to confuse the jury by bringing in many facts that weren't **pertinent** to the case.

   a. obvious
   b. continuous
   c. relevant
   d. harmful

10. We keep candles in the house to **avert** being left in the dark during power failures.

    a. prevent
    b. ensure
    c. accommodate
    d. begin

Using All of the Context Clues

When you read a chapter in a textbook or a story you like, you probably use all four types of context clues. You may find a definition here, an example there, and a contrasting word someplace else. You also put on your thinking cap and use your common sense and reasoning to figure out other words you don't know. Sometimes, though, there are no context clues, or they don't go far enough in explaining what a difficult word really means. For this reason, you need to develop other kinds of vocabulary skills, which are covered in the next chapter.

What Have You Learned?

Directions: To check your understanding of the chapter, select the word or phrase from the box below that best completes each of the following sentences. Keep in mind that two of the words will not be used.

examples	inference	definitions
context clues	parts	word group
antonym	synonym	context

1. The words around an unfamiliar word in a sentence are known as its
   _____context_____ .

2. _____Context clues_____ are hints or tips that help you figure out
   a word you don't know.

3. A _____synonym_____ has the same meaning as another
   word, whereas an antonym has an opposite meaning.

4. The two types of context clues that textbook authors often use are
   _____definitions_____ and examples.

5. When you figure out the meaning of a word by using logic and your
   reasoning skills, you are using _____inference_____ .

Directions: Using context clues, in the space provided write the letter of the choice that best defines each boldfaced word.

_____c_____ 1. The cat and her newborn kittens had to be **isolated** from the family dog after he tried to attack them.

    a. combined   c. separated

    b. heated up   d. rejected

_____d_____ 2. All of the movies I wanted to rent were taken, so as an **alternative** I went home and watched television.

    a. command   c. assignment

    b. design   d. another option

_____a_____ 3. The baby birds needed a place of **refuge** from the winter storm.

    a. shelter   c. building

    b. rejection   d. separation

_____b_____ 4. Mike's efforts to buy a car were **futile,** so he continued to ride his bike to work.

    a. helpful   c. necessary

    b. useless   d. careless

_____a_____ 5. Janice was **persistent** in asking her mother to buy a new car, so she finally gave in and bought one.

    a. stubborn   c. brief

    b. lazy   d. unenthusiastic

_____c_____ 6. The meal was prepared perfectly, but the young woman found it **repugnant.**

    a. overpriced   c. unappealing

    b. lovely   d. delicious

_____d_____ 7. Getting our car fixed after the accident was an **ordeal.**

    a. good time   c. unexpected event

    b. relaxing opportunity   d. painful experience

_____d_____ 8. Candace wore a red, low-cut dress to the party, but her sister was dressed more **decorously.**

    a. fashionably   c. fancy

    b. warmly   d. modestly

   b   9. Monica let a few weeks **elapse** before returning her ex-boyfriend's phone call.

            a. separate   c. slow down

            b. pass   d. speed up

   c   10. Gorillas can **convey** messages to humans through gestures and sounds.

            a. invent   c. communicate

            b. allow   d. approve of

NAME _____ SECTION _____

DATE _____ SCORE _____

Directions: Using context clues, in the space provided write the letter of the choice that best defines each boldfaced word.

___b___ 1. When several members of the president's staff were charged with various crimes, the public's confidence in the government **eroded.**

    a. grew   c. healed

    b. deteriorated   d. repeated

___b___ 2. People who suffer from migraine headaches are frequently advised to avoid foods that can **precipitate** an attack, such as chocolate and some cheeses.

    a. prevent   c. follow

    b. trigger   d. delay

___b___ 3. When solving a complex math problem, it is better to be **punctilious** and get it right than to be careless and risk getting it wrong.

    a. timely   c. mistaken

    b. careful   d. risky

___b___ 4. Being extremely thin has become a **compulsion** for many teenage girls.

    a. behavior   c. punishment

    b. obsession   d. separation

___a___ 5. The veterinarian gave the puppies vitamins to **stimulate** their appetites.

    a. arouse   c. stop

    b. confuse   d. delay

___b___ 6. The children looked angelic, but after their parents left they became more and more **obstreperous.**

    a. agreeable   c. sad

    b. unruly or rowdy   d. intellectual

___c___ 7. After visiting the dark cave, it was difficult to make the **transition** into the sunlight.

    a. purchase   c. change

    b. invention   d. repetition

_____a_____ 8. My **conservative** grandparents were disappointed when I served a vegetarian meal for Thanksgiving.

    a. resisting change   c. not definite

    b. opinionated   d. understanding

_____c_____ 9. The fact that Tim was ten years older than Sandy was enough to **deter** her from dating him.

    a. damage   c. prevent

    b. refuse   d. dislike

_____c_____ 10. Our senator **advocates** stricter gun control laws; she favors lengthening the waiting period for the purchase of guns.

    a. eliminates   c. supports

    b. opposes   d. indulges

NAME _____ SECTION _____

DATE _____ SCORE _____

Directions: Select the word from the box below that best defines the bold-faced word in each of the following sentences. Keep in mind that four of the words will not be used.

generous	exceed	travel plan	not intended
gruesome	not talkative	weaknesses	burned
lively	helpful	useless	
change	limit	trusting relationship	

1. The economy was in a state of continual **flux**; inflation increased one month and decreased the next. _____ change _____

2. Art is always talkative, but Ed is usually **taciturn**. _____ not talkative _____

3. Many **debilities** of old age, including poor eyesight and loss of hearing, can be treated medically. _____ weaknesses _____

4. The soap opera contained numerous **morbid** events: the death of a young child, the suicide of her father, and the murder of his older brother. _____ gruesome _____

5. After long hours of practice, Peter finally learned to type; Sam's efforts, however, were **futile**. _____ useless _____

6. The newspaper's error was **inadvertent**; the editor did not intend to include the victim's name. _____ not intended _____

7. To save money, we have decided to **curtail** the number of CDs we buy each month. _____ limit _____

8. Steam from the hot radiator **scalded** the mechanic's hand. _____ burned _____

9. Sonia's **itinerary** outlined her trip and listed Cleveland as her next stop. _____ travel plan _____

10. Steven had very good **rapport** with his father, but he was unable to get along with his mother. _____ trusting relationship _____

NAME _____ SECTION _____

DATE _____ SCORE _____

Directions: Using context clues, select the word from the box below that best defines each of the boldfaced words in the following paragraph. Keep in mind that four of the words will not be used.

Can looking at a color affect your behavior or **alter** your mood? Some researchers are **skeptical,** but others believe color can **influence** how you act and feel. A number of experiments have been conducted that **demonstrate** the effects of color. In 1979 a psychologist names Schauss **evaluated** the effect of the color pink. He found out that the color relaxed the subjects so much that they could not perform simple strength tests as well as they did when looking at other **hues.** The officer in charge of a U.S. Navy **brig** in Washington noticed Schauss's findings and allowed Schauss to test his calm-color **hypothesis** on inmates. Today, many **institutions,** such as jails, juvenile correction facilities, and holding centers, put individuals in pink rooms when their tempers **flare.**

colors	change	erupt	calm down
equaled	places of confinement	doubtful	show
theory	studied	prison	
demoralize	asylums	affect	

1. alter _____change_____   6. hues _____colors_____

2. skeptical _____doubtful_____   7. brig _____prison_____

3. influence _____affect_____   8. hypothesis _____theory_____

4. demonstrate _____show_____   9. institutions _places of confinement_

5. evaluated _____studied_____   10. flare _____erupt_____

Directions: Using context clues, select the word from the box below that best defines each of the boldfaced words in the following paragraph. Keep in mind that four of the words will not be used.

   The homeless are among the extremely poor. They are by definition people who sleep in streets, parks, shelters, and places not intended as **dwellings,** such as bus stations, lobbies, or **abandoned** buildings. Homelessness is not new. There have always been homeless people in the United States. But the homeless today differ in some ways from their **counterparts** of the 1950s and 1960s. More than 30 years ago, most of the homeless were old men, only a **handful** were women, and **virtually** no families were homeless. Today the homeless are younger, and include more women and families with young children. Today's homeless also are more **visible** to the general public because they are much more likely to sleep on the streets or in other public places in great numbers. They also suffer greater **deprivation.** Although in the past homeless men on Skid Row were **undoubtedly** poor, their average income from casual and **intermittent** work was three to four times more than what the current homeless receive. In addition, many of the older homeless had small but **stable** pensions, which today's homeless do not have.

—Thio, *Sociology,* p. 235

large group	dependable	almost	those who are similar
noticeable	blind	houses	given up completely
few	hardship	never	
definitely	integrated	not continuous	

1. dwellings _____ houses _____

2. abandoned __ given up completely __

3. counterparts __ those who are similar __

4. handful _____ few _____

5. virtually _____ almost _____

6. visible _____ noticeable _____

7. deprivation _____ hardship _____

8. undoubtedly _____ definitely _____

9. intermittent __ not continuous __

10. stable _____ dependable _____

CLIMBING MT. EVEREST
Seaborn "Beck" Weathers

This essay is taken from *Everest: Mountain Without Mercy*, a book that describes one man's attempt to climb Mt. Everest, the highest mountain in the world.

Vocabulary Preview

These are some of the difficult words in this essay. The definitions here will help you if you can't figure out the meanings from the sentence context or word parts.

constrict (par. 1) to make smaller

deteriorated (par. 4) worsened

dilated (par. 5) expanded

disembodied (par. 9) separated from the body

halting (par. 11) slow and uncertain, hesitant

remote (par. 12) distant, far away

primitive (par. 17) primary, basic

traverse (par. 1) something difficult to cross

1   As I approached the Southeast Ridge of Mt. Everest shortly before sunrise, I was feeling strong, but my eyes simply weren't focusing. Fortunately, I didn't really need to see the route, because deep steps had been kicked ahead of me. The traverse at the bottom of the Southeast Ridge required more vision, however, and I had great difficulty feeling my way along it. When we reached the Balcony, I had to tell Rob Hall that I wouldn't be able to continue climbing—for the moment. In the brightness of the sun perhaps my pupils would constrict and I could follow later, I told him optimistically.

2   "Only if you're able to leave here within the next 30 minutes," Rob told me.

3   "Well, if I can't, then I'll just head back down the mountain."

4   But Rob didn't like the idea of not knowing whether I had made it down safely or not, so he made me promise to stay put until he returned.

5   I was still waiting there for Rob when the evening light started to fade. My vision again deteriorated when my pupils dilated. I now regretted my promise

to Hall, especially because some hours earlier, around 1 P.M., others on our team had abandoned their summit attempt and offered to help me down.

6   Jon Krakauer, a teammate, was the first climber to return from the summit. He didn't mention having seen a storm coming, though in one of his accounts he reported that when high on the mountain he noticed that to the south a blanket of clouds had quickly replaced clear skies. I told Jon that I really couldn't see very well and that I needed to descend, and might need him to downclimb close enough to be my eyes.

7   Jon was willing to descend with me, but he reminded me that he was not a guide and that Mike Groom was coming 20 minutes behind him. Mike had a radio, and could let Hall know that I was heading down with him.

8   When Mike descended, he was assisting Yasuko Namba, who was badly exhausted. Neal Beidleman also came, with clients from Scott Fischer's group. Mike turned Yasuko over to Neal, then short-roped me down the Triangular Face.

9   From the face we climbed onto the South Col, and were there for only a few minutes when the storm came up—very quickly. I was cold but not particularly tired, and held onto Groom's coat sleeve. Visibility went to zip, and in the blowing snow and gathering darkness the other climbers became nothing more than fuzzy, disembodied headlamps. Totally lost, we were a pod of people following, like kids playing soccer, whoever was the current leader. We came to a standstill within feet of the sheer drop-off of the Kangshung Face, on the eastern edge of the South Col, and formed a huddle.

10   All of our oxygen had run out, and we rubbed and pounded on each others' backs, trying to keep every muscle in our bodies moving in order to generate heat and stay awake. I removed my right mitten, while leaving on the expedition-weight polypropylene glove liner, in order to place my hand inside my parka to warm it. The skin on my arm instantly froze. In that instant the wind blew my mitten away, and suddenly I was unable to zip up my parka. The spare pair of gloves in my pack might as well have been on the face of the moon, and I couldn't have opened my pack anyway.

11   After a few hours, some stars shone through a hole in the clouds, and we had a halting discussion about how to proceed. Some of us were barely able to walk, and I couldn't see. Groom and Beidleman decided to strike out in search of the camp, to send people back for us. This seemed reasonable.

12   Gradually, the whole scene became more remote. I had a sensation of floating, and didn't feel cold anymore. That must have been when I drifted off. I was not conscious when Anatoli Boukreev returned for the others.

13   Some time the next afternoon, I found myself alone on the ice. I was not terribly uncomfortable, and was convinced I was dreaming. The hardest part was coming to grips with the fact that my situation was real, and serious. I rolled over and looked at my right hand, which appeared like an unnatural, plastic, twisted gray thing attached to the end of my arm—not at all the hand that I knew. I banged it on the ice and it made a hollow sound, a sickening thunk.

14   This focused my attention. I could see my family there in front of my eyes, and managed to sit up, realizing that if I didn't get moving, I was going to lie there for eternity. None of our group was there; either they had left or

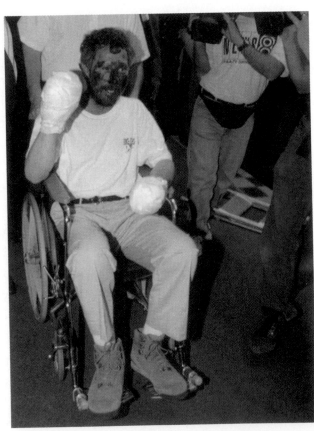

A severely frostbitten
Beck Weathers.

I had become separated from them. It was clear that help wouldn't show up now.

15   I dumped my pack and ice ax, figuring this was a one-shot deal: I would either find camp or lose my last remnant of energy and sit down to wait for the end. For about an hour and a half I wandered in different directions, unable to orient myself, hoping I'd recognize something.

16   Then I remembered that during the night someone had said that the wind blows over the South Col from the Western Cwm, from the west. Camp had to be upwind. So I turned into the wind, put my head down, and figured I'd either walk into camp or off the edge of the mountain.

17   I was propelled by a primitive desire to survive. My oxygen-starved brain wasn't working, but I was certain of one thing: that I would die, that very soon I would sit down in the snow and wait for exhaustion and the cold to overcome me. I began to hallucinate. The landscape was moving and the rocks changed shape and crawled around on me, but I accepted this and continued wandering. It was not at all frightening. I was in a very calm state, except for a feeling of sadness that I would be unable to say some of the things I wanted to to my family. I knew that I could accept death.

18   But I had a heck of a lot to live for, and wasn't going down easy. My family, standing there before me, became an enormous driving force. The changing, uneven surface of ice and rocks caused me to lose my balance and fall several times. I knew not to fall on my hands, so I rolled as I went down—which was exhausting in itself.

19   And then a miracle happened. A couple of soft, bluish rocks appeared in front of me, and their smoothness led me to think they might be tents. But right away I caught myself indulging this thought, knowing I would only be disappointed, which would affect my will to continue. I steered toward them anyway, preparing to walk right past them.

20   Suddenly, someone was standing there and it was Todd Burleson. He took one look at me, got me by the arm, and led me to camp. Pete Arhans and Todd were sure that I was going to die, too, but I'm glad they didn't tell me. When a middle-aged guy like me can survive that, it gives truth to the possibility that this kind of strength resides in each of us.

■ · ■

Directions: In the space provided, write the letter of the choice that best completes each of the following statements.

CHECKING YOUR COMPREHENSION

   d   1. The main point of the reading is that

      a. climbing Mr. Everest should only be attempted by young men with good eyesight.

      b. when facing death, it is easier to give up than to keep fighting to live.

      c. staying together in dangerous situations isn't as important as people think.

      d. most people have more inner strength than they realize.

   d   2. Paragraph 10 is primarily about

      a. how cold the temperature was.

      b. the group's efforts to stay awake.

      c. the oxygen supply.

      d. why the author's arm was frozen.

   b   3. The following statement best expresses the main idea of paragraph 17.

      a. Aware that he may die, the author fights to stay alive.

      b. The author is not afraid to die.

      c. Hallucinations are a way of knowing when death is near.

      d. Exhaustion is the result of lack of oxygen to breathe.

   c   4. At the time the others were rescued, the author was

      a. unwilling to leave.   c. unconscious.

      b. in severe pain.   d. crying.

   d   5. At first the author abandoned his attempt to climb Everest because

      a. a snowstorm came up

      b. he got separated from his guide.

      c. night came.

      d. his vision deteriorated.

USING YOUR CONTEXT CLUES

_____c_____ 6. In paragraph 1, the word **optimistically** means
  a. carefully.
  b. negatively.
  c. hopefully.
  d. thoughtfully.

_____c_____ 7. In paragraph 5, the word **regretted** means
  a. was glad about.
  b. was confident about.
  c. was sorry about.
  d. was confused about.

_____b_____ 8. In paragraphs 5 and 6, the word **summit** means
  a. useless.
  b. highest point.
  c. summation.
  d. earlier location.

_____d_____ 9. In paragraph 9, the word **zip** means
  a. close.
  b. vigorous movement.
  c. energy.
  d. nothing.

_____a_____ 10. In paragraph 15, the word **remnant** means
  a. remaining part.
  b. unimportant piece.
  c. destroyed piece.
  d. expression.

_____b_____ 11. In paragraph 16, the word **upwind** means
  a. over the top of a mountain.
  b. into the wind.
  c. away from the wind.
  d. toward the edge of a mountain.

_____a_____ 12. In paragraph 17, the word **propelled** means
  a. moved forward.
  b. stopped.
  c. stalled.
  d. exhausted.

_____c_____ 13. In paragraph 19, the word **indulging** means
  a. canceling.
  b. moving away from.
  c. giving into.
  d. ignoring.

_____d_____ 14. In paragraph 20, the word **resides** means
  a. is rewarding.
  b. is occasional.
  c. is unusual.
  d. is present.

a   15. In the sentence "I told Jon that I really couldn't see very well and that I needed to descend, and might need him to down-climb close enough to be my eyes," the word **descend** has which type of context clue?

     a. synonym   c. contrast

     b. example   d. inference

REVIEWING DIFFICULT VOCABULARY

Directions: Complete each of the following sentences by inserting a word from the Vocabulary Preview on page 48 in the space provided. A word should be used only once.

16. Due to age and weathering, the condition of the cabin's front porch had _____deteriorated_____.

17. Knowing that he would probably fail the exam, the unprepared student walked at a _____halting_____ pace toward the exam room.

18. Due to its _____remote_____ location, the mountain cabin has not been used for years.

19. As more and more people crowded into the small elevator, its space seemed to _____constrict_____.

20. _____Primitive_____ human needs include food, shelter, and safety.

Chapter 2:   Building Vocabulary: Using Context Clues

RECORDING YOUR PROGRESS

Test	Number Right	Score
Practice Test 2-1	_____ × 10 =	_____ %
Practice Test 2-2	_____ × 10 =	_____ %
Practice Test 2-3	_____ × 10 =	_____ %
Mastery Test 2-1	_____ × 10 =	_____ %
Mastery Test 2-2	_____ × 10 =	_____ %
Mastery Test 2-3	_____ × 5 =	_____ %

EVALUATING YOUR PROGRESS

Based on your test performance, rate how well you have mastered the skills taught in this chapter by checking one of the boxes below or by writing your own evaluation.

☐ **Need More Improvement**

Tip: Try using the "Vocabulary" Module on the Reading Road Trip CD-ROM or Website that accompanies this textbook to fine-tune the skills that you have learned in this chapter.

☐ **Need More Practice**

Tip: Try using the "Vocabulary" Module on the Reading Road Trip CD-ROM that accompanies this textbook to brush up on the skills you have learned in this chapter, or visit this textbook's Website at **http://ablongman.com/mcwhorter** for extra practice.

☐ **Good**

Tip: To maintain your skills, do a quick review of this chapter by using the Website that accompanies this textbook by logging on to **http://ablongman.com/mcwhorter.**

☐ **Excellent**

YOUR EVALUATION: _____

_____

_____

_____

_____

Read Me First!

Look at the photograph showing Aaron baking delicious chocolate cookies. Even though he hasn't made this dessert before, he can figure out how to do it. He reads the recipe, gathers all the ingredients together, and combines everything in the correct sequence.

When you see a word you don't know, you may also be able to figure out its meaning by looking at its "ingredients" or parts.

Chapter 3

Building Vocabulary: Using Word Parts

What Are Word Parts?

Just as Aaron baked the cookies he hadn't made before by working with the ingredients presented in a recipe, you can learn many new words by studying their "ingredients" or parts.

Although many people build their vocabulary word by word, studying word parts is a better and faster way to do it. For example, if you learn that *pre-* means *before*, then you can begin to figure out hundreds of words that begin with *pre* (premarital, premix, prepay).

Suppose you came across the following sentence in a child psychology text:

The parents thought their child was **unteachable.**

If you did not know the meaning of *unteachable*, how could you figure it out? Since there are no clues in the sentence context, you might decide to look up the word in a dictionary. An easier way, though, is to break the word into parts. Many words in the English language are made up of word parts called *prefixes*, *roots*, and *suffixes*. A **prefix** comes at the beginning of a word, and a **suffix** comes at the end of a word. The **root**—which contains a word's basic meaning—forms the middle.

Let's look at the word *unteachable* again and divide it into three parts: its prefix, root, and suffix.

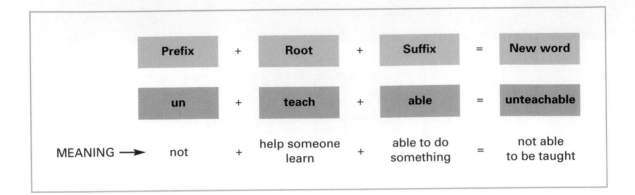

By using word parts, you can see that *unteachable* means "not able to be taught."

EXAMPLE   My friend Josh is **nonconformist.**

non- = not
conform = go along with others
-ist = one who does something
nonconformist = someone who does not go along with others

To use word parts effectively, you should learn some of the most common ones. The prefixes and roots listed in Tables 3-1 and 3-2 are a good place to start. By knowing just *some* of these prefixes and roots, you can figure out the meanings of thousands of words without looking them up in the dictionary. For instance, more than 10,000 words can begin with the prefix *non-*. Another common prefix, *pseudo-* (which means "false") is used in more than 400 words. As you can see, by learning only a few word parts, you can add many new words to your vocabulary.

Prefixes

Though some English words do not have a prefix, many of them do. Prefixes appear at the *beginnings* of words and change the meaning of the root to which they are connected. For example, if you add the prefix *re-* to

TABLE 3-1   Common Prefixes

Prefix	Meaning	Sample Word
Prefixes Referring to Amount or Number		
mono/uni	one	monocle/unicycle
bi/di/du	two	bimonthly/divorce/duet
tri	three	triangle
quad	four	quadrant
quint/pent	five	quintet/pentagon
deci	ten	decimal
centi	hundred	centigrade
milli	thousand	milligram
micro	small	microscope
multi/poly	many	multipurpose/polygon
semi	half	semicircle
equi	equal	equidistant
Prefixes Meaning "Not" (Negative)		
a	not	asymmetrical
anti	against	antiwar
contra	against, opposite	contradict
dis	apart, away, not	disagree
in/il/ir/im	not	incorrect/illogical/irreversible/impossible
mis	wrongly	misunderstand
non	not	nonfiction
un	not	unpopular
pseudo	false	pseudoscientific
Prefixes Giving Direction, Location, or Placement		
ab	away	absent
ad	toward	adhesive
ante/pre	before	antecedent/premarital
circum/peri	around	circumference/perimeter
com/col/con	with, together	compile/collide/convene
de	away, from	depart
dia	through	diameter
en/em	into, within	encase/embargo
ex/extra	from, out of, former	ex-wife/extramarital
hyper	over, excessive	hyperactive
inter	between	interpersonal
intro/intra	within, into, in	introduction
post	after	posttest
re	back, again	review
retro	backward	retrospect
sub	under, below	submarine
super	above, extra	supercharge
tele	far	telescope
thermo	heat	thermometer
trans	across, over	transcontinental

the word *read*, the word *reread* is formed, meaning "to read again." If *dis-* is added to the word *respect*, the word *disrespect* is formed, meaning "lack of respect."

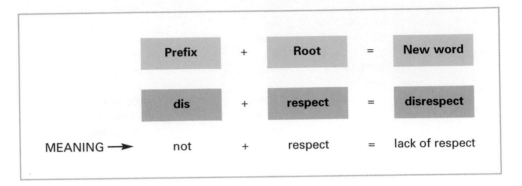

Prefix	+	**Root**	=	**New word**
dis	+	**respect**	=	**disrespect**
MEANING ⟶ not	+	respect	=	lack of respect

Exercise 3–1

Directions: Using the list of common prefixes in Table 3-1, match each word in column A with its meaning from column B. Write the letter of your choice in the space provided.

Column A		Column B
_f_	1. misplaced	a. half a circle
_d_	2. interoffice	b. build again
_i_	3. exhale	c. unusual
_a_	4. semicircle	d. between offices
_h_	5. nonprofit	e. not fully developed
_b_	6. reconstruct	f. put in the wrong position
_j_	7. triathlete	g. build up electrical power again
_c_	8. atypical	h. not for making money
_g_	9. recharge	i. breathe out
_e_	10. immature	j. one who participates in three-part sporting events

Exercise 3–2

Directions: Select a prefix from the box below that will complete the word indicated in each of the following sentences. One of the prefixes is used more than once.

bi	inter	re
dis	ir	retro
im	mis	sub

1. A person who speaks two languages is _____**bi**_____ lingual.

2. My new sweater had a snag; I returned it to the store because it was _____**im**_____ perfect.

3. The flood damage in Carl's hometown was permanent and _____**ir**_____ reversible.

4. Sheila was not given the correct date and time; she was _____**mis**_____ informed.

5. The magazine didn't interest me, so I _____**dis**_____ continued my subscription.

6. Clothing that does not pass factory inspection is considered _____**sub**_____ standard and is often sold at a discount.

7. The raise I got on April 1 will apply to last month's salary as well; it will be _____**retro**_____ active to March 1.

8. The attorneys acted as _____**inter**_____ mediaries between the angry, divorcing couple.

9. Because the results of the research study were unexpected, the research team decided to _____**re**_____ plicate the experiment.

10. The draperies in Juan's apartment are _____**dis**_____ colored because they were exposed to the sun for too long.

Roots

Think of roots as being at the core of a word's meaning. You already know many roots—like *bio* in *biology* and *sen* in *insensitive*—because they are used in everyday speech. Thirty-one of the most common and useful roots are listed in Table 3-2. Learning the meanings of these roots will help

TABLE 3-2	Common Roots	
Common Root	**Meaning**	**Sample Word**
aud/audit	hear	audible/auditory
aster/astro	star	asteroid/astronaut
bene	good, well	benefit
bio	life	biology
cap	take, seize	captive
chron(o)	time	chronology
corp	body	corpse
cred	believe	incredible
dict/dic	tell, say	dictate/predict
duc/duct	lead	introduce/conduct
fact/fac	make, do	factory/factor
graph	write	telegraph
geo	earth	geophysics
log/logo/logy	study, thought	logic/psychology
mit/miss	send	permit/dismiss
mort/mor	die, death	immortal/mortician
path	feeling	sympathy
phono	sound, voice	telephone
photo	light	photosensitive
port	carry	transport
scop	seeing	microscope
scrib/script	write	scribe/inscription
sen/sent	feel	sensitive/sentiment
spec/spic/spect	look, see	retrospect/spectacle
tend/tent/tens	stretch or strain	tendon/tension
terr/terre	land, earth	terrain/territory
theo	god	theology
ven/vent	come	convention/venture
vert/vers	turn	invert/inverse
vis/vid	see	invisible/video
voc	call	vocation

you unlock the meanings of many words. For example, if you know that the root *dic/dict* means "tell or say," then you would have a clue to the meanings of such words as *dictate* (to speak for someone to write down) or *dictionary* (a book that "tells" what words mean).

When you see a word you don't know, and you can't figure it out from the sentence context, follow these tips:

1. **Look for the root first.**
2. **Keep in mind that the spelling of a root may change a bit if it is combined with a suffix.**

(Table 3-2 has some examples of spelling changes.)

Exercise 3–3

Directions: Using the list of common roots in Table 3-2, match each word in column A with its meaning from column B. Write the letter of your choice in the space provided. To help you, the roots in each word in column A are in italics.

	Column A		Column B
i	1. *aud*ible	a.	undertaker
h	2. *miss*ive	b.	went back
j	3. *sent*iment	c.	able to respond to light
a	4. *mort*ician	d.	come between two things
d	5. inter*vene*	e.	channel or pipe that brings water from a distance
b	6. re*vert*ed	f.	use the voice
e	7. aque*duct*	g.	blessing; expression of good wishes
c	8. *photo*active	h.	letter or message
f	9. *voc*alize	i.	can be heard
g	10. *bene*diction	j.	expression of a feeling

Exercise 3–4

Directions: Select a word from the box below that best completes each of the following sentences. Refer to the list of roots in Table 3-2 if you need help.

apathetic	extraterrestrial	prescribed	spectators	verdict
deduce	graphic	scriptures	synchronized	visualize

1. After hearing the testimony, the jury brought in its _____verdict_____ quickly.

2. Religious or holy writings are called _____scriptures_____.

3. Tina closed her eyes and tried to _____visualize_____ the license plate number.

4. As they watched the football game, the _____spectators_____ became tense.

5. Henry's doctor _____prescribed_____ two types of medication for his rash.

6. The murderer seemed _____apathetic_____ when the judge pronounced her sentence.

7. Just before the race, the runners _____synchronized_____ their watches.

8. My history text contains many _____graphic_____ aids, including maps, charts, and diagrams.

9. Emily's favorite movie is about a(n) _____extraterrestrial_____, a creature not from earth.

10. By putting together many clues, the detective was finally able to _____deduce_____ who committed the crime.

Suffixes

Suffixes are word *endings*. Think of them as add-ons that make a word fit grammatically into a sentence. For example, adding the suffix *y* to the noun *cloud* forms the adjective *cloudy*. The words *cloud* and *cloudy* are used in different ways:

The rain **cloud** above me looked threatening.

It was a **cloudy,** rainy weekend.

You can often form several different words from a single root by adding different suffixes.

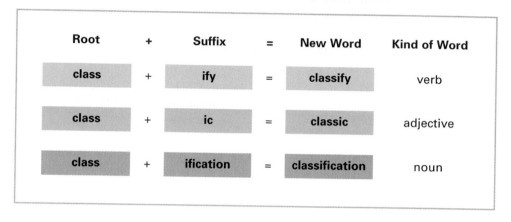

Root	+	Suffix	=	New Word	Kind of Word
class	+	ify	=	classify	verb
class	+	ic	=	classic	adjective
class	+	ification	=	classification	noun

As you know, when you find a word that you do not know, look for the root first. Then try to figure out what the word means with the suffix added. A list of common suffixes and their meanings appears in Table 3-3.

TABLE 3-3   Common Suffixes

Suffix	Sample Word	Suffix	Sample Word
Suffixes Referring to a State, Condition, or Quality			
able	touchable	ive	permissive
ance	assistance	like	childlike
ation	confrontation	ment	amazement
ence	reference	ness	kindness
ful	playful	ous	jealous
ible	tangible	ty	loyalty
ion	discussion	y	creamy
ity	superiority		
Suffixes Meaning "One Who"			
an	Italian	ent	resident
ant	participant	er	teacher
ee	referee	ist	activist
eer	engineer	or	advisor
Suffixes Meaning "Pertaining to or Referring to"			
al	autumnal	hood	brotherhood
ship	friendship	ward	homeward

Sometimes you may find that the spelling of the root word changes because of the suffix. For instance, a final *e* may be dropped, a final consonant may be doubled, or a final *y* may be changed to *i*. Keep these possibilities in mind when you're trying to identify a root word.

EXAMPLES

David's article was a **compilation** of facts.

Root: compil(e)
Suffix: -ation
New word: compilation (something that has been compiled, or put together, in an orderly way)

We were concerned with the **legality** of our decision about our taxes.

Root: legal
Suffix: -ity
New word: legality (involving legal matters)

Our college is one of the most **prestigious** in the state.

Root: prestig(e)
Suffix: -ious
New word: prestigious (having prestige or distinction)

In the examples above, which root word did not have a spelling change when the suffix was added? Did you notice that *compile* and *prestige* both lost an *e*?

Exercise 3-5

Directions: *For each list of four words, select the choice that best completes each of the following sentences. Write your answer in the space provided.*

1. *conversely, converse, conversation, conversing*

   Our phone _____ conversation _____ lasted ten minutes.

2. *assist, assistant, assisted, assists*

   My doctor's _____ assistant _____ labels each patient's blood samples.

3. *qualifications, qualify, qualifies, qualifying*

   As Bill spoke to the interviewer, he outlined his

   _____ qualifications _____ for the job.

4. *intern, interned, internship, interning*

Dr. Bernard completed her _____internship_____ at Memorial Medical Center.

5. *eating, eat, eater, eaten*

We did not realize that the blossoms of the plant could be _____eaten_____ .

6. *audition, audio, audible, audioed*

Theresa spoke so softly that her voice was not _____audible_____ .

7. *sincerer, sincere, sincerity, sincerest*

When my best friend lied to me, I began to question her _____sincerity_____ .

8. *permitted, permit, permissive, permission*

Beverly's professor granted her _____permission_____ to miss class.

9. *instructor, instructive, instructs, instructed*

The lecture on Freud was very _____instructive_____ .

10. *remembrance, remember, remembering, remembered*

A wealthy businessman donated the building in _____remembrance_____ of his deceased father.

11. *mortal, mortally, mortals, mortality*

The _____mortality_____ rate in Ethiopia is very high.

12. *presidency, president, presidential, presidentship*

The _____presidential_____ race was full of surprises.

13. *femininely, feminine, feminism, feminist*

She called herself a _____feminist_____ , but she never actively supported equal rights for women.

14. *hazarding, hazardous, hazard, hazardousness*

When there is toxic waste in a lake, it is _____ hazardous _____ to health.

15. *destiny, destined, destinies, destine*

Robert felt it was his _____ destiny _____ to become a priest.

16. *different, differences, differ, differing*

The physical _____ differences _____ among the three brothers were striking.

17. *friend, friendly, friendlier, friendship*

A true _____ friendship _____ with another person sometimes lasts a lifetime.

18. *comforted, comfortable, comforting, comfort*

I felt _____ comfortable _____ in my role as counselor.

19. *popularize, popular, popularity, popularly*

The rock group's _____ popularity _____ rose after their first hit song.

20. *apologetic, apology, apologizing, apologize*

Kelly seemed _____ apologetic _____ about the temper tantrum she had last night.

Using Word Parts

When you're reading your favorite magazine or one of your textbooks, you'll often be able to figure out new words from context, as you did in Chapter 2. Now, though, you have even stronger vocabulary skills because you know how to work with word parts. As you work with prefixes, roots, and suffixes, remember these tips:

1. Look for the *root* first and try to figure out its meaning, even if a few of its letters are missing.

2. Look for a *prefix* and see how it changes the meaning of the root word.

3. Find a *suffix* and see how it further changes or adds to the meaning.

When you use word parts every day, you will find that your vocabulary grows by leaps and bounds.

What Have You Learned?

Directions: Write true (T) or false (F) before each of the following statements.

___F___ 1. A word part that comes at the beginning of a word is known as a suffix.

___T___ 2. Prefixes change the meaning of a word.

___F___ 3. All English words have prefixes.

___T___ 4. A suffix helps a word fit grammatically into a sentence.

___T___ 5. The part of a word that carries its core meaning is known as a root.

___F___ 6. When a suffix is added to a root, the spelling of the root always changes.

Directions: In each of the following sentences, the boldfaced word contains a root and a prefix and/or suffix. Using your knowledge of word parts, in the space provided write the letter of the choice that best defines each word.

___c___   1. Enoch was a lawyer before he turned to **theology.**

     a. writing   c. study of religion

     b. teaching   d. study of life

___b___   2. The **antiwar** movement of the 1960s helped bring about U.S. withdrawal from Vietnam.

     a. before war   c. in favor of war

     b. against war   d. during war

___d___   3. If you use spaces instead of tabs in your computer document, your columns will **misalign.**

     a. be against one line   c. form a small line

     b. skip a line   d. line up wrong

___b___   4. The juggler's performance **captivated** the audience.

     a. bored   c. misjudged

     b. seized the attention of   d. quieted

___c___   5. Peter's English instructor told him he had written a **creditable** paper.

     a. very poor   c. deserving credit

     b. detailed   d. lacking credit

___b___   6. The coroner prepared a **postmortem** report on the drowning victim.

     a. before life   c. written again

     b. after death   d. confused

___b___   7. The Supreme Court's decisions are **irreversible.**

     a. capable of great injury   c. unacceptable

     b. not able to be turned around   d. flawless

___a___   8. As we watched the movie, the music seemed to **foretell** the murder of the heroine.

     a. predict   c. delay

     b. repeat   d. cover up

_____c_____ 9. My congressman pledged to put an end to **substandard** wages in our district.

    a. illegal   c. below normal

    b. under investigation   d. dishonest

_____a_____ 10. A famous **economist** predicted that unemployment would increase.

    a. person who studies economics

    b. theories of economics

    c. former studies of the economy

    d. the quality of the economy

Directions: Using your knowledge of word parts, in the space provided write the letter of the choice that best defines each word.

_____c_____ 1. multistage rocket
- a. rocket with two stages
- b. rocket with three stages
- c. rocket with several stages
- d. multipurpose rocket

_____a_____ 2. noncommittal
- a. unwilling to reveal attitude or feeling
- b. unable to perform a task
- c. unwilling to make an effort
- d. unwilling to change

_____d_____ 3. equidistant
- a. specific distances
- b. uneven distances
- c. unlike distances
- d. equal distances

_____b_____ 4. triennial
- a. occurring once a year
- b. occurring every three years
- c. occurring every two years
- d. occurring every four years

_____d_____ 5. transcultural
- a. differences in cultures
- b. within cultures
- c. among cultures
- d. extending across cultures

_____c_____ 6. chronometer
- a. machine to control velocity
- b. device to control friction
- c. instrument for measuring time
- d. instrument for measuring speed

_____a_____ 7. disaffiliated
- a. not associated
- b. partially associated
- c. weakly associated
- d. strongly associated

_____a_____ 8. territory
- a. area of land
- b. related to fear
- c. upper surface area
- d. resulting from terror

    a   9. astrology
        a. study of positions of stars   c. form of heat
        b. study of types of sound   d. type of lens

    b   10. photosensitive cell
        a. cell sensitive to heat   c. cell sensitive to color
        b. cell sensitive to light   d. cell sensitive to friction

NAME _____ SECTION _____

DATE _____ SCORE _____

Directions: Select the word part from the box below that will complete the word indicated in the following sentences. Each word part should be used only once.

dict	terr	trans	uni	vis
vert	thermo	un	ver	voc

1. The instant replay provided _____**ver**_____ ification that our team had won the football game.

2. The _____**terr**_____ ain was too rocky for planting vegetables.

3. Even though Karen dropped her expensive vase, it remained _____**un**_____ broken.

4. During the job interview, Joe was asked what he en _____**vis**_____ ioned doing in five years.

5. My cousin con _____**vert**_____ ed his Canadian currency to American dollars.

6. The minister's in _____**voc**_____ ation began the morning services.

7. All of the children in the marching band were required to wear _____**uni**_____ forms.

8. Many students were able to pre _____**dict**_____ their exam grades.

9. When I _____**trans**_____ planted the tree to a different location, it grew much bigger.

10. _____**Thermo**_____ dynamics deals with the connection between heat and mechanical energy.

Directions: Read the paragraph below. Using your knowledge of word parts, write the correct meaning for each word listed.

When Dimitri and his wife Carol began to renovate their old house, they underestimated the amount of time and effort it would take. They were careless in their planning, and they miscalculated the amount of money they would need. Since the bank was hesitant to provide more money for their project, the young couple was fearful that they would have to forgo the house of their dreams. Eventually, though, Dimitri and Carol overcame their financial problems, and their friends and families pitched in on a multitude of tasks—rewiring, painting, and even putting on a new roof. In less than a year, their old rundown house was transformed into a lovely Victorian.

1. renovate _____ restore _____

2. underestimated _____ figured as less _____

3. careless _____ not attentive; sloppy _____

4. miscalculated _____ made a mistake in estimating _____

5. hesitant _____ not inclined _____

6. fearful _____ afraid _____

7. forgo _____ give up _____

8. overcame _____ conquered _____

9. multitude _____ large number _____

10. transformed _____ changed _____

NAME _____ SECTION _____

DATE _____ SCORE _____

Directions: Using your knowledge of word parts, select the word from the box below that best completes each of the following sentences. Each word should be used only once.

flexible	benefits	endanger	snakelike	location
dramatic	tension	erroneously	strenuous	peaceful

Lu-chin loves to exercise. She knows, though, that too much exercise or exercise done ___erroneously___ could ___endanger___ her health. To get ready for a ___strenuous___ workout, she stretches and bends to make her body ___flexible___.

Once Lu-chin is warmed up, she likes to jog around the quiet, ___peaceful___ park near her home. Its winding, ___snakelike___ trails and ___dramatic___ views make it a perfect ___location___ for her early morning run. When she's done, she walks and stretches again to relieve the ___tension___ in her body. Because Lu-chin knows how to exercise correctly, her running truly ___benefits___ her health.

THE DOLPHIN AFFAIR
Dan Greenburg

In this article, first printed in the magazine *Modern Maturity*, Dan Greenburg vividly describes his experiences swimming with dolphins.

Vocabulary Preview

These are some of the difficult words in this essay. The definitions here will help you if you can't figure out the meanings from the sentence context or word parts.

ominous (par. 4) threatening, unfavorable

linguistic (par. 15) having to do with language

evolution (par. 18) change that occurs over time to an organ, person, plant, or animal

synchrony (par. 16) movement taking place at the same time and rate

pidgin (par. 17) a simplified speech used between people who speak different languages

criteria (par. 25) standards

imperceptibility (par. 33) gradually, not noticeably

caveats (par. 21) rules, warnings

---

1   I have always been fascinated by dolphins. By their intelligence, their playfulness, their kindness to humans. I'd heard that dolphins become alarmed if you're upright in the water and will do anything, including pushing you with their beaks and whapping you with their tails, to get you into a horizontal position. I'd heard that dolphins use their sonar to examine you for signs of distress. That's like having a radiologist friend x-ray you when you come over for dinner. I had a picture of dolphins as helpful, protective, concerned, worried, compulsive, somewhat controlling creatures—Jewish mothers of the sea—and I wanted to meet some. So I made plans to swim with them in Florida, then join an experimental program in Hawaii that tests their intelligence and linguistic skill.

2   Dolphins Plus in Key Largo, Florida, studies interaction between dolphins and humans and conducts dolphin-assisted therapy for people with disabilities. It houses a huge dolphin pool and lecture hall and allows small groups of visitors to swim with its dolphins.

3   I'm accompanied by my fiancée, Judith, my 13-year-old son, Zack, and local photographer Stephen Frink, a dead ringer for movie star Chuck Norris. We're taken to an 80 × 120-foot partially fenced-off section of a canal that leads into the ocean. Seven dolphins, all females, swim around in the murky water. I've been told relentlessly that they're safe to swim with, but I'm uneasy. My apprehension grows when an instructor named Christy enters and gives us our preswim briefing. "The dolphins are not trained to allow people to touch them in this program—in other programs you can—so whatever you

Dolphins mate 365 days a year—no wonder they are always smiling.

do, don't touch them. Don't reach out to them either. They might interpret that as threatening. In fact," she says, "don't swim with your hands at all—trail them at your sides or clasp them behind your back."

4   I find it frustrating not being allowed to touch them. I find it ominous not being allowed to swim with my hands. But the implication seems that if I use them now, I might not be able to use them afterwards.

5   "If a dolphin looks at you," says Christy, "break eye contact immediately. That's how they challenge each other." They challenge each other? Is she saying that adorable Flipper, the Lassie of the sea, has attitude?

6   "Also, stay ten feet away from any other human in the water," she continues. "Dolphins consider us toys, and they don't like sharing them. Most important, don't jerk your head." Head-jerks, she explains, are tantamount to saying rude things about a dolphin's mother. We're then told that dolphins are eight to ten feet long, weigh more than 350 pounds, and can swim up to 40 miles per hour. We're told that dolphins will mate 365 days a year. We're told that dolphins like kids best, women second, and men least.

7   "Okay," says Christie, "get into the water."

8   Getting into the water is the last thing I want to do right now, but I see Judith and Zack slip into the pool, so I follow. Underwater, I peer warily at the dolphins. They're off in a corner, like girls at a mixer, too shy to come over and say hi.

9   Suddenly, one of them screws up her courage and zooms across the pool—toward me—missing me by millimeters. Another dolphin decides this is amusing and whizzes toward me at what seems like double the speed. I freeze, wondering what it's like to be rammed by more than 300 pounds of speeding mammal, but she misses me by the diameter of a hair. The girls retreat to the far side of the pool and snigger. And that's it. They make no more advances, show no more interest, not even in Zack or Judith.

10   Stephen says he's not getting the shots he needs and asks us to attract the dolphins by making sounds. Attracting the dolphins toward me again is not something I'm eager to do, but I know we need the pictures. Judith hums sea chanteys. I do flawless imitations of whale song.

11   "Dad, why are you doing sad puppy sounds?" Zack asks. "Are you trying to guilt them into coming over?"

12   Christy suggests we swim across the pool on our bellies in a sort of Busby Berkeley water ballet. I ask what this is for and she says it's for the girls' amusement. Ah. Well, I do hope they're amused, but they no longer seem to notice.

13   Unable to get the pictures he wants from the deck, Stephen enters the pool. He's wearing a black and purple wetsuit with neon-colored accessories and is carrying several shiny underwater cameras and lights. The girls come to life, race across the pool, and converge on him like high school sophomores around Brad Pitt.

14   I'm a tad disappointed. No, let's be frank. I am speechless with jealousy. Your buddy begs you to let him tag along to this great party, and when you get there the women ignore you but hang onto him like lint on a black suit. I find the Dolphins Plus girls surprisingly shallow, being less impressed by a writer with a good personality than by a Chuck Norris look-alike in flashy clothing. I hope for better luck in Hawaii. . . .

15   The dolphins at the Kewalo Basin Marine Mammal Laboratory have been taught to respond to approximately 150 sign-language gestures and several thousand combinations thereof. One of these is truly amazing. Give them a list of commands, then slip the sign for ERASE anywhere into your list. The dolphins will automatically delete every command before ERASE and do all the others.

16   Their most impressive maneuver, though, is called TANDEM-CREATIVE and requires two dolphins. The TANDEM-CREATIVE sign means "Okay guys, do whatever you like, but discuss it first, do it together, and do it now." No sooner does the trainer give the sign than they're off, whistling and clicking. They race around the pool, leap into the air, and do three backward somersaults in perfect synchrony. I naively suggest that they probably just do the same trick each time. She gives me a "Watch this" look and repeats the command. This time they leap into the air, touch flippers, then swim on their backs while touching pectoral fins. Hmmm. Most of my friends couldn't even get past choosing the activity.

17   I've been learning to sign at KBMML, and have mastered roughly three dozen commands. Today I'm to perform my first "local," or one-on-one with Elele (whom the staff call Ellie). I think of it as our first date. I am nervous.

For one thing, there was the rejection by the fickle hussies at Key Largo. For another, there's the language barrier. Will I "speak" gracefully or will I utter pidgin dolphin? . . .

18   With a bravado more feigned than felt, I ascend the stand and flash PRESENT BELLY. Ellie considers this a moment, and then . . . complies! She rolls over submissively and presents her belly. I stroke it avidly. Touching a dolphin's skin is a pleasant surprise, like smooth rubber. Judith dubbed them big rubber puppies, which is as good a description as I've heard.

19   Without thinking, I flash OPEN MOUTH. She does. Uh-oh! I am now expected to stick my hand and forearm into the mouth of a creature that weighs over 350 pounds, has approximately 100 sharp teeth, and has a tail and a dorsal fin like a shark's. I poke my hand and forearm tentatively inside. The skin of my hand grazes her teeth and tongue. If she closes her jaws now, I will return as Captain Hook.

20   She doesn't. In fact, she presents all of her body parts. After thoroughly inspecting Ellie's body, which I've rarely been able to get away with on most first dates, I reward her with a dead smelt (on dates I always provide dinner).

21   The tryst ends sweetly with a HUG and a KISS. But before I do, my trainer-chaperone warns me: (1) don't hug too long, (2) don't pet below the "waist" (beneath the dorsal fin on the back or beneath the navel on the belly), and (3) keep kisses chastely close-mouthed (a needless directive). Her caveats are not whimsical. Dolphins are highly sexual and harbor no stuffy biases against inter-species romance. Indeed, women who have swum with dolphins have reported behavior more commonly associated with former Senator Packwood.

22   I flash HUG (bend forward, arms in a circle) and Ellie rises into them and rests her head on my shoulder. Awww. Then KISS (two fingers on my mouth) and she rises to touch her beak to my lips. Prigs keep their fingers between their mouths and the dolphin's. I am not a prig.

23   At the end of the week, it's time to finally say good-bye. Farewells are bittersweet. I wave my hand. Ellie waves a flipper. We hug. We kiss. I don't suggest we correspond. I suspect we both know this was just a summer fling.

■ · ■

Directions: In the space provided, write the letter of the choice that best completes each of the following statements.

CHECKING YOUR COMPREHENSION

_____c_____ 1. The main point of this selection is that
   a. dolphin research centers differ in what they allow visitors to do with the dolphins.
   b. after swimming together, a human and a dolphin will create a lifetime bond.
   c. learning to swim and communicate with dolphins is a difficult but rewarding experience.
   d. dolphins are more like humans than was ever imagined.

_____c_____ 2. The author wanted to learn more about dolphins because
   a. he wanted to see if dolphins were smarter than humans.
   b. he wanted to overcome his fear of dolphins.
   c. he had always been fascinated by dolphins.
   d. he wanted to impress his fiancée and his son.

_____b_____ 3. The following is *not* one of the instructions Christy gave during her briefing:
   a. Put your hands at your sides or behind your back.
   b. If a dolphin looks at you, look him in the eye.
   c. Stay 10 feet away from other humans in the water.
   d. Don't jerk your head.

_____b_____ 4. According to this article, the following is true of dolphins:
   a. They weigh about 100 pounds.
   b. They swim up to 40 mph.
   c. They usually obey spoken commands from humans.
   d. They like men best among humans.

_____b_____ 5. The group that dolphins like best is
   a. men.   c. older people.
   b. kids.   d. women.

_____c_____ 6. According to the reading, a dolphin's skin feels like
   a. wet paper.   c. smooth rubber.
   b. silk.   d. velvet.

_____a_____ 7. The main idea of paragraph 16 is that dolphins can
   a. communicate and make up their own tricks.
   b. touch flippers in the air.
   c. diagnose human illnesses with their sonar.
   d. perform only if they are told what to do.

_____d_____ 8. The main point of paragraph 17 is that the author
   a. has learned three dozen commands.
   b. was rejected by dolphins in Key Largo.
   c. is afraid of Ellie's sharp teeth.
   d. is nervous about his "date' with Ellie.

_____b_____ 9. In paragraph 3, the author refers to Steve as a "dead ringer for movie star Chuck Norris." By looking at paragraph 14, you can figure out that **dead ringer** means
   a. someone flashy.
   b. someone who looks just like another person.
   c. someone with a good personality.
   d. someone dangerous.

_____a_____ 10. When the author got into the pool with Ellie, she
   a. followed all of his commands.
   b. hid at the other end of the pool.
   c. leapt into the air and did a back flip.
   d. knocked him over.

USING CONTEXT AND WORD PARTS

_____a_____ 11. In paragraph 1, the word **radiologist** means
   a. one who takes x-rays.
   b. having a specific quality of voice.
   c. pertaining to the study of x-rays.
   d. to say again.

_____c_____ 12. In paragraph 1, the word **horizontal** means
   a. upright.
   b. over the horizon.
   c. in the same direction as the horizon.
   d. crossing the horizon.

_____a_____ 13. In paragraph 3, the word **relentlessly** means

  a. over and over again.   c. recently.

  b. casually.   d. less and less.

_____b_____ 14. In paragraph 3, the word **apprehension** means

  a. disappointment.   c. appeal.

  b. fear.   d. appearance.

_____c_____ 15. In paragraph 3, the word **preswim** means

  a. small swim.   c. before swimming.

  b. while swimming.   d. swim again.

REVIEWING DIFFICULT VOCABULARY

_____d_____ 16. In paragraph 4, the word **implication** means

  a. wrong idea.   c. command.

  b. rule.   d. logical suggestion.

_____d_____ 17. In paragraph 10, the word **flawless** means

  a. making no sense.   c. helpless.

  b. quiet.   d. without any faults.

_____c_____ 18. In paragraph 13, the word **converge** means

  a. communicate.   c. come together.

  b. make gestures.   d. become interested.

_____c_____ 19. In paragraph 18, the word **bravado** means

  a. lack of bravery.   c. act of showing off.

  b. brave act.   d. rapid movement.

_____c_____ 20. In paragraph 21, the word **inter-species** means

  a. above species.   c. between species.

  b. within species.   d. with many species.

Chapter 3: Building Vocabulary: Using Word Parts

RECORDING YOUR PROGRESS

Test	Number Right			Score	
Practice Test 3-1	_____	× 10	=	_____	%
Practice Test 3-2	_____	× 10	=	_____	%
Practice Test 3-3	_____	× 10	=	_____	%
Mastery Test 3-1	_____	× 10	=	_____	%
Mastery Test 3-2	_____	× 10	=	_____	%
Mastery Test 3-3	_____	× 5	=	_____	%

EVALUATING YOUR PROGRESS

Based on your test performance, rate how well you have mastered the skills taught in this chapter by checking one of the boxes below or by writing your own evaluation.

☐ **Need More Improvement**

Tip: Try using the "Vocabulary" Module on the Reading Road Trip CD-ROM or Website that accompanies this textbook to fine-tune the skills that you have learned in this chapter.

☐ **Need More Practice**

Tip: Try using the "Vocabulary" Module on the Reading Road Trip CD-ROM that accompanies this textbook to brush up on the skills you have learned in this chapter, or visit this textbook's Website at **http://ablongman.com/mcwhorter** for extra practice.

☐ **Good**

Tip: To maintain your skills, do a quick review of this chapter by using the Website that accompanies this textbook by logging on to **http://ablongman.com/mcwhorter.**

☐ **Excellent**

YOUR EVALUATION: _____

_____

_____

_____

_____

Read Me First!

Look at the photograph below—a movie still from the classic film *King Kong.* Just by looking at the photo, you can get a *general idea* of what this movie is about—a giant gorilla is terrorizing a large city, especially the woman in his clutches. Until you see the whole movie, though, you won't know the movie's *main idea*—the most important point the film is making.

When you study a paragraph, you also start with its general idea and then try to figure out its main point.

Chapter 4

Locating Main Ideas

What Is a Main Idea?

When a friend asks you to go to a movie you haven't heard of, you probably ask "What's it about?" As you watch the movie, you come to understand the characters and the story. Eventually, you grasp the point the film is making—you realize what all the conversations and action, taken together, mean.

Understanding a paragraph involves a similar process. You first need to know what the paragraph is about, then you have to understand each of the sentences and how they relate to one another. Finally, to understand the paragraph's main point, you need to grasp what all the sentences, taken together, mean.

The one general subject a whole paragraph is about is called the **topic.** The most important point a whole paragraph makes is called the **main idea.** For example, read the following paragraph:

> Despite its increase in popularity, hypnotism has serious limitations that restrict its widespread use. First of all, not everyone is capable of being hypnotized. Second, a person who does not cooperate with the hypnotist is unlikely to fall into a hypnotic trance. Finally, there are limits to the commands a subject will obey when hypnotized. In many cases, subjects will not do anything that violates their moral code.

In this paragraph, the topic is "hypnotism," and the main idea is that "hypnotism has serious limitations that restrict its widespread use."

Here the main point of the paragraph is stated in the first sentence. The rest of the sentences then support or back up the main idea. As you will see later, however, the main idea doesn't always come first.

Understanding General versus Specific Ideas

To identify topics and main ideas in paragraphs, it helps to understand the difference between general and specific. A *general* idea applies to a large number of individual items. The term *clothing* is general because it refers to a large collection of individual items—pants, suits, blouses, shirts, and so on. A *specific* idea or term is more detailed or particular. It refers to an individual item. The word *scarf*, for example, is more specific than the word *clothing*. The phrase *plain red scarf* is even more specific.

EXAMPLES

General: Pies
Specific: chocolate cream
apple
cherry

General: Fruit
Specific: grapes
lemons
pineapple

General: Countries
Specific: Britain
Finland
Brazil

General: Word Parts
Specific: prefix
root
suffix

Exercise 4-1

Directions: Circle the letter that represents the most general term in each group of words.

1. (a) math   (b) college courses   (c) sociology   (d) computer science

2. (a) roses   (b) tulips   (c) flowers   (d) daffodils

3. (a) music   (b) hip-hop   (c) jazz   (d) classical

4. (a) comedies   (b) thrillers   (c) movies   (d) dramas

5. (a) curly   (b) hairstyles   (c) braided   (d) ponytail

6. (a) pounds   (b) ounces   (c) kilograms   (d) weights

7. (a) soda   (b) coffee   (c) beverage   (d) wine

8. (a) soap operas   (b) news   (c) TV programs   (d) sports special

9. (a) home furnishings   (b) carpeting   (c) drapes   (d) wall hangings

10. (a) sociology   (b) social sciences   (c) anthropology   (d) psychology

---

Exercise 4–2

Directions: For each list of items, circle the letter of the choice that best applies to that grouping.

1. Dogs, canaries, tigers, elephants, panda bears
   a. household pets   c. endangered animals
   b. animals   d. zoo animals

2. Alcohol, tobacco, heroin
   a. liquids   c. addictive substances
   b. illegal substances   d. legal substances

3. For better health, to fit into old clothes, for vanity
   a. reasons to visit your doctor   c. reasons to take vitamins
   b. reasons to go on a diet   d. reasons to buy new clothes

4. Mosquito, wasp, gnat, butterfly
   a. living creatures   c. insects
   b. pests   d. harmful insects

5. Martha Washington, Hillary Clinton, Jacqueline Kennedy
   a. famous twentieth-century women
   b. famous American parents
   c. wives of American presidents
   d. famous wives

Now that you are familiar with the difference between general and specific, you will be able to use these ideas in the rest of the chapter.

Identifying the Topic

You already know that the topic is the general subject of an entire paragraph. Every sentence in a paragraph in some way discusses or explains this topic. To find the topic of a paragraph, ask yourself: What is the one idea the author is discussing throughout the paragraph? Read the following paragraph with that question in mind:

Nutrition is the process of taking in and using food for growth, repair, and maintenance of the body. The science of nutrition is the study of foods and how the body uses them. Many North Americans define nutrition as eating a healthful diet. But what is healthful? Our food choices may be influenced by fads, advertising, or convenience. We may reflect on the meaning of nutrition while pushing a cart down a supermarket aisle, or while making a selection from a restaurant menu.

—Byer and Shainberg, *Living Well: Health in Your Hands*, p. 256

In this example, the author is discussing one topic—nutrition—throughout the paragraph. Notice that the word *nutrition* is used several times.

Look again at the paragraph about hypnotism on page 87. How many times does the author use the word *hypnotism* or a version of that word? As you can see, the repeated use of a word often serves as a clue to the topic.

Exercise 4-3

Directions: After reading each of the following paragraphs, circle the letter of the choice that best represents the topic of the paragraph.

1. Some plants require more light than others as a result of the colors of their leaves. Plants with shades of white, yellow, or pink in their leaves need more light than plants with completely green foliage. For example, a Swedish ivy plant with completely green leaves requires less light per day than a variegated Swedish ivy that contains shades of white, yellow, and green in its leaves.

   a. how plants grow   c. light

   (b.) plants and light   d. green foliage

2. Mental illness is usually diagnosed from abnormal behavior. A woman is asked the time of day, and she begins to rub her arms and recite the Apostles' Creed. A man is so convinced that someone is "out to get him" that he refuses to leave his apartment. Unusual behaviors like these are taken as evidence that the mental apparatus is not working quite right, and mental illness is the resulting diagnosis.

   —Schaie and Geiwitz, *Adult Development and Aging*, pp. 371–372

   a. psychology   (c.) mental illness

   b. mental health   d. evidence

3. Discrimination doesn't go away: it just aims at whatever group appears to be out of fashion at any given moment. One expert feels that *age* is the major factor in employment discrimination today, although studies have shown older workers may be more reliable than young workers

and just as productive. The Age Discrimination in Employment Act gives protection to the worker between forty and sixty-five. If you're in this age range, your employer must prove that you have performed unsatisfactorily before he can legally fire you. This act also prohibits age discrimination in hiring, wages, and benefits.

—George, *The New Consumer Survival Kit*, p. 212

(a.) age discrimination   c. employment

b. older workers   d. protection of workers

4. Magazines are a means of communication halfway between newspapers and books. Until the 1940s most consumer (general) magazines offered both fiction and nonfiction articles as well as poetry and short humor selections. With television providing so much entertainment for the American home, many magazines discovered a strong demand for non-fiction articles, their almost exclusive content today.

—Agee, Ault, and Emery, *Introduction to Mass Communication*, p. 153

a. communication   c. newspapers and books

b. nonfiction articles   (d.) magazines

5. Slavery has taken a number of different forms. War captives and their descendants formed a class of slaves in some societies; in others, slaves were owned and could be bought and sold. The rights granted to a slave varied, too. In ancient Greece, a slave could marry a free person, but in the southern United States before the Civil War, slaves were not allowed even to marry each other because they were not permitted to engage in legal contracts. Still, slaves in the South often lived together as husband and wife throughout their adult lives, forming families that remained tightly knit until they were separated at the auction block.

—Hicks and Gwynne, *Cultural Anthropology*, p. 270

a. rights of slaves   (c.) forms of slavery

b. slavery in Greece   d. slavery in the southern
                                  United States

Finding the Main Idea

You learned earlier that the **main idea** of a paragraph is its most important point. The main idea is also the most *general* statement the writer makes about the topic. Pick out the most general statement among the following sentences.

1. People differ according to height.
2. Hair color distinguishes some people from others.
3. People differ in a number of ways.
4. Each person has his or her own personality.

Did you choose item 3 as the most general statement? Now we will change this list into a paragraph by rearranging the sentences and adding a few facts.

> People differ in numerous ways. They differ according to physical characteristics, such as height, weight, and hair color. They also differ in personality. Some people are friendly and easygoing. Others are more reserved and formal.

In this brief paragraph, the main idea is expressed in the first sentence. This sentence, known as the **topic sentence**, is the most general statement in the paragraph. All the other sentences are specific details that explain this main idea.

Tips for Finding the Main Idea

Here are some tips that will help you find the main idea.

1. **Identify the topic.** As you did earlier, figure out the general subject of the entire paragraph. In the previous sample paragraph, "how people differ" is the topic.

2. **Locate the most general sentence (the topic sentence).** This sentence must be broad enough to include all of the other ideas in the paragraph. The topic sentence in the sample paragraph ("People differ in numerous ways") covers all of the other details in that paragraph. The tips in the next section will help you locate topic sentences.

3. **Study the rest of the paragraph.** The main idea must make the rest of the paragraph meaningful. It is the one idea that ties all of the other details together. In the sample paragraph, sentences 2, 3, 4, and 5 all give specific details about how people differ.

Tips for Locating the Topic Sentence

Although a topic sentence can be located anywhere in a paragraph, it is usually *first* or *last*.

Topic Sentence First In most paragraphs, the topic sentence comes first. The author states his or her main point and then explains it.

Good listeners follow specific steps in order to achieve accurate under-standing. First, whenever possible, good listeners prepare in advance for the speech or lecture they are going to attend. They study the topic to be discussed and find out about the speaker and his or her beliefs. Second, when they arrive at the place where the speech is to be given, they choose a seat where it is easy to see, hear, and remain alert. Finally, when the speech is over, effective listeners review what was said and evaluate the ideas that were expressed.

In the first sentence, the writer states that good listeners follow specific steps. The rest of the paragraph lists those steps.

Topic Sentence Last   The second most likely place for a topic sentence to appear is last in a paragraph. When using this arrangement, a writer leads up to the main point and then states it at the end. Here is an almost identical paragraph to the preceding one, but with the topic sentence last.

Whenever possible, good listeners prepare in advance for the speech or lecture they plan to attend. They study the topic to be discussed and find out about the speaker and his or her beliefs. When they arrive at the place where the speech is to be given, they choose a seat where it is easy to see, hear, and remain alert. And when the speech is over, they review what was said and evaluate the ideas that were expressed. Thus, effective listeners follow spe-cific steps in order to achieve accurate understanding.

This paragraph lists all the steps that good listeners follow. Then, at the end, the writer states the main idea.

Topic Sentence in Middle   If a topic sentence is placed neither first nor last, then it may appear somewhere in the middle of a paragraph. In this arrange-ment, the sentences before the topic sentence lead up to or introduce the main idea. Those that follow the main idea explain or describe it.

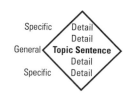

Whenever possible, good listeners prepare in advance for the speech or lecture they plan to attend. They study the topic to be discussed and find out about the speaker and his or her beliefs. Effective listeners, then, take specific steps to achieve accurate understanding of the lecture. Furthermore, when they arrive at the place where the speech is to be given, they choose a seat where it is easy to see, hear, and remain alert. Finally, when the speech is over, effective listeners review what was said and evaluate the ideas that were expressed.

This paragraph begins with two examples of what good listeners do. Then the writer states the main idea and continues with more examples.

Topic Sentence First and Last   Occasionally writers put the main idea at the beginning of a paragraph and again at the end. Writers may do this to emphasize the main point or to clarify it.

General   **Topic Sentence**
         Detail
Specific   Detail
         Detail
General   **Topic Sentence**

<u>Good listeners follow specific steps in order to achieve accurate understanding</u>. First, whenever possible, good listeners prepare in advance for the speech or lecture they are going to attend. They study the topic to be discussed and find out about the speaker and his or her beliefs. Second, when they arrive at the place where the speech is to be given, they choose a seat where it is easy to see, hear, and remain alert. Finally, when the speech is over, they review what was said and evaluate the ideas that were expressed. <u>Effective listening, then, is an active process in which listeners deliberately take certain actions to ensure that accurate communication has occurred.</u>

The first and last sentences both state, in slightly different ways, the main idea of the paragraph—that good listeners follow certain steps.

Exercise 4–4

Directions: Underline the topic sentence in each of the following paragraphs. Keep in mind that one of the paragraphs has a topic sentence at the beginning and at the end.

1. Fast foods tend to be short on fresh fruits and vegetables, and are low in calcium, although calcium can be obtained in shakes and milk. Pizza is a fast-food exception. It contains grains, meat, vegetables, and cheese, which represent four of the food groups. Pizza is often only about 25 percent fat, most of which comes from the crust. <u>Overall, studies have shown pizza to be highly nutritious.</u>

—Byer and Shainberg, *Living Well: Health in Your Hands*, p. 289

2. Earlier we examined the concept of irreversibility, the idea that once something is said, it cannot be unsaid. <u>Perhaps the most common method for defending or justifying something that has been said and may be perceived negatively is "the excuse."</u> Excuses pervade all forms of communication and behavior. Although we emphasize their role in conversation, recognize that the excuse is applicable to all human behaviors, not just the conversational ones.

—Adapted from DeVito, *Human Communication*, p. 170

3. You could be the greatest genius since Thomas Edison, but if no one knows about your talent or is in a position to judge it, you're wasting your time. Being in the right field is important. <u>But within that field, it's also a good idea to maintain a high degree of visibility.</u> If you've got the

potential to be a brilliant corporate planner, you may be wasting your time working for a small company. You'd be better off working for a large corporation where you have the opportunity to take off in many directions, learn how the different departments work together, and thus have a larger arena to test your skills.

—Weinstein, *Jobs for the 21st Century*, p. 118

4. <u>Dirty words are often used by teenagers in telling off-color stories and this can be considered part of their sex education.</u> As their bodies grow and change, both boys and girls wonder and worry. To keep from being overwhelmed by these fears, they turn them into jokes or dirty-word stories. By telling and retelling off-color stories, they learn that they aren't the only ones in the group disturbed about their future roles in courtship and marriage. Using dirty words and stories to laugh at sexual doubts and fears may make them less frightening.

—Brothers, "What Dirty Words Really Mean" from Good Housekeeping

5. Deciding to buy a product or service takes preparation. Since you have already spent time to gather information and compare what is available, you should spend a little more time prior to arriving at a final decision. <u>In this respect it is best to go home before making a selection.</u> At home it is easier to evaluate all of the information while you're not under any sales or time pressure to make a purchase. In addition, at home you can take a final look at your financial plans to be sure the purchase will fit your budget.

—Brown, pp. 20–21

6. <u>The 1950s were to most Americans a time of great security.</u> After World War II, the people prospered in ways they had never known before. Our involvement in the Korean war was thought to be successful from the point of view of national image. We saw ourselves as *the* world power, who had led the fight for democracy. When Dwight D. Eisenhower was elected president, we entered a period in American history where everything was all right, everyone was getting richer, and tomorrow would always be better than today.

—Weirich, *Personal Financial Management*, p. 155

7. Suppose you are part of an audience today to whom you will make a speech tomorrow. What do you notice about how people in the audience are dressed? Is their clothing formal or informal, conservative, preppy, casual, or wild? What is their economic background? What is their level of education? Where do their interests lie? What is their

ethnic background? <u>The more you know about your audience, the more you can target your speech to their needs, values, and interests, and the more interesting your speech will be.</u>

8. <u>The words "effortless exercise" are a contradiction in terms.</u> Muscles grow in strength only when subjected to overload. Flexibility is developed only by extending the normal range of body motion. Endurance is developed only through exercise that raises the pulse rate enough to achieve a training effect on the heart, lungs, and circulatory system. In all cases, the benefits from exercise come from extending the body beyond its normal activity range. What this requires is, precisely, effort.

—Dorfman, *Well Being: An Introduction of Health*, p. 263

9. <u>Burger King Corporation offers both a service and a product to its customers.</u> Its service is the convenience it offers the consumer—the location of its restaurants and its fast food service. Its product is *the total Burger King experience*, which starts from the time you drive into the restaurant's parking lot and ends when you drive out. It includes the speed of service, the food you order, the price you pay, the friendliness and courtesy you are shown, the feeling of satisfaction—in short, an experience. <u>Burger King, then, is marketing a positive experience, as promised by its advertising and promotional efforts and delivered by its product.</u>

—Fox and Wheatley, *Modern Marketing*, p. 142

10. In the United States, Australia, and Western Europe people are encouraged to be independent. Members of these cultures are taught to get ahead, to compete, to win, to achieve their goals, to realize their unique potential, to stand out from the crowd. In many Asian and African countries, people are taught to value an interdependent self. Members of these cultures are taught to get along, to help others, and to not disagree or stand out. <u>Thus, there are significant cultural differences in the way people are taught to view themselves.</u>

—Adapted from DeVito, *Human Communication*, p. 78

Learning More about Paragraphs

When you read a paragraph now, you should be pretty good at figuring out its topic and finding its topic sentence. Obviously, though, there is more to a paragraph than these two items. What about all of the other sentences?

These are the **details**—the sentences that explain the main idea. To connect sentences, writers use **transitions,** words like *first, however,* and *finally.* You will learn more about details and transitions in the next chapter.

What Have You Learned?

Directions: Circle the letter of the choice that best completes each statement.

1. The topic of a paragraph is the
   (a.) subject of the paragraph.
   b. main idea of the paragraph.
   c. noun that is the subject of a sentence.
   d. object of the predicate

2. The best clue to use in identifying the topic of a paragraph is
   a. the arrangement of the sentences.
   b. the use of directional words.
   (c.) a frequently repeated key word.
   d. the order of details.

3. The sentence that expresses the main idea of a paragraph is known as the
   a. opening sentence.   (c.) topic sentence.
   b. general sentence.   d. main sentence.

4. In what position are you most likely to find the topic sentence in a paragraph?
   (a.) first   c. last
   b. second   d. in the middle

5. Occasionally, writers who want to clarify or emphasize a main idea might put a topic sentence
   a. first.   c. last.
   (b.) first and last.   d. in the middle.

NAME _____ SECTION _____

DATE _____ SCORE _____

Directions: In the space provided, write the letter of the choice that best applies to that grouping.

___c___ 1. Touchdown, homerun, 3-pointer, 5 under par
    a. types of errors in sports   c. types of scoring in sports
    b. types of activities   d. types of sports

___b___ 2. Oprah Winfrey, David Letterman, Jay Leno, Dr. Laura Schlesinger
    a. rock stars   c. comedians
    b. talk-show hosts   d. movie stars

___c___ 3. For companionship, to play with, because you love animals
    a. reasons to visit the zoo   c. reasons to get a pet
    b. reasons to feed your cat   d. reasons to become a veterinarian

___a___ 4. Taking a hot bath, going for a walk, watching a video, listening to music
    a. ways to relax   c. ways to listen
    b. ways to help others   d. ways to solve problems

___d___ 5. Road Runner, Donald Duck, Mickey Mouse, Tweety Bird
    a. movie characters   c. historical figures
    b. live animals   d. cartoon characters

___c___ 6. Lamp, toaster, radio, chainsaw
    a. machinery   c. electrical devices
    b. luxuries   d. good birthday gifts

___b___ 7. Listen, be helpful, be generous, be forgiving
    a. ways to get a job   c. ways to learn
    b. ways to keep a friend   d. ways to appreciate a movie

___a___ 8. Lake Huron, Mississippi River, Atlantic Ocean, Gulf of Mexico
    a. bodies of water   c. areas of conflict
    b. vacation spots   d. U.S. landmarks

__d__ 9. Take your blood pressure, record your weight, ask how you're feeling
   a. tasks doctors usually perform
   b. tasks mothers usually perform
   c. tasks friends usually perform
   d. tasks nurses usually perform

__c__ 10. Soccer, baseball, basketball, football
   a. sports that use similar scoring systems
   b. sports that are popular all over the world
   c. team sports that use a ball
   d. the safest sports

NAME _____ SECTION _____

DATE _____ SCORE _____

Directions: For each general idea, write four specific ideas that "fit" within it. An example is provided for each entry. **Responses will vary.**

1. <u>General idea</u>: types of exercise   <u>sit-ups</u>

   <u>knee-bends</u>   <u>jogging</u>   <u>lifting weights</u>   <u>swimming</u>

2. <u>General idea</u>: fast-food restaurants   <u>McDonald's</u>

   <u>Burger King</u>   <u>Wendy's</u>   <u>Hardees</u>   <u>Sonic</u>

3. <u>General idea</u>: musical instruments   <u>saxophone</u>

   <u>piano</u>   <u>trumpet</u>   <u>drums</u>   <u>harp</u>

4. <u>General idea</u>: types of personalities   <u>outgoing</u>

   <u>shy</u>   <u>friendly</u>   <u>distant</u>   <u>moody</u>

5. <u>General idea</u>: models of cars   <u>Ford Mustang</u>

   <u>Honda Civic</u>   <u>Volkswagen Beetle</u>   <u>Dodge Intrepid</u>   <u>Toyota Camry</u>

6. <u>General idea</u>: breakfast drinks   <u>coffee</u>

   <u>tea</u>   <u>milk</u>   <u>orange juice</u>   <u>grapefruit juice</u>

7. <u>General idea</u>: food categories   <u>meat</u>

   <u>vegetables</u>   <u>fish</u>   <u>fruit</u>   <u>dairy products</u>

8. <u>General idea</u>: summer sports   <u>swimming</u>

   <u>baseball</u>   <u>tennis</u>   <u>golf</u>   <u>rowing</u>

9. <u>General idea</u>: popular singers   <u>Whitney Houston</u>

   <u>Faith Hill</u>   <u>Britney Spears</u>   <u>Garth Brooks</u>   <u>Tony Bennett</u>

10. <u>General idea</u>: tools   <u>hammer</u>

   <u>saw</u>   <u>screwdriver</u>   <u>spade</u>   <u>trowel</u>

Directions: For each of the following paragraphs, (1) in the space provided, write the letter of the choice that best represents the topic of the paragraph, and (2) underline the topic sentence.

_____b_____ 1. <u>There are a number of reasons why there has been an increase in the demand for nurses, not the least of which is the aging of the U.S. population.</u> Older people use hospitals more and have chronic ailments that require more nursing. Moreover, as hospitals reduce the length of stay of patients, people who are discharged earlier than in previous years need more home care, usually provided by nurses. While demand has been rising, the supply of nurses has decreased somewhat—there are now fewer women between the ages of 18 and 24. Because this is the group from which nurses traditionally come, there have been fewer potential nurses. In addition, women have more alternatives in the labor market than they did years ago.

—Miller, *Economics Today*, p. 84

    a. aging population   c. age distribution of women

    b. demand for nurses   d. other job choices for nurses

_____c_____ 2. When good writers use the word revision, they don't mean the sort of minor changes implied in the old elementary school phrase "Copy it over in ink." Revision doesn't even mean writing your paper over again. <u>Instead, it means reading your draft carefully in order to make effective changes in the existing text.</u> It means stepping outside the draft you've created; looking at its strengths and weaknesses as if you were a reader seeing it for the first time; and deciding what parts of the draft need to be expanded, clarified, elaborated, illustrated, reworded, restructured, modified—or just plain cut.

—Anson and Swegler, *The Longman Handbook for Writers and Readers*, p. 78

    a. writing   c. what revision means

    b. what drafting means   d. rewording a paper

_____b_____ 3. Young women who suffer from *anorexia nervosa*, an eating disorder, severely limit their food intake to the point of significant weight loss and near starvation. Many young women also have *bulimia nervosa*, another serious eating disorder, which involves frequent binges (overeating) followed by purges (self-induced vomiting or the use of laxatives). In the United States approximately 10 million women experience one of these disorders. Both of these life-threatening eating disorders involve an obsessive relationship with food, and women who have these disorders must be treated professionally before permanently damaging their bodies.

a. young women   c. bulimia nervosa

b. eating disorders   d. anorexia

<u>d</u>   4. Narratives are stories, and they are often useful as supporting materials in a speech. Narratives give the audience what it wants: a good story. Listeners seem to perk up automatically when a story is told. If the narrative is a personal one, it will make you more believable and show you as a real person. Listeners like to know about speakers, and the personal narrative meets this desire. Notice how you remember the little stories noted personalities tell in television interviewers.

—DeVito, *The Elements of Public Speaking*, p. 164

a. supporting materials   c. listeners

b. speeches   d. narratives in speeches

<u>b</u>   5. We might like to think of ourselves as so sophisticated that physical attractiveness does not move us. We might like to claim that sensitivity, warmth, and intelligence are more important to us. However, we might never learn about other people's personalities if they do not meet our minimal standards for physical attractiveness.

—Rathus, *Human Sexuality*, p. 189

a. learning about personalities

b. importance of physical attractiveness

c. factors in dating

d. factors in relationships

NAME _____ SECTION _____

DATE _____ SCORE _____

Directions: After reading the following passage, in the space provided write the letter of the choice that best completes each of the statements below.

The most common form of Internet abuse is spam. *Spam* is unsolicited impersonal e-mail from a party who is unknown to you or with whom you have no consenting relationship. Anyone who sends out an announcement to millions of e-mail addresses is a spammer. Most e-mail spam is commercial in nature. But spam can also contain political calls for action, religious sermons, or the incoherent ravings of someone with a mental problem.

If you're worried about avoiding spam, you'll need to learn more about the various ways that spammers obtain e-mail addresses. Whenever you are asked to provide personal information over the Web or via e-mail, you should know what, if any, privacy policies will be applied to protect your privacy online. No laws in the United States protect the privacy rights of consumers, so users must be savvy about what goes on behind the scenes. If a company offers you a "free" e-mail account, how much information do you have to give up in order to participate? Data resellers generate a lot of revenue by selling Internet user profiles to advertisers, marketing organizations, and scam artists. Whenever anyone on the Internet offers you a free service in exchange for information, understand that you are probably being bought and sold. If the service is worth it to you, fine. But most people don't realize that they are really trading personal privacy for a free e-mail account or free space on a Web page server.

—Lehnert, *Light on the Internet*, pp. 53, 55

___b___ 1. The topic of the first paragraph is

  a. e-mail.   c. political calls for action.
  b. spam.   d. privacy issues.

___a___ 2. In the first paragraph, the topic sentence begins with the words

  a. "The most common."   c. "Most e-mail."
  b. "Anyone who."   d. "But spam."

___c___ 3. In paragraph 1, the word **unsolicited** means

  a. unusual.   c. not requested.
  b. dangerous.   d. not proven.

___d___ 4. In paragraph 1, the word **consenting** means

  a. convenient.   c. close.
  b. caring.   d. agreed upon.

   b   5. In paragraph 1, the word **incoherent** means
- a. not pleasant.
- c. not quiet.
- b. not understandable.
- d. not teachable.

   d   6. The topic of the second paragraph is
- a. how to generate spam.
- b. the privacy rights of consumers.
- c. free e-mail accounts.
- d. how spammers obtain e-mail addresses.

   a   7. In the second paragraph, the topic sentence begins with the words
- a. "If you're worried."
- c. "Data resellers."
- b. "No laws."
- d. "But most people."

   d   8. According to the selection, which of the following is *not* correct?
- a. A religious sermon might be spam.
- b. Data resellers sell personal information to advertisers and others.
- c. You may lose personal privacy to get a free e-mail account.
- d. U.S. laws protect the privacy of personal e-mail.

   a   9. According to the selection, one way that spammers obtain e-mail addresses is by
- a. buying them from data resellers.
- b. violating laws that protect the privacy rights of consumers.
- c. responding to requests for information.
- d. sending out requests for names.

   b   10. The two paragraphs in this reading support the idea that a topic sentence usually comes
- a. in the middle.
- c. last.
- b. first.
- d. first and last

NAME _____ SECTION _____

DATE _____ SCORE _____

Directions: After reading the following passage, in the space provided write the letter of the choice that best completes each of the statements below.

Many people start relationships because of loneliness. Loneliness and being alone are not synonymous. Loneliness is a state of painful isolation, of feeling cut off from others. Being alone, a state of solitude, can be quite desirable, since it allows us to work, study, or reflect on the world around us. Solitude is usually a matter of choice; loneliness is not.

Lonely people tend to spend a lot of time by themselves, eat dinner alone, spend weekends alone, and participate in few social activities. They are unlikely to date. Some lonely people report having many friends, but a closer look suggests that these "friendships" are shallow. Lonely people are unlikely to share confidences. Loneliness tends to peak during adolescence. This is when most young people begin to supplant family ties with peer relationships. Loneliness is often connected with feelings of depression and with a feeling of being "sick at heart."

Loneliness is even reported among some married people. In one study, lonely wives tended to feel less liking and love for their partners and expressed less marital satisfaction. Lonely husbands reported less liking for their wives and less intimacy in their relationships.

—Rathus, *Human Sexuality*, p. 221

_____b_____ 1. The topic of the first paragraph is

    a. how to begin relationships.

    b. solitude and loneliness.

    c. solitude.

    d. isolation and pain.

_____b_____ 2. The topic sentence of the first paragraph begins with the words

    a. "Many people start."

    b. "Loneliness and being."

    c. "Being alone."

    d. "Solitude is."

_____b_____ 3. In paragraph 1, the word **synonymous** means

    a. different.

    b. the same.

    c. serious.

    d. relevant.

_____c_____ 4. In the first paragraph, what is the easiest way to figure out the meaning of the word **isolation?**

    a. by using word parts

    b. by using a dictionary

    c. by using sentence context

    d. by rereading the paragraph.

_____a_____ 5. The topic of the second paragraph is

    a. how lonely people behave.

    b. what lonely people want.

    c. the difference between loneliness and solitude.

    d. why lonely people are depressed.

_____a_____ 6. In the second paragraph, the topic sentence begins with the words

    a. "Lonely people tend."

    b. "Some lonely people."

    c. "Lonely people are."

    d. "Loneliness is often."

_____d_____ 7. In paragraph 2, the word **confidences** means

    a. factual information

    b. knowledge of others.

    c. family histories.

    d. personal stories.

_____b_____ 8. In paragraph 2, the word **supplant** means

    a. reject.

    b. replace.

    c. lessen.

    d. encourage.

_____d_____ 9. The topic of the third paragraph is
   a. marriage.
   b. lonely wives.
   c. lonely husbands.
   d. loneliness among married people.

_____c_____ 10. According to the selection,
   a. loneliness is desirable.
   b. lonely people date quite a bit.
   c. solitude can be desirable.
   d. married people are usually lonely.

NAME _____   SECTION _____

DATE _____   SCORE _____

DON'T ASK
Deborah Tannen

Men and women differ in many ways, including how they communicate. You'll probably recognize some of the differences Deborah Tannen describes in this excerpt from her book *You Just Don't Understand*.

Vocabulary Preview

These are some of the difficult words in this essay. The definitions here will help you if you can't figure out the meanings from the sentence context or word parts.

paradox (par. 4) contradiction

metamessages (par. 4) meanings that appear beneath the surface; hidden meanings

hierarchical (par. 5) arranged in a specified order

framed (par. 5) placed within a context

implicit (par. 6) not directly stated

asymmetrical (par. 8) having a lack of harmony or balance

status (par. 8) position or rank; one's standing in relation to others

---

1   Talking about troubles is just one of the many conversational tasks that women and men view differently, and that consequently causes trouble in talk between them. Another is asking for information.

2   A man and a woman were standing beside the information booth at the Washington Folk Life Festival, a sprawling complex of booths and displays. "You ask," the man was saying to the woman. "I don't ask."

3   Sitting in the front seat of the car beside Harold, Sybil is fuming. They have been driving around for half an hour looking for a street he is sure is close by. Sybil is angry not because Harold does not know the way, but because he insists on trying to find it himself rather than stopping and asking someone. Her anger stems from viewing his behavior through the lens of her own: If she were driving, she would have asked directions as soon as she realized she didn't know which way to go, and they'd now be comfortably

ensconced in their friends' living room instead of driving in circles, as the hour gets later and later. Since asking directions does not make Sybil uncomfortable, refusing to ask makes no sense to her. But in Harold's world, driving around until he finds his way is the reasonable thing to do, since asking for help makes him uncomfortable. He's avoiding that discomfort and trying to maintain his sense of himself as a self-sufficient person.

4   Why do many men resist asking for directions and other kinds of information? And, it is just as reasonable to ask, why is it that many women don't? By the paradox of independence and intimacy, there are two simultaneous and different metamessages implied in asking for and giving information. Many men tend to focus on one, many women on the other.

5   When you offer information, the information itself is the message. But the fact that you have the information, and the person you are speaking to

CLOSE TO HOME   JOHN McPHERSON

"Ha! I TOLD you I could find my way back to
the interstate without stopping to ask directions!"

doesn't, also sends a metamessage of superiority. If relations are inherently hierarchical, then the one who has more information is framed as higher up on the ladder, by virtue of being more knowledgeable and competent. From this perspective, finding one's own way is an essential part of the independence that men perceive to be a prerequisite for self-respect. If self-respect is bought at the cost of a few extra minutes of travel time, it is well worth the price.

6   Because they are implicit, metamessages are hard to talk about. When Sybil begs to know why Harold won't just ask someone for directions, he answers in terms of the message, the information: He says there's no point in asking, because anyone he asks may not know and may give him wrong directions. This is theoretically reasonable. There are many countries, such as, for example, Mexico, where it is standard procedure for people to make up directions rather than refuse to give requested information. But this explanation frustrates Sybil, because it doesn't make sense to her. Although she realizes that someone might give faulty directions, she believes this is relatively unlikely, and surely it cannot happen every time. Even if it did happen, they would be in no worse shape than they are in now anyway.

7   Part of the reason for their different approaches is that Sybil believes that a person who doesn't know the answer will say so, because it is easy to say, "I don't know." But Harold believes that saying "I don't know" is humiliating, so people might well take a wild guess. Because of their different assumptions, and the invisibility of framing, Harold and Sybil can never get to the bottom of this difference; they can only get more frustrated with each other. Keeping talk on the message level is common, because it is the level we are most clearly aware of. But it is unlikely to resolve confusion since our true motivations lie elsewhere.

8   To the extent that giving information, directions, or help is of use to another, it reinforces bonds between people. But to the extent that it is asymmetrical, it creates hierarchy: Insofar as giving information frames one as the expert, superior in knowledge, and the other as uninformed, inferior in knowledge, it is a move in the negotiation of status.

9   It is easy to see that there are many situations where those who give information are higher in status. For example, parents explain things to children

and answer their questions, just as teachers give information to students. An awareness of this dynamic underlies one requirement for proper behavior at Japanese dinner entertainment, according to anthropologist Harumi Befu. In order to help the highest-status member of the party to dominate the conversation, others at the dinner are expected to ask him questions that they know he can answer with authority.

10   Because of this potential for asymmetry, some men resist receiving information from others, especially women, and some women are cautious about stating information that they know, especially to men. For example, a man with whom I discussed these dynamics later told me that my perspective clarified a comment made by his wife. They had gotten into their car and were about to go to a destination that she knew well but he did not know at all. Consciously resisting an impulse to just drive off and find his own way, he began by asking his wife if she had any advice about the best way to get there. She told him the way, then added, "But I don't know. That's how I would go, but there might be a better way." Her comment was a move to redress the imbalance of power created by her knowing something he didn't know. She was also saving face in advance, in case he decided not to take her advice. Furthermore, she was reframing her directions as "just a suggestion" rather than "giving instructions."

— ∎ —

Directions: In the space provided, write the letter of the choice that best completes each of the following statements.

CHECKING YOUR COMPREHENSION

____a____   1. The main point of the passage is
    a. men and women differ on asking for information because of how they think about relationships.
    b. men and women ask for directions in different ways.
    c. women are willing to ask for help because they are bad at remembering directions.
    d. you shouldn't give information to others because you will embarrass them.

_____c_____ 2. In paragraph 3, the main reason Sybil is angry is because
  a. they are late arriving at their friend's home.
  b. they are lost.
  c. Harold will not ask for directions.
  d. Harold doesn't know the way.

_____b_____ 3. According to paragraph 7,
  a. information is more important than what motivates Harold and Sybil.
  b. Harold and Sybil have unspoken assumptions about what motivates people.
  c. Harold and Sybil know they have similar approaches to asking for information.
  d. Harold and Sybil can never understand each other.

_____d_____ 4. According to Harold's reasoning, when asked for directions, most people will
  a. try to embarrass him for having asked for help.
  b. be uncomfortable and avoid his question.
  c. lead him to his destination.
  d. give wrong directions rather than say "I don't know."

_____b_____ 5. In the last example in the passage, the wife said she wasn't sure her directions were the best because
  a. she had forgotten how to reach their destination.
  b. she was being considerate of how her husband would feel.
  c. she would prefer to ask for directions along the way.
  d. she wanted to confuse her husband with unclear advice.

_____b_____ 6. The topic of paragraph 3 is
  a. driving.   c. Sybil's anger.
  b. asking for directions.   d. Harold's discomfort.

_____a_____ 7. The topic sentence of paragraph 6 begins with the words
  a. "Because they are."   c. "Although she realizes."
  b. "This is theoretically."   d. "Even if it did."

_____c_____ 8. The topic of paragraph 8 is
  a. creating bonds.   c. giving information.
  b. communication.   d. being an expert.

    a   9. The topic sentence of paragraph 9 begins with the words
   a. "It is easy."   c. "An awareness."
   b. "For example."   d. "In order."

    d   10. The topic sentence of paragraph 10 begins with the words
   a. "They had gotten."   c. "Furthermore, she."
   b. "Consciously resisting."   d. "Because of this."

USING CONTEXT CLUES AND WORD PARTS

    a   11. In paragraph 3, the word **ensconced** means
   a. settled.   c. expected.
   b. waiting.   d. enlisted.

    a   12. In paragraph 3, the word **self-sufficient** means
   a. able to take care of oneself.
   b. able to rely on others for care.
   c. able to trust others.
   d. able to present one's own problems.

    c   13. In paragraph 5, the word **superiority** means
   a. being worse than someone else.
   b. being different from someone else.
   c. being better than someone else.
   d. being the same as someone else.

    a   14. In paragraph 5, the word **prerequisite** means
   a. something that is necessary.
   b. something that is important.
   c. something that is confusing.
   d. something that is distracting.

    c   15. In paragraph 7, the word **humiliating** means
   a. courageous.
   b. helpful to one's purpose.
   c. harmful to one's self-respect.
   d. cowardly.

REVIEWING DIFFICULT VOCABULARY

Directions: Complete each of the following sentences by inserting a word from the Vocabulary Preview on page 108 in the space provided. A word should be used only once.

16. Because José had not _____framed_____ the question correctly, I didn't understand what he meant.

17. In terms of income, the poor, the middle-class, and the wealthy can be arranged in a _____hierarchical_____ order.

18. If two sisters love each other but also get so angry that they hate each other, this situation might be called a _____paradox_____ .

19. Since Wanda is well educated, has a good-paying job, and has famous parents, her _____status_____ is higher than mine.

20. One leg of Amy's old jeans is three inches shorter than the other. The legs of her jeans are _____asymmetrical_____ .

Chapter 4: Locating Main Ideas

RECORDING YOUR PROGRESS

Test	Number Right			Score
Practice Test 4-1	_____	× 10	=	_____ %
Practice Test 4-2	_____	× 10	=	_____ %
Practice Test 4-3	_____	× 10	=	_____ %
Mastery Test 4-1	_____	× 10	=	_____ %
Mastery Test 4-2	_____	× 10	=	_____ %
Mastery Test 4-3	_____	× 5	=	_____ %

EVALUATING YOUR PROGRESS

Based on your test performance, rate how well you have mastered the skills taught in this chapter by checking one of the boxes below or by writing your own evaluation.

☐ **Need More Improvement**
Tip: Try using the "Main Idea" Module on the Reading Road Trip CD-ROM or Website that accompanies this textbook to fine-tune the skills that you have learned in this chapter.

☐ **Need More Practice**
Tip: Try using the "Main Idea" Module on the Reading Road Trip CD-ROM that accompanies this textbook to brush up on the skills you have learned in this chapter, or visit this textbook's Website at **http://ablongman.com/mcwhorter** for extra practice.

☐ **Good**
Tip: To maintain your skills, do a quick review of this chapter by using the Website that accompanies this textbook by logging on to **http://ablongman.com/mcwhorter.**

☐ **Excellent**

YOUR EVALUATION: _____

_____

_____

_____

_____

Read Me First!

Look at the photograph below, which shows everyone having a good time at a party. Did this party just "happen," or did someone have an idea and then follow it up with work and planning? Suppose you decide to have a birthday party for your best friend. Your *main idea* is that it will be a surprise party and that you will serve pizza, your friend's favorite food. In order for the party be successful, though, you also need to pay attention to the *details*—inviting people, doing the grocery shopping, getting a birthday cake, and so forth.

Studying a paragraph can be a little bit like planning a party. First you find the paragraph's main idea, and then you look for the details that support it.

Copyright © 2002 by Kathleen T. McWhorter

Chapter 5

Identifying Supporting Details

What Are Supporting Details?

Just as grocery shopping and inviting friends are details that help you throw a party, the details writers use in a paragraph help them back up the point they want to make. **Supporting details** are those facts and ideas that prove or explain the main idea of a paragraph. As you read, you will notice that some details are more important than others. Pay particular attention to the **key details**—the most important details that directly explain the main idea. You should also note **minor details**—details that may provide additional information, offer an example, or further explain one of the key details.

Figure 5-1 on page 118 shows how details relate to the main idea. As you recall from Chapter 4, the main idea is usually stated in a topic sentence.

Read the following paragraph and then study the diagram in Figure 5-2 (p. 118).

> The skin of the human body has several functions. First, it serves as a protective covering. In doing so, it accounts for 17 percent of the body weight. Skin also protects the organs within the body from damage or harm. The skin serves as a regulator of body functions. It controls body temperature and water loss. Finally, the skin serves as a receiver. It is sensitive to touch and temperature.

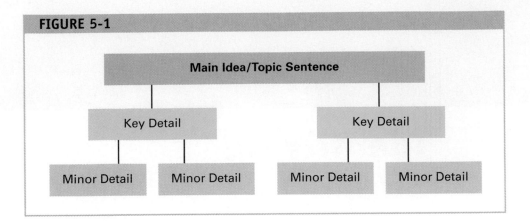

FIGURE 5-1

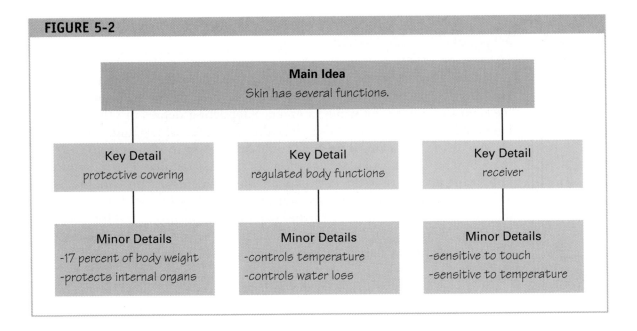

FIGURE 5-2

From Figure 5-2 you can see the key details that state the three main functions of the skin. The minor details, such as "controls temperature," provide further information and are less important than the key details.

Look at the paragraph again, and notice how the author has used **transitions**—words that lead you from one key detail to the next. The words *first*, *also*, and *finally* are a few of the transitions that can help you find the key details in a paragraph. Be on the lookout for transitions as you read; they will be discussed more fully later in this chapter.

Exercise 5-1

A. Directions: *Read the following paragraph and then complete the diagram that follows. Some of the items have been filled in for you.*

Communication occurs with words and gestures, but did you know it also occurs through the sense of smell? Odor can communicate at least four types of messages. First, odor can signal attraction. Animals give off scents to attract members of the opposite sex. Humans use fragrances to make themselves more appealing or attractive. Smell also communicates information about tastes. The smell of popcorn popping stimulates the appetite. If you smell a chicken roasting you can anticipate its taste. A third type of smell communication is through memory. A smell can help you recall an event that occurred months or even years ago, especially if the event was an emotional one. Finally, smell can communicate by creating an identity or image for a person or product. For example, a woman may wear only one brand of perfume. Or a brand of shaving cream may have a distinct fragrance, which allows users to recognize it.

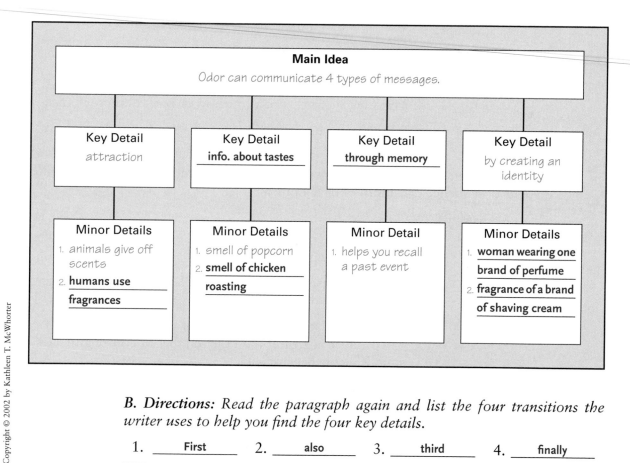

B. Directions: *Read the paragraph again and list the four transitions the writer uses to help you find the four key details.*

1. _____First_____ 2. _____also_____ 3. _____third_____ 4. _____finally_____

The diagram you completed in the exercise above is a **map**—a visual way of organizing information. By filling in—or drawing—maps you can "see" how ideas in a paragraph or essay are related. Chapter 9 gives you more information about mapping (see page 263) and about other ways of organizing information.

Exercise 5–2

Directions: *Each of the following topic sentences states the main idea of a paragraph. After each topic sentence are sentences containing details that may or may not support the topic sentence. Read each sentence and put a "K" beside those that contain key details that support the topic sentence.*

1. *Topic sentence:* Many dramatic physical changes occur during adolescence between the ages of 13 and 15.

   Details:

   ____K____ a. Voice changes in boys begin to occur at age 13 or 14.

   ____K____ b. Facial proportions may change during adolescence.

   ____K____ c. Adolescents, especially boys, gain several inches in height.

   _____ d. Many teenagers do not know how to react to these changes.

   ____K____ e. Primary sex characteristics begin to develop for both boys and girls.

2. *Topic sentence:* The development of speech in infants follows a definite sequence or pattern of development.

   Details:

   ____K____ a. By the time an infant is six months old, he or she can make twelve different speech sounds.

   _____ b. Mindy, who is only three months old, is unable to produce any recognizable syllables.

   ____K____ c. During the first year, the number of vowel sounds a child can produce is greater than the number of consonant sounds he or she can make.

   ____K____ d. Between six and twelve months, the number of consonant sounds a child can produce continues to increase.

   _____ e. Parents often reward the first recognizable word a child produces by smiling or speaking to the child.

3. *Topic sentence:* The main motives for attending a play are the desire for recreation, the need for relaxation, and the desire for intellectual stimulation.

   Details:

   ___K___ a. By becoming involved with the actors and their problems, members of the audience temporarily forget about their personal cares and concerns and are able to relax.

   _____ b. In America today, the success of a play is judged by its ability to attract a large audience.

   ___K___ c. Almost everyone who attends a play expects to be entertained.

   _____ d. Even theater critics are often able to relax and enjoy a good play.

   ___K___ e. There is a smaller audience that looks to theater for intellectual stimulation.

4. *Topic sentence:* Licorice is used in tobacco products because it has specific characteristics that cannot be found in any other single ingredient.

   Details:

   _____ a. McAdams & Co. is the largest importer and processor of licorice root.

   ___K___ b. Licorice blends with tobacco and provides added mildness.

   ___K___ c. Licorice provides a unique flavor and sweetens many types of tobacco.

   _____ d. The extract of licorice is present in relatively small amounts in most types of pipe tobacco.

   ___K___ e. Licorice helps tobacco retain the correct amount of moisture during storage.

5. *Topic sentence:* An *oligopoly* is a market structure in which only a few companies sell a certain product.

   Details:

   ___K___ a. The automobile industry is a good example of an oligopoly, even though it gives the appearance of being highly competitive.

   ___K___ b. The breakfast cereal, soap, and cigarette industries, although basic to our economy, operate as oligopolies.

_____ c. Monopolies refer to market structures in which only one industry produces a particular product.

_____ d. Monopolies are able to exert more control and price fixing than oligopolies.

___K___ e. In the oil industry there are only a few producers, so each producer has a fairly large share of the sales.

Exercise 5-3

Directions: Read the following paragraph and answer the questions that follow.

The larger-scale and more technologically sophisticated a society, the weaker its ties of marriage, for several reasons. First, in large-scale societies, especially mobile ones like Western society, individuals continually meet new people of the opposite sex. Second, people are likely to live longer in technologically advanced societies, and longevity sometimes leads to marital discontent. Third, many of the functions of marriage in large-scale, technologically sophisticated societies are fulfilled by other institutions. A married person's economic support, for example, does not depend on cooperation with a spouse when both spouses earn paychecks outside their joint household and can continue to do so even if they part.

—Hicks and Gwynne, *Cultural Anthropology*, p. 258

1. Does the topic sentence occur first, last, or in the middle of the paragraph? _____ first _____

2. List the paragraph's three key details:

   Individuals continually meet new people of opposite sex.

   Living longer can lead to marital discontent.

   Many functions of marriage are fulfilled by other institutions.

3. What transition words does the writer use to take the reader from one key detail to the next? _____ first, second, third _____

4. In the third sentence, what does the word *longevity* mean?

   _____ living longer _____

5. Is the last sentence the main idea of the paragraph, a key detail, or a minor detail? _____ minor detail _____

Recognizing Transitions

As you know, **transitions** are linking words or phrases that lead the reader from one idea to another. If you get into the habit of recognizing transitions, you will see that they often help you read a paragraph more easily.

In the following paragraph, notice how the underlined transitions lead you from one detail to the next.

When Su-ling gets ready to study at home, she follows a certain procedure. <u>First of all</u>, she tries to find a quiet place, far away from her kid sisters and brothers. This place might be her bedroom, <u>for example</u>, or it might be the porch or the basement, depending on how much noise the younger children are making. <u>Next</u>, she finds a snack to eat while she is studying, <u>such as</u> chips, an apple, or a candy bar. Sometimes, <u>however</u>, she skips the snack, especially if she is on a diet. <u>Finally</u>, Su-ling takes her books and notes to the quiet spot she has found. She usually does her most difficult homework first <u>because</u> she is more alert at the beginning.

Not all paragraphs contain such obvious transitions, and not all transitions serve as such clear markers of details. As you can see, transitions may be used for a variety of reasons. They may alert you to what will come next in the paragraph, they may tell you that an example will follow, or they may predict that a different, opposing idea is coming. Table 5-1 lists some of the most common transitions and indicates what they will tell you.

TABLE 5-1 Common Transitions

Type of Transition	Example	What They Tell the Reader
Time—sequence	first, later, next, finally	The author is arranging ideas in the order in which they happened.
Example	for example, for instance, to illustrate, such as	An example will follow.
Enumeration	first, second, third, last, another, next	The author is marking or identifying each major point. (Sometimes these may be used to suggest order of importance.)
Continuation	also, in addition, and, further, another	The author is continuing with the same idea and is going to provide additional information.
Contrast	on the other hand, in contrast, however	The author is switching to a different, opposite, or contrasting idea than previously discussed.
Comparison	like, likewise, similarly	The writer will show how the previous idea is similar to what follows.
Cause—effect	because, thus, therefore, since, consequently	The writer will show a connection between two or more things, how one thing caused another, or how something happened as a result of something else.

Exercise 5–4

Directions: Select the transitional word or phrase from the box below that best completes each of the following sentences. Two of the transitions in the box may be used more than once.

on the other hand similarly	for example later	because next	in addition however

1. As a young poet, e. e. cummings was traditional in his use of punctuation and capitalization. _____Later_____, he began to create his own grammatical rules.

2. Many fruits are high in calories; vegetables, ___on the other hand___, are usually low in calories.

3. In order to sight-read music, you should begin by scanning it. _____Next_____, you should identify the key and tempo.

4. Many rock stars have met with tragic ends. _____For example_____, John Lennon was gunned down, Buddy Holly and Ritchie Valens were killed in a plane crash, and Janis Joplin died of a drug overdose.

5. Hernando's sister made a delicious birthday cake for him. _____In addition_____, she surprised him with a big party.

6. Touching the grooves on a record is not advisable _____because_____ oils and minerals in the skin get into the grooves and reduce the quality of sound.

7. Some scientists believe that intelligence is determined equally by heredity and environment. Other scientists, _____however_____, believe that heredity accounts for about 60 percent of intelligence and environment for the other 40 percent.

8. Tigers tend to grow listless and unhappy in captivity. _____Similarly_____, pandas grow listless and have a difficult time reproducing in captivity.

9. American voters tend to vote according to the state of the economy. _____For example_____, if the economy is good, they tend to vote for the

party in power and if the economy is poor, they tend to vote for the party not in power.

10. Liz refused to go to her friend's wedding _____because_____ she knew her ex-husband would be there.

Exercise 5–5

Directions: *Many transitions have similar meanings and can sometimes be used interchangeably. Match each transition in column A with a similar transition in column B. Write the letter of your choice in the space provided.*

	Column A		Column B
_e_	1. because	a.	therefore
_g_	2. in contrast	b.	also
_j_	3. for instance	c.	likewise
_a_	4. thus	d.	after that
_i_	5. first	e.	since
_h_	6. one way	f.	finally
_c_	7. similarly	g.	on the other hand
_d_	8. next	h.	one approach
_b_	9. in addition	i.	in the beginning
_f_	10. to sum up	j.	for example

Putting It All Together

In Chapters 4 and 5 you have learned the four essential ingredients of a paragraph and how to find them. You know how to locate the general *topic* of a paragraph and its *main idea* in a topic sentence. You also know how to identify *details* and how to use *transitions* to help you. In short, you can recognize and put together all of the important parts of a paragraph. Sometimes, though, as you have probably noticed in your reading, the main idea of a paragraph is not always stated directly. Instead of being in a topic sentence—like the paragraphs you've been working with—a main idea may be **implied.** Paragraphs with implied main ideas will be covered in Chapter 6.

What Have You Learned?

Directions: To check your understanding of the chapter, select the word or phrase from the box below that best completes each of the following sentences. Keep in mind that five of the choices will not be used.

finally	next
minor details	because
first	transitions
main idea	key details
for example	on the other hand

1. The details in a paragraph are intended to prove or explain the
   _____main idea_____ .

2. The most important details in a paragraph are its _____key details_____ .

3. _____Transitions_____ are words or phrases that lead the reader from
   one idea to another.

4. Words such as *first*, *next*, and _____finally_____ tell you that the
   writer is putting ideas in the order in which they happened.

5. The phrase _____on the other hand_____ tells you that the writer is switching
   to a different idea.

NAME _____ SECTION _____

DATE _____ SCORE _____

Directions: Read the following paragraph and then complete the diagram below. Some of the items have been filled in for you.

There are four main types of sunglasses. The traditional *absorptive* glasses soak up all the harmful sun rays. *Polarizing* sunglasses account for half the market. They're the best buy for knocking out glare, and reflections from snow and water, but they may admit more light rays than other sunglasses. *Coated* sunglasses usually have a metallic covering that itself reflects light. They are often quite absorptive, but a cheap pair of coated glasses may have an uneven or nondurable coating that could rub off after a short period of time. New on the market are the somewhat more expensive *photochromatic* sunglasses. Their chemical composition causes them to change color according to the brightness of the light: in the sun, they darken; in the shade, they lighten. This type of sunglasses responds to ultraviolet light only, and will not screen out infrared rays, so they're not the best bet for continual exposure to bright sun.

—George, *The New Consumer Survival Kit*, p. 114

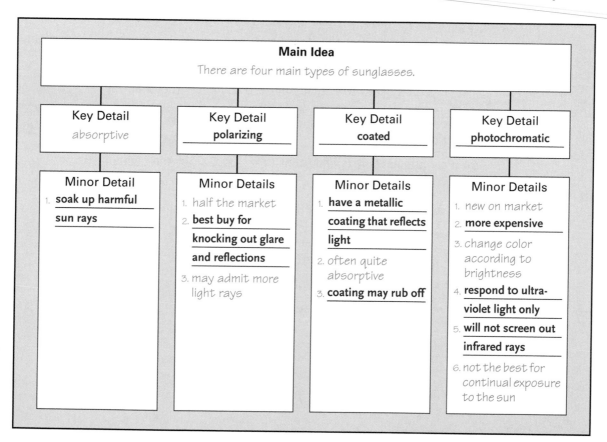

NAME _____ SECTION _____

DATE _____ SCORE _____

Directions: Select the transitional word or phrase from the box below that best completes each of the following sentences. Use each transition only once.

also	because
second	finally
on the other hand	first
another	to illustrate
likewise	such as

When you begin to put together a new computer, you should _____first_____ read the directions. _____Second_____, make sure that you have all of the various components, _____such as_____ the monitor, keyboard, and mouse. If you have everything, you can proceed with the assembly. _____On the other hand_____, if you are missing an item, you might have to contact the store where you bought the computer. You might _____also_____ have to wait for the missing component.

Once you begin to actually put the computer together, _____another_____ point to remember is to work carefully, following the directions step by step. _____Because_____ you are working with electronic equipment, it is important to connect all of the components correctly. _____To illustrate_____, if the printer is not plugged in properly, you will not be able to print out an email or an assignment for one of your classes. _____Likewise_____, the monitor must be connected at the right place or you won't have a screen on which to work. _____Finally_____, when you have attached all of the components, you are ready to turn on your new computer and enjoy it.

NAME _____ SECTION _____

DATE _____ SCORE _____

Directions: After reading the paragraph below, in the space provided write the letter of the choice that best completes each of the statements that follow.

The role of affirmative action in our multicultural society lies at the center of a national debate about how to steer a course in race and ethnic relations. In affirmative action, quotas based on race (and gender) are used in hiring and college admissions. Liberals, both white and minority, defend affirmative action, saying that it is the most direct way to level the playing field of economic opportunity. If whites are passed over, this is an unfortunate cost we must pay if we are to make up for past discrimination. Conservatives, in contrast, both white and minority, agree that opportunity should be open to all, but say that putting race (or sex) ahead of people's ability to perform a job is reverse discrimination. Because of their race (or sex), qualified people who had nothing to do with past discrimination are being discriminated against. They add that affirmative action stigmatizes the people who benefit from it because it suggests that they hold their jobs because of race (or sex), rather than merit.

—Henslin, *Essentials of Sociology*, p. 239

___c___ 1. The topic of the paragraph is
  a. race relations.   c. affirmative action.
  b. discrimination.   d. economic opportunity.

___a___ 2. The topic sentence occurs
  a. first.   c. last.
  b. second.   d. first and last.

___b___ 3. The third sentence, which begins with the word "Liberals," is
  a. a transition.   c. the paragraph's main idea.
  b. a key detail.   d. a minor detail.

___c___ 4. When the author moves to his second key detail, the transition he uses to provide a signal for the reader is
  a. *because.*   c. *in contrast.*
  b. *however.*   d. *but.*

___d___ 5. The last sentence of the paragraph is
  a. its main idea.   c. a transitional statement.
  b. a key detail.   d. a minor detail.

Directions: After reading the paragraph below, in the space provided write the letter of the choice that best completes each of the statements.

Several types of experiences influence how people feel about being touched. Our experiences as a child are one thing that affects our attitudes toward touching. Little girls, for example, are generally kissed and hugged more than little boys. As a result, women often like touching more than men. Our feelings about being touched also depend on our cultural background. Latin Americans and southern Europeans, for example, casually touch each other more than northern Europeans and most Americans. Social context as well influences our willingness to touch and be touched. Even men who are usually uneasy about touching may hug one another at an exciting sporting event.

___d___ 1. The general topic of the paragraph is

    a. types of childhood experiences.

    b. how men and women feel about each other.

    c. how the fear of touching influences our lives.

    d. what affects our feelings about touching.

___a___ 2. The topic sentence of the paragraph begins with the words

    a. "Several types."   c. "Social context."

    b. "As a result."   d. "Even men."

___b___ 3. The key supporting details of the paragraph are

    a. Latin Americans, southern Europeans, and men at sporting events.

    b. childhood experiences, cultural background, and social context.

    c. willingness to be touched, and discomfort at being touched.

    d. little girls, little boys, and differences in being touched.

___a___ 4. The first key supporting detail is signaled by the transitional word or phrase

    a. *one thing.*   c. *also.*

    b. *for example.*   d. *as well.*

___a___   5. Sentence 3, which begins with the words "Little girls," is
           a. a minor detail.   c. a transition
           b. a key detail.   d. the paragraph's main idea.

___d___   6. The transition "as a result" in sentence 4 indicates
           a. the writer is putting ideas in order.
           b. an example will follow.
           c. the writer is continuing with the same idea.
           d. the writer will show how one thing caused another.

___b___   7. You know the author is moving to his second key supporting detail because he uses the transitional word or words
           a. *one.*   c. *for example.*
           b. *also.*   d. *as well.*

___a___   8. Sentence 6, which begins with the words "Latin Americans," provides
           a. minor details.   c. key details.
           b. the paragraph's main idea.   d. additional transitions.

___c___   9. The last key detail is about
           a. why northern Europeans dislike touching.
           b. why women like touching.
           c. how social context affects touching.
           d. how cultural background affects touching.

___d___   10. According to the paragraph,
           a. men never like to hug each other.
           b. Latin Americans casually touch each other more than southern Europeans.
           c. women who were never hugged as children will still like to be touched.
           d. two men might hug one another at an exciting baseball game.

NAME _____ SECTION _____

DATE _____ SCORE _____

Directions: After reading the selection below, in the space provided write the letter of the choice that best completes each of the statements that follow.

Corporations may be either public or private. The stock of a public corporation is widely held and available for sale to the general public. For example, anyone who has the money can buy shares of Caterpillar, Digital Equipment, or Time Warner. The stock of a private corporation, on the other hand, is held by only a few people and is not available for sale to the general public. The controlling group of stockholders may be a family, a management group, or even the firm's employees. Gallo Wine, Levi Strauss, and United Parcel Service are all private corporations. Because few investors will buy unknown stocks, most new corporations start out as private corporations. As the corporation grows and investors see evidence of success, it may issue shares to the public as a way to raise additional money. For example, Netscape Communications publicly issued stock for the first time in 1995. The firm quickly sold 81 million shares and raised over a billion dollars for new product development and expansion.

Corporations have several advantages. The biggest advantage is limited liability: The liability of investors is limited to their personal investments in the corporation. In the event of failure, the courts may seize and sell a corporation's assets but cannot touch the personal possessions of investors. For example, if you invest $1,000 in a corporation that goes bankrupt, you may lose your $1,000, but no more. In other words, $1,000 is the extent of your liability. Another corporate advantage is continuity. Because it has a legal life independent of its founders and owners, a corporation can, at least in theory, go on forever. Shares of stock, for example, may be sold or passed on from generation to generation. Moreover, most corporations also benefit from the continuity provided by professional management. Finally, corporations have advantages in raising money. By selling more stock, for instance, they can expand the number of investors and the amount of available funds. Continuity and the legal protections afforded to corporations also tend to make lenders more willing to grant loans.

—Griffin and Ebert, *Business*, p. 43

_____c_____ 1. The topic sentence of the first paragraph begins with the words

    a. "The firm."   c. "Corporations may."

    b. "The controlling group."   d. "Because few."

_____b_____ 2. The second sentence in paragraph 1, which begins with the words "The stock of a public corporation," is

    a. the paragraph's main idea.   c. a minor detail.

    b. a key detail.   d. an additional transition.

_____d_____ 3. When the writer moves the discussion in paragraph 1 to private corporations, he uses the transition
    a. *for example.*   c. *in contrast.*
    b. *because.*   d. *on the other hand.*

_____a_____ 4. The last sentence of paragraph 1 is
    a. a minor detail.   c. a key detail.
    b. a transition.   d. the paragraph's main idea.

_____b_____ 5. The key supporting details of paragraph 2 are
    a. corporate advantages and disadvantages.
    b. limited liability, continuity, and raising money.
    c. investing and selling stock.
    d. corporations, founders, and owners.

_____c_____ 6. In paragraph 2, the word **liability** means
    a. accuracy.   c. responsibility.
    b. honesty.   d. awareness.

_____b_____ 7. In paragraph 2, the word **continuity** means
    a. having the ability to change.
    b. going on without interruption.
    c. knowing something is true.
    d. having the experience to succeed.

_____a_____ 8. The last key detail in paragraph 2 begins with the transition
    a. *finally.*   c. *for example.*
    b. *also.*   d. *moreover.*

_____b_____ 9. According to the selection,
    a. people should not invest in corporations.
    b. new corporations usually begin as private corporations.
    c. corporations often have difficulty raising money.
    d. Levi Strauss is a public corporation.

_____d_____ 10. When the writer wants to add some specific information, he often uses the transition
    a. *another.*   c. *in other words.*
    b. *on the other hand.*   d. *for example.*

NAME _____   SECTION _____

DATE _____   SCORE _____

HOW TO ACE A JOB INTERVIEW
Richard Koonce

There are many ways to handle yourself during a job interview, but some are better than others. Richard Koonce offers a number of helpful suggestions.

Vocabulary Preview

These are some of the difficult words in this essay. The definitions here will help you if you can't figure out the meanings from the sentence context or word parts.

quibble (par. 1) argue; find fault

prospective (par. 2) possible

terrain (par. 5) setting or territory

showcase (par. 5) reveal in a favorable way

refinement (par. 5) improvement

concise (par. 5) brief and meaningful

vignettes (par. 5) descriptions

etiquette (par. 11) acceptable behavior; manners

---

1   Next to public speaking, most people think that enduring a job interview is one of the most stressful experiences. I wouldn't quibble with that. However, a lot of people not only manage to master the art of effective interviewing as they go about job searches, but actually grow to enjoy the interview experience.

2   Good thing! Job interviews are something we all have to deal with from time to time in our careers. So, it pays to know how to handle yourself effectively when you're sitting across the desk from a prospective employer. Indeed, knowing how to navigate the terrain of job interviews can pay off big time for your career, land you a better job than the one you initially interview for, and position you for the job success and satisfaction you deserve.

3   How do you ace a job interview? Here are some tips. Recognize that when you interview for a job, employers are looking for evidence of four things:

A job interview.

your ability to do the job, your motivation, your compatibility with the rest of the organization, and your self-confidence. If you understand how all those things play into an interviewer's questions (and an employer's hiring decisions), you'll have a better chance of getting hired.

4   Often the first thing an employer wants to know is, "Will you fit in?" Presuming a company has seen your resume ahead of time and invited you for an interview, it may assume you have certain skills. Now they want to know, "Will you be compatible with everyone else that works here?" Fitting in is a real hot button for employers. That's because it's expensive to go through the rehiring process if someone doesn't work out.

5   Along with determining compatibility, employers want to know that you're motivated to do a job. And, they want to know why you want to work for their organization. So be ready with career highlights that illustrate why hiring you would be a good decision for the organization. Showcase your talents as an instructional designer for example, or tell the interviewer about the process improvement efforts you've put in place in your current job that ensure continuous refinement of training courses. Concise oral vignettes like these can make a great impression on interviewers.

6 Throughout the interview, breathe deeply, speak slowly, and focus on projecting yourself confidently. This is important. Employers want to see self-confidence in job seekers. A lot of job seekers are too modest. They downplay their accomplishments. Don't embellish or exaggerate, but don't be a shrinking violet either. Rehearse ahead of time the answers to key questions that you expect to be asked, especially that all-time favorite: "Tell me about yourself."

7 Some other points to keep in mind:

8 Before the interview, do some research on the company you're interviewing with. That will enable you to demonstrate the knowledge of the company when you meet the interviewer. It may also prompt questions that you'll want to get answers to, even as questions are being asked of you. There are lots of research options. You can tap into the Internet and pull down everything from company profiles to Dun and Bradstreet financial reports. You can talk to friends or co-workers that may know something about the organization. And don't forget to watch the paper for late-breaking developments about the company. (If you read in the paper the day of your interview that your prospective employer is about to file Chapter 11, you may want to think twice about working there!) Arrive for the interview early enough to go to the restroom to check yourself out. The last thing you want is to arrive for your interview beaded with sweat, having just sprinted there from the subway stop two blocks away.

9 Once in the interview, concentrate on making a pleasant and strong first impression. Eighty percent of the first impression an interviewer gets of you is visual—and it's formed in the first two minutes of the meeting! So, men, wear a well-made suit, crisply starched white or blue shirt, and polished shoes. Women, you can get away with more color than men, but dress conservatively in dresses, or jacket and skirt combinations. Wearing a colorful scarf is a good way to weave in color, but keep jewelry to a minimum.

10 As you answer questions, be sure to emphasize as often as you can the reasons why your skills, background, and experience make you a good fit for the job that you're interviewing for.

11 After the interview, immediately send a thank-you note to the interviewer. This is a critical point of interview etiquette. Many job candidates eliminate themselves from competition for a job because they don't do this.

12   Finally, learn from every job interview you have. Don't be hard on yourself if things don't go your way. Even job interviews that don't go well can be great learning experiences. And in my own life, I can look back on interviews where I'm glad I didn't get the job!

— ▪ —

Directions: In the space provided, write the letter of the choice that best completes each of the following statements.

CHECKING YOUR COMPREHENSION

_b_   1. The main point of the selection can be stated as follows:

    a. If you arrive early enough for an interview, you will feel relaxed and confident.

    b. If you understand the four things employers are looking for in an interview, you will have a better chance of getting the job.

    c. If you seem to "fit in" with the company, you will probably get hired.

    d. If you do research on the company ahead of time, you will be able to impress the interviewer.

_c_   2. In a job interview, employers are primarily looking for your ability to do the job, your motivation, your self-confidence, and

    a. your ability to speak clearly about your skills and background.

    b. your willingness to work hard and be dedicated to the company.

    c. your compatibility with the rest of the organization.

    d. your understanding of the company's history and products.

_d_   3. What is the "all-time-favorite" question an interviewer usually asks?

    a. Why are you interested in this position?

    b. Tell me about your current job.

    c. What salary are you looking for?

    d. Tell me about yourself.

_____a_____ 4. According to paragraph 9, an employer's first impression of you is based mainly on
- a. your appearance.
- b. your enthusiasm.
- c. your tone of voice.
- d. your job skills.

_____b_____ 5. What does the author suggest that you do immediately after a job interview?
- a. phone the interviewer
- b. send a thank-you note to the interviewer
- c. relax and wait to hear if you got the job
- d. send a letter to the president of the company

USING WHAT YOU KNOW ABOUT SUPPORTING DETAILS

_____c_____ 6. In paragraph 1, the transition _however_ tells the reader that
- a. an example will follow.
- b. the author will show how one thing caused another.
- c. the author will switch to a contrasting idea.
- d. the author will identify each major point.

_____a_____ 7. In paragraph 4, where does the topic sentence occur?
- a. first
- c. in the middle
- b. second
- d. last

_____b_____ 8. In paragraph 5, the sentence that begins with the words "so be ready" is a
- a. minor detail.
- c. transition.
- b. key detail.
- d. topic sentence.

_____c_____ 9. In paragraph 8, the sentence that begins with the words "You can tap into the Internet" is
- a. the paragraph's main idea.
- b. a topic sentence.
- c. a minor detail.
- d. a key detail.

_____d_____ 10. The author uses a transition at the beginning of the last five paragraphs in order
    a. to indicate that he is switching to contrasting ideas.
    b. to indicate how something happened as a result of something else.
    c. to indicate how each idea is similar to the preceding one.
    d. to indicate that he is arranging ideas in the order in which they would occur.

USING CONTEXT CLUES AND WORD PARTS

_____b_____ 11. In paragraph 1, the word **enduring** means
    a. enjoying.   c. preparing for.
    b. suffering through.   d. resisting.

_____a_____ 12. In paragraph 2, the word **navigate** means
    a. find your way around.   c. leave behind.
    b. come to terms with.   d. come close to.

_____d_____ 13. In paragraph 3, the word **compatibility** means the ability to
    a. compromise.   c. make friends.
    b. work hard.   d. fit in.

_____c_____ 14. In paragraph 5, the word **ensure** means
    a. eliminate.   c. make certain.
    b. cause doubt about.   d. need help for.

_____a_____ 15. In paragraph 6, the word **embellish** means
    a. add extra details.   c. add errors.
    b. make mistakes.   d. make noise.

REVIEWING DIFFICULT VOCABULARY

Directions: Complete each of the following sentences by inserting a word from the Vocabulary Preview on page 132 in the space provided. A word should be used only once.

16. Screaming at a waitress in a restaurant is not considered good

_____**etiquette**_____ .

17. After her first date with Juan, Amy knew that he might be her
    _____prospective_____ husband.

18. When my brother told me he would pay me interest on the loan, I told
    him I couldn't _____quibble_____ with that.

19. It is difficult for Alfredo to _____showcase_____ his talents because he
    is so shy.

20. Instead of being long and windy, Sheila's story was _____concise_____
    and to the point.

RECORDING YOUR PROGRESS

Test	Number Right			Score	
Practice Test 5-1	_____	× 10	=	_____	%
Practice Test 5-2	_____	× 10	=	_____	%
Practice Test 5-3	_____	× 10	=	_____	%
Mastery Test 5-1	_____	× 10	=	_____	%
Mastery Test 5-2	_____	× 10	=	_____	%
Mastery Test 5-3	_____	× 5	=	_____	%

EVALUATING YOUR PROGRESS

Based on your test performance, rate how well you have mastered the skills taught in this chapter by checking one of the boxes below or by writing your own evaluation.

☐ **Need More Improvement**

Tip: Try using the "Supporting Details" Module on the Reading Road Trip CD-ROM or Website that accompanies this textbook to fine-tune the skills that you have learned in this chapter.

☐ **Need More Practice**

Tip: Try using the "Supporting Details" Module on the Reading Road Trip CD-ROM that accompanies this textbook to brush up on the skills you have learned in this chapter, or visit this textbook's Website at **http://ablongman.com/mcwhorter** for extra practice.

☐ **Good**

Tip: To maintain your skills, do a quick review of this chapter by using the Website that accompanies this textbook by logging on to **http://ablongman.com/mcwhorter.**

☐ **Excellent**

YOUR EVALUATION: _____

_____

_____

_____

_____

Read Me First!

Study the cartoon below. The point the cartoonist is making is clear—"The dog ate my homework" is a common excuse given by students. Notice, however, that this point is not stated directly; instead, it is implied. To get the cartoonist's point, you have to study the details and dialogue in the cartoon and then figure out what the cartoonist is trying to say.

When you read a paragraph that lacks a topic sentence, you need to use the same reasoning process. You have to study all of the details and figure out the writer's main point. This chapter will show you how to figure out implied main ideas.

"Oh no, not homework again."

Chapter 6

Understanding Implied Main Ideas

What Does Implied Mean?

Just as you figured out the cartoonist's main point, you often have to figure out the implied main ideas of speakers and writers. When an idea is **implied,** it is suggested, but not stated outright. Suppose your favorite shirt is missing from your closet and you know that your roommate often borrows your clothes. Thus you say to your roommate, "If my blue plaid shirt is back in my closet by noon, I'll forget it was missing." This statement does not directly accuse your roommate of borrowing the shirt, but your message is clear—Return my shirt! Your statement implies or suggests to your roommate that he has borrowed the shirt and should return it.

Speakers and writers often imply ideas rather than state them directly.

Here is another statement. What is the writer implying?

EXAMPLE

I wouldn't feed that dessert to a dog.

You can figure out that the writer dislikes the dessert and considers it inedible even though this is not stated directly.

Exercise 6-1

Directions: For each of the following statements, circle the letter of the choice that best explains what the writer is implying or suggesting.

1. Jane's hair looked as if she just came out of a wind tunnel.
   a. Jane needs a haircut.
   b. Jane's hair is messed up.
   c. Jane needs a hat.
   d. Jane's hair needs coloring.

2. Dino would not recommend Professor Wright's class to his worst enemy.
   a. Dino likes Professor Wright's class.
   b. Dino dislikes Professor Wright's class.
   c. Professor Wright's class is popular.
   d. Professor Wright's class is unpopular.

3. The steak was overcooked and tough, the mashed potatoes were cold, the green beans were withered, and the chocolate pie was mushy.
   a. The dinner was tasty.
   b. The dinner was nutritious.
   c. The dinner was prepared poorly.
   d. The dinner was served carelessly.

4. Professor Rodriguez assigns three 5-page papers, gives pop quizzes, and requires both a midterm and final exam. In addition to reading chapters in the text every week, Leah must read three or four other articles. It is difficult to keep up.
   a. Professor Rodriguez' course is demanding.
   b. Professor Rodriguez is not a good teacher.
   c. Professor Rodriguez likes to give homework.
   d. Professor Rodriguez' course is unpopular.

5. The floor of the theater was scattered with popcorn; my feet stuck to the floor where soda had been spilled; the aisles were cluttered with candy wrappers.
   a. The theater's management is not well-trained.
   b. The theater is well-attended.
   c. The theater has not been cleaned.
   d. The theater was crowded.

Remembering General versus Specific Ideas

When trying to figure out the implied main idea in a paragraph, it is important to remember the distinction between general and specific. From Chapter 4 you know that a *general* idea applies to many items or ideas, whereas a *specific* idea refers to a particular item. The word *color*, for instance, is general because it refers to many other specific colors—purple, yellow, red, and so forth. The word *shoe* is general because it can apply to many types, such as running shoes, high heels, loafers, and bedroom slippers. (For more information on general and specific ideas, see Chapter 4, p. 88.)

Exercise 6-2

Directions: For each set of specific items or ideas, circle the letter of the choice that best applies to them. When choosing a general idea, be careful that it is not too general or too narrow.

1. Sledding, skiing, ice-hockey, snowmobiling
   a. men's activities
   b. Olympic events
   c. winter sports
   d. recreational activities

2. Cleaning the house, having a yard party, planting flowers, having a garage sale
   a. homeowner activities
   b. daily chores
   c. general responsibilities
   d. weekend jobs

3. Answering the phone politely, taking accurate messages, being outgoing and positive
   a. how to be successful
   b. how to keep a job
   c. how to be a good receptionist
   d. how to assert yourself

4. Cutting calories, jogging, eliminating desserts, working out at a gym
   a. ways to exercise
   b. ways to lose weight
   c. ways to make friends
   d. ways to improve your well-being

5. To lower heating costs, to reduce drafts, to keep your house warmer
   a. reasons to insulate your house
   b. reasons to stay inside
   c. reasons to turn up the heat
   d. reasons to move south in the winter

You also know from Chapter 4 that the main idea of a paragraph is not only its most important point but also it most *general* idea. *Specific* details back up or support the main idea. In the paragraphs you studied in Chapters 4 and 5, the main idea was always stated in a topic sentence. In this chapter, however, because main ideas are implied, you have to look at the specific details to figure out the main idea. Like main ideas that are stated directly, implied main ideas are usually larger, more important, and general than the details.

What larger, more general idea do the following specific details and the accompanying photograph point to?

The wind was blowing at 35 mph.

The wind chill was 5 degrees below zero.

Snow was falling at the rate of 3 inches per hour.

Together these three details and the photograph suggest that a snowstorm or blizzard was occurring.

What general idea do the following specific sentences suggest?

The child refused to speak.

The child crossed his arms and turned his back.

The child then threw himself face down on the floor.

You probably determined that the child was angry or having a temper tantrum.

Exercise 6–3

Directions: Read the specific details in each exercise, and then select the word or phrase from the box below that best completes the general idea in the sentence that follows. Make sure that each general idea fits all of its specific details. Three words or phrases in the box will not be used.

| in an accident | a power outage | going too fast | dying |
| tonsillitis | the flu | a burglary | closed |

1. The child has a headache.

   The child has a queasy stomach.

   The child has a mild fever.

   General Idea: The child has _____the flu_____.

2. The plant's leaves were withered.
   Its blossoms had dropped.
   Its stem was drooping.

   General Idea: The plant was _____dying_____.

3. The windshield of the car was shattered.
   The door panel was dented.
   The bumper was crumpled.

   General Idea: The car had been ____in an accident____.

4. The lights went out.
   The clock radio flashed.
   The refrigerator stopped running.

   General Idea: There was ____a power outage____.

5. The supermarket door was locked.
   The parking lot was nearly empty.
   A few remaining customers were checking out.

   General Idea: The supermarket was _____closed_____.

Exercise 6–4

Directions: Study the photo shown here and then answer each of the following questions.

1. What do you think is happening in the photograph?

   The two people are involved in an automobile accident.

2. What general idea is the photographer trying to express through the photograph?

   The two people are arguing: The woman is accusing the man of some wrongdoing;

   the man is not accepting blame.

How to Find Implied Main Ideas in Paragraphs

As you know, when a writer leaves his or her main idea unstated, it is up to you, the reader, to look at the details in the paragraph and figure out the writer's main point.

The details, when taken together, will all point to a general and more important idea. You might want to think of such a paragraph as the pieces of a puzzle. You must put together the pieces or details to determine the meaning of the paragraph as a whole. Use the following steps as a guide to find implied main ideas:

1. **Find the topic.** As you know from earlier chapters, the *topic* is the general subject of the entire paragraph. Ask yourself: "What is the one thing the author is discussing throughout the paragraph?"

2. **Figure out what is the most important idea the writer wants you to know about that topic.** Look at each detail and decide what larger idea is being explained.

3. **Express this main idea in your own words.** Make sure that the main idea is a reasonable one. Ask yourself: "Does it apply to all of the details in the paragraph?"

EXAMPLE

Some advertisers rely on star power. Commercials may use celebrities, for example, to encourage consumers to purchase a product. Other commercials may use an "everyone's buying it" approach, arguing that thousands of consumers could not possibly be wrong in their choice, so the product must be worthwhile. Still other commercials may use visual appeal to catch the consumers' interest and persuade them to make purchases.

—Solomon, *Consumer Behavior: Buying, Having, and Being,* Fourth Edition, pp. 49–50

The general topic of this paragraph is commercials. More specifically, the paragraph is about the various persuasive devices used in commercials. Three details are given: (1) star power, (2) the everyone's-buying-it approach, and (3) visual appeal. Each of the three details is a different persuasive device. The main point the writer is trying to make, then, is that commercials use a variety of persuasive devices to appeal to consumers. You can figure out this writer's main idea even though no single sentence states this directly. You might visualize this paragraph as follows:

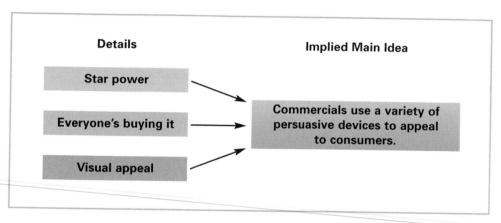

Here is another paragraph. Read it and then fill in the diagram that follows:

EXAMPLE

Yellow is a bright, cheery color; it is often associated with spring and hopefulness. Green, since it is a color that appears frequently in nature (trees, grass, plants), has come to suggest growth and rebirth. Blue, the color of the sky, may suggest eternity or endless beauty. Red, the color of both blood and fire, is often connected with strong feelings such as courage, lust, and rage.

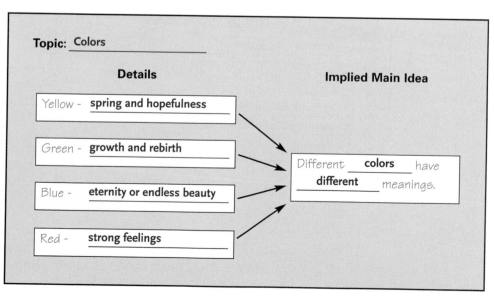

After you come up with a main idea, make sure it is broad enough. Every sentence in the paragraph should support the idea you have chosen. Work through the paragraph sentence by sentence. Check to see if each sentence explains or gives more information about the main idea. If some sentences do not explain your chosen idea, it probably is not broad enough. You may need to expand your idea and make it more general.

Exercise 6-5

Directions: After reading each of the following paragraphs, complete the diagram that follows.

1. In 1920 there was one divorce for every seven marriages in the United States. Fifty years later the rate had climbed to one divorce for every three marriages, and today there is almost one divorce for every two marriages. The divorce rate in the United States is now the highest of any major industrialized nation, while Canada is in a rather distant second place.

—Coleman and Cressey, *Social Problems*, p. 130

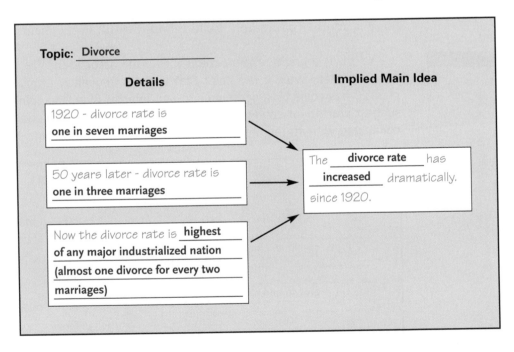

Topic: Divorce

Details

1920 - divorce rate is **one in seven marriages**

50 years later - divorce rate is **one in three marriages**

Now the divorce rate is **highest of any major industrialized nation (almost one divorce for every two marriages)**

Implied Main Idea

The ___**divorce rate**___ has ___**increased**___ dramatically. since 1920.

2. Immigration has contributed to the dramatic population growth of the United States over the past 150 years. It has also contributed to the country's shift from a rural to an urban economy. Immigrants provided

inexpensive labor, which allowed industries to flourish. Native-born children of immigrants, benefiting from education, moved into professional and white collar jobs, creating a new middle class. Immigration also increased the U.S. mortality rate. Due to crowded housing and unhealthy living conditions, disease and fatal illness were common.

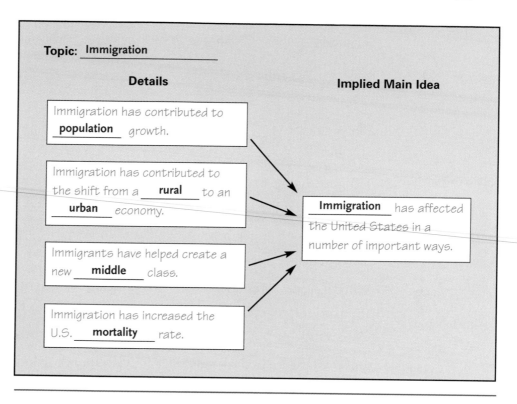

Working with Paragraphs

Now that you have read Chapters 4 through 6, you know a lot about paragraphs. You know, for instance, that they always have a *topic* and a *main idea*. In some paragraphs, the main idea is stated directly in a *topic sentence*. In other paragraphs, like the ones you worked with in this chapter, the main idea is *implied* or suggested. In all paragraphs, the main idea is backed up by *details*. As you move on to Chapter 7, you will learn some ways to keep track of the kinds of information you've been learning. The methods in that chapter will help you with all kinds of reading—for this course, for other college courses, and for reading you do on the job or just for fun.

What Have You Learned?

Directions: To check your understanding of the chapter, select the word or phrase from the box below that best completes each of the following sentences. Three words or phrases in the box are not correct.

important	in the writer's words	general
missing	specific	details
in your own words	implied	identity

1. When an idea is _____implied_____, it is suggested but not stated directly.

2. To figure out the main idea in a paragraph, it is important to understand the distinction between ____general____ and ____specific____.

3. Main ideas are larger, more general, and more ____important____ than details.

4. When a writer does not state the main idea directly, you have to look at a paragraph's specific ____details____ in order to figure out the main idea.

5. Once you figure out the main idea in a paragraph, you should be able to express this idea ____in your own words____.

NAME _____ SECTION _____
DATE _____ SCORE _____

PRACTICE TEST 6-1

Directions: Read the specific details in each exercise and then select the word or phrase from the box below that best completes the general idea in the sentence that follows. Five words in the box are not correct.

cancelled	validated	impatient
spoiled	St. Patrick's Day	speeding ticket
dining	Superbowl	overexposure
eating disorder	late	allergy
camping	vandalized	party

1. The window was shattered.
   Dresser drawers were emptied; clothing was thrown about.
   Furniture was overturned.

   General Idea: The apartment had been _____vandalized_____.

2. The broccoli soup was left sitting unrefrigerated all afternoon.
   The soup was served to everyone at the banquet.
   Everyone who ate the soup got sick.

   General Idea: The soup was _____spoiled_____.

3. The child was in the hot sun for four hours.
   She began to feel queasy.
   Her skin reddened.

   General Idea: She was suffering from _____overexposure_____ to the sun.

4. The family unpacked tents.
   Everyone wore boots and warm clothing.
   Their food was hung from a rope in a tree.

   General Idea: The family was _____camping_____.

5. Players on both teams were introduced.
   The national anthem was sung.
   The stadium was filled with cheering fans.

   General Idea: The _____Superbowl_____ was about to begin.

6. Janine, a teenager, was dangerously thin.

   She thought she needed to lose more weight.

   She often forced herself to vomit.

   General Idea: Janine suffered from an _____eating disorder_____.

7. The lecture hall in which the class was scheduled to meet was locked.

   There was a message posted on the door.

   Several classmates read the message and walked away.

   General Idea: The class was _____cancelled_____.

8. It was a rainy day in March in Buffalo.

   Many people wore green.

   There were parades, and restaurants served corned beef and cabbage.

   General Idea: It was _____St. Patrick's Day_____.

9. A woman was seated alone at a table in a restaurant.

   She tapped her foot impatiently.

   She kept glancing at her watch.

   General Idea: She was meeting someone who was _____late_____.

10. Jeremy was driving 55 miles per hour.

    The speed limit in the residential area was 35 mph.

    In his rearview mirror he saw a police car with its lights flashing.

    General Idea: Jeremy was going to get a/an _____speeding ticket_____.

Directions: After reading each of the following paragraphs, complete the diagram that follows by filling in each blank line.

1. Severe punishment may generate such anxiety in children that they do not learn the lesson the punishment was designed to teach. Moreover, as a reaction to punishment that they regard as unfair, children may avoid punitive parents, who therefore will have fewer opportunities to teach and guide the child. In addition, parents who use physical punishment provide aggressive models. A child who is regularly slapped, spanked, shaken, or shouted at may learn to use these forms of aggression in interactions with peers.

—Newcombe, *Child Development*, p. 354

Topic: Severe Punishment

Details

Punishment may prevent **learning** .

Punishment may cause children to **avoid** their parents, who will then have fewer **chances/opportunities** to teach and guide their children.

Parents who use physical punishment may provide **aggressive** models for their children, who may then learn to use aggression with their **peers** .

Implied Main Idea

Physical punishment has four negative **effects** .

2. Traffic is directed by color. Pilot instrument panels, landing strips, road and water crossings are regulated by many colored lights and signs. Factories use colors to distinguish between thoroughfares and work areas. Danger zones are painted in special colors. Lubrication points and removable parts are accentuated by color. Pipes for transporting water, steam, oil, chemicals, and compressed air are designated by different colors. Electrical wires and resistances are color coded.

—Gerritsen, *Theory and Practice of Color*, p. 9

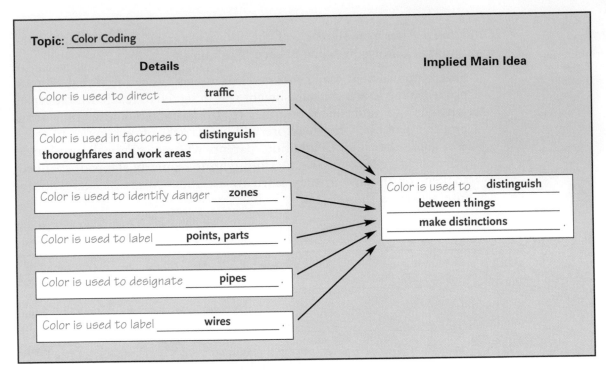

Topic: Color Coding

Details

Color is used to direct ___**traffic**___.

Color is used in factories to ___**distinguish thoroughfares and work areas**___.

Color is used to identify danger ___**zones**___.

Color is used to label ___**points, parts**___.

Color is used to designate ___**pipes**___.

Color is used to label ___**wires**___.

Implied Main Idea

Color is used to ___**distinguish between things make distinctions**___.

3. Jack Schultz and Ian Baldwin found last summer that trees under attack by insects or animals will release an unidentified chemical into the air as a distress signal. Upon receiving the signal, nearby trees step up their production of tannin—a poison in the leaves that gives insects indigestion. The team learned, too, that production of the poison is in proportion to the duration and intensity of the attack.

—"Trees Talk to One Another," *Science Digest*, January 1984, p. 47

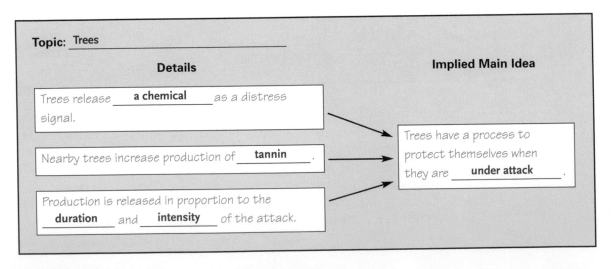

Topic: Trees

Details

Trees release ___**a chemical**___ as a distress signal.

Nearby trees increase production of ___**tannin**___.

Production is released in proportion to the ___**duration**___ and ___**intensity**___ of the attack.

Implied Main Idea

Trees have a process to protect themselves when they are ___**under attack**___.

NAME _____ SECTION _____

DATE _____ SCORE _____

Directions: After reading each of the following paragraphs, select the letter of the choice that best answers the questions below.

Paragraph A

When President Lincoln was shot, the word was communicated by telegraph to most parts of the United States, but because we had no links to England, it was five days before London heard of the event. When President Reagan was shot, journalist Henry Fairlie, working at his typewriter within a block of the shooting, got word of it by telephone from his editor at the *Spectator* in London, who had seen a rerun of the assassination attempt on television shortly after it occurred.

—Naisbitt, *Megatrends*, p. 23

_____a_____ 1. What is the topic?

  a. communication of information

  b. President Lincoln

  c. assassinations

  d. President Reagan

_____c_____ 2. What main idea is the writer implying?

  a. U.S. presidents are in danger.

  b. The telegraph is outdated.

  c. The speed of communication has increased dramatically.

  d. Communication links between countries need to be built.

Paragraph B

The perceived richness or quality of the material in clothing, bedding, or upholstery is linked to its "feel," whether rough or smooth, flexible or inflexible. A smooth fabric such as silk is equated with luxury, although denim is considered practical and durable. Fabrics that are composed of scarce materials or that require a high degree of processing to achieve their smoothness or fineness tend to be more expensive and thus are seen as being higher class. Similarly, lighter, more delicate textures are assumed to be feminine. Roughness is often positively valued for men, and smoothness is sought by women.

—Solomon, *Consumer Behavior: Buying, Having, and Being*, Fourth Edition, pp. 49–50

___a___   3. What is the topic?

      a. the feel of fabrics

      b. expense in producing fabrics

      c. luxury clothing

      d. roughness in clothing

___d___   4. What is the writer saying about the topic?

      a. Denim is a practical and durable fabric.

      b. Men and women differ in their perception of quality.

      c. Fabrics made of scarce materials are expensive.

      d. The feel of a fabric influences how consumers regard its quality.

Paragraph C

A study by the market research department of the *New York Times* found that when choosing between two similar food or beverage products, 81 percent of consumers would choose one they could both smell and see over one they could only see. Samuel Adams beer was one of the first non-perfume products to be advertised with a scent strip that smelled of hops, and Rolls Royce distributed ads scented with the smell of leather. However, a note of caution: This technique adds at least 10 percent to the cost of producing an ad, so marketers will need to watch their dollars and scents.

—Solomon, *Consumer Behavior: Buying, Having, and Being*, Fourth Edition, p. 48

___d___   5. What is the topic?

      a. market research study

      b. beer advertisements

      c. cost of advertisements

      d. the use of smells in advertising

___b___   6. What main idea is the writer implying?

      a. People have difficulty choosing between similar products.

      b. Advertisers are beginning to use scent as part of their advertisements.

      c. Advertising is expensive.

      d. Advertisers should control their spending.

_b_ 7. Which one of the following details does *not* support the paragraph's implied main idea?

    a. Samuel Adams beer used scent strips.

    b. Consumers must always choose between two similar products.

    c. Rolls Royce used scented ads.

    d. Consumers prefer to both see and smell products.

Paragraph D

Your e-mail address will eventually become available to a lot of people you don't know. Some of these people may contact you with unsolicited information or with queries that you are not qualified to answer. If you are in a work situation in which it is appropriate to forward a query to someone else, then you have a legitimate right to pass mail on without further comment. Exercise your good judgment in these situations. Perhaps you will choose to reply to a message that interests you even if it might have been misdirected. But if you find yourself pressed for time and you discover yourself talking to perfect strangers about things that you aren't being paid to discuss, you need to get serious and ignore more of your mail. At the very least, forward legitimate queries to other people if you aren't the appropriate respondent.

—Lehnert, *Internet 101: A Beginner's Guide to the Internet and World Wide Web*, p. 95

_d_ 8. What is the topic?

    a. legitimate queries   c. inappropriate e-mail responses

    b. unsolicited information   d. responding to e-mail

_b_ 9. What is the writer saying about the topic?

    a. All e-mail messages deserve acknowledgement or responses.

    b. It is not always necessary to respond to e-mail messages.

    c. Work situations require a different type of e-mail response than personal situations.

    d. You should protect you e-mail address and restrict its use.

_a_ 10. Which one of the following details does *not* support the paragraph's implied main idea?

    a. Use of e-mail programs will get easier in future years.

    b. E-mail can be forwarded to the appropriate respondent.

    c. Some e-mail can be ignored.

    d. It may not be your job to answer some e-mail.

Directions: After reading each of the following paragraphs, select the letter of the choice that best completes the statements that follow.

Paragraph A

When a homemaker is killed in an auto accident, that person's family can often sue for the value of the services that were lost. Attorneys (who rely on economists) are often asked to make an attempt to estimate this value to present to the court. They add up the cost of purchasing baby-sitting, cooking, housecleaning, and tutoring services. The number turns out to be quite large, often in excess of $30,000 a year. Of course one of the problems in measuring the value of unpaid housework in such a way is that we could often purchase the services of a full-time live-in house-keeper for less money than if we paid for the services of the various components of housekeeping. And what about quality? Some homemakers serve fabulous gourmet meals; others simply warm up canned and frozen foods. Should they be valued equally? Another problem lies in knowing when to stop counting. A person can hire a valet to help him or her get dressed in the morning. Should we therefore count the time spent in getting dressed as part of unpaid work? Both men and women perform services around the house virtually every day of the year. Should all of those unpaid services be included in a "new" measure of GDP (Gross Domestic Product)? If they were, measured GDP would be increased dramatically.

—Miller, *Economics Today*, Eighth Edition, p. 185

_____a_____ 1. The implied main idea of the paragraph is

    a. It is difficult to place a dollar value on a homemaker's services.

    b. Homemakers are not all valued equally.

    c. Full-time housekeepers are expensive.

    d. Homemakers provide a variety of services.

_____b_____ 2. The statement that can reasonably be inferred from the details given in the paragraph is that

    a. all homemakers are underpaid.

    b. not all homemakers provide the same services.

    c. homemakers cannot fairly represent themselves in legal disputes.

    d. most homemakers are not recognized fairly by the people in their households.

_____d_____ 3. A valet is a

    a. tutor.

    b. cook.

    c. homemaker.

    d. personal assistant.

_____a_____ 4. It is cheaper to hire a full-time live-in housekeeper than it is to hire

    a. a number of different workers to handle each part of housekeeping.

    b. a valet.

    c. inexperienced workers.

    d. two half-time employees.

_____d_____ 5. When the author says one of the problems is "knowing when to stop counting," he means

    a. costs add up quickly if one doesn't keep track.

    b. it is impossible to count a housekeeper's hours of work.

    c. assigning number values to homemakers' work is insulting.

    d. it is difficult to know what services to include in determining value.

Paragraph B

In 1970 the federal government passed the Comprehensive Drug Abuse, Prevention and Control Act (also known as the Controlled Substance Act). That act did not contain a rigid penalty system but rather established only upper bounds for the fines and prison terms to be imposed for offenses. In 1984 the act was amended in order to impose fixed penalties, particularly for dealers. For anyone caught with more that 1 kilogram of heroin, 50 grams of cocaine base, or 1,000 kilograms of marijuana, the applicable penalty was raised to imprisonment from 10 years to life plus a fine of $4 million. A variety of other prison penalties and fines were outlined in that amendment. Another amendment passed in 1988 included the death penalty for "drug kingpins."

—Miller, _Economics Today_, Eighth Edition, p. 513

_____c_____ 6. The implied main idea of this paragraph is

    a. Drug laws are focused on users, not dealers.

    b. Drug laws are becoming less effective.

    c. Drug laws have become increasingly more strict.

    d. Drug laws are effective in reducing drug abuse.

c   7. Drug laws have more severe penalties for
    a. drug users.   c. dealers.
    b. underage users.   d. countries that supply drugs.

b   8. The author arranged his details in the paragraph
    a. from least to most important.
    b. in the order in which events happened.
    c. from most to least important.
    d. in no particular order.

c   9. The 1984 amendment was probably designed to penalize
    a. recreational users.   c. dealers.
    b. underage users.   d. repeat offenders.

d   10. As used in the paragraph, the term *rigid* means
    a. weak.   c. lenient.
    b. fair.   d. strict.

NAME _____ SECTION _____

DATE _____ SCORE _____

Directions: Read the following excerpt from an essay titled "My Grandmother, the Bag Lady" by Patsy Neal. Then read each statement and decide whether it is a reasonable implied idea that can be drawn from the information presented in the passage. If the statement is reasonable, write **R** in the space provided; if it is not reasonable, write **NR**.

Almost all of us have seen pictures of old, homeless ladies, moving about the streets of big cities with everything they own stuffed into a bag or a paper sack.

My grandmother is 89 years old, and a few weeks ago I realized with a jolt that she, too, had become one of them. Before I go any further, I had best explain that I did not see my grandmother's picture on TV. I discovered her plight during a face-to-face visit at my mother's house—in a beautiful, comfortable, safe, middle-class environment with good china on the table and turkey and chicken on the stove.

My grandmother's condition saddened me beyond words, for an 89-year-old should not have to carry around everything she owns in a bag. It's enough to be 89, without the added burden of packing the last fragments of your existence into a space big enough to accommodate only the minutest of treasures.

Becoming a bag lady was not something that happened to her overnight. My grandmother had been in a nursing home these last several years; at first going back to her own home for short visits, then less frequently as she became older and less mobile.

No matter how short these visits were, her greatest pleasure came from walking slowly around her home, touching every item lovingly and spending hours browsing through drawers and closets. Then, I did not understand her need to search out all her belongings.

As she spent longer days and months at the nursing home, I could not help noticing other things. She began to hide her possessions under the mattress, in her closet, under the cushion of her chair, in every conceivable, reachable space. And she began to think that people were "stealing" from her.

____R____ 1. The behavior of the author's grandmother changed as a result of living in a nursing home.

____NR____ 2. The grandmother is homeless.

____R____ 3. The grandmother's bag may contain items she valued, such as jewelry, photographs, or family mementoes.

   R   4. The grandmother felt as if she could not trust others in the nursing home.

  NR   5. The grandmother is fond of her granddaughter.

   R   6. The author feels sorry for her grandmother.

   R   7. The grandmother's physical condition has gradually worsened.

   R   8. When returning to her own home from the nursing home, the grandmother enjoyed being surrounded by her own possessions.

  NR   9. The author is pleased with the lifestyle a nursing home offers.

  NR   10. The writer thinks that the elderly are not capable of owning and managing property.

PRIMARY COLORS
Kim McLarin

This essay, originally published in the *New York Times Magazine*, describes a mother's response to her interracial child.

Vocabulary Preview

These are some of the difficult words in this essay. The definitions here will help you if you cannot figure out the meanings from the sentence context or word parts.

retrospect (par. 5) reviewing the past

eccentricities (par. 6) oddities

mischievous (par. 8) playful in a naughty or teasing way

abduction (par. 9) kidnapping

disconcerting (par. 10) upsetting

condemnation (par. 13) strong criticism or disapproval

allegiances (par. 13) loyalties

denounce (par. 13) to criticize openly

align (par. 14) join with others

---

1   A few weeks after my daughter was born, I took her to a new pediatrician for an exam. The doctor took one look at Samantha and exclaimed: "Wow! She's so light!" I explained that my husband is white, but it didn't seem to help. The doctor commented on Sam's skin color so often that I finally asked what was on her mind.

2   "I'm thinking albino," she said.

3   The doctor, who is white, claimed she had seen the offspring of many interracial couples, but never a child this fair. "They're usually a darker, coffee-with-cream color. Some of them are this light at birth, but by 72 hours you can tell they have a black parent."

4   To prove her point, she held her arm next to Samantha's stomach. "I mean, this could be my child!"

5   It's funny now, in retrospect. But at the time, with my hormones still raging from childbirth, the incident sent me into a panic. Any fool could

see that Samantha wasn't albino—she had black hair and dark blue eyes. It must be a trick. The doctor, who had left the room, probably suspected me of kidnapping this "white" child and was outside calling the police. By the time she returned I was ready to fight.

6   Fortunately, her partner dismissed the albino theory, and we escaped and found a new pediatrician, one who knows a little more about genetic eccentricities. But the incident stayed with me because, in the months since, other white people have assumed Samantha is not my child. This is curious to me, this inability to connect across skin tone, especially since Samantha has my full lips and broad nose. I'll admit that I myself didn't expect Sam to be quite so pale, so much closer to her father's Nordic coloring than my own umber tones. My husband is a blue-eyed strawberry blond; I figured that my genes would take his genes in the first round.

7   Wrong.

8   Needless to say, I love Sam just as she is. She is amazingly, heartbreakingly beautiful to me in the way that babies are to their parents. She sweeps me away with her mischievous grin and her belly laugh, with the coy way she tilts her head after flinging the cup from her highchair. When we are alone and I look at Samantha, I see Samantha, not the color of her skin.

9   And yet I admit that I wouldn't mind if she were darker, dark enough so that white people would know she was mine and black people wouldn't give

her a hard time. I know a black guy who, while crossing into Canada, was suspected of having kidnapped his fair-skinned son. So far no one has accused me of child abduction, but I have been mistaken for Samantha's nanny. It has happened so often that I've considered going into business as a nanny spy. I could sit in the park and take notes on your child-care worker. Better than hiding a video camera in the living room.

10   In a way it's disconcerting, my being mistaken for a nanny. Because, to be blunt, I don't like seeing black women caring for white children. It may be because I grew up in the South where black women once had no choice but to leave their own children and suckle the offspring of others. The weight of that past, the whiff of a power imbalance, still stains such pairings for me. That's unfair, I know, to the professional, hard-working (mostly Caribbean) black nannies of New York. But there you are.

11   On the flip side, I think being darker wouldn't hurt Samantha with black people, either. A few weeks ago, in my beauty shop, I overheard a woman trashing a friend for "slathering" his light-skinned children with sunscreen during the summer.

12   "Maybe he doesn't want them getting skin cancer," suggested the listener. But my girl was having none of that.

13   "He doesn't want them getting black!" she said, as full of righteous condemnation as only a black woman in a beauty shop can be. Now, maybe the woman was right about her friend's motivation. Or maybe she was 100 percent wrong. Maybe because she herself is the color of butterscotch she felt she had to declare her allegiances loudly, had to place herself prominently high on the unofficial black scale and denounce anyone caught not doing the same. Either way, I know it means grief for Sam.

14   I think that as time goes on my daughter will probably align with black people anyway, regardless of the relative fairness of her skin. My husband is fine with that, as long as it doesn't mean denying him or his family.

15   The bottom line is that society has a deep need to categorize people, to classify and, yes, to stereotype. Race is still the easiest, most convenient way of doing so. That race tells you, in the end, little or nothing about a person is beside the point. We still feel safer believing that we can sum up one another at a glance.

━━ · ━━

Directions: Select the letter of the choice that best completes each of the following statements.

CHECKING YOUR COMPREHENSION

a 1. The main point of this selection is that
   a. people classify others on the basis of skin color because it is what they notice first.
   b. being the mother of an interracial child has more negative than positive moments.
   c. having an interracial child is easier in the North than in the South.
   d. although people are still aware of race, most people realize that race is not important.

a 2. The main idea of paragraph 10 is that
   a. the author has negative feeling about black women caring for white children.
   b. black women have always cared for white children.
   c. Caribbean nannies are hardworking professionals.
   d. the author is used to seeing nannies because she grew up in the South.

d 3. One reason the author wishes her daughter were darker is that she
   a. wants Sam to identify more with her father's family.
   b. doesn't want Sam to have to use sunscreen.
   c. wants to travel to Canada with Sam.
   d. doesn't want black people to criticize Sam.

a 4. The details in paragraphs 1 through 6 are presented
   a. in the order in which they occurred.
   b. in random order.
   c. from the child's perspective.
   d. from the pediatrician's perspective.

_____c_____ 5. Which statement best describes Sam's physical appearance?

    a. Sam is an albino.

    b. Sam flings her cup from her highchair.

    c. Sam has fair skin, dark hair and blue eyes.

    d. Sam has dark skin and dark hair.

USING WHAT YOU KNOW ABOUT IMPLIED MAIN IDEAS

_____b_____ 6. The main idea of paragraph 9 is that

    a. having people think she is not the mother has several advantages.

    b. people usually think a dark-skinned adult is not the parent of a light-skinned child.

    c. white people have more difficulty than black people in accepting skin tone differences in a parent and child.

    d. having a light-skinned child is easier for the author than having a dark-skinned child.

_____b_____ 7. The incident at the pediatrician's office upset the author because she was afraid that

    a. her daughter might have a genetic abnormality.

    b. the doctor thought Samantha was not her child.

    c. her child might have been switched at birth.

    d. the doctor would harm Samantha.

_____c_____ 8. The main idea of paragraph 8 is that

    a. Sam is a beautiful, teasing child.

    b. the author is most aware of Sam's skin tone when she is with other people.

    c. skin color does not come between the author and her daughter.

    d. the author feels guilty for wishing Sam were darker.

_____c_____ 9. The author finds a new pediatrician because the first one

    a. calls in her partner to help her.

    b. has never examined an interracial child.

    c. seems to know very little about genetics and interracial children.

    d. accuses the author of kidnapping child.

_d_ 10. Which statement most accurately summarizes the author's attitude toward the incident with the first pediatrician?

  a. She feared she would be arrested.

  b. She still does not understand the incident.

  c. She believes the pediatrician should lose her license to practice medicine.

  d. She was upset at the time, but now understands that others will make the same mistakes.

USING CONTEXT AND WORD PARTS

_d_ 11. In paragraph 1, **pediatrician** is a doctor who

  a. cares for feet.

  b. treats the elderly.

  c. deals with emotional problems.

  d. cares for children.

_b_ 12. In paragraph 6, **umber** means

  a. having reddish tones.   c. without color.

  b. a shade of brown.   d. pale.

_b_ 13. In paragraph 10, **imbalance** means

  a. knowing too little.   c. having too much power.

  b. not evenly spread out.   d. not understood.

_b_ 14. In paragraph 11, **slathering** means

  a. artificially coloring.   c. scrubbing thoroughly.

  b. covering thickly.   d. applying unevenly.

_a_ 15. In paragraph 15, **categorize** means

  a. to put into groups.   c. reverse.

  b. join.   d. explain.

REVIEWING DIFFICULT VOCABULARY

Directions: Complete each of the following sentences by inserting a word from the Vocabulary Preview on page 165 in the space provided.

16. In _____retrospect_____, I wish I had majored in biology instead of history.

17. The judge's _____condemnation_____ of the rapist was severe.

18. My grandmother's _____eccentricities_____ make her even more lovable and charming.

19. The news of his father's illness was very _____disconcerting_____ to Jamall.

20. The child's _____abduction_____ was the feature story on the national news.

Chapter 6: Understanding Implied Main Ideas

RECORDING YOUR PROGRESS

Test	Number Right		Score
Practice Test 6-1	_____	× 10 =	_____%
Practice Test 6-2	_____	× 10 =	_____%
Practice Test 6-3	_____	× 10 =	_____%
Mastery Test 6-1	_____	× 10 =	_____%
Mastery Test 6-2	_____	× 10 =	_____%
Mastery Test 6-3	_____	× 5 =	_____%

EVALUATING YOUR PROGRESS

Based on your test performance, rate how well you have mastered the skills taught in this chapter by checking one of the boxes below or by writing your own evaluation.

☐ **Need More Improvement**
Tip: Try using the "Main Idea" Module on the Reading Road Trip CD-ROM that accompanies this textbook to fine-tune the skills that you have learned in this chapter.

☐ **Need More Practice**
Tip: Try using the "Main Idea" Module on the Reading Road Trip CD-ROM that accompanies this textbook to brush up on the skills you have learned in this chapter, or visit this textbook's Website at **http://ablongman.com/mcwhorter** for extra practice.

☐ **Good**
Tip: To maintain your skills, do a quick review of this chapter by using the Website that accompanies this textbook by logging on to **http://ablongman.com/mcwhorter.**

☐ **Excellent**

YOUR EVALUATION: _____

_____

_____

_____

_____

Read Me First!

Suppose you were planning a two-week vacation through the state of Texas next summer. You might use a basic map like the one below to figure out your driving time and to highlight the main places you wanted to see. You could also use computer software to determine the best route to take. In addition, you might jot down a list of major cities and the attractions you didn't want to miss. Under "San Antonio," for example, you would probably write "the Alamo."

Just as there are several ways to keep track of information when you plan a vacation, there are several ways to keep track of information when you read.

Chapter 7

Keeping Track of Information

Why Keep Track of Information?

As you plan a vacation, you often begin to collect all sorts of information—newspaper articles on various cities, brochures, restaurant suggestions from friends, and so forth. If you don't keep track of the various pieces of information, you soon discover that they are hard to find and thus not very useful. For a trip to Texas, for instance, you might decide to sort what you've collected by city, putting everything for San Antonio in one large envelope, everything for Dallas in another envelope, and so forth.

When you read, the ideas and details you are learning about also become more useful if you can organize them in some way. In the preceding chapters, you discovered how to find main ideas and the details that support them. This chapter will show you five ways to keep track of this kind of information: (1) highlighting, (2) marking, (3) outlining, (4) mapping, and (5) summarizing. You may decide to use only a few of these methods, or you may decide to use different ones for different kinds of reading assignments. Whatever approach you take, keep in mind that all of these methods can help you remember what you have read—an important skill for studying and taking tests in college.

Highlighting and Marking

Highlighting and marking important facts and ideas as you read are effective ways to keep track of information. They are also big time-savers for college students. Suppose it took you four hours to read an assigned chapter in sociology. One month later you need to review that chapter to prepare for an exam. If you did not highlight or mark the chapter the first time, then you might have to spend another four hours rereading it. However, if you had highlighted and marked as you read, you could review the chapter fairly quickly.

Highlighting Effectively   Here are a few basic suggestions for highlighting effectively:

1. **Read a paragraph or section first.** Then go back and highlight what is important.
2. **Highlight important portions of any topic sentence.** Also highlight any supporting details you want to remember (see Chapter 5).
3. **Be accurate.** Make sure your highlighting reflects the content of the passage.
4. **Highlight the right amount.** If you highlight too little, you may miss valuable information. On the other hand, if you highlight too much, you are not zeroing-in on the most important ideas, and you will wind up rereading too much material when you study. As a general rule of thumb, highlight no more than 20 to 30 percent of the material.

Read the following paragraph. Notice that you can understand its meaning from the highlighted parts alone.

> Obviously, everybody spends part of his or her life as a single person. Traditionally, it was common that as adolescents entered adulthood, they felt compelled to find both jobs and marriage partners. Today, expectations and goals are changing. As an adolescent moves through high school, and perhaps college, he or she faces a number of decisions regarding the future. Marrying right after school is no longer a top priority for many, and the social stigma against remaining single is rapidly disappearing. In fact, single adults are now one of the fastest-growing factions in the United States; in the past two decades, the number of singles has more than doubled and now represents more than one-fourth of all households.

Exercise 7-1	*Directions: Read the following paragraph, which has been highlighted two different ways. Look at each highlighted version, then write your answers to the questions that follow in the spaces provided.*

Example 1

Money (or actually the lack of it) is a major source of stress for many people. In a sense, this is one of the most "valid" stressors because so many of our basic survival needs require money. Anyone struggling to survive on a small income is likely to feel plenty of stress. But money has significance beyond its obvious value as a medium of exchange. Even some of the wealthiest people become stressed over money-related issues. To some people, wealth is a measurement of human value and their self-esteem is based on their material assets. Stress management for such people requires taking an objective look at the role money plays for them.

—Byer and Shainberg, *Living Well: Health in Your Own Hands,*
Second Edition, pp. 78–79

Example 2

Money (or actually the lack of it) is a major source of stress for many people. In a sense, this is one of the most "valid" stressors because so many of our basic survival needs require money. Anyone struggling to survive on a small income is likely to feel plenty of stress. But money has significance beyond its obvious value as a medium of exchange. Even some of the wealthiest people become stressed over money-related issues. To some people, wealth is a measurement of human value and their self-esteem is based on their material assets. Stress management for such people requires taking an objective look at the role money plays for them.

1. The topic sentence begins with the word _____ money _____ .

2. Is Example 1 or Example 2 the better example of effective highlighting? _____ Example 2 _____

3. Why isn't the highlighting in the other example effective?
   too much highlighting; wouldn't save time when studying _____

4. According to the writer, what two kinds of people may be stressed by money or the lack of it?

   a. **anyone on a small income** _____ b. **wealthy people** _____

Marking   Although highlighting can be very helpful, sometimes you may want to circle a word, ask a question, or write some other kind of note to yourself as you read. In these instances, try making notes in the margin in addition to highlighting.

Here are just a few ways to use marking:

1. **Circle words you do not know.**

2. **Mark definitions with "def".**

3. **Make notes to yourself**—such as "good example," "test question," "reread," or "ask instructor."

4. **Put question marks next to confusing words/passages.**

In the following passage a student taking an introduction to business course has used marking as well as highlighting.

def

U.S. Companies have several (options) as to the products they sell outside the United States. They can sell the same product abroad that they sell at home, they can modify the product for foreign markets, or they can develop an entirely new product for foreign markets.

The simplest strategy is known as *product extension*, which involves offering the same product in all markets, domestic and foreign. This approach has worked successfully for companies including Pepsico, Coca-Cola, Kentucky Fried Chicken, and Levis. Pepsi and Coke are currently battling for market share in both Russia and Vietnam, countries with small but growing soft-drink markets. Both firms are producing and selling the same cola to the Russian and Vietnamese markets that they sell to other markets around the world. Not all companies that have attempted it, however, have found success with product extension. When Duncan Hines introduced its rich, moist American cakes to England, the British found them too messy to hold while sipping tea. Japanese consumers disliked the coleslaw produced by Kentucky Fried Chicken; it was too sweet for their tastes. KFC responded by cutting the sugar in half.

good examples of product extension not working

—Kinnear, Bernhardt, and Krentler, *Principles of Marketing*, Fourth Edition, p. 132

Notice how the student has used marking to circle a word he's not sure of, to point out a definition, and to comment on some examples.

Exercise 7-2

Directions: Read the following paragraphs, which are a continuation of the preceding passage. Highlight and mark the paragraphs in a way that would help you remember the material and study it later.

def

When companies modify a product to meet local preferences or conditions, this strategy is know as *product adaptation*. Cosmetics companies produce different colors to meet the differing preferences of European consumers. French women like bold reds while British and German women prefer pearly pink shades of lipstick and nail color. Nestle's sells varieties of coffee to suit local tastes worldwide. Unilever produces frozen versions of local delicacies such as (Bami Goreng) and Madras Curry for markets in Indonesia and India.

def

Product invention consists of developing a new product to meet a market's needs and preferences. The opportunities that exist with this strategy are great since many unmet needs exist worldwide, particularly in developing and less-developed economies. Marketers have not been quick, however, to attempt product invention. For example, despite the fact that an estimated 600 million people worldwide still scrub clothes by hand, it was

Why so slow? the early 1980s before a company (Colgate-Palmolive) developed an inexpensive, all plastic, manual washing machine with the tumbling action of an automatic washer for use in homes without electricity.

—Kinnear, Bernhardt, and Krentler, *Principles of Marketing*, p. 132

Outlining

Making an outline is another good way to keep track of what you have read. **Outlining** involves listing major and minor ideas and showing how they are related. When you make an outline, follow the writer's organization. An outline usually follows a format like the one below:

I. Major topic
   A. First major idea
      1. First key supporting detail
      2. Second key supporting detail
   B. Second major idea
      1. First key supporting detail
         a. Minor detail or example
         b. Minor detail or example
      2. Second key supporting detail
II. Second major topic
   A. First major idea

Suppose you had just read a brief essay about your brother's vacation in Texas. An outline of the essay might begin like this:

I. Favorite cities
   A. San Antonio—beautiful, interesting history
      1. Alamo
      2. Riverwalk
   B. Houston—friendly people
      1. Seeing Houston Astros play
         a. Excitement of game
         b. Getting lost after leaving Astrodome

Notice that the most important ideas are closer to the left margin. The rule of thumb to follow is this: The less important the idea, the more it should be indented.

Here are a few suggestions for using the outline format:

1. **Don't worry about following the outline format exactly.** As long as your outline shows an organization of ideas, it will work for you.

2. **Use words and phrases or complete sentences,** whichever is easier for you.

3. **Use your own words, and don't write too much.**

4. **Pay attention to headings.** Be sure that all the information you place underneath a heading explains or supports that heading. In the outline above, for instance, the entries "San Antonio" and "Houston" are correctly placed under the major topic "Cities." Likewise, "the Alamo" and "Riverwalk" are under "San Antonio."

Read the following paragraph on fashions, and then study its outline.

Why do fashions occur in the first place? One reason is that some cultures, like ours, *value change:* what is new is good, even better. Thus, in many modern societies clothing styles change yearly, while people in traditional societies may wear the same style for generations. A second reason is that many industries promote quick changes in fashion to increase sales. A third reason is that fashions usually trickle down from the top. A new style may occasionally originate from lower-status groups, as blue jeans did. But most fashions come from upper-class people who like to adopt some style or artifact as a badge of their status. But they cannot monopolize most status symbols for long. Their style is adopted by the middle class, maybe copied or modified for use by lower-status groups, offering many people the prestige of possessing a high-status symbol.

—Thio, *Sociology,* Fifth Edition, p. 534

I. Why fashions occur
   A. Some societies like change.
      1. Modern societies—yearly changes
      2. Traditional societies—may be no change for many years
   B. Industries encourage changes to increase sales
   C. Changes generally start at top.
      1. Blue jeans an exception—came from lower class
      2. Usually start as upper-class status symbol, then move to other classes

---

In this outline, the major topic of the paragraph, "Why fashions occur," is listed first. The writer's three main reasons are listed as A, B, and C. Supporting details are then listed under the reasons. When you look at this outline, you can easily see the writer's most important points.

Exercise 7–3

Directions: *After reading the following passage and the incomplete outline that follows, fill in the missing information in the outline in the space provided.*

CHANGING MAKEUP OF FAMILIES AND HOUSEHOLDS

The traditional definition of a typical U.S. household was one that contained a husband, a nonworking wife, and two or more children. That type of household accounts for only about 9 percent of households today. In its place we see many single-parent households, households without children, households of one person, and other nontraditional households.

A number of trends have combined to create these changes in families and households. Americans are staying single longer—more than one-half of the women and three-quarters of the men between 20 and 24 years old in the United States are still single. Divorce rates are at an all-time high. It is predicted that almost two-thirds of first marriages may end up in divorce. There is a widening gap between the life expectancy of males and females. Currently average life expectancy in the United States is 74 years for men and 78 years for women. Widows now make up more than one-third of one-person households in the United States. These trends have produced a declining average size of household.

The impact of all these changes is significant for marketers. Nontraditional households have different needs for goods and services than do traditional households. Smaller households often have more income per person than larger households, and require smaller houses, smaller cars, and smaller package sizes for food products. Households without children often spend more on personal entertainment and respond more to fads than do traditional households. More money may be spent on travel as well.

—Kinnear, Bernhardt, and Krentler, *Principles of Marketing*, Fourth Edition, pp. 39–40

I. Typical U.S. household has changed
   A. Traditional household
      1. Husband
      2. Nonworking wife
      3. Two or more children
   B. Households of today
      1. Single parent
      2. No children
      3. Only one person
II. Trends that created these changes
    A. Americans stay single longer

      1. One-half of women age 20–24

      2. Three-quarters of men age 20–24

   B. Divorce rates higher

      1. May be two-thirds of first marriages

   C. Gap between male and female life expectancies

      1. Women (78 years) live longer than men (74).

      2. Women are one-third of one-person households.

III. Impact of changes for marketers

   A. Different goods and services needed for traditional vs. nontraditional households

   B. Characteristics of smaller households

      1. More income per person

      2. Need smaller houses, cars, food packages

      3. Spend more on entertainment and fads

      4. Spend more on travel

Mapping

In Chapter 5 you learned a little bit about **mapping** (p. 120), which is a visual method of organizing information. It involves drawing diagrams to show how ideas in a paragraph or chapter are related. Some students prefer mapping to outlining because they feel it is freer and less tightly structured.

Maps can take many forms. You can draw them in any way that shows the relationships between ideas. Figures 7-1 and 7-2 show two sample maps of the paragraph about fashions on page 180. Look at the maps and then look again at the outline of the fashions paragraph. Notice how the important information is included in each method—it's just presented differently.

As you draw a map, think of it as a picture or diagram that shows how ideas are connected. You can hand draw them or use a word processor. Use the following steps, which can be seen in Figures 7-1 and 7-2:

1. **Identify the overall topic or subject.** Write it in the center or at the top of the page.
2. **Identify major ideas that relate to the topic.** Using a line, connect each piece of information to the central topic.
3. **As you discover supporting details that further explain an idea already mapped, connect those details with new lines.**

FIGURE 7-1 Sample hand-drawn map

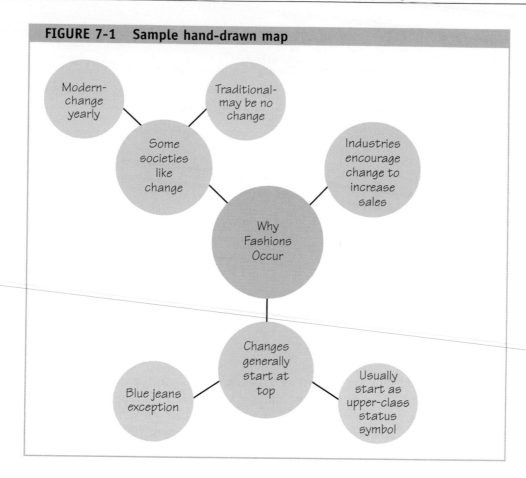

FIGURE 7-2 Sample computer-drawn map

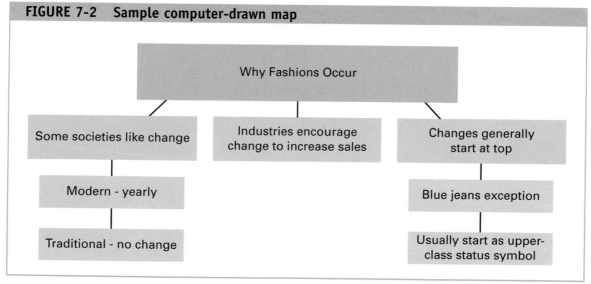

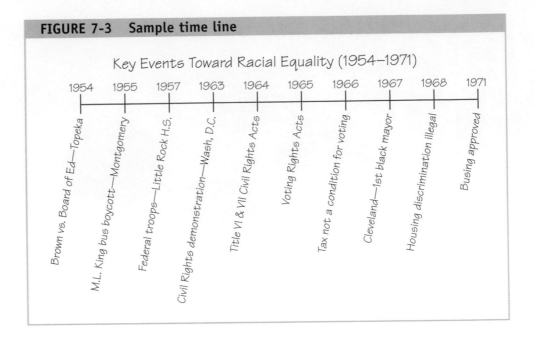

FIGURE 7-3   Sample time line

Key Events Toward Racial Equality (1954–1971)

Once you are skilled at drawing maps, you can become more creative, drawing different types of maps to fit what you are reading. For example, you can draw a *time line* (see Figure 7-3) to show historical events in the order in which they occurred. A time line starts with the earliest event and ends with the most recent. Another type of map is one that shows a process—the steps involved in doing something (see Figure 7-4). When you study chronological order and process in Chapter 8 (p. 219), you will discover more uses for these kinds of maps.

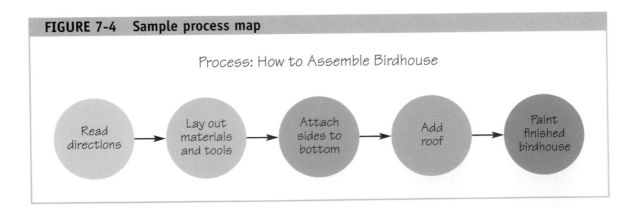

FIGURE 7-4   Sample process map

Process: How to Assemble Birdhouse

Exercise 7–4

Directions: *Read the following paragraph and complete the map below, filling in the writer's main points in the spaces provided. Then answer the question that follows the map.*

When your college work load increases, it is tempting to put things off. Here are some suggestions to help you overcome *procrastination*, which is the tendency to postpone tasks that need to be done. First, clear your desk. Move everything except the materials for the task at hand. Once you start working, you will be less likely to be distracted. Second, give yourself five minutes to start. If you are having trouble beginning a task, working on it for just five minutes might spark your motivation. Next, divide the task into manageable parts. Working with just a part of a task is usually less overwhelming. Then, start somewhere, no matter where. It is better to do something rather than sit and stare. Finally, recognize when you need more information. Sometimes you may avoid a task because you're not sure how to do it. Discuss your questions with classmates or with your professor.

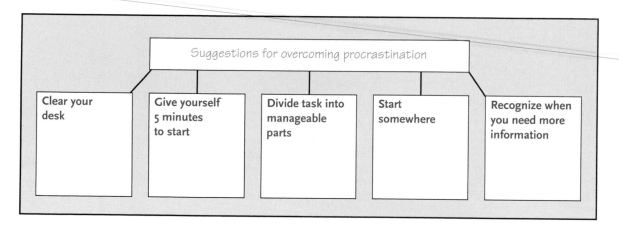

Suggestions for overcoming procrastination

| Clear your desk | Give yourself 5 minutes to start | Divide task into manageable parts | Start somewhere | Recognize when you need more information |

1. What five transition words does the writer use to introduce the main points?

   a. First   b. Second   c. Next   d. Then   e. Finally

Exercise 7–5

Directions: *After reading the following paragraphs, complete each section of the map in which a blank line appears. Fill in the writer's main points as well as some supporting details.*

Animal diets vary *enormously,* and so do methods of feeding. Certain parasites—tapeworms, for instance—are absorptive feeders; lacking a mouth or digestive tract, they absorb nutrients through their body surface. In contrast, the majority of animals, including the great whales, are ingestive feeders; they eat (ingest) living or dead organisms, either plants or animals or both, through a mouth.

Animals that ingest both plants and animals are called omnivores. We humans are omnivores, as are crows, cockroaches, and raccoons. In contrast, plant-eaters, such as cattle, deer, gorillas, and a vast array of aquatic species that graze on algae are called herbivores. Carnivores, such as lions, sharks, hawks, spiders, and snakes, eat other animals.

—Campbell, Mitchell, and Reece, *Biology*, p. 430

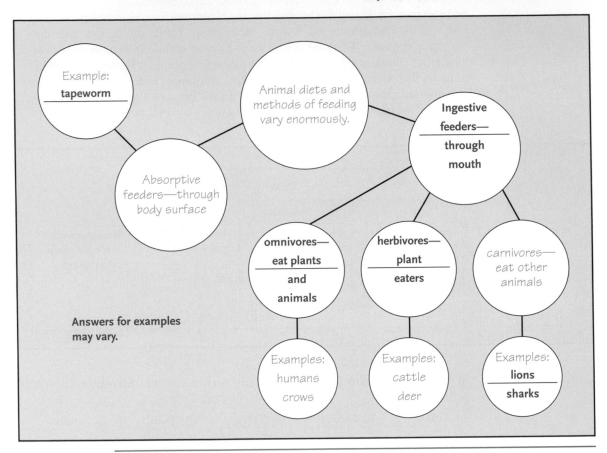

Summarizing

Summarizing is another good way to remember and keep track of information. A **summary** is a brief statement that pulls together the most important ideas in something you have read. It is much shorter than an outline and contains less detailed information. At times, you may want to summarize a paragraph, an essay, or even a chapter.

To write a good summary you need to understand the material and to identify the writer's major points. Here are some tips to follow:

1. **Underline each major idea in the material.**

2. **Write one sentence that states the writer's most important idea.** This sentence will be the topic sentence of your summary.

3. **Be sure to use your own words rather than those of the author.**

4. **Focus on the author's major ideas,** not on supporting details.

5. **Keep the ideas in the summary in the same order as in the original material.**

Read the following summary of "Changing Makeup of Families and Households," which appeared in Exercise 7-3 on page 181.

The typical U.S. household has changed from a husband, nonworking wife, and two or more children to a smaller sized unit that might contain a single parent, no children, or even only one person. Three trends have caused this change: people are staying single longer, divorce rates are higher, and women are outliving men by four years or more. Because of these changes, marketers have found that the current, smaller household needs different goods and services, has more income per person, tends to purchase smaller items, and spends more on entertainment, fads, and travel than the typical household of the past.

Notice that this summary contains only the most important ideas. Details are not included. The first sentence shows how the typical household has changed, the second sentence lists the three trends that are causing this change, and the last sentence lists the implication for marketers.

| **Exercise 7–6** | *A. **Directions:** Write true (T) or false (F) in the space provided before each of the following statements.* |

<u>　F　</u> 1. Summaries usually contain a lot of detailed information.

<u>　T　</u> 2. When writing a summary, it is important to use your own words.

<u>　T　</u> 3. The ideas in a summary should be in the same order as in the original material.

B. Directions: *After reading the following paragraphs, circle the letter of the choice that best summarizes each one.*

4. When a group is too large for an effective discussion or when its members are not well informed on the topic, a *panel* of individuals may be selected to discuss the topic for the benefit of others, who then become an audience. Members of a panel may be particularly well informed on the subject or may represent divergent views. For example, your group may be interested in UFOs (unidentified flying objects) and hold a discussion for your classmates. Or your group might tackle the problems of tenants and landlords. Whatever your topic, the audience should learn the basic issues from your discussion.

   —Gronbeck et al., *Principles of Speech Communication*, p. 302.

   a. Panel members are usually well informed on the subject, even though they may express different views. Members of a panel on UFOs, for example, may disagree about whether they exist.

   b. Whatever topic a panel discusses, it is important that the audience learns basic information about the topic. For this reason, only well-informed people should participate in panels.

   c. If a group is very large, or if its members are not familiar with a particular topic, a panel of people is sometimes chosen to talk about the topic. The rest of the group should get essential information from the panel's discussion.

   d. Panels work effectively in large groups, such as in classrooms. Panels also work well when a group's members don't know very much about a topic. For example, a panel might talk about the problems of tenants and landlords to a group that was not familiar with such problems.

5. The process of becoming hypnotized begins when the people who will be hypnotized find a comfortable body position and become thoroughly relaxed. Without letting their minds wander to other matters, they focus their attention on a specific object or sound, such as a metronome or the hypnotist's voice. Then, based on both what the hypnotherapist [hypnotist] expects to occur and actually sees occurring, she or he tells the clients how they will feel as the hypnotic process continues. For instance, the hypnotist may say, "You are feeling completely relaxed" or "Your eyelids are becoming heavy." When people being hypnotized recognize that their feelings match the hypnotist's comments, they are likely to believe that some change is taking place. That belief seems to increase their openness to other statements made by the hypnotist.

   —Uba and Huang, *Psychology*, p.148

a. The first step in being hypnotized is for people to feel comfortable and at ease. Then, they pay close attention to a particular item or sound while the hypnotist tells them how they will feel. If they believe their feelings are the same as what the hypnotist is saying, they will be more likely to accept other comments the hypnotist makes.

b. If the hypnotist says, "Your eyelids are becoming heavy," then the person being hypnotized would believe such a statement. The person being hypnotized would also continue to believe other statements the hypnotist makes.

c. The most important part of being hypnotized is to feel comfortable and relaxed. If you are uncomfortable at the beginning, you might not be willing to accept what the hypnotist is saying. To feel relaxed try to focus on changes that are taking place.

d. If the hypnotist says that "You are feeling completely relaxed," people being hypnotized have to believe that this is true. If such belief does not occur, then it is unlikely that hypnosis will happen. Once the subject feels relaxed, his or her eyelids get heavy.

Good Reasons to Keep Track of Information

As you know, you will do a lot of reading in your college courses, and you will often be tested on what you have read. If you keep track of information as you go along, you will remember more of the material, and studying for tests or exams will be much easier. Instead of rereading everything, you can study from the notes, outlines, or maps you have already made. You now know five ways to keep track of information—highlighting, marking, outlining, mapping, and summarizing. Try out a few of these methods as you read the next chapters.

What Have You Learned?

Directions: To test your understanding of the chapter and to review its major points, write true (T) or false (F) before each of the following statements.

_____T_____ 1. If people highlight too much material, they are probably not focusing on the most important ideas.

_____F_____ 2. Highlighting is helpful if you want to circle a word, ask a question, or make a note to yourself as you read.

___T___   3. Outlining involves listing major and minor ideas and showing how they are related.

___F___   4. When you make an outline, the most important ideas are closer to the right margin.

___F___   5. Mapping is more structured than outlining.

___T___   6. A summary is a brief statement that pulls together the most important ideas in something you have read.

___F___   7. A time line is a kind of summary.

Directions: After reading the following article titled "Road Rage," select the words and phrases from the box that follows the selection that best complete the summary. Use each word or phrase only once. Several extra words that you will not use are included.

ROAD RAGE

If you haven't heard or seen anything about Road Rage in the last few months, you've probably been avoiding the media. There have been countless stories about this new and scary phenomenon, considered a type of aggressive driving. You have most likely encountered aggressive driving and/or Road Rage recently if you drive at all.

While drunk driving remains a critical problem, the facts about aggressive driving are surely as ominous. For instance, according to the National Highway Transportation Safety Association, 41,907 people died on the highways last year. Of those fatalities, the agency estimates that about two-thirds were caused at least in part by aggressive driving behavior.

Why is this phenomenon occurring more than ever now, and why is it something that seemed almost nonexistent a few short years ago? Experts have several theories, and all are probably partially correct. One suggestion is sheer overcrowding. In the last decade, the number of cars on the roads has increased by more than 11 percent, and the number of miles driven has increased by 35 percent; however, the number of new road miles has only increased by 1 percent. That means more cars in the same amount of space; and the problem is magnified in urban areas. Also, people have less time and more things to do. With [people working and] trying to fit extra chores and activities into the day, stress levels have never been higher. Stress creates anxiety, which leads to short tempers. These factors, when combined in certain situations, can spell Road Rage.

Are You Immune to Road Rage?

You may think you are the last person who would drive aggressively, but you might be surprised. For instance, have you ever tailgated a slower driver, honked long and hard at another car, or sped up to keep another driver from passing? If you recognize yourself in any of these situations, watch out!

Avoid the "Rage" (Yours and Other Drivers')

Whether you are getting angry at other drivers, or another driver is visibly upset with you, there are things you can do to avoid any major confrontation. If you are susceptible to Road Rage, the key is to discharge your emotion in a healthy way. [I]f you are the target of another driver's rage, do everything possible to get away from the other driver safely, including avoiding eye contact and getting out of their way. The following safety tips can help you avoid Road Rage.

- Avoid eye contact!
- If you need to use your horn, do it sparingly.
- Get out of the way. Even if the other guy is speeding, it's safest to not make a point by staying in your lane.
- If someone is following you after an on-the-road encounter, drive to a public place or the nearest police station.
- Report any aggressive driving incidents to the police department immediately. You may be able to prevent further occurrences by the same driver.
- Above all, always use your seat belt! Seat belt use saves 9,500 lives annually.

Even though the problem of Road Rage may seem daunting, there are large-scale preventative measures currently underway to reduce the risk of aggressive driving and related fatalities. For instance, there is a major push to inform and educate the public about the problem, to improve enforcement techniques designed to punish and deter aggression, and to design safer roads.

According to the Coalition for Consumer Health and Safety, unsafe driving reflects not only the irresponsible behavior of a small minority of all drivers, but also the slow erosion of safe, courteous driving standards among the majority of all drivers. By disseminating information about the dangers of aggressive driving and emphasizing courteous driving, the Coalition hopes to teach drivers about the value of driving carefully and courteously, and cool Road Rage.

precautions	politely	stress	quickly
fatal accidents	enforcement	roads	helpful
overcrowding	emotions	immune	
road rage	drivers	aggression	

Summary

_____Road rage_____ is a form of aggressive driving that may account for approximately two-thirds of _____fatal accidents_____ . Experts think road rage may be caused by _____overcrowding_____ and by _____stress_____ , which, in turn, produces short tempers. Many people who think they are _____immune_____ to road rage do, at times, drive aggressively. To avoid road rage, try to release your _____emotions_____ in a nonaggressive, healthy way. Drivers should take _____precautions_____ to avoid becoming the target of road rage. Road rage can be prevented through education, _____enforcement_____ of laws, and the creation of safer _____roads_____. The Coalition for Consumer Health and Safety is attempting to teach drivers to drive carefully and _____politely_____ and thereby avoid road rage.

NAME _____   SECTION _____

DATE _____   SCORE _____

Directions: After reading the following passage, taken from a communication textbook, select the letter of the choice that best completes the statements that follow.

HUMOROUS APPEALS

1   The use of humor can be tricky, particularly since what is funny to one person may be offensive or incomprehensible to another. Specific cultures may have different senses of humor and use funny material in diverse ways. For example, commercials in the United Kingdom are more likely to use puns and satire than they are in the United States.

2   Does humor work? Overall, humorous advertisements do get attention. One study found that recognition scores for humorous liquor ads were better than average. However, the verdict is mixed as to whether humor affects recall or product attitudes in a significant way. One function it may play is to provide a source of *distraction*. A funny ad inhibits the consumer from counterarguing, thereby increasing the likelihood of message acceptance.

3   Humor is more likely to be effective when the brand is clearly identified and the funny material does not "swamp" the message. This danger is similar to that of beautiful models diverting attention from copy points. Subtle humor is usually better, as is humor that does not make fun of the potential consumer. Finally, humor should be appropriate to the product's image. An undertaker or a bank might want to avoid humor, but other products adapt to it quite well. Sales of Sunsweet pitted prunes improved dramatically based on the claim, "Today the pits, tomorrow the wrinkles."

4   An antismoking public campaign recently sponsored by the State of Arizona illustrates how humor can be used to transmit a serious message to an audience that may not be otherwise receptive to it. In a television commercial, a teenager sitting in a movie theater with his date spits gooey chewed tobacco in a cup. His date, who doesn't realize this, reaches over and takes a drink. The caption says, "Tobacco: a tumor-causing, teeth-staining, smelly, puking habit." The campaign is also selling merchandise with the slogan through its Smelly, Puking Habit Merchandise Center.

—Solomon, *Consumer Behavior: Buying, Having, and Being,*
Fourth Edition, pp. 252–253

_____a_____ 1. In paragraph 1, which of the following word groups is *most* important to highlight?

 a. use of humor can be tricky

 b. in diverse ways

 c. particularly since what is funny

 d. commercials in the United Kingdom

_____c_____ 2. In paragraph 1, which word or phrase serves as a transition?

 a. in the United States

 b. specific cultures

 c. for example

 d. more likely

_____d_____ 3. In paragraph 2, which of the following word groups is *most* important to highlight?

 a. one study found

 b. in a significant way

 c. one function it may play

 d. humorous advertisements do get attention

_____d_____ 4. Paragraph 2 begins with the question "Does humor work?" According to the passage, the best answer to that question is

 a. yes.

 b. no.

 c. only if humor serves as a distractor.

 d. the verdict is mixed.

_____a_____ 5. The main idea of paragraph 3 is that

 a. there are several guidelines to follow in using humor in advertisements.

 b. undertakers and bankers might want to avoid humor.

 c. subtle humor is usually better.

 d. "Today the pits, tomorrow the wrinkles."

_____d_____ 6. In paragraph 3, all of the following word groups are important to highlight except

 a. funny material does not "swamp" the message.

 b. subtle humor is usually better.

 c. humor should be appropriate to the product's image.

 d. sales of Sunsweet pitted prunes improved dramatically.

<u>b</u>   7. In paragraph 3, the Sunsweet pitted prune advertisement is

        a. the unstated main idea.   c. the main point.

        b. an example.   d. a transition.

<u>a</u>   8. In paragraph 4, the term **receptive** means

        a. open to.   c. angered by.

        b. opposed to.   d. object to.

<u>a</u>   9. The main idea of paragraph 4 is that humor can be used

        a. with audiences not willing to accept the advertiser's message.

        b. with teenagers.

        c. with controversial products.

        d. without offending the audience.

<u>b</u>   10. In paragraph 4, which of the following word groups is *most* important to highlight?

        a. reaches over and takes a drink

        b. humor can be used to transmit a serious message

        c. sponsored by the State of Arizona

        d. Smelly, Puking Habit Merchandise Center

NAME _____ SECTION _____

DATE _____ SCORE _____

Directions: After reading the following passage, taken from a health textbook, fill in the missing information in the outline that follows.

CAFFEINE

Caffeine is the most popular and widely consumed drug in the United States. Almost half of all Americans drink coffee every day, and many others use caffeine in some other form, mainly for its well-known "wake-up" effect. Drinking coffee is legal, even socially encouraged. Many people believe caffeine is a nondrug item and not really addictive. Besides, it tastes good. Coffee and other caffeine-containing products seem harmless; with no cream or sugar added, they are calorie-free and therefore a good way to fill yourself up if you are dieting. If you share these attitudes, you should think again, because research in the last decade has linked caffeine to certain health problems.

Caffeine is a drug derived from the chemical family called *xanthines*. Two related chemicals, *theophylline* and *theobromine,* are found in tea and chocolate, respectively. The xanthines are mild central nervous system stimulants. They enhance mental alertness and reduce the feeling of fatigue. Other stimulant effects include increases in heart muscle contraction, oxygen consumption, metabolism, and urinary output. These effects are felt within 15 to 45 minutes of ingesting a caffeine-containing product.

Side effects of the xanthines include wakefulness, insomnia, irregular heartbeat, dizziness, nausea, indigestion, and sometimes mild delirium. Some people also experience heartburn. As with some other drugs, the user's psychological outlook and expectations will influence the stimulant effects of xanthine-containing products.

—Donatelle, *Health: The Basics,* Fourth Edition, p. 213

I. Caffeine—popular and widely consumed _____ **drug** _____.

    A. Uses and benefits

        1. Wake-up effect _____

        2. Good taste _____

        3. Calorie free _____

    B. May create health problems

II. Physical effects of caffeine as a member of the drug family xanthine

    A. Mild stimulant

    B. Enhances alertness, reduces fatigue

    C. Increases heart muscle contractions

    D. Increases oxygen consumption

    E. Increases metabolism

    F. Increases urinary output

III. Side effects

    A. Wakefulness

    B. Insomnia

    C. Dizziness

    D. Nausea

    E. Indigestion

    F. Mild delirium

    G. Heartburn

    H. User's state of mind may influence the effects of caffeine products

NAME _____ SECTION _____

DATE _____ SCORE _____

Directions: After reading the following passage taken from a health text-book, fill in the missing information in the map that follows.

THIS THING CALLED LOVE

What is love? Finding a definition of love may be more difficult than listing characteristics of a loving relationship. The term *love* has more entries in *Bartlett's Familiar Quotations* than does any other word except *man*. This four-letter word has been written about and engraved on walls; it has been the theme of countless novels, movies, and plays. There is no one definition of *love,* and the word may mean different things to people depending on cultural values, age, gender, and situation.

Many social scientists maintain that love may be of two kinds: *companionate* and *passionate*. Companionate love is a secure, trusting attachment, similar to what we may feel for family members or close friends. In companionate love, two people are attracted, have much in common, care about each other's well-being, and express reciprocal liking and respect. Passionate love is, in contrast, a state of high arousal, filled with the ecstasy of being loved by the partner and the agony of being rejected. The person experiencing passionate love tends to be preoccupied with his or her partner and to perceive the love object as being perfect. According to Hatfield and Walster, passionate love will not occur unless three conditions are met. First, the person must live in a culture in which the concept of "falling in love" is idealized. Second, a "suitable" love object must be present. If the person has been taught by parents, movies, books, and peers to seek partners having certain levels of attractiveness or belonging to certain racial groups or having certain socioeconomic status and none is available, the person may find it difficult to allow him- or herself to become involved. Finally, for passionate love to occur, there must be some type of physiological arousal that occurs when a person is in the presence of the object of desire. Sexual excitement is often the way in which such arousal is expressed.

In his article "The Triangular Theory of Love," researcher Robert Sternberg attempts to clarify further what love is by isolating three key ingredients:

- *Intimacy*: The emotional component, which involves feelings of closeness.

- *Passion*: The motivational component, which reflects romantic, sexual attraction.

- *Decision/commitment*: The cognitive component, which includes the decision you make about being in love and the degree of commitment to your partner.

According to Sternberg's model, the higher the levels of intimacy, passion, and commitment, the more likely a person is to be involved in a healthy, positive love relationship.

—Donatelle, *Health: The Basics*, Fourth Edition, p. 99

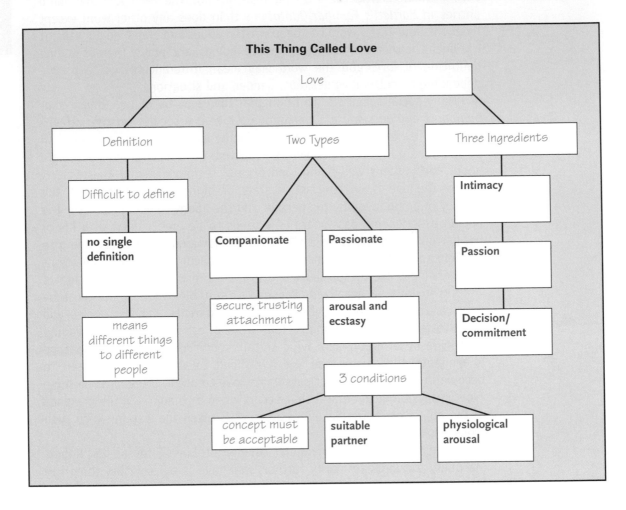

Directions: After reading the following passage, fill in the missing information in the outline that follows.

ACTIVE AND PASSIVE LISTENING

The general key to effective listening in interpersonal situations is to listen actively. Perhaps the best preparation for active listening is to act physically and mentally like an alert listener. For many people, this may be the most abused rule of effective listening. Recall, for example, how your body almost automatically reacts to important news: Almost immediately, you assume an upright posture, cock your head to the speaker, and remain relatively still and quiet. You do this almost reflexively because this is the way you listen most effectively. Even more important than this physical alertness is mental alertness. As a listener, participate in the communication as an equal partner with the speaker, as one who is emotionally and intellectually ready to engage in the sharing of meaning.

Active listening is expressive. Let the listener know that you are participating in the communication process. Nonverbally, maintain eye contact, focus your concentration on the speaker rather than on others present, and express your feeling facially. Verbally, ask appropriate questions, signal understanding with "I see" or "yes," and express agreement or disagreement as appropriate.

Passive listening is, however, not without merit. Passive listening—listening without talking or directing the speaker in any obvious way—is a powerful means of communicating acceptance. This is the kind of listening that people ask for when they say, "Just listen to me." They are essentially asking you to suspend your judgment and "just listen." Passive listening allows the speaker to develop his or her thoughts and ideas in the presence of another person who accepts but does not evaluate, who supports but does not intrude. By listening passively, you provide a supportive environment. Once that has been established, you may wish to participate in a more active way, verbally and nonverbally.

A. Active listening

   1. Physical alertness

      a. Sit straight

      b. Tilt your _____head_____

      c. Remain quiet

2. _____ Mental _____ alertness

   a. Be an equal partner

   b. Be ready to share _____ meaning _____

B. Letting the listener know you are participating

   1. Nonverbal clues

      a. _____ Maintain eye contact _____

      b. Pay attention to the speaker

      c. Express feeling with your _____ face _____

   2. _____ Verbal _____ clues

      a. Ask _____ questions _____

      b. Signal understanding with words

      c. Express _____ agreement _____ or disagreement

C. Passive listening

   1. Definition

      a. Listening without _____ talking _____

      b. Listening without giving the speaker
         _____ direction _____

   2. Benefits

      a. Communicates acceptance

      b. Allows speakers to develop their own ideas

      c. Provides supportive environment

SCHOOL'S OUT? BUT THIS IS ONLY APRIL
USA Today

Have you wondered why college semesters are so short? In this argumentative essay, the author argues that shorter semesters are cheating students.

> **Vocabulary Preview**
>
> These are some of the difficult words in this essay. The definitions here will help you if you cannot figure out the meanings from the sentence context or word parts.
>
> **elite** (par. 4) superior group or class
> **abbreviated** (par. 5) shortened
> **depreciated** (par. 7) lessened in value
> **rigor** (par. 9) strictness
> **comprehensive** (exams) (par. 9) exams covering the entire course

1   Students at the University of Pittsburgh finish their classes Friday. Rice University's course work wraps up next week. And at Tulane, the last day of classes is April 29.

2   The calendar says it is springtime. But for college students, summer is here.

3   These early vacation breaks are part of a shortening of the school year at colleges nationwide. Data collected by the National Association of Scholars shows that the length of the average college year has shrunk 35 days since 1964. Yet over the same period, inflation-adjusted college cost have doubled.

4   The result: Students and their families are paying more for less. In fact, at the nation's elite universities, the combination of higher tuition and condensed class time means an education prices out at about $1,000 a week.

5   The reason for the abbreviated academic calendar is largely economic. Universities discovered they can save money on operating expenses by shortening the school year.

6   Teachers like it because they have more time for research. Students don't complain because they can earn more in their summer jobs. And the practice of trimming away a class day here, while tacking on another holiday there, is less obvious—and controversial—than other cost-cutting strategies.

7 So who's hurt? The student earning a depreciated diploma, for starters.

8 During the same period that colleges sliced away one-fifth of their academic calendars, they also shortened the length of the standard class by 3.5 minutes. As a result of this double decrease, educators teach less and students are given a shorter time to absorb class material.

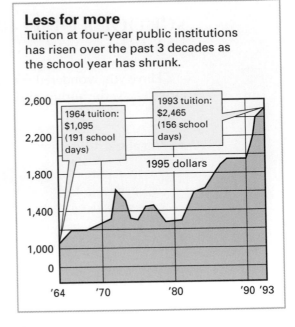

Less for more
Tuition at four-year public institutions has risen over the past 3 decades as the school year has shrunk.

1964 tuition: $1,095 (191 school days)

1993 tuition: $2,465 (156 school days)

1995 dollars

9 Researchers who track the trend see it as part of the overall decline in rigor at American universities. They say it is no coincidence that the shorter school year has been phased in at the same time colleges have lightened academic demands on students by dropping thesis requirements, abolishing comprehensive exams, and reducing scientific lab work.

10 Yet by reducing class time, colleges aren't cutting students any breaks in the long run. The complex subject matter covered in many university courses is best learned through repeated, long-term exposure. And because students are spending less time in class, they have fewer opportunities to glean knowledge and expertise from their professors.

11 Researchers also believe the pressures of the compressed schedule contribute to the growing number of students unable to complete their degree requirements within the traditional four years. This month, the American College Testing program reported a record low for students earning their bachelor's degrees on schedule. Even within five years of college enrollment, only 52.8% of college students earn a degree.

12 That may not be a problem for universities. After all, they save money by shortening the school year and then collect extra tuition from students who can't finish their course work during the shrunken semester.

13   Yet the students getting a college education—and the families who are funding it—are investing more and getting less.

14   For them, summer has arrived. But that's no reason to celebrate.

━━ ▪ ━━

Directions: Select the letter of the choice that best completes each of the following statements.

CHECKING YOUR COMPREHENSION

a   1. The main point of the selection is that
   a. shortened school years are cheating college students.
   b. students learn as much as they need to in shorter classes.
   c. universities have found a way to cut costs harmlessly.
   d. a shorter school year is beneficial to students who need summer jobs to earn tuition money.

d   2. The main idea of paragraph 11 is that because of shorter schedules
   a. students are not motivated to study as hard.
   b. more students are attending college.
   c. colleges are costing more and becoming more self-sufficient.
   d. students may need more than four years to get their degrees.

b   3. The main point of paragraph 6 is
   a. most students are now able to begin their summer jobs sooner.
   b. a shorter school year has some advantages for teachers, students, and universities.
   c. universities need to find less obvious and controversial ways to save money.
   d. shorter classes mean more classes can be offered in a day.

a   4. Since 1964, the average class length has become shorter by
   a. 3.5 minutes.   c. 35 days.
   b. 7 minutes.   d. half.

_____c_____ 5. According to this selection, college subject matter is best learned through

    a. taking comprehensive exams each term.

    b. writing a thesis.

    c. repetition over a long period of time.

    d. studying during the summer.

USING WHAT YOU KNOW ABOUT KEEPING TRACK OF INFORMATION

_____a_____ 6. In paragraph 4, which group of words is the most important to highlight?

    a. students and their families are paying more for less

    b. at the nation's elite universities

    c. the combination of higher tuition and condensed class time

    d. prices out at about $1,000 per week

Questions 7, 8, 9

The following map of paragraphs 5 and 6 is referred to in questions 7–9.

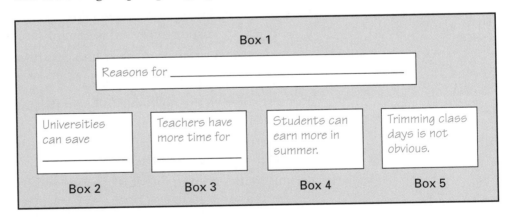

_____b_____ 7. Box 1 can best be completed with the words

    a. increasing class time.

    b. shortened academic years.

    c. reducing tuition.

    d. restricting the school year.

___d___ 8. Box 2 can be best completed with the word
   a. time.   c. tuition.
   b. staff.   d. money.

___c___ 9. Box 3 can best be completed with the words
   a preparing lectures.   c research and study.
   b. grading papers.   d. talking with students.

___b___ 10. Which of the following statements best summarizes paragraph 10?
   a. Professors can share knowledge and expertise with their students.
   b. When class time is reduced, students have less time to learn material and have less exposure to their professors.
   c. University courses require repeated exposure to information, and shortened school years cheat students.
   d. Colleges are not concerned with student learning.

USING CONTEXT AND WORD PARTS

___d___ 11. In paragraph 6, **trimming away** means
   a revising.   c. viewing.
   b. altering.   d. cutting.

___a___ 12. In paragraph 6, **tacking on** means
   a. adding.   c. reducing.
   b. altering.   d. condensing.

___c___ 13. In paragraph 8, **absorb** means
   a. memorize.   c. take in.
   b. repeat.   d. adjust.

___b___ 14. In paragraph 9, **abolishing** means
   a. repeating.   c. increasing.
   b. eliminating.   d. emphasizing.

___b___ 15. In paragraph 10, **glean** means
   a. submit.   c. discuss.
   b. gather.   d. distribute.

REVIEWING DIFFICULT VOCABULARY

Directions: Match each word in column A with its meaning in column B. Write the letter of your choice in the space provided.

	Column A	Column B
d	16. elite	a. of lessened value
e	17. abbreviated	b. covering the entire course
a	18. depreciated	c. strictness
c	19. rigor	d. superior group
b	20. comprehensive	e. shortened

RECORDING YOUR PROGRESS

Test	Number Right	Score
Practice Test 7-1	_____ × 10 =	_____ %
Practice Test 7-2	_____ × 10 =	_____ %
Practice Test 7-3	_____ × 10 =	_____ %
Mastery Test 7-1	_____ × 10 =	_____ %
Mastery Test 7-2	_____ × 10 =	_____ %
Mastery Test 7-3	_____ × 5 =	_____ %

EVALUATING YOUR PROGRESS

Based on your test performance, rate how well you have mastered the skills taught in this chapter by checking one of the boxes below or by writing your own evaluation.

☐ **Need More Improvement**

Tip: Try using the "Outlining, Summarizing, Mapping & Paraphrasing" Module on the Reading Road Trip CD-ROM that accompanies this textbook to fine-tune the skills that you have learned in this chapter.

☐ **Need More Practice**

Tip: Try using the "Outlining, Summarizing, Mapping & Paraphrasing" Module on the Reading Road Trip CD-ROM that accompanies this textbook to brush up on the skills you have learned in this chapter, or visit this textbook's Website at **http://ablongman.com/mcwhorter** for extra practice.

☐ **Good**

Tip: To maintain your skills, do a quick review of this chapter by using the Website that accompanies this textbook by logging on to **http://ablongman.com/mcwhorter.**

☐ **Excellent**

YOUR EVALUATION: _____

_____

_____

_____

_____

Read Me First!

Imagine that your bedroom looks like one of the pictures below. If you were looking for your favorite sweatshirt and a clean pair of socks, finding them would be a problem in the room on the left. The other room, however, is pretty neat and organized, so socks and sweatshirts are probably in a particular drawer or on a certain shelf. Being organized may not always be fun, but it makes it easier to find what you're looking for.

Organization is also important in paragraphs and in longer pieces of writing. Good writers try to follow a clear *pattern* when they write so that readers can easily find and understand the important points they are making.

Chapter 8

Recognizing the Basic Patterns of Organization

What Are Patterns of Organization?

Just as there is no one way to organize a room, there is no one way to organize a paragraph or essay. Writers use a variety of *patterns of organization*, depending on what they want to accomplish. These patterns, then, are the different ways that writers present their ideas.

To help you think about patterns a bit, complete each of the following steps:

1. Study each of the following drawings for a few seconds (count to ten as you look at each one).
2. Cover up the drawings and try to draw each from memory.
3. Check to see how many you had exactly correct.

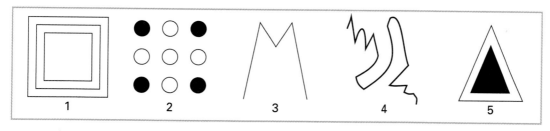

You probably drew all but the fourth correctly. Why do you think you got that one wrong? How does it differ from the others?

Drawings 1, 2, 3, and 5 have patterns. Drawing 4, however, has no pattern; it is just a group of randomly arranged lines.

From this experiment you can see that it is easier to remember drawings that have a pattern—a clear form of organization. The same is true of written material. If you can see how a paragraph or essay is organized, it is easier to understand and remember. In this chapter you will learn about some of the common patterns writers use and how to recognize them: (1) example, (2) definition, (3) chronological order and process, and (4) listing.

Example

One of the clearest ways to explain something is to give an example. This is especially true when a subject is unfamiliar. Suppose, for instance, that your younger brother asks you to explain what anthropology is. You might give him examples of the topics you study, such as apes and early humans, and the development of modern humans. Through examples, your brother would get a fairly good idea of what anthropology is all about.

When organizing a paragraph, a writer often states the main idea first and then follows it with one or more examples. The preceding paragraph takes this approach. The main idea in the topic sentence is supported by the example about explaining anthropology to a younger brother. In some paragraphs, of course, a writer might use several examples. And in a longer piece of writing, a separate paragraph may be used for each example.

Here is one way that the example pattern in a paragraph can be visualized:

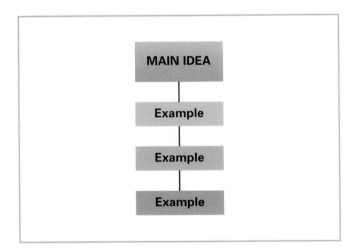

Notice how this example pattern is developed in the following paragraph:

Static electricity is all around us. We see it in lightning. We receive electric shocks when we walk on a nylon rug on a dry day and then touch something (or someone). We can see sparks fly from a cat's fur when we pet it in the dark. We can rub a balloon on a sweater and make the balloon stick to the wall or the ceiling. Our clothes cling together when we take them from the dryer.

—Newell, *Chemistry: An Introduction*, p. 11

In the preceding paragraph, the writer explains static electricity through the use of everyday examples. You could visualize the paragraph as follows:

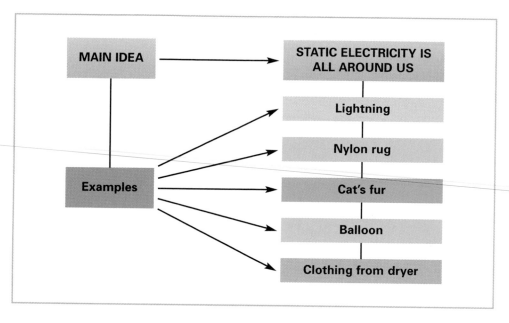

As you recall from Chapter 5, sometimes writers use transitional words—*for example, for instance,* or *such as*—to signal the reader that an example is to follow. The writer of the following paragraph uses transitions in this way:

Charlie agrees with the old saying that "a dog is a man's best friend." When he comes home from work, *for instance,* his dog Shadow is always happy to see him. He wags his tail, licks Charlie's hand, and leaps joyously around the room. Shadow is also good company for him. The dog is always there, *for example,* when Charlie is sick or lonely or just needs a pal to take for a walk. Many pets, *such as* cats and parakeets, provide companionship for their owners. But Charlie would put his dog Shadow at the top of any "best friend" list.

By using examples and transitions, the writer explains why Shadow is Charlie's best friend. Although writers don't always use transitions with examples, be on the lookout for them as you read.

Exercise 8-1

Directions: The following paragraphs, all of which are about stress, use the example pattern. Read each of them and answer the questions that follow in the space provided.

A. Any single event or situation by itself may not cause stress. But, if you experience several mildly disturbing situations at the same time, you may find yourself under stress. For instance, getting a low grade on a biology lab report by itself may not be stressful, but if it occurs the same week during which you car "died," you argued with a close friend, and you discovered your checking account is overdrawn, then it may contribute to stress.

1. What transition does the writer use to introduce the examples?

   for instance

2. List the four examples the writer provides as possible causes of stress.

   a. low grade on biology lab report

   b. car "dies"

   c. argument with a close friend

   d. checking account overdrawn

B. Every time you make a major change in your life you are susceptible to stress. Major changes include a new job or career, marriage, divorce, birth of a child, or the death of someone close. Beginning college is a major life change. Try not to create multiple life changes, which multiply the potential for stress.

3. Does the topic sentence occur first, second, or last? first

4. The writer gives six examples of major changes. List them briefly.

   a. new job or career   d. birth of a child

   b. marriage   e. death of someone close

   c. divorce   f. beginning college

C. Because you probably depend on your job to pay part or all of your college expenses, your job is important to you and you feel pressure to perform well in order to keep it. Some jobs are more stressful than others. Those, for example, in which you work under constant time pressure tend to be stressful. Jobs that must be performed in loud, noisy, crowded, or unpleasant conditions—a hot kitchen, a noisy machine shop, with coworkers who don't do their share—can be stressful. Consider changing jobs if you are working in very stressful conditions.

5. Does the topic sentence occur first, second, or last? second

6. What transition does the writer use to introduce the first type of jobs?
   <u>for example</u>

7. To help you understand "jobs that must be performed in loud, noisy, crowded, or unpleasant conditions," the writer provides three examples. List these examples in the diagram below.

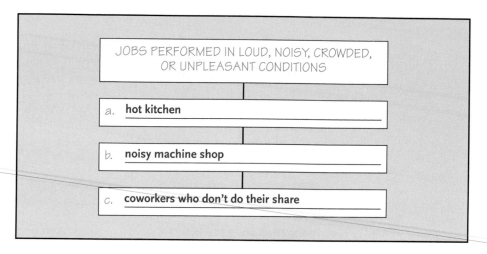

JOBS PERFORMED IN LOUD, NOISY, CROWDED, OR UNPLEASANT CONDITIONS

     a.   **hot kitchen**

     b.   **noisy machine shop**

     c.   **coworkers who don't do their share**

D. People who respond well to stress focus on doing the best they can, not on how they might fail. It's not that the potential problems have disappeared, it's that successful people believe in the possibility of success. Once success is seen as possible, you can focus on completing the task to the best of your ability. For example, instead of saying "I cannot do this on time," leave out the word *not*. Ask yourself: "How *can* I finish this task on time?" and "How well *can* I do this?"

8. Does the topic sentence occur first, second, or last? <u>first</u>

9. What transition does the author use to introduce the example?
   <u>for example</u>

10. What does the example tell you to do?
    <u>ask yourself how you can finish a task</u>

Definition

Another pattern writers follow is definition. Let's say that you see an opossum while driving in the country and you mention this to a friend. Since your friend does not know what an opossum is, you have to define it. Your definition should describe an opossum's characteristics or features, explaining how it is different from other animals. Thus, you might define an opossum as follows:

> An opossum is an animal with a ratlike tail that lives in trees. It carries its young in a pouch. It is active at night and pretends to be dead when trapped.

This definition can be shown as follows:

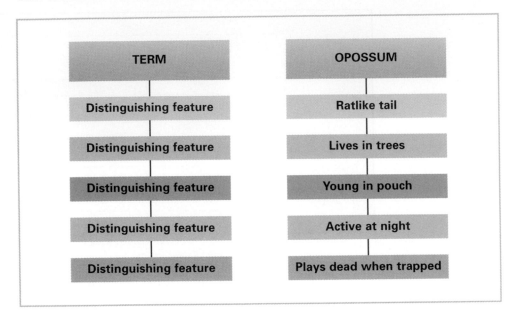

As you read passages that use the definition pattern, keep these questions in mind:

1. What is being defined?
2. What makes it different from other items or ideas?

Apply these questions to the following paragraph:

> Ragtime music is a piano style that developed at the turn of the twentieth century. Ragtime music usually has four themes. The themes are divided into four musical sections of equal length. In playing ragtime music, the left hand plays chords and the right hand plays the melody. There is an uneven accenting between the two hands.

When you ask yourself the preceding questions, you can see, first of all, that *ragtime music* is being defined. In addition, the definition lists four ways that ragtime is different from other piano styles: (1) there are four themes, (2) the left hand plays chords, (3) the right hand plays the melody, and (4) there is uneven accenting.

Combining Definition and Example

It is important to note that definitions are often combined with examples. For instance, if someone asks you to define the term *comedian*, you might begin by saying that a comedian is an entertainer who tells jokes and makes people laugh. You might also give some examples of well-known comedians, such as David Letterman or Eddie Murphy. When definition and example are used together in this way, you can visualize this pattern as follows:

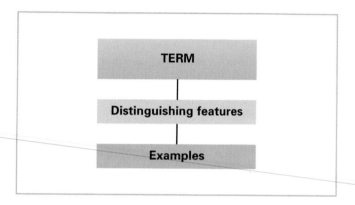

You will often encounter the definition and example pattern in your textbooks. An author will define a term and then use examples to explain it further, as shown in this passage from a psychology text:

> Everyone has **central traits**—a few dominant traits that are thought to summarize an individual's personality. For example, Oprah Winfrey's central traits might include a desire to do good works, honesty, a sense of humor, and a strong work ethic.

> —Uba and Huang, *Psychology*, p. 483

First the author defines *central traits*, and then she uses the example of Oprah Winfrey to make the definition more understandable. You have probably already noticed that textbook authors often put an important term in **boldface** type just before they define it. This makes it easier for students to find definitions as they read or study for tests.

Exercise 8-2

Directions: Read each of the following paragraphs and answer the questions that follow:

A. A partnership is a form of ownership used primarily in small business firms. Two or more owners comprise a partnership. The partners establish the conditions of the partnership, contribution of each partner to the business, and division of profits. They also decide on the amount of authority, duties, and liability each will have.

—Pickle and Abrahamson, *Introduction to Business*, p. 40

1. What term is being defined? <u>partnership</u>

2. The writer mentions several distinguishing features of this term. List three of them. **Answers may vary.**

   <u>used in small businesses; two or more owners; partners establish conditions,</u>

   <u>contribution of partners, division of profits, authority, duties, and liability</u>

   B. Stress is a natural response to the expectations, demands, and challenges of life. When you are asked to perform more (or better) than you think you can, stress may result. For example, stress can occur when you don't have enough time to study for an upcoming exam (you are expected to study but you cannot find enough time). In addition, stress occurs when your boss wants you to work for her on the weekend so she can take time off. (She expects you to work, but you cannot give up study time to work extra hours.)

3. What term is being defined? <u>stress</u>

4. Does this paragraph have a definition and example pattern? <u>yes</u>

5. What two transitional phrases does the writer use?

   <u>for example; in addition</u>

   C. The Small Business Administration (SBA) is an independent agency of the federal government that was created by Congress when it passed the Small Business Act in 1953. The purposes of the SBA are to assist people in getting into business, to help them stay in business, to help small firms win federal contracts, and to act as a strong advocate for small business.

   —Pickle and Abrahamson, *Introduction to Business*, p. 119

6. What term is being defined? Enter it in the diagram on the next page.

7. In defining this term, the writer mentions four distinguishing features. List them in the diagram on the next page.

8. Does this paragraph have a definition and example pattern? <u>no</u>

   D. **Assimilation** is what you do when you fit new information into your present system of knowledge and beliefs or into your mental categories of things and people. Suppose that little Harry learns the category for "dog" by playing with the family schnauzer. If he then sees the neighbor's collie and says "doggie!" he has assimilated the new information about the neighbor's pet into his category for dogs. **Accommodation** is what you do when, as a result of undeniable new information, you must change or modify your existing categories. If Harry sees the neighbor's Siamese cat and still says

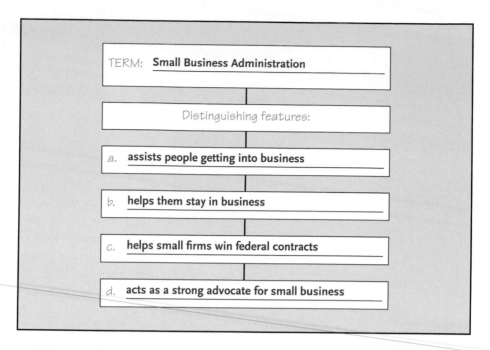

TERM: **Small Business Administration**

Distinguishing features:

a. **assists people getting into business**

b. **helps them stay in business**

c. **helps small firms win federal contracts**

d. **acts as a strong advocate for small business**

"doggie!" his parents are likely to laugh and correct him. Harry will have to modify his category for *dogs* to exclude cats, and he will have to create a category for *cats*. In this way, he accommodates the new information that a Siamese cat is not a dog.

—Wade and Tavris, *Psychology*, Fifth Edition, p. 499

9. What two terms are being defined?

   assimilation and accommodation

10. After defining each of these terms, how does the writer make them clearer? **Answers may vary.**

    through examples/stories about Harry

Chronological Order and Process

The terms *chronological order* and *process* both refer to the order in which something occurs or is done. When writers tell a story, they usually present events in chronological order. In other words, they start with the first event, continue with the second, and so on. For example, if you were telling a friend that a police officer stopped you for speeding, you would probably start with the fact of being "pulled over," continue with the conversation between you and the officer, and end with the result—did you get a ticket? You would put events in order according to the *time* they occurred, beginning with the first event.

Common Transitions in Chronological Order and Process		
first	before	following
second	after	last
later	then	during
next	in addition	when
another	also	until
as soon as	finally	meanwhile

When you read stories for an English class or material in a history of political science text, you will often encounter chronological order. When writers use this pattern, they often include time transitions, such as *first*, *next*, and *finally* (see box). They may also use actual dates to help readers keep track of the sequence of events.

EXAMPLE

In the early 1930s, the newly established Federal Bureau of Narcotics took on a crucial role in the fight against marijuana. Under the directorship of Harry J. Anslinger, a rigorous campaign was waged against the drug and those using it. By 1937 many states had adopted a standard bill making marijuana illegal. In that same year, the federal government stepped in with the Marijuana Tax Act, a bill modeled after the Harrison "Narcotics" Act. Repressive legislation continued, and by the 1950s severe penalties were imposed on those convicted of possessing, buying, selling, or cultivating the drug.

—Barlow, p. 332

As you can see in this paragraph from a history text, the writer uses chronological order to discuss the actions taken to limit the use of marijuana. He uses three phrases with dates to show the reader the time sequence—in the early 1930s, by 1937, and by the 1950s. As you read, look for such phrases as well as for time transitions.

Writers also follow a time sequence when they use the **process pattern**—when they explain how something is done or made. When writers explain how to put together a bookcase, how to knit a sweater, or how bees make honey, they use steps to show the appropriate order.

EXAMPLE

To plant a tulip bulb, follow a few easy steps. First, dig a hole large enough for the bulb and about six inches deep. Next, place the bulb in the hole, making sure that the pointed end of the tulip is facing up. Then fill the hole firmly with dirt and sprinkle some bulb fertilizer on top. Finally, water the spot where you have planted the tulip.

This writer uses four time transitions—*first, next, then,* and *finally*—to make the order clear for the reader. Note that she also uses the word *steps* in the topic sentence. In the process pattern and in other patterns as well, the topic sentence often provides a clue as to the kind of pattern that will be used.

You can visualize and draw the chronological order and process patterns as follows:

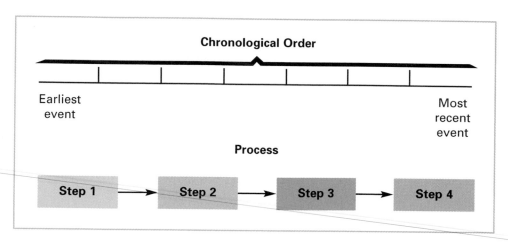

Sample maps showing chronological order and process appear in Chapter 7 (see Figures 7-3 and 7-4, p. 184).

Exercise 8–3

Directions: Using either chronological order or process, put each of the following groups of sentences in the correct order. Insert a number from 1 to 4 for each sentence in the space provided, beginning with the topic sentence.

1. __2__ Vassar College opened its doors in 1865, followed by Smith in 1871, Wellesley in 1877, and Bryn Mawr in 1880.

   __1__ In spite of varied protests, the 1800s saw the admission of women into higher education.

   __4__ Today the great majority of the more than 2000 institutions of higher learning in the United States are coeducational.

   __3__ Meanwhile, the University of Michigan had admitted women in 1870, and by the turn of the century coed colleges and universities were becoming commonplace.

   —from Kephart and Jedlicka, *The Family, Society, and the Individual*, p. 332

2. __3__ Next, it involves evaluating why the reaction or response occurred as it did.

_____2_____   First, it involves monitoring the impact or influence of our messages on the other person.

_____4_____   Finally, it involves adjusting or changing our future messages.

_____1_____   In communication, the process of *feedback* has three steps.

—from Weaver, *Understanding Personal Communication*, p. 123

3.   ____2____   The blips meant one thing: high levels of radiation.

____3____   The technicians began a frantic search for the problem at their own plant, but they found nothing.

____1____   At 9:00 A.M. on Monday, April 28, 1986, technicians at a nuclear plant sixty miles north of Stockholm began to see alarming blips across their computer screens.

____4____   They concluded that the problem was not with their own facilities but perhaps with the Soviet Union's nuclear plant to the south, at Chernobyl.

—from Wallace, *Biology*, Seventh Edition, p. 572

4.   ____3____   He soon had one-third of all Americans over 65 enrolled in his Townsend clubs, demanding that the federal government provide $200 a month for every person over 65—the equivalent of about $2,000 a month today.

____2____   The Great Depression made matters even worse, and in 1930 Francis Townsend, a social reformer, started a movement to rally older citizens.

____4____   Because the Townsend Plan was so expensive, Congress embraced President Franklin Roosevelt's more modest Social Security plan in June 1934.

____1____   In the 1920s, before Social Security provided an income for the aged, two-thirds of all citizens over 65 had no savings and could not support themselves.

—from Henslin, *Essentials of Sociology*, Second Edition, p. 272

5.   ____4____   When you revise, you step back to see whether you have expressed your thoughts adequately; you review your message and rewrite it.

____1____   Writing a business message may be organized into three simple stages.

_____3_____   In the writing stage, you decide on the organization and put your message on paper, including details and examples.

_____2_____   During the planning stage, you think about your basic message, your audience, and the best way to convey your thoughts.

—Thill and Bovee, *Excellence in Business Communication*, Fourth Edition, p. 79

Listing

Although writers often want to put events or items in a specific time sequence, sometimes they just want to list them. **Listing,** then, is used when a particular order isn't so important. If you were telling a friend about three movies or TV shows you liked, you might just list them. It wouldn't matter which movie or show was listed first.

EXAMPLE   Maria goes to the movies often, and she likes old movies as well as new ones. Three of them, however, are her favorites. She loves *Gone with the Wind* because she is a Civil War buff and a big fan of Clark Gable. *Titanic* is another favorite because of the dramatic love story, the tragedy that occurred, and the intense drama. Maria also likes *Grumpy Old Men*; it makes her laugh a lot, and she appreciates the comic acting of the late Jack Lemmon and Walter Matthau.

In the preceding paragraph, the writer might have put any of the movies first. The order simply depends on how the writer wants to present the material. Specific steps or time sequences are not important. Note, however, that the writer uses the transitions *another* and *also* to link the movies together.

You can visualize the listing pattern as follows:

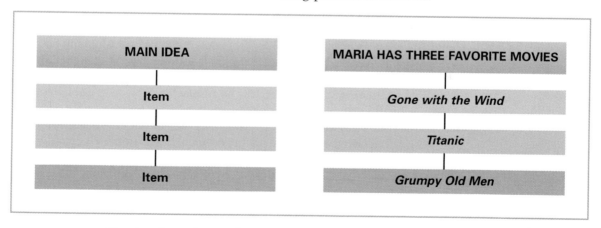

MAIN IDEA	MARIA HAS THREE FAVORITE MOVIES
Item	*Gone with the Wind*
Item	*Titanic*
Item	*Grumpy Old Men*

Textbook authors often use listing when they want to present information. The order is the way *they* want to present the material. It is not determined by time or steps.

EXAMPLE

Audiences favor speakers who communicate in a personal rather than an impersonal style, who speak *with* them rather than *at* them. There are several ways to develop a personal style. First, use personal pronouns, such as *I, me, he, she,* and *you,* which will create bridges to the audience. Using personal pronouns is better than using impersonal expressions such as "One is lead to believe . . . ." In addition, try to involve the audience by asking questions. When you direct questions to your listeners, they feel that they are part of the public speaking experience. You should also try to create immediacy—a sense of connected-ness—with your audience. You can do this in numerous ways, such as by using personal examples, complimenting the audience, or referring to what you and the audience have in common.

—from DeVito, *Elements of Public Speaking*, Seventh Edition

The author of this passage, Joseph DeVito, could have listed his advice in a different order. He might, for example, have discussed immediacy first and personal pronouns last. The decision was up to him because he was not talking about something related to time.

As in the paragraph about Maria's favorite movies, textbook writers also use transitions to link the items in a list. In the preceding example, the transitions *first, in addition,* and *also* tie together the three ways of developing a personal style. Other transitions—such as *one* and *finally*—are also used in the listing pattern.

Exercise 8–4

Directions: After reading the paragraph below, circle the letter of the choice that best answers the questions that follow.

Many companies—including Johnson & Johnson, McDonald's, and Burger King—have adopted written codes of ethics that formally acknowledge their intent to do business in an ethical manner. Indeed, the number of such companies has risen dramatically in the last three decades. In 1968, for example, polls revealed that 32 percent of the companies surveyed maintained ethical codes. A mere two years later, the number was 75 percent. Today, over 90 percent of all Fortune 500 firms have such codes. These codes serve one or more of the following functions. First, they increase public confidence in the firm. They also lessen the potential for government regulation by indicating a commitment to self-control. In addition, they improve internal operations by providing a consistent blueprint for acceptable conduct. Last but not least, they prescribe a response when unethical behavior does occur.

—Griffin and Ebert, *Business*, Fifth Edition, p. 83

1. The topic of the paragraph is
   a. public confidence in business.
   b. written codes of ethics.
   c. Fortune 500 firms.
   d. unethical behavior.

2. In the third, fourth, and fifth sentences, the writer presents an example. What pattern of organization do these sentences follow?

   (a.) chronological order   c. definition

   b. process   d. listing

3. At the end of the paragraph, the writer mentions several functions of the codes. What pattern of organization do these functions follow?

   a. process   (c.) listing

   b. chronological order   d. example

4. What four transition words does the writer use to link the functions of the codes?

   _____First_____   _____also_____   _____In addition_____   _____Last but not least_____

5. Complete the following outline of the paragraph. Some items have been filled in for you.

   I. Main idea: Many companies now have written codes of ethics.
      A. The number of such companies has risen_____.
         1. 32 percent had codes in 1968.
         2. 75 percent had codes in 1970_____.
         3. 90 percent have codes today.
      B. The codes serve several functions.
         1. They increase public confidence_____.
         2. They lessen potential for government regulation.
         3. They improve internal operations_____.
         4. They prescribe a response to unethical behavior_____.

Combining Patterns of Organization

As you saw in Exercise 8-4, some pieces of writing may have more than one pattern. In the beginning of this chapter, for instance, you learned how definition and example could be combined, with a writer defining a term and then giving examples to clarify the definition. As you read textbooks, novels, magazine articles, and newspapers, you will see that writers often combine other patterns as well. Within a story that is in chronological order, for instance, a writer might include a list of items. And writers almost always use examples, regardless of the overall pattern they are following. In the next chapter you will learn about two more patterns—comparison/contrast and cause/effect—and how these patterns, too, are often combined with lists, examples, and definitions.

What Have You Learned?

Directions: To check your understanding of the chapter, select the word or phrase from the box below that best completes each of the following sentences. Keep in mind that three of the words in the box will not be used.

listing	next	definition
patterns of organization	distinguishing features	main ideas
for instance	chronological order	thus
process	example	

1. The different ways that writers present their ideas is called
   _____ patterns of organization _____ .

2. Textbook writers often use the _____ definition _____
   and example pattern to help explain unfamiliar subjects.

3. When writers tell a story, they usually present events in
   _____ chronological order _____ .

4. A(n) _____ listing _____ pattern is used when a
   particular order is not important.

5. A transition that signals an example is to follow is
   _____ for instance _____ .

6. A definition always includes _____ distinguishing features _____ .

7. The _____ process _____ pattern is used to explain
   how something is done or made.

8. A transition that signals chronological order is
   _____ next _____ .

NAME _____ SECTION _____

DATE _____ SCORE _____

Directions: Select the letter of the choice that best answers each of the following questions.

____c____ 1. If you want to explain *defense mechanisms* to someone who is unfamiliar with the term, the best pattern to use is probably

    a. chronological order.   c. example.

    b. process.   d. listing.

____b____ 2. To write a paragraph describing how to load a disk into a computer, which pattern would you most likely use?

    a. listing   c. definition

    b. process   d. example

____c____ 3. Which of the following topics would most likely be developed using the chronological order pattern?

    a. the psychology of humor

    b. a comparison of personality theories

    c. stages of child development

    d. types of intimacy

____a____ 4. If Carla wants to write a paragraph about her four favorite musical groups, which pattern will she probably use?

    a. listing   c. process

    b. chronological order   d. definition and example

____c____ 5. Suppose you were explaining rap music to someone. If you talked about rap music's distinctive beat and how it is different from other types of music, what pattern would you be using?

    a. process   c. definition

    b. chronological order   d. listing

____d____ 6. If, after giving the explanation in question 5, you also provided some examples—like the songs of Queen Latifah—what pattern would you be using?

    a. listing and example

    b. process and example

    c. chronological order and example

    d. definition and example

_____c_____ 7. If a paragraph begins with the topic sentence "Various gestures and facial expressions play an important role in communication," which of the following patterns is the paragraph most likely to follow?

a. definition   c. example

b. chronological order   d. listing

_____d_____ 8. If a paragraph begins with the topic sentence "Encouraging a preschool child to become interested in reading involves a specific sequence of activities," which of the following patterns is the paragraph most likely to follow?

a. example   c. definition

b. listing   d. process

_____a_____ 9. If you were taking an essay exam in a health course and one question read "Explain the term *wellness*," what pattern would you use to organize your answer?

a. definition   c. chronological order

b. listing   d. process

_____b_____ 10. If you were writing a paper on the important events that led up to the Civil War, what pattern would be the best to use?

a. process   c. example

b. chronological order   d. definition

Directions: For each of the following statements, select the letter of the choice that best describes its particular pattern of organization.

<u>a</u>   1. Transitions are words and phrases that show relationships between ideas. For instance, time transitions such as *before, soon,* and *now* show time relationships.
   a. chronological order   c. definition and example
   b. process   d. listing

<u>d</u>   2. To borrow money, consumers can choose among several sources: banks, finance companies, and insurance companies.
   a. chronological order   c. definition and example
   b. process   d. listing

<u>b</u>   3. During a medical assessment, a nurse who notes a change in a patient's emotional or physical state notifies the attending physician. The doctor, in turn, assesses the problem and makes a diagnosis.
   a. chronological order   c. definition and example
   b. process   d. listing

<u>b</u>   4. To open, cut the box along the dotted lines. Then, remove the plastic bag and empty the cake mix into a bowl.
   a. definition   c. example
   b. process   d. listing

<u>a</u>   5. Pedro's father graduated from college in 1980. Four years later, he was running his own delivery service.
   a. chronological order   c. definition
   b. process   d. listing

<u>c</u>   6. Small cities often struggle to survive in today's economy. In the town of Camden, for instance, there is never enough money for essential services.
   a. chronological order   c. example
   b. process   d. listing

_c_ 7. Hummingbirds have several distinctive features: their wings beat 50 times per second; they burn energy faster than any other animal; they can fly backwards, sideways, and upside-down.

    a. chronological order   c. listing
    b. process   d. example

_b_ 8. Before you paint a room, follow a few simple steps. First, wash the walls and woodwork with a mild soap.

    a. example   c. definition
    b. process   d. listing

_d_ 9. One method psychologists use is observation. Observation involves watching others and recording what occurs. For instance, psychologists often observe children through one-way mirrors.

    a. chronological order   c. listing
    b. process   d. definition and example

_a_ 10. When Michael began his story, the children were noisy and jumping around. Soon, though, they began to listen and finally quieted down.

    a. chronological order   c. example
    b. process   d. listing

Directions: After reading each of the following passages, complete the exercises that follow.

A.   Personality disorders are character traits that create difficulties in personal relationships. One type of disorder is called *antisocial personality disorder*. It is characterized by aggressive and harmful behavior that first occurs before the age of 15. Such behavior includes lying, stealing, fighting, and resisting authority. During adulthood, people with this disorder often have difficulty keeping a job or accepting other responsibilities.

    Another disorder is the *paranoid personality disorder*. Individuals with this disorder are overly suspicious, cautious, and secretive. They may have delusions that people are watching them or talking about them. They often criticize others but have difficulty accepting criticism.

    Finally, *compulsive personality disorder* is a type of disorder in which people attach great importance to organization. They strive for efficiency and may spend a great deal of time making lists and schedules. But they are also indecisive and seldom accomplish anything they set out to do. They often make unreasonable demands on other people and have difficulty expressing emotions.

—from *World Book*, Volume 13, pp. 795–796

1. Complete the following map by writing the three types of personality disorder mentioned by the writer.

MAIN IDEA: PERSONALITY DISORDERS ARE CHARACTER TRAITS THAT CREATE DIFFICULTIES IN PERSONAL RELATIONSHIPS

a. **antisocial**

b. **paranoid**

c. **compulsive**

2. List two transitions used in the passage. **Answers may vary.**

    a. **one** _____   b. **another/finally** _____

3. Name the main pattern of organization used in this passage. **listing** _____

B.   Job opportunities for women have changed dramatically since colonial times. Unless they were employed as servants, colonial women had little occupational opportunity. Even during the early 1800s, after certain types of jobs had been opened to women, female wage earners continued to be stigmatized by inferior social status.

The first large-scale influx of female workers took place in the New England factories. Most of the workers were unmarried farm girls, some hardly more than children. They were welcomed, nevertheless, because they not only were conscientious employees but would work for low wages.

During the Civil War an increasing number of occupations were opened to women, a phenomenon that was to be repeated in the First and Second World Wars. During World War II, women were employed as welders, mechanics, machinists, taxi drivers, and streetcar operators; in fact, with the exception of heavy-duty laboring jobs, females could be found in virtually every branch of industry. Also, because of their excellent record, women were made a permanent part of the armed forces.

Today there are more than 52 million women in the workforce. Of those not in the labor force, the great majority are retired or have home responsibilities. From the sociological perspective it is important to note that currently even mothers with small children are likely to be employed outside the home. "Regardless of marital status or the presence of young children, labor force participation has become the norm for women." Since 1986, more than half of all women with children under three years of age have been in the labor force.

—Kephar and Sedlika, *The Family, Society, and the Individual,* pp. 332–333

4. Complete the following map.

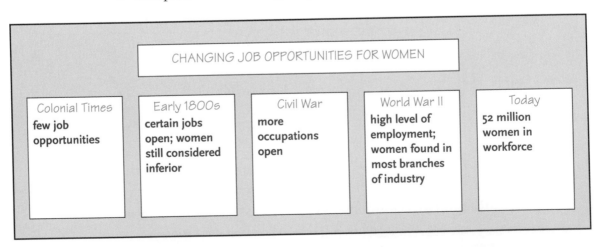

CHANGING JOB OPPORTUNITIES FOR WOMEN

Colonial Times	Early 1800s	Civil War	World War II	Today
few job opportunities	certain jobs open; women still considered inferior	more occupations open	high level of employment; women found in most branches of industry	52 million women in workforce

5. The organizational pattern used in this passage is <u>chronological order</u>

Directions: After reading each of the following passages, select the letter of the choice that best answers the questions.

A.   The action and reaction forces make up a *pair* of forces; forces always occur in pairs. There is never a single force in any situation. For example, in walking across the floor, we push against the floor, and the floor in turn pushes against us. Likewise, the tires of a car push against the pavement, and the pavement pushes back on the tires. When we swim, we push the water backward, and the water pushes us forward. The reaction forces, those acting in the direction of our resulting movements, are what account for our motion in these cases. These forces depend on friction; a person or car on ice, for example, may not be able to exert the action force to produce the needed reaction force by the ice.

—Hewitt, *Conceptual Physics*, p. 56

_____a_____ 1. The main idea of this paragraph appears in the
      a. first sentence.   c. fourth sentence.
      b. third sentence.   d. last sentence.

_____d_____ 2. The main pattern of organization used in this paragraph is
      a. chronological order.   c. definition.
      b. listing.   d. example

_____c_____ 3. A transitional word or phrase used in this paragraph is
      a. when.   c. for example.
      b. in these cases.   d. these.

B.   Horticulture, the study and cultivation of garden plants, is a large industry. Recently it has become a popular area of study. There are four areas of study in the horticulture field. First, there is pomology, the science and practice of growing and handling fruit trees. Then there is olericulture, which is concerned with growing and storing vegetables. A third field, floriculture, is the science of growing, storing, and designing flowering plants. The last category, ornamental and landscape horticulture, is concerned with using grasses, plants, and shrubs in landscaping.

_____c_____ 4. The main idea of this paragraph is
      a. Horticulture is the study and cultivation of plants.
      b. Horticulture is a large industry.
      c. Horticulture has four branches of study.
      d. Horticulture is a popular field of study.

_____b_____ 5. The main pattern of organization used in this paragraph is
    a. chronological order.   c. definition.
    b. listing.   d. example.

_____a_____ 6. The term **pomology** can best be defined as the study and care of
    a. fruit trees.   c. plants used in landscaping.
    b. flowering plants.   d. vegetables.

_____d_____ 7. Which one of the following words or phrases is _not_ used as a transition in this paragraph?
    a. first   c. the last category
    b. a third field   d. there are

C.   Mimosa is the name of a group of trees, shrubs, and herbs which have featherlike leaves. The mimosa grows chiefly in warm and tropical lands. The tree is similar to the acacia. The seed, or fruit, grows in flat pods. The small flowers may be white, pink, lavender, or purple. Mimosa grows throughout Asia, Africa, Mexico, and Australia. In the United States, it grows along the valley of the Rio Grande and in many states, including West Virginia, Virginia, Alabama, Kentucky, Louisiana, and Indiana.

—_World Book_, Volume 13, p. 474b

_____a_____ 8. Which sentence states the main idea of the paragraph?
    a. first sentence   c. third sentence
    b. second sentence   d. last sentence

_____b_____ 9. The pattern of organization used in this paragraph is
    a. process.   c. chronological order.
    b. definition.   d. example.

_____c_____ 10. Which of the following is _not_ a distinguishing characteristic of mimosa?
    a. The mimosa grows in warm, tropical lands.
    b. The mimosa tree is similar to the acacia.
    c. Mimosa is the name of a group of trees, shrubs, and herbs.
    d. Mimosa seed grows in flat pods.

Directions: After reading the excerpt below, taken from a travel and tourism textbook, select the letter of the choice that best answers the questions that follow the passage.

HOW PEOPLE EVALUATE SERVICE

1   When you go to a water park for the first time, do you have some idea of what benefits you will receive from that particular attraction? Of course you do. And how did you develop these service expectations? You may have talked with friends who had been to the water park (word-of-mouth communications). You may be going to the water park because you believe it will be fun and provide relief from the heat (personal needs). You may have been to other water parks and therefore have a general impression of what water parks are like (past experience). And, finally, you may have seen commercials on TV giving you an impression of the park (marketing communications). These factors combine and lead to expectations about the type of experience you will have during this tourism service encounter.

2   Once you enter the park, what elements of the experience will be important in shaping your ideas about the quality of this park? People generally consider five factors when judging the quality of a service.

3   *Tangibles* are those physical aspects of the service that we can see and with which we interact—the physical appearance of the facilities, the equipment we use or which service employees use for us, the appearance and uniforms of the employees, any signs of other communications materials that are provided. For instance, in our water park example, you may be provided with a brochure that includes a map and information about support facilities such as lockers and places to buy a snack or soft drink.

4   *Reliability* refers to the ability of service personnel to perform the promised service accurately and consistently. For example, if the water park provides you with the opportunity to learn how to snorkel, do the instructors teach you well enough so that you can snorkel without drinking half of the pool?

5   *Responsiveness* involves service employees' willingness to help customers and their promptness in providing service. You expect snack bar personnel to wait on you as soon as possible and to provide your food without unnecessary delay.

6 *Assurance* is a catch-all quality that involves the faith we have in the service personnel. Do they seem well trained? Are they knowledgeable about the park as a whole? Do they seem trustworthy? After all, the lifeguards at a water park literally have guests' lives in their hands.

7 Finally, *empathy* is the "warm, fuzzy" piece of service quality, the part of quality that is heartfelt. Empathy is the quality element that shows that service personnel care about you and understand your needs and frustrations. It involves setting operating hours for the convenience of guests, not management or employees. It includes caring about waiting times and fairness in waiting line systems. For example, our hypothetical water park's management realizes that many people will be waiting in lines in their bare feet on hot pavement. For guest comfort, they have located shade trees and shade umbrellas over the line areas so that you can jump from one shady area to the next while waiting your turn.

—Coah, et al., *Tourism: The Business of Travel*

_____c_____ 1. What is the general subject of this passage?
- a. service expectations
- b. marketing communications
- c. evaluation of service
- d. empathy

_____a_____ 2. Paragraph 1 is primarily concerned with
- a. the process of developing expectations.
- b. definitions and expectations.
- c. types of expectations.
- d. lists of expectations.

_____a_____ 3. Paragraph 3 includes both
- a. definition and example.
- b. process and listing.
- c. chronological order and example.
- d. process and listing.

_____d_____ 4. The best synonym for the word **tangibles** as used in paragraph 3 is
- a. the equipment you can use.
- b. your interactions with service employees.
- c. the appearance and uniforms of employees.
- d. the physical items you see and interact with.

_____a_____ 5. In paragraph 7, **empathy** is explained primarily by the use of
   a. example.
   b. process.
   c. chronological order.
   d. comparison.

_____a_____ 6. The main point of the entire selection is that
   a. five factors are involved in evaluating service.
   b. evaluating service is very personal and time consuming.
   c. the evaluation of service should be done by professionals, not guests.
   d. your impressions of service managers are important.

_____c_____ 7. The example used throughout this selection is that of
   a. a theme park.
   b. a guest lodge.
   c. a water park.
   d. customer satisfaction.

_____b_____ 8. The two patterns of organization used throughout this selection are
   a. definition and chronological order.
   b. definition and example.
   c. process and chronological order.
   d. listing and chronological order.

_____b_____ 9. The term **empathy** in paragraph 7 can be defined as
   a. an awareness of conveniences.
   b. a sympathetic understanding and caring.
   c. a concern for fairness.
   d. an emphasis on comfort.

_____b_____ 10. In paragraph 1 what function do the words in parentheses perform?
   a. They give examples.
   b. They name what is described earlier in the sentence.
   c. They define marketing terms.
   d. They offer reasons to continue reading.

NAME _____ SECTION _____

DATE _____ SCORE _____

HOW TO MANAGE YOUR DOCTOR
Diane Cyr

Have you ever been displeased with the care you received from a doctor? In this essay Cyr offers advice on how to make sure you get quality health care from your physician.

Vocabulary Preview

These are some of the difficult words in this essay. The definitions here will help you if you can't figure out the meanings from the sentence context or word parts.

mythological (par. 3) imaginary, beyond belief

savants (par. 3) scholars, learned people

empathy (par. 3) understanding of another's situation

demeanor (par. 4) the way a person behaves

malady (par. 10) illness, disorder, or disease

caveat (par. 11) rule, warning

coyness (par. 18) shyness, bashfulness

1   Maybe all that a person really needs out of life is for Dr. C. Everett Koop to tell them they're okay.

2   Just look at the man: admiral-straight, shoulders squared, bow-tie perpendicular to the famously tufted chin. With his stony brow and compressed expression, the former U.S. surgeon general is not the sort of person you would want to see across your plate of chili fries. He is, however, exactly the sort—confident, knowledgeable, full of authority—you would want to see across the examining table. "As a pediatric surgeon," he says, "the thing I got the greatest kick out of was when I could send the child's parents out feeling they were in the right place and with the right doctor and it was all going to be okay. It was being able to find their anxiety spot and settle it for them."

3   Would that all physicians today could do the same. In fact, doctors like Koop seem almost mythological. It's not hard to find the Body-by-Jake type doctors, reassuring but sketchily informative. Nor is it hard to find respected

medical savants high on knowledge but low on empathy.

4   But just try to find someone with Koop's demeanor and stamina. At age 81, the founder of Shape Up America is still scarily fit, frequently putting in 90-hour work weeks that include chairing Dartmouth's C. Everett Koop Institute, the National Safe Kids Campaign, Personal Medical Records, Inc., and a host of other causes. He is blunt, calling the United States an "obese nation," and noting aloud that achieving quality of life means saying no

to that extra slice of pizza. He is respected, knowledgeable, informed, and passionate. You would believe Koop was the type of person to practice surgical knots at age eight, which he did.

5   So when Koop tells a listener, as he does in his Time-Life medical video series, "You'll not only be healthier, but you'll also look and feel better," you believe it. Just one problem: How do you find other doctors who can do the same for you?

6   Not easy, says Koop, who is fluent in doctor-patient statistics. "Seventy percent of doctors, by poll, think they have not been properly trained in how to talk to patients," he says. According to another five-year-old study, he notes, "only one in 52 patients leaves an interview with their doctor telling them what needs to be told."

7   It's not just the doctor with the problem. Since few patients know how their bodies operate (can you define "triglyceride"?), they often treat health-care professionals like car mechanics, giving them unearned authority. They're reluctant to converse, ask "stupid" questions, or take up the doctor's time. As a result, they never know if they're getting the best treatment, or even if the best person is treating them. So they take the prescription, the bill, and the occasional doubts, and they're out of there.

8   Picking a good doctor, then, is really a dual issue. The best doctors, of course, know what they're talking about—but it's the best patients who know how to get the information out of them. The bottom line is

this: "Doctors like to take care of patients who are knowledgeable." It's the familiar Koop hard line. Be responsible. "Under the present health system," he says, "you had better take charge of your health because no one else is going to do it."

9   Here's where to start.

10   **Know your body.** Yes, body-conscious baby boomers do have a health advantage. Most at least know what their body parts should look like, and when something hurts that shouldn't. "Baby boomers are so much more understanding of their bodies than their parents were," says Koop. "Doctors find that easier to deal with." Better, boomers also like to hang out on the World Wide Web, which has a site for nearly every symptom, malady, and diagnosis that exists. Once you've got a diagnosis, "the Internet is great for understanding what you have," says Koop.

11   One caveat, though: Bad Health information can be worse than no information. So pay attention to brand. "If you're looking something up from the University of Minnesota, or the Mayo Clinic, you have reason to believe those people know what they're talking about," Koop says. "But if you find a farmer in West Virginia who says, 'I put cobwebs in my ears,' that's probably not reliable."

12   **Don't go in cold.** More Koop statistics: Male doctors, on average, interrupt their patients within 18 seconds of asking, "What's wrong?" (Female doctors wait almost a minute.) In a typical 20-minute interview, most doctors spend just one minute teaching their patients about their diagnosis.

13   The solution isn't necessarily to find a chatty doctor. It's to make your doctor tell you what you need to know. "Sit down and write out the questions you want answered three to five days before your visit," Koop says. "The day before, cross out the ones that aren't pertinent. Then don't leave until your questions are answered."

14   Start with the basics: What do I want to talk about? What do these symptoms usually mean? What else might they mean? How can I find out? What are my treatment choices? What are the advantages and disadvantages? Bring a tape recorder and take down what's said, and ask a nurse to write out a layperson's description.

15   Better to put a doctor on the spot than on a pedestal. "He *has* to be put on the spot," says Koop. "Even if he is at the point of having his hand

on the doorknob, you say, 'You haven't answered my questions.'" Which means. . . .

16   **Act on your behalf.** Among Koop's medical anecdotes, there's one about the doctor who diagnosed a child with a Wilm's kidney tumor. Just before surgery by the doctor-recommended urologist, the child's father discovered that a nearby hospital—not under the plan—was actually the center of excellence for the procedure. The father took the child there, sued to have the procedure covered, and won.

17   It pays, in other words, to play hardball with your health. "If a doctor says, 'I take out lots of kidneys,' you can say, 'How many children with tumors of the kidney do you see every year?'" Koop notes, "If he says one, say goodbye. If there's the slightest doubt, see another physician. Insurance companies are easy in payment with this because they want to be sure there's no unnecessary surgery, either."

18   It also pays to be assertive in bringing up uncomfortable health topics, like incontinence, impotence, or mental illness. You should mention alternative therapies you've tried, like over-the-counter herbs or therapeutic massages. Coyness doesn't pay in either case. First off, self-treatment might contradict or antagonize a doctor's prescribed treatment. Second, the more willing you are to discuss awkward issues, the more productive you can make the discussion. (Remember, doctors may not like talking, either.)

19   **Follow your instincts.** Once you've got a health concern, make sure first of all that you find a doctor who's knowledgeable in the specific area you're dealing with. From there, see if you're comfortable discussing "stupid" questions or embarrassing issues. Listen to whether your questions are answered or merely brushed aside. If you're not getting the right "vibe," trust your instinct and move on.

20   And don't rush your choice. If you're running a 102-degree temperature, you're probably not in the best frame of mind to begin choosing your primary-care physician. Instead, you can first try calling a nurse, nurse practitioner, or physician's assistant. They can either get the attention of a health provider, or even save you a trip by offering you practical, helpful advice over the phone.

21   Other tips: If you have a diagnosis, find an accredited specialist in that particular field. Call a local country medical office to discover any nearby

medical centers of excellence. Check "best doctor" reference guides. Even if you've got managed care, it's likely that you have an ample range of physician choices, so use them. "You can request a change if you don't get along," says Koop. "Personally, I choose doctors I know, who are expert in what they do to me, but who are also people who can be empathetic to me and my family."

22   And if you've had a bad experience, Koop says, let the managed-care company know about it, along with your employer. "The human resources person should be sensitive to what employees like and don't like about the system," says Koop.

23   **Then follow the directions.** Getting the best medical advice is one thing. Taking it is another. Any proven weight-loss treatment won't work if you keep stuffing yourself, and if you're prescribed two weeks of bed rest, don't get up after one. In matters of health, it pays to follow the rules. And it pays to understand what you're doing and why. "There's no doubt in my mind," says Koop, "one of the most valuable messages you can hear today is that you must take charge of your health."

24   In a perfect world, in fact, perhaps the ultimate health-care solution might simply be to be Dr. C. Everett Koop. Blessed as he is with inhuman energy and decent habits, he is further endowed with two other gifts: He not only can diagnose himself, but also is old enough to get Medicare to cover it. "I always know what I have, so if I know it's my heart, I pick out a cardiologist; if I'm having arrhythmia, I go to someone whose specialty is heart rhythm," he says.

— · —

Directions: Select the letter of the choice that best answers each of the following questions.

CHECKING YOUR COMPREHENSION

    c   1. The main purpose of this article is to
        a. interview C. Everett Koop about his health habits.
        b. push for changes in the health care system.
        c. tell readers how to choose and interact with a doctor.
        d. describe the characteristics of a good doctor.

_____c_____ 2. The main idea of paragraph 7 is that

a. doctors are like car mechanics.

b. patients ask stupid questions.

c. patients do not know how to discuss things with their doctors.

d. patients usually take medicine without knowing why.

_____a_____ 3. The main idea of paragraph 11 is that

a. where you get medical information is important.

b. people in Minnesota are smarter than people in West Virginia.

c. the brand of medicine you take is important.

d. getting good information is difficult.

_____b_____ 4. How much time do most doctors spend explaining an illness to a patient?

a. 18 seconds   c. 5 minutes

b. 1 minute   d. 20 minutes

_____b_____ 5. Once you've received good medical advice, Dr. Koop would advise you to

a. take most of the medicine prescribed.

b. follow your doctor's directions.

c. stay in bed until you're feeling better.

d. go back to work after your fever goes down.

USING WHAT YOU NEED TO KNOW ABOUT BASIC PATTERNS

_____c_____ 6. What overall pattern of organization does the author follow throughout most of the selection?

a. definition   c. process

b. chronological order d. listing

_____d_____ 7. How can you tell that the author is following this pattern?

a. She organizes her information according to specific dates.

b. Her information could be put in any order.

c. She explains terms and gives their distinguishing features.

d. She follows certain steps to explain how to do something.

_____a_____ 8. In the middle of paragraph 4, the phrase calling the United States an "obese nation" is

    a. an example of bluntness.

    b. a definition of stamina.

    c. the main idea of the paragraph.

    d. a transitional phrase.

_____b_____ 9. In paragraph 17, the transitional phrase *in other words* tells the reader that the author is

    a. moving to a new topic.

    b. explaining a point in a different way.

    c. showing the difference between two things.

    d. beginning a list of items.

_____c_____ 10. In paragraph 20, the transition *instead* means that the author is about to

    a. offer an example.   c. offer a different view.

    b. add a similar point.   d. put items in time order.

USING CONTEXT AND WORD PARTS

_____a_____ 11. In paragraph 3, the word **sketchily** means

    a. lacking in completeness.   c. lacking in knowledge.

    b. lacking in respect.   d. lacking in carefulness.

_____b_____ 12. In paragraph 6, the word **fluent** means

    a. acts favorably toward.   c. is hesitant about.

    b. speaks easily about.   d. is a follower of.

_____d_____ 13. In paragraph 13, the word **pertinent** means

    a. reliable.   c. hard.

    b. answerable.   d. relevant.

_____c_____ 14. In paragraph 16, the word **anecdotes** means

    a. problems.   c. stories.

    b. recommendations.   d. decisions.

_____b_____ 15. In paragraph 21, the word **accredited** means

    a. lacking certification.   c. being well liked.

    b. having official approval.   d. being knowledgeable.

REVIEWING DIFFICULT VOCABULARY

Directions: Complete each of the following sentences by inserting a word from the Vocabulary Preview on page 238 in the space provided.

16. Dino had a lot of _____empathy_____ for his mother, Maria, as she struggled with a serious eye disease.

17. Maria's _____malady_____ involved a gradual loss of sight, which would eventually result in blindness.

18. Despite this problem, Maria's _____demeanor_____ remained very much the same: She was perky and talkative and energetic.

19. As Dino noted, _____coyness_____ was never part of his mother's personality—she was always very outgoing.

20. The doctors gave the family one _____caveat_____: As Maria's eyesight worsens, make sure someone is always with her.

Chapter 8: Recognizing Basic Patterns of Organization

RECORDING YOUR PROGRESS

Test	Number Right		Score	
Practice Test 8-1	_____	× 10 =	_____	%
Practice Test 8-2	_____	× 10 =	_____	%
Practice Test 8-3	_____	× 10 =	_____	%
Mastery Test 8-1	_____	× 10 =	_____	%
Mastery Test 8-2	_____	× 10 =	_____	%
Mastery Test 8-3	_____	× 5 =	_____	%

EVALUATING YOUR PROGRESS

Based on your test performance, rate how well you have mastered the skills taught in this chapter by checking one of the boxes below or by writing your own evaluation.

☐ **Need More Improvement**
Tip: Try using the "Patterns of Organization" Module on the Reading Road Trip CD-ROM that accompanies this textbook to fine-tune the skills that you have learned in this chapter.

☐ **Need More Practice**
Tip: Try using the "Patterns of Organization" Module on the Reading Road Trip CD-ROM that accompanies this textbook to brush up on the skills you have learned in this chapter, or visit this textbook's Website at **http://ablongman.com/mcwhorter** for extra practice.

☐ **Good**
Tip: To maintain your skills, do a quick review of this chapter by using the Website that accompanies this textbook by logging on to **http://ablongman.com/mcwhorter.**

☐ **Excellent**

YOUR EVALUATION: _____

_____

_____

_____

_____

Read Me First!

When you walk into a grocery store, you know it will be organized in a particular way. The cereals will be in one aisle, the snacks will be in another aisle, and so forth. This organization allows you to see, for example, how two brands of cereal are alike and different—both may have the same calories, but one might be more expensive. When you look at products in this way, you are comparing and contrasting them. Writers often use the pattern of *comparison* and *contrast* in paragraphs and in longer pieces of writing. It helps them explain how items, people, or events are alike and different.

In Chapter 8 you learned five basic patterns of organization: example, definition, chronological order, process, and listing. In this chapter you will learn two additional patterns: comparison/contrast and cause/effect.

Chapter 9

Recognizing Comparison/Contrast and Cause/Effect Patterns

Comparison/Contrast Patterns

You use comparison and contrast every day—not just in the grocery store. For example, when you decide which Italian restaurant to go to, what to wear to a job interview, or which movie to see, you are thinking about similarities and differences.

Writers use comparison or contrast to explain how something is similar to or different from something else. **Comparison** treats similarities, whereas **contrast** emphasizes differences. For example, a writer who is *comparing* two car models would focus on their shared features: radial tires, air conditioning, power steering, power brakes. But a writer who is *contrasting* the two cars would discuss how the cars differ in gas mileage, body shape, engine power, and so forth.

As you read, you will find passages that only compare, some that only contrast, and some that do both.

Exercise 9-1

Directions: *Choose one of the following subjects: two friends, two jobs, two restaurants, or two vacations. Then, using the box below as a guide, make a list of five similarities and five differences.*

Example:

Subject: two professors

Items A and B: Professor Miller and Professor Wright

Similarities

1. Both require class attendance.

2. Both give essay exams.

3. Both have sense of humor.

4. Both are fair.

5. Both wear casual clothes.

Differences

1. Only Miller assigns a term paper.

2. Wright demands class participation, but Miller does not.

3. Miller is much younger.

4. Wright is married, while Miller is single.

5. They graduated from different universities.

Subject: _____

Items A and B: _____

Similarities

1. Answers will vary.

2.

3.

4. .

5.

Differences

1.

2.

3.

4.

5.

Comparison

A writer who is concerned only with similarities may identify the items to be compared and then list the ways they are alike. The following paragraph shows how chemistry and physics are similar.

> Although physics and chemistry are considered separate fields of study, they have much in common. First, both are physical sciences and are concerned with studying and explaining physical occurrences. Second, to study and record these occurrences, each field has developed a precise set of signs and symbols. These might be considered a specialized language. Finally, both fields are closely tied to the field of mathematics and use mathematics in predicting and explaining physical occurrences.

> —Hewitt, *Conceptual Physics*, pp. 82–84

Such a pattern can be diagrammed as follows:

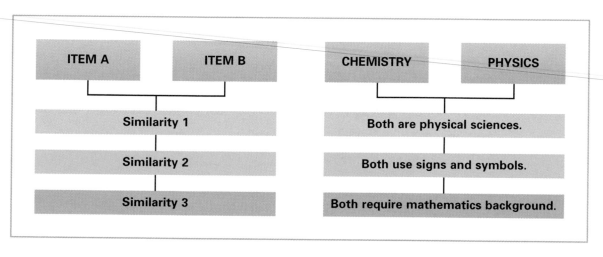

Look at the paragraph again, and notice the clues the writer provides about what kind of pattern he is following. In the first sentence—the topic sentence—the phrase *in common* tells you that the paragraph will be about the similarities between physics and chemistry. The writer also uses the words *both* and *each*, which signal that a comparison is being made. As you read, be on the lookout for words that indicate comparison or contrast.

When writers use comparison or contrast, sometimes they also include transitions to introduce each important point they are making. In the paragraph about physics and chemistry, for example, the writer uses the transitions *first*, *second*, and *finally* to help the reader follow the main points of the comparison. Although such transitions are not always used in comparison and contrast, you will often find them in longer selections.

Common Words in Comparison and Contrast			
To Show Similarities		**To Show Differences**	
alike	likewise	unlike	in contrast
same	both	different	despite
similar	just as	difference	nevertheless
similarity	each	on the other hand	however
like	in common	instead	but

Exercise 9–2

Directions: Select the comparison word or phrase from the box below that best completes each sentence in the paragraph. Write your answer in the space provided. Use each choice only once.

same	in common	both
similarity	alike	

Although Gretchen's two brothers are ten years apart in age, they are very much _____alike_____. Andrew and Tim like to swim, they enjoy golf and jogging, and they are _____both_____ good cooks. They also have _____in common_____ the love of playing practical jokes on their friends and relatives, especially on Gretchen. Another _____similarity_____ is that while Andrew teaches physical education at a middle school, Tim coaches the high school football team. What is most important to Gretchen is that her two brothers are the _____same_____ in one special way— they are both terrific people.

Contrast

A writer concerned only with the differences between sociology and psychology might write the following paragraph:

Sociology and psychology, although both social sciences, are very different fields of study. Sociology is concerned with the structure, organization, and behavior of groups. Psychology, on the other hand, focuses on individual behavior. While a sociologist would study characteristics of groups of people, a psychologist would study individual motivation and behavior. Psychology and sociology also differ in the manner in which research is conducted. Sociologists obtain data and information through observation and surveys. Psychologists, however, obtain data through carefully designed experiments.

Such a pattern can be diagrammed as follows:

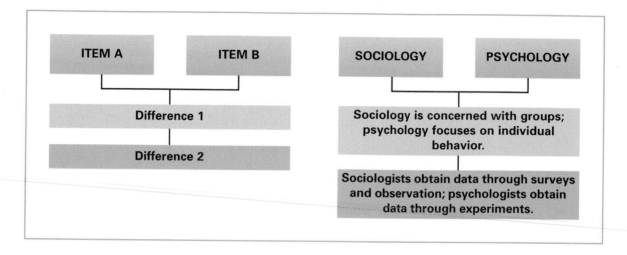

Look at the preceding paragraph again, and circle the contrast clues you can find (use the box on p. 252 to help you). Did you circle the following words and phrases: *different, on the other hand, differ,* and *however*?

Exercise 9–3

A. Directions: *Select the contrast word or phrase from the box below that best completes each sentence in the paragraph. Write your answer in the space provided. Use each choice only once, but keep in mind that in some sentences, there is more than one possible right answer.*

contrast	despite
different	unlike
on the other hand	however
difference	

After visiting Chicago and New York City several times, Jeremy has decided that they are very _____different_____ cities. First of all, Chicago's mass-transit system is _____unlike_____ the one in

New York. In Chicago, you need a car to reach many areas of the city. In New York, __on the other hand or however__, you can get to most places by subway or bus. Another _____contrast_____ is Chicago's lakefront versus New York's rivers. In Chicago, you can actually live near the downtown area and walk along a beautiful sand beach. In New York, __however/on the other hand__, there is no beach near the main business districts. Finally, Jeremy has discovered a major _____difference_____ between Chicago's and New York City's winter weather. _____Despite_____ their northern locations, Chicago's cold temperatures and snowfall amounts are much more extreme than those in New York City. Since Jeremy doesn't mind cold weather, he enjoys either city in the winter.

B. Directions: *List the three transitions that the writer uses to introduce her three main points.*

1. ___First of all___   2. ___Another___   3. ___Finally___

Using Both Comparison and Contrast

Writers often want to discuss similarities as well as differences. They might, for instance, want to compare *and* contrast the Miami Dolphins and Dallas Cowboys, presidents Franklin Roosevelt and Harry Truman, or San Francisco and Los Angeles.

When writers use comparison and contrast together, they may discuss everything about their first item (say, the Miami Dolphins) and then discuss everything about their second item (say, the Dallas Cowboys). Often, though, writers move back and forth from item to item, discussing similarities and differences as they go along. This pattern is shown in the following paragraph from a sociology textbook, which compares and contrasts primary and secondary groups.

The term primary group, coined by Charles H. Cooley (1909) refers to small informal groups who interact in a personal, direct, and intimate way. A secondary group, on the other hand, is a group whose members interact in an impersonal manner, have few emotional ties, and come together for a specific purpose. Like primary groups, secondary groups are usually small and involve face-to-face contacts. Although the interactions may be cordial or friendly, they are more formal than primary group interactions. Secondary groups, however, are often just as important as primary groups. Most of our time is spent in secondary groups—committees, professional groups, sales-related groups, classroom groups, or neighborhood groups. The key difference between primary and secondary groups is in the quality of the relationship and the extent of personal intimacy and involvement. Primary groups are person-oriented, whereas secondary groups tend to be goal-oriented.

—Eshelman and Cashion, *Sociology: An Introduction*, Second Edition, p. 88

Exercise 9–4

Directions: *After reading the preceding paragraph, circle the letter of the choice that best answers each of the following questions.*

1. Although the writer is comparing and contrasting primary and secondary groups, what other pattern (from Chapter 8) does he use in the first two sentences?

   a. example   c. process

   (b.) definition   d. listing

2. The writer uses many words to indicate similarities and differences. Which of the following is *not* used as a contrast word?

   a. on the other hand   c. difference

   b. whereas   (d.) like

3. The paragraph includes many similarities and differences between primary and secondary groups. List some of the similarities and differences below.

Primary and Secondary Groups

Similarities

1. both small
2. both involve face-to-face contacts/friendly
3. both important

Answers may vary. Examples are given.

Differences

1. primary are personal and intimate; secondary are impersonal
2. secondary more formal
3. secondary come together for specific purpose
4. more time spent in secondary groups
5. primary groups are person-oriented; secondary are goal-oriented

---

Cause/Effect Patterns

Writers use the *cause/effect* pattern to explain why an event or action causes another event or action. For example, if you are describing an automobile accident to a friend, you would probably follow a cause/effect pattern. You would tell what caused the accident and what happened as a result.

When a single cause has multiple effects, it can be visualized as follows:

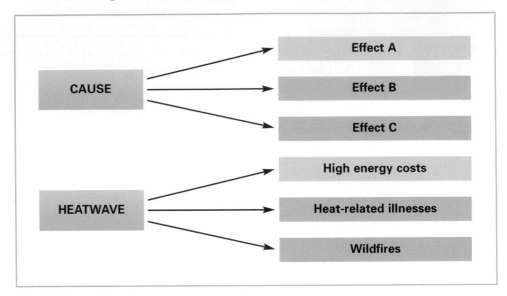

Sometimes, however, multiple causes result in a single effect. This kind of cause/effect pattern can be visualized this way:

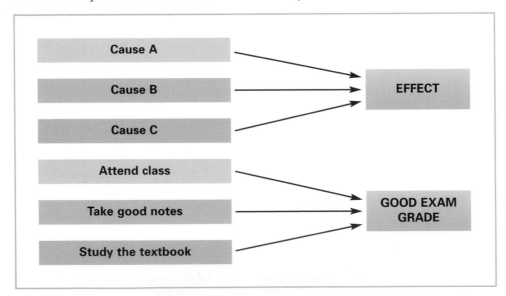

Read the following paragraph, which discusses the multiple causes of a single effect.

Research has shown that mental illnesses have various causes, but the causes are not fully understood. Some mental disorders are due to physical changes in the brain resulting from illness or injury. Chemical imbalances in the brain may cause other mental illnesses. Still other disorders are mainly due to conditions in the environment that affect a person's mental state. These conditions include unpleasant childhood experiences and severe emotional stress. In addition, many cases of mental illness probably result from a combination of two or more of these causes.

Exercise 9–5

Directions: After reading the preceding paragraph, answer the following questions in the space provided.

1. What effect is the writer discussing? mental illness

2. The writer mentions several causes of the effect. List four of them. **Answers may vary.**
   a. physical changes
   b. chemical imbalances
   c. environment/childhood experiences/stress
   d. combination of causes

As you worked on Exercise 9-5, did you notice that the topic sentence tells the reader that the paragraph will be about causes? Topic sentences often provide this important clue in a cause/effect paragraph, so pay close attention to them.

You also may have noticed that the writer uses specific words to show cause and effect. In addition to the word *causes*, he uses the phrases *due to* and *result from*. Writers often use such words to show why one event is caused by another. Look at the following statement:

Louis forgot to wear his glasses to the restaurant. Consequently, he couldn't read the menu.

The word *consequently* ties the cause—no glasses—to the effect—not being able to read the menu. Here is another example:

Bill couldn't wait for Nicole because he was already late for work.

In this sentence the word *because* ties the effect—Bill couldn't wait—to the cause—he was already late for work. In both of these examples, the cause and effect words help explain the relationship between two events. As you read, watch for words that show cause and effect; some common ones are listed in the box below.

Common Words in Cause and Effect			
cause	since	effect	one result is
because	due to	consequently	therefore
because of	reasons	as a result	thus

Exercise 9-6

A. Directions: *After reading the paragraph below, select the cause and effect word in the box below that best completes each sentence in the paragraph. Write your answer in the space provided. Keep in mind that one word in the box will not be used.*

consequently	reason
because of	result
effects	causes

The three-car accident on Route 150 had several serious _____effects_____ . First, and most tragically, two people died when their car overturned. In addition, traffic into the city was delayed for several hours _____because of_____ the accident. _____Consequently_____, those who were headed to the fairgrounds for the 4th of July fireworks never got to see the colorful display. Another _____result_____, which occurred long afterward, was that the state legislature lowered the speed limit in the area where the accident had occurred. After the legislation passed, several congressmen admitted that the accident was the main _____reason_____ for the change.

B. Directions: *After reading the preceding paragraph, answer the following questions in the space provided.*

1. What cause is being discussed? ___car accident___

2. What four effects does the writer mention?

a. two people died

b. traffic was delayed

c. people missed the fireworks

d. speed limit was lowered

3. Does the topic sentence tell you that this will be a cause/effect paragraph? _____yes_____

4. Aside from the cause and effect words, list four transitions that the writer uses to lead the reader through the information.

a. ___First___ b. ___In addition___ c. ___Another___ d. ___After___

Moving Beyond Patterns

In Chapters 8 and 9 you have learned about many of the common patterns writers use—example, definition, chronological order, process, listing, comparison/contrast, and cause/effect. You have seen how these patterns help readers understand what a writer is saying and how writers may use more than one pattern in a piece of writing. In Chapter 10 you will have a chance to think about other issues involved in reading, such as whether an author is biased or is writing with a particular purpose in mind.

What Have You Learned?

Directions: To check your understanding of the chapter, select the word or phrase from the box below that best completes each of the sentences that follow. Write your answer in the space provided. Keep in mind that some of the choices will not be used and some may be used more than once.

topic sentence	process
comparison/contrast	cause/effect
definition	final statement

1. The pattern that is most concerned with relationships between events is ___cause/effect___.

2. Words or phrases such as *on the other hand* and *however* often suggest the _____comparison/contrast_____ pattern.

3. In the _____topic sentence_____ a writer often provides an important clue about the pattern he or she is using.

4. Words such as *consequently* and *because* often suggest the _____cause/effect_____ pattern.

5. The pattern that is most concerned with similarities and differences is _____comparison/contrast_____.

Directions: Each of the following statements reflects a particular pattern of organization from either Chapter 8 or 9. Select the letter of the choice that indicates the correct pattern for each passage.

____d____ 1. Eleanor Roosevelt received threatening letters after her husband became president. Therefore, the secret service insisted she carry a pistol.

    a. example   c. comparison/contrast

    b. process   d. cause/effect

____c____ 2. A polliwog goes through numerous stages before becoming a frog.

    a. comparison/contrast   c. process

    b. definition   d. cause/effect

____b____ 3. Several factors, including unemployment, poverty, and decreased police protection, are responsible for the high crime rate in this city.

    a. listing   c. chronological order

    b. cause/effect   d. comparison/contrast

____c____ 4. High school friendships are often different from newer friendships. Old friends can share memories, but new friends are more likely to share current interests.

    a. chronological order   c. comparison/contrast

    b. cause/effect   d. definition and example

____d____ 5. Tim decided to save time by washing his dark clothes with his white ones. As a result, his white dress shirts are now an ugly graying pink.

    a. process   c. listing

    b. comparison/contrast   d. cause/effect

____b____ 6. Carlos arrived at work at 8:30 A.M., attended a meeting at 10:30, and went to lunch at noon.

    a. listing   c. cause/effect

    b. chronological order   d. comparison/contrast

    c   7. Like butter, all margarine (with the exception of the low-fat versions) is 99 percent fat and contains about one hundred calories per tablespoon. Margarine, however, contains less saturated fat than butter.

        a. listing   c. comparison/contrast

        b. example   d. cause/effect

    a   8. Julie gave her instructor several reasons why she hadn't completed her term paper, but her instructor gave her a failing grade anyway.

        a. cause/effect   c. comparison/contrast

        b. process   d. example

    d   9. Dachshunds are reddish-brown dogs of German origin with long bodies and short legs.

        a. comparison/contrast   c. cause/effect

        b. listing   d. definition

    a   10. The two baseball teams had a lot in common. Both had star home-run hitters, excellent managers, and good defensive players.

        a. comparison/contrast   c. cause/effect

        b. process   d. definition and example

Directions: After reading each paragraph, complete the map or outline that follows.

A.　　The differences in the lifestyles of the city and the suburbs should be thought of as differences of degree, not kind. Suburban residents tend to be more family-oriented and more concerned about the quality of education their children receive than city dwellers. On the other hand, because the suburbs consist largely of single-family homes, most young and single people prefer city life. Suburbanites are usually wealthier than city residents and more apt to have stable career or occupational patterns. As a result, they seem to be more hardworking and achievement oriented than city residents. They may also buy goods and services that offer visible evidence of their financial success.

—Eshelman and Cashion, *Sociology: An Introduction*, Second Edition, p. 583

Contrasting City Dwellers and Suburbanites

Difference #1　　_____Suburban residents_____ tend to be more family-oriented.

Difference #2　　_____Suburban residents_____ are usually more concerned with education.

Difference #3　　Many young and single people prefer to live in the _____city_____.

Difference #4　　_____Suburbanites_____ are usually wealthier.

Difference #5　　_____Suburbanites_____ seem to be more hardworking and achievement-oriented.

Difference #6　　_____Suburbanites_____ may be more concerned with visible evidence of financial success.

B.   Colors surely influence our perceptions and our behaviors. People's acceptance of a product, for example, is largely determined by its package. The very same coffee taken from a yellow can was described as weak, from a dark brown can too strong, from a red can rich, and from a blue can mild. Even our acceptance of a person may depend on the colors worn. Consider, for example, the comments of one color expert: "If you have to pick the wardrobe for your defense lawyer in court and choose anything but blue, you deserve to lose the case. . . ." Black is so powerful it could work against a lawyer with the jury. Brown lacks sufficient authority. Green would probably elicit a negative response.

—DeVito, *Messages: Building Interpersonal Communication Skills,*
Third Edition, p. 153

I. Color—influences how we see things and how we behave.
   A. <u>Acceptance of a product</u>   is determined by its wrapping or container.
      1. Example: <u>coffee cans</u>
   B. <u>Acceptance of people</u>   is influenced by colors worn.
      1. Defense lawyers should wear blue.
      2. <u>Black</u>   is too powerful.
      3. Brown does not suggest authority.
      4. <u>Green</u>   might elicit a negative response.

Directions: After reading each of the paragraphs below, select the letter of the choice that best answers each question that follows.

A.   France and the United States present an interesting contrast of cultural factors that affect how retailers market their products. U.S. homemakers spend more time watching television and reading magazines, and they rely more on friends and advertising before purchasing a new product. In contrast, French homemakers spend more time shopping, examining items on shelves, and listening to the opinions of retailers. Therefore, it has been easier to presell U.S. homemakers, whereas in France discounts to distributors and place of purchase displays have been more effective.

—Adapted from Daniels and Radebaugh, *International Business:*
Environments and Operations, Eighth Edition, p. 679

_____a_____ 1. This paragraph is concerned primarily with

    a. contrasts.   c. causes and effects.

    b. a process.   d. comparisons.

_____d_____ 2. The purpose of the paragraph is to explain how the French and Americans

    a. have similar shopping habits.

    b. both rely on advertising.

    c. shop for bargains and discounts.

    d. differ in how they make purchases.

_____c_____ 3. A transitional word or phrase that indicates the writer will shift from discussing French homemakers to American homemakers is

    a. therefore.   c. in contrast.

    b. interesting contrast.   d. present.

_____a_____ 4. It is easier to influence U.S. homemakers before they enter a store because they

    a. pay more attention to advertising.

    b. look for discounts.

    c. are more educated.

    d. shop for quality.

_____b_____ 5. Which stores should be the most concerned with in-store displays and the arrangement of merchandise?

    a. American stores   c. grocery stores

    b. French stores   d. retail stores

B.   Small businesses are likely to have less formal purchasing processes. A small retail grocer might, for example, purchase a computer system after visiting a few suppliers to compare prices and features, but a large grocery store chain might collect bids from a specified number of vendors and then evaluate those bids according to detailed corporate guidelines. Usually, fewer individuals are involved in the decision-making process for a small business. The owner of the small business, for example, may make all decisions, and a larger business may operate with a buying committee of several people.

—Kinnear, Bernhardt, and Krentler, *Principles of Marketing*, p. 218

_____d_____ 6. This paragraph is primarily concerned with
  a. similarities among businesses.
  b. differences among small businesses.
  c. similarities among chair retailers.
  d. differences between small and large businesses.

_____a_____ 7. Small retail grocers and grocery store chains are
  a. mentioned as examples to illustrate differences.
  b. the topics of the paragraph.
  c. used to show similarities.
  d. the reasons why large and small stores differ.

_____c_____ 8. According to the paragraph, one way large and small businesses differ is in how they
  a. advertise.   c. make purchases.
  b. establish criteria. d. make bids.

_____a_____ 9. Another way large and small businesses differ is in
  a. the number of people who make decisions.
  b. the types of decisions that are made.
  c. how budgets are prepared.
  d. how computer systems are installed.

_____b_____ 10. A transitional word or phrase that suggests the overall patterns of the paragraph is
  a. likely.   c. usually.
  b. but.   d. for example.

Directions: After reading the following passage by Rick Weiss, select the letter of the choice that best answers each question below.

ACUPUNCTURE*

1   Perhaps no other alternative therapy has received more attention in this country or gained acceptance more quickly than acupuncture. Most Americans had never even heard of it until 1971, when *New York Times* foreign correspondent James Reston wrote a startling first person account of the painkilling effects of acupuncture following his emergency append-ectomy in China. Today the needling of America is in full swing. Last year alone, Americans made some 9 to 12 million visits to acupuncturists for ailments as diverse as arthritis, bladder infections, back pain, and morning sickness.

2   In a culture that is overwhelmingly shy of needles, what could account for such popularity?

3   Safety, for one thing. There is something to be said for a medical practice that's been around for 5,000 years, with billions of satisfied patients. If acupuncture were dangerous, even its stodgiest critics concede, somebody would have noticed by now.

4   Many people are also encouraged by doctors' growing willingness to refer patients for acupuncture—or to learn the ancient art themselves—despite its unconventional claims. Acupuncturists say that health is simply a matter of tweaking into balance a mysterious life force called *qi* (pronounced *chee*), which is said to move through invisible meridians in the body. That's hardly a mainstream view, yet of the 9,000 practicing acupuncturists in this country, fully a third are M.D.s.

5   Most important, there's mounting evidence that acupuncture has some-thing important to offer, especially when it comes to pain. In one big study, acupuncture offered short-term relief to 50 to 80 percent of patients with acute or chronic pain. And in the only controlled trial that followed patients for six months or more, nearly six out of ten patients with low back pain

_____

*Acupuncture involves the use of needles to treat physical pains and illnesses.

continued to show improvement, compared to a control group that showed no improvement. Other studies have shown that acupuncture may be useful in treating nausea, asthma, and a host of other common ills.

—Weiss, "Acupuncture" from *Health*

___d___ 1. The subject of this passage is
   a. how acupuncture works.
   b. the medical properties of acupuncture.
   c. alternative medical treatments.
   d. the popularity of acupuncture.

___a___ 2. The article focuses primarily on
   a. the causes of acupuncture's popularity.
   b. why acupuncture relieves pain.
   c. the differences between acupuncture and traditional medicine.
   d. the process of acupuncture.

___a___ 3. Acupuncture first became known in the United States through
   a. an article written by James Reston.
   b. reports from travelers to the Orient.
   c. the successful treatment of arthritis sufferers.
   d. Americans' fear of needles.

___c___ 4. One reason acupuncture has grown in popularity is
   a. the life force called *qi*.   c. its safety
   b it is easy to obtain.   d. the low cost of treatments.

___d___ 5. Acupuncture has been used to treat all of the following except
   a. back pain   c. morning sickness
   b. bladder infections d. bone fractures

___b___ 6. Some acupuncturists think acupuncture is effective because it
   a. divides the body into meridians.
   b. brings the life force *qi* into balance.
   c. is an ancient medical treatment.
   d. has billions of satisfied customers.

_____d_____ 7. In paragraph 4 the word *unconventional* means
  a. ordinary.   c. disturbing.
  b. important.   d. nontraditional.

_____c_____ 8. At the beginning of paragraph 5, the transitional phrase *most important* suggests that the author will
  a. argue against widespread use of acupuncture.
  b. present a contrasting point of view.
  c. give his most compelling reason.
  d. summarize his ideas.

_____a_____ 9. Which statement best describes the current position of the medical profession toward acupuncture?
  a. Doctors are becoming more willing to refer patients for acupuncture.
  b. Acupuncture is declining in popularity.
  c. Most doctors think acupuncture is risky.
  d. Acupuncture is not a legitimate form of medicine.

_____a_____ 10. In paragraph 1, the main idea is stated in the
  a. first sentence.   c. third sentence.
  b. second sentence.   d. last sentence.

Directions: After reading the following passage, select the letter of the choice that best answers each question below.

In 1980, the Asian children far outperformed the American children on a broad battery of mathematical tests. On computation and word problems, there was virtually no overlap between schools, with the lowest-scoring Beijing schools doing better than the highest-scoring Chicago schools.

By 1990, the gap between the Asian and American children had grown ever greater. Only 4 percent of the Chinese children and 10 percent of the Japanese children had scores as low as those of the average American child. These differences could not be accounted for by educational resources: the Chinese had worse facilities and larger classes than the Americans. On the average, the American children's parents were far better-off financially and were better educated than the parents of the Chinese children. Nor could the test differences be accounted for by differences in the children's fondness for math: 85 percent of the Chinese kids said they like math, but so did almost 75 percent of the American children. Nor did it have anything to do with intellectual ability in general, because the American children were just as knowledgeable and capable as the Asian children on tests of general information.

Today, the same differences exist, and they are accentuated by the growing need for mathematical skills in the electronic age.

—Adapted from Wade and Tavris, *Psychology*, Fifth Edition, p. 494

_____c_____ 1. The main subject of the passage is

    a. American children.

    b. Asian children.

    c. mathematical abilities of children.

    d. intellectual capacity of children.

_____d_____ 2. The primary organizational pattern used throughout the passage is

    a. cause/effect.   c. definition.

    b. process.   d. comparison/contrast.

<u> a </u>   3. The main point of the passage is that

        a. Asian children score higher on mathematics tests than do American children.

        b. American children are superior in mathematics to Asian children.

        c. The gap between mathematical abilities of Asian and American children is lessening.

        d. The differences in mathematical abilities between Asian and American children can be explained by educational resources.

<u> d </u>   4. Which of the following is considered to be an educational resource?

        a. parental income   c. parental education

        b. fondness for mathematics   d. class size

<u> a </u>   5. The differences in mathematical abilities

        a. is not explained.

        b. is due to overall intellectual ability.

        c. can be attributed to educational resources.

        d. is easily explained by attitudes toward mathematics.

<u> c </u>   6. A "broad battery" of tests refers to

        a. tests repeated each year.

        b. teacher-written tests.

        c. wide range of tests.

        d. commercially published tests.

<u> b </u>   7. By 1990, what percentage of Japanese children scored as low as the average American child?

        a. 4 percent   c. 50 percent

        b. 10 percent   d. 80 percent

<u> d </u>   8. The statistics comparing the performance of Asian and American children are arranged

        a. by test score.   c. by type of test.

        b. by the age of the children. d. chronologically.

<u>c</u>   9. What word or phrase suggests the overall organizational pattern used throughout the passage?

a. In general

b. on the average

c. These differences

d. because

<u>a</u>   10. According to the passage, which of the following statements is accurate?

a. More Chinese than American children report that they like math.

b. Chinese parents are better educated than American parents.

c. The Chinese have superior educational facilities.

d. The income of American parents is the same as Chinese parents.

WHY DO WOMEN LIVE LONGER?
Robert A. Wallace

Taken from a college biology textbook, *Biology: The World of Life*, this reading explores the age-old question posed in its title.

Vocabulary Preview

These are some of the difficult words in this essay. The definitions here will help you if you can't figure out the meanings from the sentence context or word parts.

proposed (par. 2) to make an offer

susceptible (par. 2) easily influenced or affected by

produce (par. 2) to yield

implicated (par. 3) involved; connected with

suggested (par. 5) to propose—offer for consideration

immune system (par. 5) a system that protects the body from disease

heritage (par. 6) tradition; something passed from generation to generation

phenomenon (par. 6) unusual or significant event

mammalian (par. 6) pertaining to mammals (animals that nurture their young through mammary glands)

render (par. 8) to cause or make

---

1   People are living longer than ever, but for some reason, women are living longer than men. A baby boy born in the United States in 1994 can expect to live to be about 73, a baby girl, about 79. (In Canada, the figures are 75 and 82.) This is indeed a wide gap, and no one really knows why it exists. The greater longevity of women, however, has been known for centuries. It was, for example, described in the seventeenth century. However, the difference was smaller then—the gap is growing.

2   A number of reasons have been proposed to account for the differences. The gap is greatest in industrialized societies, so it has been suggested that women are less susceptible to the strains of "the rat race" that produce such

debilitating conditions as heart disease and alcoholism. Sociologists also tell us that women are encouraged to be less adventurous than men (and this may be why they are more careful drivers, involved in fewer accidents).

3   Even smoking has been implicated in the age discrepancy. It was once suggested that working women are more likely to smoke and as more women entered the work force, the age-gap would begin to close, because smoking is related to earlier deaths. Now, however, we see more women smoking and they still tend to live longer although their lung cancer rate is climbing sharply.

4   One puzzling aspect of the problem is that women do not appear to be as healthy as men. That is, they report far more illnesses. But when a man reports an illness, it is more likely to be serious.

5   Some researchers have suggested that men may die earlier because their health is more strongly related to their emotions. For example, men tend to

A woman exercising.

die sooner after losing a spouse than women do. Men even seem to be more weakened by loss of a job. (Both of these are linked with a marked decrease in the effectiveness of the immune system.) Among men, death follows retirement with an alarming promptness.

6   Perhaps we are searching for the answers too close to the surface of the problem. Perhaps the answers lie deeper in our biological heritage. After all, the phenomenon is not isolated to humans. Females have the edge among virtually all mammalian species, in that they generally live longer. Furthermore, in many of these species the differences begin at the moment of conception; there are more male miscarriages. In humans, after birth, more baby boys than baby girls die.

7   Another biological explanation involves differences in the sex hormones. Estrogen, for example, may help protect against heart disease. Also, the female hormones apparently render the immune system more efficient.

8   In any case, women do tend to live longer than men and this is necessarily shaping such programs as our extended care facilities, our hospitals, and (in an increasingly aging population) the direction of our medical research.

▬ ▪ ▬

Directions: Select the letter of the choice that best answers each of the following questions.

CHECKING YOUR COMPREHENSION

____c____   1. What is the main point of the selection?
    a. Women appear to be healthier than men.
    b. Hormones help protect women against heart disease.
    c. Women live longer than men, but we're not sure why.
    d. Scientists are certain why women live longer than men.

____a____   2. The gap between the ages that men and women can expect to live is
    a. growing.   c. staying about the same.
    b. decreasing.   d. reversing.

_____b_____ 3. In the past, what factor may have contributed to men's dying sooner than women?

    a. exercise   c. eating habits

    b. smoking   d. obesity

_____c_____ 4. According to the selection, which of the following has *not* been suggested as a reason why women live longer?

    a. Women are affected less by "the rat race."

    b. Women are encouraged to be less adventurous.

    c. Women are less likely to go to the doctor.

    d. Females live longer in other species.

_____d_____ 5. According to paragraphs 6 and 7, women may live longer than men because of

    a. chemical factors.   c. social differences.

    b. hormone imbalances.   d. biological factors.

USING WHAT YOU KNOW ABOUT OTHER PATTERNS

_____d_____ 6. When the author discusses the reasons why women live longer than men, what overall pattern is he following?

    a. listing   c. process

    b. chronological order   d. cause/effect

_____b_____ 7. When the author talks about the differences between men and women, what other pattern is he using?

    a. cause/effect   c. listing

    b. comparison/contrast   d. example

_____c_____ 8. At the beginning of the second sentence in paragraph 4, the transition *That is* means

    a. in addition.   c. in other words.

    b. because.   d. on the other hand.

_____a_____ 9. In paragraph 6, the transition *Furthermore* tells the reader that the author is

    a. making another, related point.

    b. moving to a new topic.

    c. showing a contrast between two things.

    d. showing a connection between two things.

____b____ 10. What pattern of organization does the author follow within paragraphs 5 and 7?
a. definition
b. example
c. process
d. listing

USING CONTEXT AND WORD PARTS

____c____ 11. In paragraph 1, the word **longevity** means
a. good health.
b. lengthening.
c. long life.
d. endurance.

____a____ 12. In paragraph 2, the phrase **account for** means
a. explain.
b. number.
c. list.
d. define

____d____ 13. In paragraph 2, the word **debilitating** means
a. curable.
b. desirable.
c. minor.
d. weakening.

____c____ 14. In paragraph 3, the word **discrepancy** means
a. discussion.
b. problem.
c. difference.
d. dispute.

____a____ 15. In paragraph 4, the word **puzzling** means
a. hard to understand.
b. significant.
c. less important.
d. unbelievable.

REVIEWING DIFFICULT VOCABULARY

Directions: Complete each of the following sentences by inserting a word from the Vocabulary Preview on page 273 in the space provided.

16. When Henry's mother kept getting sick, the doctor said there might be something wrong with her _____immune system_____.

17. The presidential election of the year 2000 was quite a _____phenomenon_____.

18. Because Joey's parents were both very critical of him, he was more

_____susceptible_____ to the criticism of his teachers.

19. After the jury had considered all of the evidence, they decided to

_____render_____ a verdict against the defendant.

20. The evidence showed that the murderer had been

_____implicated_____ in several previous shootings.

Chapter 9: Recognizing Comparison/Contrast and Cause/Effect Patterns

RECORDING YOUR PROGRESS

Test	Number Right		Score
Practice Test 9-1	_____ × 10 =		_____ %
Practice Test 9-2	_____ × 10 =		_____ %
Practice Test 9-3	_____ × 10 =		_____ %
Mastery Test 9-1	_____ × 10 =		_____ %
Mastery Test 9-2	_____ × 10 =		_____ %
Mastery Test 9-3	_____ × 5 =		_____ %

EVALUATING YOUR PROGRESS

Based on your test performance, rate how well you have mastered the skills taught in this chapter by checking one of the boxes below or by writing your own evaluation.

☐ **Need More Improvement**

Tip: Try using the "Patterns of Organization" Module on the Reading Road Trip CD-ROM that accompanies this textbook to fine-tune the skills that you have learned in this chapter.

☐ **Need More Practice**

Tip: Try using the "Patterns of Organization" Module on the Reading Road Trip CD-ROM that accompanies this textbook to brush up on the skills you have learned in this chapter, or visit this textbook's Website at **http://ablongman.com/mcwhorter** for extra practice.

☐ **Good**

Tip: To maintain your skills, do a quick review of this chapter by using the Website that accompanies this textbook by logging on to **http://ablongman.com/mcwhorter.**

☐ **Excellent**

YOUR EVALUATION: _____

_____

_____

_____

_____

Read Me First!

Look carefully at the picture below, which was taken by the well-known photographer Paul Schutzer in 1965. Many of Schutzer's photographs are of wartime scenes and were published in *Life* magazine during the Vietnam War. What is your overall impression of the photograph? What details in the photo give you that impression? What purpose do you think Schutzer had in mind when he took this photograph?

When you ask questions like these, you are using *inference*—you are going beyond the "facts" of the photograph and thinking about what the photographer meant to convey. This chapter will show you how to use inference as you read.

Understanding Inference and the Writer's Purpose

What Is Inference?

Just as you use inference when you study a photograph, you also use it when you try to figure out why a friend is sad or what an author's message is in a particular piece of writing. An **inference** is an educated guess or prediction about something unknown based on available facts and information. It is the logical connection that you draw between what you observe or know and what you do not know.

Here are a few everyday situations. Make an inference for each.

- You are driving on an expressway and you notice a police car with flashing red lights behind you. You check your speedometer and notice that you are going ten miles over the speed limit.

- A woman seated alone in a bar nervously glances at everyone who enters. Every few minutes she checks her watch.

In the first situation, a good inference might be that you are going to be stopped for speeding. However, it is possible that the officer only wants to pass you to get to an accident ahead or to stop someone driving faster than you. In the second situation, one inference is that the woman is waiting to meet someone who is late.

When you make inferences about what you read, you go beyond what a writer says and consider what he or she *means*. You have already done this, to some extent, in Chapters 2 and 6 as you inferred the meanings of words from context (see pp. 31–36) and figured out implied main ideas (see pp. 143–151). Thus you know that writers may directly state some ideas but hint at others. It is left to the reader, then, to pick up the clues or suggestions and to figure out the writer's unstated message. This chapter will show you how to do so.

How to Make Inferences

Making an inference is a thinking process. As you read, you are following the writer's thoughts. You are also alert for ideas that are suggested but not directly stated. Because inference is a logical thought process, there is no simple, step-by-step procedure to follow. Each inference depends on the situation, the facts provided, and the reader's knowledge and experience.

However, here are a few guidelines to keep in mind as you read. These will help you get in the habit of looking beyond the factual level.

1. **Be sure you understand the literal meaning.** Before you can make inferences, you need a clear grasp of the facts, the writer's main ideas, and supporting details.

2. **Notice details.** Often a particular detail provides a clue that will help you make an inference. When you spot a striking or unusual detail, ask yourself: Why did the writer include this piece of information? Remember that there are many kinds of details, such as descriptions, actions, and conversations.

3. **Add up the facts.** Consider all the facts taken together. Ask yourself: What is the writer trying to suggest from this set of facts? What do all these facts and ideas point toward?

4. **Look at the writer's choice of words.** A writer's word choice often suggests his or her attitude toward the subject. Notice, in particular, descriptive words, emotionally charged words, and words that are very positive or negative.

5. **Understand the writer's purpose.** An author's purpose, which is discussed in the next section, affects many aspects of a piece of writing. Ask yourself: Why did the author write this?

6. **Be sure your inference is supportable.** An inference must be based on fact. Make sure there is sufficient evidence to justify any inference you make.

Keep the preceding guidelines in mind as you read the following passage. Try to infer why Cindy Kane is standing on the corner of Sheridan and Sunnyside.

> An oily midnight mist had settled on the city streets . . . asphalt mirrors from a ten-o'clock rain now past . . . a sleazy street-corner reflection of smog-smudged neon . . . the corner of Sheridan and, incongruously, Sunnyside . . . Chicago.
>
> A lone lady lingers at the curb . . . but no bus will come.
>
> She is Cindy Kane, twenty-eight. Twenty-eight hard years old. Her iridescent dress clings to her slender body. Her face is buried under a Technicolor avalanche of makeup.
>
> She is Cindy Kane.
>
> And she has a date.
>
> With someone she has never met . . . and may never meet again.
>
> Minutes have turned to timelessness . . . and a green Chevy four-door pulls slowly around the corner.
>
> The driver's window rolls down. A voice comes from the shadow . . .
>
> "Are you working?"
>
> Cindy nods . . . regards him with vacant eyes.
>
> He beckons.
>
> She approaches the passenger side. Gets in. And the whole forlorn, unromantic ritual begins all over again. With another stranger.
>
> —from Paul Arandt, *Paul Harvey's The Rest of the Story*, p. 116

If you made the right inferences, you realized that Cindy Kane is a prostitute and that she is standing on the corner waiting for a customer. Let us look at some of the clues the writer gives that lead to this inference.

- **Descriptive details:** By the way the writer describes Cindy Kane, you begin to suspect that she is a prostitute. She is wearing an iridescent, clinging dress and a lot of makeup, which convey an image of a gaudy, unconventional appearance. As the writer describes the situation, he slips in other clues. He establishes the time as around midnight ("An oily midnight mist"). His reference to a "reflection of smog-smudged neon" suggests an area of bars or nightclubs.

- **Action details:** The actions, although few, also provide clue about what is happening. The woman is lingering on the corner. When the car approaches, she gets in.

- **Conversation details:** The only piece of conversation, the question, "Are you working?" is one of the strongest clues the writer provides.

- **Word choice:** The writer has chosen words that help to convey the image and situation of a prostitute. Cindy is described as "hard," and her makeup is "a Technicolor avalanche." In the last paragraph, the phrase "forlorn, unromantic ritual" provides a final clue.

Exercise 10–1

Directions: Read each of the following passages. Using inference, determine whether the statements following each passage are true (T) or false (F). Insert your answer in the space provided before each statement.

A.   Eye-to-eye contact and response are important in real-life relationships. The nature of a person's eye contact patterns, whether he or she looks another squarely in the eye or looks to the side or shifts his gaze from side to side, tells a lot about the person. These patterns also play a significant role in success or failure in human relationships. Despite its importance, eye contact is not involved in television watching. Yet children spend several hours a day in front of the television set. Certain children's programs pretend to speak directly to each individual child. (Mr. Rogers is an example, telling the child "I like you, you're special," etc.) However, this is still one-way communication and no response is required of the child. How might such a distortion of real-life relationships affect a child's development of trust, or openness, of an ability to relate well to other people?

—from Weaver, *Understanding Personal Communication*, p. 291

____T____   1. To develop a strong relationship with someone, you should look directly at him or her.

____F____   2. The writer has a positive attitude toward television.

____F____   3. The writer thinks that television helps children relate well to other people.

____T____   4. The writer would probably recommend that children spend more time talking to others and playing with other children.

B.   There is little the police or other governmental agencies can't find out about you these days. For starters, the police can hire an airplane and fly over your backyard filming you sunbathing and whatever else is visible from above. A mail cover allows the post office, at the request of another government or police agency, to keep track of people sending you mail and organizations sending you literature through the mail. Police or other governmental agencies may have access to your canceled checks and deposit records to find out who is writing checks to you and to whom you are writing checks. Even the trash you discard may be examined to see what you are throwing away.

No doubt by now you've realized that all of this information provides a fairly complete and accurate picture about a person, including his or her health, friends, lovers, political and religious activities, and even beliefs. Figure that, if the Gillette razor company knows when it's your eighteenth birthday to send you a sample razor, your government, with its super, inter-connecting computers, knows much more about you.

—from Lewis Katz, *Know Your Rights*, p. 54

___F___ 5. The writer seems to trust government agencies.

___T___ 6. The writer would probably oppose forcing libraries to give the police information about the books you read.

___T___ 7. The writer is in favor of strengthening citizens' rights to privacy.

C.   George Washington is remembered not for what he was but for what he should have been. It doesn't do any good to point out that he was an "inveterate landgrabber," and that as a young man he illegally had a surveyor stake out some prize territory west of the Alleghenies in an area decreed off limits to settlers. Washington is considered a saint, and nothing one says is likely to make him seem anything less. Though he was a wily businessman and accumulated a fortune speculating in frontier lands, he will always be remembered as a farmer—and a "simple farmer" at that.

Even his personal life is misremembered. While Washington admitted despising his mother and in her dying years saw her infrequently, others maintain that he remembered his mother fondly and considered him a devoted son. While his own records show he was something of a dandy and paid close attention to the latest clothing designs, ordering "fashionable" hose, the "neatest shoes," and coats with "silver trimmings," practically no one thinks he was vain. Though he loved to drink and dance and encouraged others to join him, the first president is believed to have been something of a prude.

—from Richard Shenkman, *Legends, Lies, and Cherished Myths of American History*, pp. 37–38

___T___ 8. Washington is usually remembered as saintlike because he was one of the founding fathers and our first president.

___T___ 9. The writer considers Washington dishonest and vain.

___F___ 10. The writer believes that eventually Americans' attitudes toward Washington will change.

Exercise 10-2

Directions: After reading the following selection, circle the letter of the choice that best answers each of the questions below.

THE FATHER AND HIS DAUGHTER

A little girl was given so many picture books on her seventh birthday that her father, who should have run his office and let her mother run the home, thought his daughter should give one or two of her new books to a little neighbor boy named Robert, who had dropped in, more by design than by chance.

Now, taking books, or anything else, from a little girl is like taking candy from a baby, but the father of the little girl had his way and Robert got two of her books. "After all, that leaves you with nine," said the father, who thought he was a philosopher and a child psychologist, and couldn't shut his big fatuous mouth on the subject.

A few weeks later, the father went to his library to look up "father" in the Oxford English Dictionary, to feast his eyes on the praise of fatherhood through the centuries, but he couldn't find volume F–G, and then he discovered that three others were missing, too—A–B, L–M, V–Z. He began a probe of his household, and learned what had become of the four missing volumes.

"A man came to the door this morning," said his little daughter, "and he didn't know how to get from here to Torrington, or from Torrington to Winstead, and he was a nice man, much nicer than Robert, and so I gave him four of your books. After all, there are thirteen volumes in the Oxford English Dictionary, and that leaves you nine."

Moral

This truth has been known from here to Menander: what's sauce for the gosling's not sauce for the gander.

—from James Thurber, "The Father and His Daughter,"
from *Further Fables of Our Time*, pp. 51–53

1. What is the first clue the writer gives that the father's actions are going to lead him into trouble?
   a. "taking books, or anything else"
   b. "was given so many picture books on her seventh birthday"
   c. "who should have run his office and let her mother run the home"
   d. "more by design than by chance"

2. What can you infer about the writer's attitude toward the father?
   a. He dislikes the father and considers him overbearing.
   b. He thinks the father is a good child psychologist.
   c. He thinks the daughter likes her mother better than her father.
   d. He admires the father's educational background.

3. What inference does the daughter make from her father's actions?

   a. One should always make donations to strangers.

   b. It is okay to give away items when one has many.

   c. Generosity is a virtue.

   d. Books are the best items to give away.

4. Which of the following is *not* a clue about the father's personality?

   a. "the father of the little girl had his way"

   b. "like taking candy from a baby"

   c. "who thought he was a philosopher"

   d. "couldn't shut his big fatuous mouth"

5. In terms of the story, what does the moral mean at the end of the selection?

   a. The father was upset because his daughter misunderstood him.

   b. The daughter should have known not to give away her father's books.

   c. The daughter was angry that her father gave her books to Robert.

   d. The father was unhappy that the rules he made for his daughter were then applied to him.

Understanding a Writer's Purpose

Writers have many different reasons or purposes for writing. These purposes affect their style of writing, the language they use, and the details they include. Once you understand a writer's purpose, it becomes easier to make inferences about a particular piece of writing.

Read the following statements and try to decide why each was written:

1. About 14,000 ocean-going ships pass through the Panama Canal each year. This averages nearly forty ships per day.

2. *New Unsalted Dry Roasted Almonds*. Finally, a snack with a natural flavor and without salt. We simply shell the nuts and dry-roast them until they're crispy and crunchy. Try a jar this week.

3. Humans are the only animals that blush or have a need to.

4. If a choking person has fallen down, first turn him or her face up. Then knit together the fingers of both your hands and apply pressure with the heel of your bottom hand to the victim's abdomen.

The statements above were written (1) to give information, (2) to persuade you to buy almonds, (3) to amuse you and make a comment on human behavior, and (4) to give instructions.

In each of the examples, the writer's purpose was fairly clear, as it will be in most textbooks, newspaper articles, and reference books. However, in many other types of writing, authors have less obvious purposes. In these cases, an author's purpose must be inferred.

Sometimes a writer wants to express an opinion indirectly or to encourage readers to think about a particular issue or problem. Writers achieve their purposes by controlling what they say and how they say it. This section will focus on the techniques writers use to achieve the results they want.

Style and Intended Audience

Are you able to recognize a friend just by his or her voice? Can you identify family members by their footsteps? You are able to do so because each person's voice and footsteps are unique. Have you noticed that writers have unique characteristics as well? One writer may use many examples; another may use few. One may use relatively short sentences, whereas another may use long, complicated ones. The characteristics that make a writer unique are known as **style.** By changing style, writers can create different effects.

Writers may vary their styles to suit their intended audiences. For example, someone writing a science article for a newspaper or general magazine, such as *Time* or *Newsweek*, would use fairly straightforward language and would be careful to explain or define any uncommon scientific or technical terms. The same person, writing for medical doctors in the *Journal of American Medicine*, could assume that readers would be familiar with the subject and thus could use more sophisticated language and details.

Depending on the group of people for whom an author is writing, he or she may change the level of language, choice of words, and method of presentation. One step toward identifying an author's purpose, then, is to ask yourself: Who is the intended audience? Your response will be your first clue to determining why the author wrote the article.

Exercise 10-3

Directions: After reading each of the following statements, circle the letter of the choice that best describes the audience for whom each was written.

1. Chances are you're going to be putting money away over the next five years or so. You are hoping for the right things in life. Right now, a smart place to put your money is in mutual funds or bonds.

a. people who are struggling to pay for basic needs like rent and food

b. people who are very wealthy and have been investing their money for many years

(c.) people with enough income that they can think of investing some for the future

d. people who are using their extra income to pay off credit-card debt and student loans.

2. Think about all the places your drinking water has been before you drink another drop. Most likely it has been chemically treated to remove bacteria and chemical pollutants. Soon you may begin to feel the side effects of these treatments. Consider switching to filtered, distilled water today.

a. people who have no interest in environmental issues

b. chemists

c. employees of the Environmental Protection Agency

(d.) people who are concerned about the environment and their health

3. Introducing the new, high-powered Supertuner III, a stereo system guaranteed to keep your mother out of your car.

a. drivers who love music

(b.) teenagers who own cars

c. parents of teenage drivers

d. specialists in stereo equipment

4. The life cycle of many species of plants involves an alternation of generations in which individuals of the gametophyte generation produce gametes that fuse and develop into individuals of a sporophyte generation.

—Adapted from Wallace, *Biology: The World of Life*, p. 271

(a.) biology students

b. readers of general-interest magazines

c. gardeners

d. managers of landscaping companies

5. As a driver, you're ahead of the repair game if you can learn to spot car trouble before it's too late. If you can learn the difference between the drips and squeaks that occur under normal conditions and those that mean big trouble is just down the road, then you'll be ahead of expensive repair bills and won't find yourself stranded on a lonely road.

a. mechanics

b. managers of auto-parts stores

c. car owners who do the repairs and maintenance on their own cars

(d.) car owners who are unfamiliar with a car's trouble signs and maintenance

Tone

The tone of a speaker's voice helps you interpret what he or she is saying. If a friend says to you, "Would you mind closing the door?" you can tell by her tone of voice whether she is being polite, insistent, or angry.

Writers also convey a tone, or feeling, through writing. **Tone** refers to the attitude or feeling a writer expresses about his or her subject. A writer's tone may be sentimental, angry, humorous, sympathetic, instructive, persuasive, and so forth. Here are a few examples of different tones. Note the words each writer uses to express a particular tone.

- **Instructive:** When purchasing a piece of clothing, one must be concerned with quality as well as with price. Be certain to check for the following: double-stitched seams, matched patterns, and ample linings.

- **Sympathetic:** The forlorn, frightened-looking child wandered through the streets alone, searching for someone who would show an interest in helping her find her parents.

- **Persuasive:** Child abuse is a tragic occurrence in our society. Strong legislation is needed to control the abuse of innocent victims and to punish those who are insensitive to the rights and feeling of others.

In the first example, the writer offers advice in a straightforward way, using the words *must* and *be certain*. In the second example, the writer wants you to feel sorry for the child. In the third example, the writer tries to convince the reader that action must be taken to prevent child abuse. The use of such words as *tragic, innocent,* and *insensitive* establish this tone.

A writer's tone is intended to rub off on you, so to speak. A writer whose tone is humorous hopes you will be amused. A writer whose tone is persuasive hopes you will accept his or her viewpoint. Thus, tone can be important in determining an author's purpose. Tone also alerts you to a writer's possible biases about a subject. When trying to determine a writer's purpose, then, you should ask yourself certain questions: What tone does the writer use? How is the writer trying to make me feel about the subject?

Exercise 10–4

Directions: After reading each of the following passages, circle the letter of the choice that best describes the tone that the writer is expressing.

1. No one says that nuclear power is risk free. There are risks involved in all methods of producing energy. However, the scientific evidence is clear and obvious. Nuclear power is at least as safe as any other means used to generate electricity.

   a. angry

   b. persuasive

   c. sentimental

   d. casual

2. Cross-country skis have heel plates of different shapes and materials. They may be made of metal, plastic, or rubber. Be sure that they are tacked on the ski right where the heel of your boot will fall. They will keep snow from collecting under your foot and offer some stability.

   a. persuasive

   b. sympathetic

   (c.) instructive

   d. humorous

3. The condition of our city streets is outrageous. The sidewalks are littered with paper and other garbage—you could trip while walking to the store. The streets themselves are in even worse condition. Deep potholes and crumbling curbs make it unsafe to drive. Where are our city tax dollars going if not to correct these problems?

   (a.) angry

   b. instructive

   c. sympathetic

   d. impersonal

4. I am a tired American. I am tired of watching criminals walk free while they wait for their day in court. I'm tired of hearing about victims getting as much as or more hassle than criminals. I'm tired of reading about courts of law that even accept a lawsuit in which a criminal sues his or her intended victim.

   a. persuasive

   b. instructive

   c. logical

   (d.) disgusted

5. In July of 1986 my daughter, Lucy, was born with an underdeveloped brain. She was a beautiful little girl—at least to me and my husband—but her disabilities were severe. By the time she was two weeks old we knew that she would never walk, talk, feed herself, or even understand the concept of mother and father. It's impossible to describe the effect that her five-and-a-half-month life had on us; suffice it to say that she was the purest experience of love and pain that we will ever have, that she changed us forever, and that we will never cease to mourn her death, even though we know that for her it was a triumphant passing.

   a. instructive

   (b.) emotional

   c. persuasive

   d. angry

Language: Denotation and Connotation

You already know that writers use different words to achieve different purposes. A reporter writing an objective, newspaper account of a murder might use very different words than would a brother of the slain person. In this section you will learn more about the meanings of words and how they are clues to a writer's purpose.

Which of the following would you like to be a part of: a crowd, mob, gang, audience, congregation, or class? Each of these words has the same basic meaning: "an assembled group of people." But each has a different *shade* of meaning. *Crowd* suggests a large, disorganized group. *Audience,* on the other hand, suggests a quiet, controlled group.

This example shows that words have two levels of meaning—a literal meaning and an additional shade of meaning. These two levels of meaning are called denotation and connotation. A word's **denotation** is the meaning stated in the dictionary—its literal meaning. A word's **connotation** is the additional implied meanings that a word may take on. A word's connotation often carries either a positive or negative, favorable or unfavorable, impression. The words *mob* and *gang* have a negative connotation because they imply a disorderly, disorganized group. *Congregation, audience,* and *class* have a positive connotation because they suggest an orderly, organized group.

Here are a few more examples. Would you prefer to be described as *slim* or *skinny*? As *intelligent* or *brainy*? As *tall* or *gangly*? As *particular* or *picky*? Notice that each pair of words has a similar denotation, but each word within the pair has a different connotation.

Depending on the words they choose, writers can suggest favorable or unfavorable impressions of the person, object, or event they are describing. For example, through the writer's choice of words, the two sentences below create two entirely different impressions. As you read them, underline the words that have a positive or negative connotation.

- The unruly crowd forced its way through the restraint barriers and ruthlessly attacked the rock star.
- The enthusiastic group of fans burst through the fence and rushed toward the rock star.

It is important to pay attention to a writer's choice of words, especially when you are reading persuasive material. Often a writer may communicate subtle or hidden messages or encourage you to feel positively or negatively toward the subject.

Read the following paragraph on violence in sports and, as you read, underline the words that have a strong positive or negative connotation.

So it goes. Knifings, shootings, beatings, muggings, paralysis, and death become part of our play. Women baseball fans are warned to walk with friends and avoid taking their handbags to games because of strong-arm robberies and purse snatchings at San Francisco's Candlestick Park. A professional football coach, under oath in a slander case, describes some of his own players as part of a "criminal element" in his sport. The commissioner of football proclaims that playing field outlaws and bullies will be punished, but to anybody with normal eyesight and a working television set the action looks rougher than ever. In Europe and South America—and, chillingly, for the first time in the United States—authorities turn to snarling attack dogs to control unruly mobs at athletic events.

—from Robert C. Yeager, *Seasons of Shame: the New Violence in Sports*, p. 6

Exercise 10–5

Directions: *For each of the following pairs of words, underline the word with the more positive connotation.*

1. <u>request</u>   demand

2. <u>overlook</u>   neglect

3. ridicule   <u>tease</u>

4. <u>glance</u>   stare

5. <u>display</u>   expose

6. garment   <u>gown</u>

7. gaudy   <u>showy</u>

8. clumsy   <u>awkward</u>

9. <u>artificial</u>   fake

10. <u>take</u>   snatch

11. jalopy   <u>limousine</u>

12. <u>large</u>   oversized

13. gobble   <u>dine</u>

14. <u>inquire</u>   interrogate

15. token   <u>keepsake</u>

Understanding More of What You Read

Now that you know about inference and about the various clues to look for in a piece of writing, you should gain a better understanding of everything you read—textbooks, newspapers, magazine, and so forth. Determining a writer's purpose is one of the best clues to look for as you read. When you pay attention to style, audience, tone, and language, you come to understand the writer's motivation—the effect he or she is trying to have on you, the reader.

What Have You Learned?

Directions: Match each term in column A with its correct definition in column B. Write the letter of your choice in the space provided.

	Column A		Column B
_c_	1. denotation	a.	an educated guess or prediction about something unknown based on available facts and information
_e_	2. audience	b.	the characteristics that make a piece of writing unique
_b_	3. style	c.	a word's literal meaning
_f_	4. connotation	d.	the attitude or feeling a writer expresses about a subject
_d_	5. tone	e.	the group of people for whom an author is writing
_a_	6. inference	f.	the additional implied meanings that a word may take on

NAME _____ SECTION _____
DATE _____ SCORE _____

A. *Directions:* Select the letter of the choice that best describes the tone expressed in each of the following statements.

___c___ 1. The best thing to do when you feel the urge to exercise is to lie down until the feeling goes away.

    a. instructive   c. humorous

    b. persuasive   d. angry

___a___ 2. Put the book back on the shelf when you are through reading it.

    a. instructive   c. humorous

    b. disapproving   d. nostalgic

___d___ 3. I can remember when our house was surrounded by tall, majestic trees and furry little animals. Now when I look outside my window all I see is a highway.

    a. instructive   c. thankful

    b. persuasive   d. nostalgic

___b___ 4. We need to start caring more about the rights of baby seals. They are defenseless against the ruthless hunters who kill them for their pelts.

    a. instructive   c. forceful

    b. persuasive   d. nostalgic

___c___ 5. Lincoln is one of our most famous and respected presidents. His most notable and important accomplishment was the freeing of slaves in the southern United States.

    a. persuasive   c. admiring

    b. forceful   d. disapproving

B. *Directions:* After reading the following passage, select the letter of the choice that best answers the questions below. You will have to use inference in order to answer the questions.

THE LION'S SHARE

The lion, the jackal, the wolf, and the hyena had a meeting and agreed that they would hunt together in one party and share equally among them whatever game they caught.

They went out and killed an antelope. The four animals then discussed which one of them would divide the meat. The lion said, "Whoever divides the meat must know how to count."

Immediately the wolf volunteered, saying, "Indeed, I know how to count." He began to divide the meat. He cut off four pieces of equal size and placed one before each of the hunters.

The lion was angered. He said, "Is this the way to count?" And he struck the wolf across the eyes, so that his eyes swelled up and he could not see.

The jackal said, "The wolf does not know how to count. I will divide the meat." He cut three portions that were small and a fourth portion that was very large. The three small portions he placed before the hyena, the wolf, and himself. The large portion he put in front of the lion, who took his meat and went away.

"Why was it necessary to give the lion such a large piece?" the hyena said. "Our agreement was to divide and share equally. Where did you ever learn how to divide?"

"I learned from the wolf," the jackal answered.

"Wolf? How can anyone learn from the wolf? He is stupid," the hyena said.

"The jackal was right," the wolf said. "He knows how to count. Before, when my eyes were open, I did not see it. Now, though my eyes are wounded, I see it clearly."

—Dresser, *The Rainmaker's Dog*, pp. 110–11

_____a_____ 6. The lion was angered because

    a. he did not receive a large share of meat.

    b. the wolf make an error in counting.

    c. the meat was not divided equally.

    d. the wolf treated him unfairly.

_____a_____ 7. Which statement best describes the jackal's learning experience?

    a. The jackal learned from the wolf's mistake.

    b. The jackal learned not to trust the hyena.

    c. The jackal learned how to divide evenly.

    d. The jackal learned that the lion is violent.

_____c_____ 8. What did the wolf mean when he said, "though my eyes are wounded, I see it clearly"?

    a. He dislikes the lion.

    b. He resents the way the lion treated him.

    c. He understands the mistake that he made.

    d. He realizes that all jungle animals are ruthless.

_____c_____ 9. What lesson can be learned from this story?

    a. Don't trust your friends.

    b. Do it yourself if you want something done correctly.

    c. Sometimes it is wise to pay tribute to those who are more powerful than you are.

    d. Animals are natural enemies.

_____b_____ 10. Which of the following was most useful in making inferences about the story?

    a. descriptions of the animals

    b. conversation by the animals

    c. unusual word meanings

    d. interesting writing style

NAME _____ SECTION _____

DATE _____ SCORE _____

Directions: After reading the following passage, select the letter of the choice that best answers the questions below.

WHAT'S BEST FOR THE CHILD

1   In many states, there are no regulations governing the number of infants a day care staff member may care for. In those where there are, many states allow five or six. In Wisconsin, where I live, the maximum is four infants per worker. [According to the National Association for the Education of Young Children, 29 states require this four-to-one ratio, while only three—Kansas, Maryland, and Massachusetts—require a three-to-one ratio. Most of the remaining states have five-to-one ratios.]

2   Consider the amount of physical care and attention a baby needs—say 20 minutes for feeding every three hours or so, and 10 minutes for diapering every two hours or so, and time for the caregiver to wash her hands thoroughly and sanitize the area after changing each baby. In an eight-and-a-half-hour day, then, a caregiver working under the typical four-to-one ratio will have 16 diapers to change and 13 feedings to give. Four diaper changes and three feedings apiece is not an inordinate amount of care over a long day from the babies' point of view.

3   But think about the caregiver's day: Four hours to feed the babies, two hours and 40 minutes to change them. If you allow an extra two and a half minutes at each changing to put them down, clean up the area, and thoroughly wash your hands, you can get by with 40 minutes for sanitizing. (And if you think about thoroughly washing your hands 16 times a day, you may begin to understand why epidemics of diarrhea and related diseases regularly sweep through infant-care centers.)

4   That makes seven hours and 20 minutes of the day spent just on physical care—if you're lucky and the infants stay conveniently on schedule.

5   Since feeding and diaper changing are necessarily one-on-one activities, each infant is bound to be largely unattended during the five-plus hours that the other three babies are being attended to. So, if there's to be any stimulation at all for the child, the caregiver had better chat and play up a storm while she's feeding and changing.

6   Obviously, such a schedule is not realistic. In group infant care based on even this four-to-one ratio, babies will not be changed every two hours and they will probably not be held while they're fed.

7   They also will not get the kind of attention and talk that is the foundation of language development. If a child is deprived of language stimulation for eight to ten hours a day, how much compensation—how much "quality time"—can concerned parents provide in the baby's few other waking hours at home?

—from Dorothy Conniff, "What's Best for the Child," *The Progressive*

_____b_____   1. The writer's primary purpose is to
   a. explain the advantages of day care.
   b. explain the limitations of infant care in day care centers.
   c. argue for the legislation governing day care centers.
   d. explain why illnesses are common in day care centers.

_____a_____   2. What is the author suggesting in the last sentence in paragraph 3?
   a. Caregivers do not wash their hands as frequently or carefully as they should.
   b. Washing one's hands 16 times a day is too much.
   c. Caregivers should use alternative sanitizing methods.
   d. Caregivers do not care about the spread of disease.

_____d_____   3. In paragraph 7, the author is suggesting that
   a. language development is more important than physical care.
   b. infants in day care centers do not need stimulation.
   c. parents should talk to their infants as much as possible.
   d. parents cannot make up for the lack of stimulation of infants in a day care center.

_____a_____   4. Based on the reading, the author is most likely to favor which of the following?
   a. legislation to decrease the number of infants a worker is responsible for
   b. legislation to require sanitary procedures
   c. legislation to require intellectual stimulation of all infants
   d. legislation to require parents to spend quality time with their infants

_b_ 5. In paragraph 2, the term **inordinate** means
   a. inadequate.   c. undefined.
   b. excessive.   d. undervalued.

_b_ 6. This passage seems written primarily for which of the
      following audiences?
   a. day care givers   c. legislators
   b. parents   d. teachers

_b_ 7. Which of the following words has a negative connotation as
      used in the passage?
   a. regulations   c. stimulation
   b. epidemics   d. storm

_a_ 8. Which of the following terms best describes the tone of this
      passage?
   a. concerned   c. accepting
   b. humorous   d. angry

_c_ 9. The author supports the main ideas in this passage primarily
      by using
   a. stories about infants.
   b. examples of infant neglect.
   c. facts and statistics about infant care.
   d. comparisons among day care centers.

_b_ 10. Which statement best summarizes the author's view of infant
       day care?
   a. Infants should not be allowed to attend day care centers
      when they are ill.
   b. Day care centers are frequently unable to provide adequate
      language stimulation, play, and one-on-one care to infants.
   c. Infants' parents should provide language stimulation by
      playing tapes.
   d. Day care should not be allowed for children under age one.

NAME _____ SECTION _____

DATE _____ SCORE _____

A. Directions: After reading the following passage, select the letter of the choice that best answers the questions below.

STIFF LAWS NAIL DEADBEATS

1   The sight of deadbeat dad king Jeffrey Nichols nabbed, cuffed, and jailed in New York for ducking $580,000 in child support ought to shake up other scofflaws.

2   A few years ago, Nichols almost surely would have escaped his responsibilities. His wealth enabled him to run to Toronto, Boca Raton, Fla., and Charlotte, Vt., and he got away with it for five years. He defied three states' court orders to pay up.

3   He was finally caught because in the past few years, local, state, and federal governments have finally gotten serious about child support.

4   A law Congress passed in 1992 required the FBI to chase child-support cheats when they cross state lines. Nichols became a target, culminating in his arrest.

5   As the scale of such enforcement has grown, it has prompted occasional criticism—particularly about the use of Internal Revenue Service records to track down deadbeats. But there's no doubt it's needed

6   There are 7 million deadbeat parents, 90% of them dads. If all paid what they are supposed to, their children would have $34 billion more—money that sometimes has to come from the taxpayers instead.

—McMiller, *USA Today*

_____a_____ 1. In paragraph 1, the writer is suggesting that the sight of Nichols in handcuffs may
    a. encourage other deadbeat dads to pay.
    b. create legal problems.
    c. encourage more children to apply for child support.
    d. help track down other deadbeat dads.

_____d_____ 2. In paragraph 1, the word **scofflaws** means
    a. lawyers.   c. fathers.
    b. parents.   d. lawbreakers.

_____b_____ 3. In paragraph 2, the word **defied** means
    a. appealed.   c. reported.
    b. did not obey.   d. discouraged.

_____a_____ 4. The author's purpose is to
    a. argue that deadbeat dads should be made to pay up.
    b. explain how Nichols got what he deserved.
    c. show that most deadbeat parents are males.
    d. explain why children deserve more money.

_____a_____ 5. The tone of this passage could best be described as
    a. serious.   c. argumentative.
    b. casual.   d. annoying.

_____b_____ 6. For which one of the following audiences is the article intended?
    a. deadbeat dads who escape responsibilities
    b. citizens who are concerned about how tax dollars are spent
    c. children who do not receive the support they deserve
    d. men like Jeffrey Nichols

_____d_____ 7. Which one of the following words, as used in this passage, has a negative connotation?
    a. enforcement   c. taxpayers
    b. target   d. cheats

_____a_____ 8. How could the use of the Internal Revenue Service records help track down deadbeat dads?
    a. The records reveal income. c. The records report expenses.
    b. The records report   d. The records reveal job titles.
       marital status.

_____a_____ 9. The writer uses the case of Jeffrey Nichols to
    a. give an example of a deadbeat dad.
    b. defend Nichols.
    c. show how much money taxpayers are losing each year.
    d. make deadbeat dads feel guilty.

_____b_____ 10. Which one of the following words does *not* usually have a negative connotation?
    a. ducking   c. deadbeat
    b. taxpayers   d. cheats

A. Directions: Study the photograph below and then use inference to answer the questions that follow. Write your answers in the space provided.

1. What does the photo reveal about the couple?

   They are unemployed and in poverty.

2. What events may have brought the couple to their current circumstance?

   loss of jobs, illnesses, lack of employable skills

3. What is the relationship among the individuals shown in the photo?

   The man and woman are a couple and are likely the parents of the child.

4. What details in the photo suggest that it was taken in an urban setting?

   buildings, highway, bridge or highway overhead, multiple train tracks

B. Directions: After reading the following passage, select the letter of the choice that best answers the questions below.

WHAT YOU DON'T KNOW ABOUT NATIVE AMERICANS

1   Most Americans, even those deeply concerned about issues of justice, tend to speak of Indian issues as tragedies of the distant past. So ingrained is this position that when the occasional non-Indian does come forward on behalf of *today's* Indian cause—Marlon Brando, William Kunstler, Robert Redford, Jane Fonda, David Brower—they are all dismissed as romantics. People are a bit embarrassed for them, as if they'd stepped over some boundary of propriety.

2   The Indian issue is *not* part of the distant past. Many of the worst anti-Indian campaigns were undertaken scarcely 80 to 100 years ago. Your great-grandparents were already alive at the time. The Model-T Ford was on the road.

3   And the assaults continue today. While the Custer period of direct military action against Indians may be over in the United States, more subtle though equally devastating "legalistic" manipulations continue to separate Indians from their land and their sovereignty.

—Mander, *Utne Reader*

___a___ 5. The main point of the passage is that
    a. the problems of Native Americans are not just history; they continue today.
    b. Native Americans experience anti-Indian campaigns.
    c. famous people who speak out for Native Americans are considered romantics.
    d. Native Americans experienced many tragedies.

___d___ 6. Paragraph 3 focuses on
    a. solutions.   c. military actions.
    b. Custer's victories.   d. legal manipulations.

___c___ 7. Which phrase best describes the tone of the passage?
    a. scientific   c. serious and concerned
    b. casual and informal   d. light and humorous

___d___ 8. Which describes the audience for whom this was written?
    a. Native Americans not living on a reservation
    b. lawyers who represent Native Americans
    c. history teachers
    d. Americans who do not know much about Native American issues

___b___ 9. Which of these words has a strong negative connotation?
    a. issue   c. great-grandparents
    b. assaults   d. Model-T Fords

___d___ 10. The statement "The Model T Ford was on the road." was included in paragraph 2 to
    a. focus on the past.   c. call attention to big business.
    b. emphasize that the issue is an American problem.   d. emphasize that the issue is part of modern times.

NAME _____ SECTION _____

DATE _____ SCORE _____

Directions: After reading the following brief story, select the letter of the choice that best answers the questions below.

The caller's voice does not hold together well. I can tell he is quite old and not well. He is calling from Maryland.

"I want four boxes of the Nut Goodies," he rasps at me after giving me his credit card information in a faltering hurry.

"There are 24 bars in each box," I say in case he doesn't know the magnitude of his order. Nut Goodies are made here in St. Paul and consist of a patty of maple cream covered with milk chocolate and peanuts. Sort of a Norwegian praline.

"OK, then make it five boxes but hurry this up before my nurse gets back. "

He wants the order billed to his home address but sent to a nursing home.

"I've got Parkinson's," he says. "I'm 84."

"OK sir, I think I've got it all. They're on the way." I put a rush on it.

"Right. Bye," he says, and in the pause when he is concentrating God knows how much energy on getting the receiver back in its cradle, I hear a long, dry chuckle.

One hundred and twenty Nut Goodies.

Way to go, buddy.

—from Jerry Mander, *The Absence of the Sacred: The Failure of Technology and the Rise of Indian Nations*

___a___ 1. The caller is most likely

    a. not supposed to eat candy.

    b. angry with his nurse.

    c. unable to pay for his order.

    d. unhappy.

___c___ 2. Which word best describes the tone of this passage?

    a. disgusting   c. sympathetic

    b. instructive   d. forceful

___b___ 3. A praline is

    a. a Norwegian plate.   c. a type of nut.

    b. a type of candy.   d. a Norwegian tradition.

_____d_____ 4. Why does the caller chuckle at the end of the conversation?

    a. The order-taker made a joke.

    b. The caller thought his nurse had returned.

    c. The caller thought he would get better service.

    d. The caller thinks he has gotten away with something.

_____a_____ 5. What is the writer's purpose?

    a. to share an amusing incident

    b. to criticize nursing home care

    c. to sell Norwegian pralines

    d. to defend living conditions of the elderly

_____c_____ 6. The concluding phrase "Way to go, buddy" suggests

    a. disapproval.   c. approval.

    b. disappointment.   d. lack of understanding.

_____d_____ 7. The word **faltering** suggests

    a. pride.   c. assurance.

    b. importance.   d. weakness.

_____b_____ 8. What phrase best describes the person taking the call?

    a. indifferent.   c. prejudiced.

    b. polite.   d. elderly.

_____d_____ 9. The word **magnitude** means

    a. cost.   c. importance.

    b. weight.   d. size.

_____b_____ 10. Why did the order-taker put a rush on the order?

    a. He or she was afraid the nurse would discover the order.

    b. He or she felt sorry for the caller.

    c. He or she disliked the company that sold the pralines.

    d. He or she wanted to add extra costs to the order.

NAME _____   SECTION _____

DATE _____   SCORE _____

HIDDEN TREASURES: UNLOCKING STRENGTHS IN THE PUBLIC SOCIAL SERVICES

Mary Bricker-Jenkins

Taken from a college textbook titled *The Strengths in Social Work Practice*, this reading recounts a social worker's early experience working with a client.

Vocabulary Preview

These are some of the difficult words in this essay. The definitions here will help you if you can't figure out the meanings from the sentence context or word parts.

labyrinthine (para. 2) confusing and complicated

requisite (para. 4) required; necessary

invoked (para. 4) resorted to; called upon

competency-based (para. 7) a system of evaluation in which a participant's ability to perform specific tasks is measured.

field research (para. 7) studies completed in real-life situations

1   Fresh out of college with a B.A. in English, I began my social work career as a social investigator with the New York Department of Welfare. At that time, we were implementing the 1962 Defined Service Amendments to the Social Security Act. The plan was to "casework" everybody out of poverty—or at least those who were "willing to help themselves." We were to emphasize the social rather than the investigative part of our roles. Having just completed my training week, I made an appointment with Matilda Jones for her quarterly recertification visit.

2   Matilda had four children. Two were literally lost in the foster care system. Following agency advice, Matilda had voluntarily placed her children during a time of family crisis. Also at our urging, she had not visited them for a long time; the practical wisdom of the time suggested that Matilda should not visit in order to give everyone a "time to adjust." Now we were unable to locate the children in the labyrinthine maze of contract agencies to whom we had entrusted their care. Matilda's third child had already been labeled "high

risk" at his school—a school he attended when Matilda was able to get him there, which was not very often. Matilda had just brought her newborn home from the hospital; he had several conditions that reflected poor prenatal care and marginal obstetrical services.

3   These were the days before the separation of income maintenance and services, so I went prepared by my training to recertify the family's eligibility for AFDC as well as to offer social services. I could see Matilda in the window of her tenement as I turned off Broadway and walked cautiously through the rubble of the West Side Urban Renewal district. From her observation post at the front end of her railroad apartment, she signaled to the men hanging out on the street below to give me safe passage. It was 10:00 A.M. and she was having her breakfast: a piece of toast and a can of beer.

4   Matilda had learned the system when I was still in grade school. She was ready for me. She had her rent receipt, her electric bill, her clothing inventory, her list of clothing and furniture needs for the baby, and the baby's health department card. She was prepared to discuss the baby's paternity. I made the requisite notes in my little caseworker's book, then closed it and invoked my training. I said, "Mrs. Jones, you know all of this paperwork is very important, but there are other important things we could do together. I really want to work with you on problems and issues and concerns that are important to you. Now I am going to leave my book closed, and I'd really like to talk with you, just talk about stuff together, and about things we could do together that'll result in better things happening in your life."

5   Matilda studied me for a very long moment before she leaned into the space between us and said, "Look, white girl, I wanna tell you something. I got to document my life to you—because I am poor. I got to show you all my papers, prove I paid my bills, take my baby to your pig doctor, and show you this card that says I take care of my baby—all because I'm poor. I even have to talk about my sex life with you—because I'm poor. I gotta do all that—but I don't have to take your social workin'.

6   "Now I'm gonna tell you three things about your social workin'," she continued. "Number one, it ain't got nothin' to do with my life. Number two, I can't eat it. And number three, it don't dull the pain like my Pabst Blue Ribbon. Now you get along, white girl—and you think about that."

7   I have thought about that for 30 years. One of the results has been my participation in efforts to build a strengths-oriented practice in the public social services. Two components of that effort in which I have been involved included designing a statewide competency-based training program and conducting field research on the characteristics and activities of effective workers in that state.

— · —

Directions: Select the letter of the choice that best answers the questions that follow.

CHECKING YOUR COMPREHENSION

___c___   1. A main point the author makes is that
  a. the 1962 law was ineffective.
  b. social workers know more than their clients.
  c. Matilda was angry and embarrassed by the social worker's visit.
  d. social work is only useful to those "willing to help themselves."

___a___   2. As a result of her early experiences, the social worker
  a. made improvements in the social services system.
  b. reported Matilda to be uncooperative.
  c. left the field due to workload and frustration.
  d. refused to discuss Matilda's case.

___b___   3. The article was written by a
  a welfare recipient.   c. novelist.
  b. social worker.   d. lawyer.

___c___   4. Matilda's first two children could no longer be located due to the fault of
  a. their mother.
  b. their foster parents.
  c. the contract agencies to whom the children were entrusted.
  d. the New York public schools.

_____c_____ 5. The purpose of the social investigator's visit was to

    a. help Matilda pay her bill.

    b. help Matilda locate her children.

    c. recertify Matilda to receive welfare assistance.

    d. instruct Matilda on how to work within the system.

USING WHAT YOU KNOW ABOUT INFERENCE AND THE WRITER'S PURPOSE

_____a_____ 6. The audience that the author most likely intended this selection for is

    a. social workers.   c. medical doctors.

    b. welfare recipients.   d. religious leaders.

_____b_____ 7. The author's main purpose for writing this selection is to

    a. analyze the causes of poverty.

    b. show problems with earlier approaches to social work.

    c. show the good methods of casework used.

    d. report on a client's recertification visit.

_____a_____ 8. The tone of the author toward herself and the social welfare system is

    a. concerned and critical.

    b. light and humorous.

    c. distant and impersonal.

    d. positive and admiring.

_____a_____ 9. Which of the following details best supports the inference that Matilda lived in a dangerous neighborhood?

    a. She signaled to the men hanging out on the street below to give me safe passage.

    b. I could see Matilda in the window of her tenement as I turned off Broadway.

    c. Matilda studied me for a long moment before she leaned into the space between us.

    d. It was 10:00 A.M. and she was having her breakfast: a piece of toast and a can of beer.

_____a_____ 10. Which of the following statements best reveals Matilda's attitude toward the social worker?

    a. Look, white girl, I wanna tell you something.

    b. Matilda studied me for a very long moment.

    c. She was ready for me.

    d. She was having her breakfast: a piece of toast and a can of beer.

CONTEXT AND WORD PARTS

_____b_____ 11. In paragraph 1, the word **implementing** means to

    a. authorize.   c. argue against.

    b. put into practice.   d. revise.

_____b_____ 12. In paragraph 2, **prenatal care** refers to care given

    a. before conception.   c. after birth.

    b. before birth.   d. throughout infancy.

_____a_____ 13. In paragraph 2, the word **marginal** means

    a. limited.   c. professional.

    b. thorough.   d. expensive.

_____a_____ 14. In paragraph 3, the word **recertify** means to

    a. certify again.   c. deny.

    b. process an appeal.   d. question.

_____c_____ 15. In paragraph 4, the word **inventory** means

    a. shopping list.

    b. items received as gifts.

    c. records of one's possessions.

    d. items that have been thrown away.

REVIEWING DIFFICULT VOCABULARY

Directions: Complete each of the following sentences by inserting a word from the Vocabulary Preview on page 307 in the space provided.

16. To work as a home care aide, you must have the

_____ requisite _____ skills for working with patients.

17. The graduate student conducted _____field research_____ on the behavior of apes in captivity.

18. The politician accused of fraud refused to testify and _____invoked_____ the Fifth Amendment, protesting his right to remain silent.

19. Elmwood Elementary School uses a _____competency-based_____ testing program to decide which students need remedial instruction.

20. The bus weaved its way through the _____labyrinthine_____ web of traffic.

Chapter 10: Understanding Inference and the Writer's Purpose

RECORDING YOUR PROGRESS

Test	Number Right		Score
Practice Test 10-1	_____ × 10 =	_____%
Practice Test 10-2	_____ × 10 =	_____%
Practice Test 10-3	_____ × 10 =	_____%
Mastery Test 10-1	_____ × 10 =	_____%
Mastery Test 10-2	_____ × 10 =	_____%
Mastery Test 10-3	_____ × 5 =	_____%

EVALUATING YOUR PROGRESS

Based on your test performance, rate how well you have mastered the skills taught in this chapter by checking one of the boxes below or by writing your own evaluation.

☐ **Need More Improvement**
Tip: Try using the "Inference" Module on the Reading Road Trip CD-ROM that accompanies this textbook to fine-tune the skills that you have learned in this chapter.

☐ **Need More Practice**
Tip: Try using the "Inference" Module on the Reading Road Trip CD-ROM that accompanies this textbook to brush up on the skills you have learned in this chapter, or visit this textbook's Website at **http://ablongman.com/mcwhorter** for extra practice.

☐ **Good**
Tip: To maintain your skills, do a quick review of this chapter by using the Website that accompanies this textbook by logging on to **http://ablongman.com/mcwhorter.**

☐ **Excellent**

YOUR EVALUATION: _____

_____

_____

_____

_____

Student Resource Guide A

Understanding Sentences: A Review

Sentences are among the basic building blocks of language. To understand paragraphs, articles, and textbook chapters, you first have to understand the sentences with which each is built. Some sentences are short and easy to understand (*Close the door.*); others are long, complicated, and difficult to follow. This section provides a brief review of how to understand these difficult sentences.

A **sentence** is a group of words that express at least one complete thought or idea. Every sentence, then, expresses at least one main point. The main point is a statement about someone or something. Here are the steps to follow in understanding what a sentence means.

1. **Find the subject and predicate.**
2. **Understand sentences with two main points.**
3. **Understand sentences that express one main point and one related idea.**
4. **Understand how modifiers change meaning.**
5. **Express the idea(s) in your own words.**

Step 1: Finding the Subject and Predicate

Every sentence is made up of at least two parts, a subject and a predicate. The **subject,** often a noun, identifies the person or object the sentence is about. The main part of the **predicate**—the verb—tells what the person or

315

object is doing or has done. Usually a sentence contains additional information about the subject and/or the predicate.

EXAMPLE

The average <u>American</u> <u>consumed</u> six gallons of beer last year.

The key idea of this sentence is "American consumed." It is expressed by the subject and predicate. The simple subject of this sentence is American; it explains who the sentence is about. The rest of the sentence gives more information about the verb by telling what (beer) and how much (six gallons last year) was consumed. Here are a few more examples:

EXAMPLES

The <u>ship</u> <u>entered</u> the harbor early this morning.

<u>Lilacs</u> <u>bloom</u> in the spring.

Questions to Ask

In many long and complicated sentences, the key idea is not as obvious as in the previous examples. To find the key idea, ask these questions:

1. Who or what is the sentence about?
2. What is happening in the sentence?

Here is an example of a complicated sentence that might be found in a psychology textbook:

EXAMPLE

Intelligence, as measured by IQ, depends on the kind of test given, the skill of the examiner, and the cooperation of the subject.

In this sentence, the answer to the question, "Who or what is the sentence about?" is *intelligence*. The verb is *depends*, and the remainder of the sentence explains the factors upon which intelligence depends. Let us look at a few more examples:

EXAMPLES

<u>William James</u>, often thought of as the father of American psychology, <u>tested</u> whether memory could be improved by exercising it.

<u>Violence</u> in sports, both at amateur and professional levels, <u>has increased</u> dramatically over the past ten years.

Multiple Subjects and Multiple Verbs

Some sentences may have more than one subject and/or more than one verb in the predicate.

EXAMPLES

subject   subject
Poor <u>diet</u> and <u>lack</u> of exercise can cause weight gain.

verb   verb
My brother always <u>worries</u> and <u>complains</u> about his job.

subject   subject   verb   verb
Many <u>homes</u> and <u>businesses</u> <u>are burglarized</u> or <u>vandalized</u> each year.

subject   verb   verb   verb
The angry <u>customer</u> <u>was screaming</u>, <u>cursing</u>, and <u>shouting</u>.

Exercise A–1

Directions: Find the key idea in each of the following sentences. Draw a line under the subject and circle the verb.

Example: The <u>instructor</u> (assigned) a fifteen-page article to read.

1. Every summer my <u>parents</u> (travel) to the eastern seacoast.

2. <u>Children</u> (learn) how to behave by imitating adults.

3. <u>William Faulkner</u>, a popular American author, (wrote) about life in the South.

4. <u>Psychologists</u> (are interested) in studying human behavior in many different situations.

5. Terminally ill <u>patients</u> (may refuse) to take their prescribed medication.

6. The <u>use</u> of cocaine, although illegal, (is) apparently (increasing.)

7. The most accurate <u>method</u> we have of estimating the age of the earth (is based) on our knowledge of radioactivity.

8. <u>Elements</u> (exist) either as compounds or as free elements.

9. <u>Attention</u> (may be defined) as a focusing of perception.

10. The specific <u>instructions</u> in a computer program (are written) in a computer language.

Step 2: Understanding Sentences with Two Main Points

Sentences that express two or more equally important ideas are called **coordinate sentences.** Coordinate sentences got their name because they coordinate, or tie together, two or more ideas. They do this for three reasons: (1) to emphasize the relationship between ideas; (2) to indicate their equal importance; and/or (3) to make the material more concise and easier to read. In the following example notice how two related ideas can be combined.

EXAMPLES

Two Related Ideas
Marlene was in obvious danger.
Joe quickly pulled Marlene from the street.

Combined Sentence
Marlene was in obvious danger, and Joe quickly pulled her from the street.

In this case the combined sentence establishes that the two equally important events are parts of a single incident.

As you read coordinate sentences, be sure to locate both subjects and predicates. If you do not read carefully or if you are reading too fast, you might miss the second idea. Often you can recognize a sentence that combines two or more ideas by its structure and punctuation. Coordinate ideas are combined in one of two ways:

1. With a semicolon:

EXAMPLE

The union members wanted to strike; the company did nothing to discourage them.

2. With a comma and one of the following joining words: *and, or, but, nor, so, for, yet.* These words are called coordinating conjunctions. See Table A-1 for the meaning clues each provides.

EXAMPLES

Some students decided to take the final exam, and others chose to rely on their semester average.

The students wanted the instructor to cancel the class, but the instructor decided to reschedule it.

TABLE A-1	Coordinating Conjunctions—Words That Join Two Important Ideas	
Joining Words	**Meaning Clues**	**Example**
and	Links similar and equally important ideas	Jim is in my biology class, <u>and</u> Pierce is in my psychology class.
but, yet	Connects opposite ideas or change in thought	Professor Clark had given a homework assignment, <u>yet</u> she did not collect it.
for, so	Indicates reasons or shows that one thing is causing another	Most English majors in our college take a foreign language, <u>for</u> it is a requirement.
or, not	Suggests choice or options	We could make a fire in the fireplace, <u>or</u> we could get out some extra blankets.

Step 3: Understanding Sentences with One Main Point and One Related Idea

Sentences that express one main point and one related idea are called subordinate sentences. Subordinate sentences contain one key idea and one or more less important, or subordinate, ideas that explain the key idea. These less important ideas each have their own subject and predicate, but they depend on the main sentence to complete their meaning. For example, in the following sentence you cannot understand fully the meaning of the underlined portion until you read the entire sentence.

EXAMPLE   <u>Because Stewart forgot to make a payment</u>, he had to pay a late charge on his loan.

In this sentence, the more important idea is that Stewart had to pay a late charge since that portion of the sentence could stand alone as a complete sentence. The reason for the late charge is presented as background information that amplifies and further explains the basic message.

As you read subordinate sentences, be sure to notice the relationship between the two ideas. The less important idea may provide a description or explain a condition, cause, reason, purpose, time, or place set out in the more important idea. Here are a few additional examples of sentences that relate two or more ideas. In each the base idea is underlined and the function of the less important idea is indicated in brackets above it.

EXAMPLES

description

<u>My grandfather</u>, who is eighty years old, <u>collects stamps</u>.

time

<u>American foreign policy changed</u> when we entered the Vietnam War.

condition

<u>I'll be late for my dental appointment</u> unless my class is dismissed early.

reason

Since I failed my last history exam, <u>I decided to drop the course</u>.

Notice that if the subordinate idea comes first in the sentence, a comma follows it. If the key, complete idea comes first, a comma is not used.

As you read subordinate sentences, pay attention to the connecting word used. It should signal the relationship of ideas. You must be sure to pick up the signal. You should know *why* the two ideas have been combined and *what* they have to do with each other. Table A-2 lists some common connecting words, called subordinating conjunctions, and tells you what each signals.

TABLE A-2	Subordinating Conjunctions—Words That Join an Important Idea with a Less Important Idea	
Joining Words	**Meaning Clues**	**Example**
before, after, while, during, until, when, once	Indicates time	<u>After</u> taking the test, Leon felt relieved.
because, since, so that	Gives reasons	<u>Because</u> I was working, I was unable to go bowling.
if, unless, whether, even if	Explains conditions	<u>Unless</u> I leave work early, I'll miss class.
although, as far as, in order to, however	Explains circumstance	<u>Although</u> I used a dictionary, I still did not fully understand the word.

Exercise A-2

Directions: After reading each of the following sentences, in the space provided insert the letter that best indicates how the underlined idea is related to the rest of the sentence. Select one of the following choices for each.

a. Indicates time

b. Gives a reason

c. Explains a condition

d. Explains a circumstance

   d   1. <u>Although I broke my leg</u>, I am still able to drive a car.

   c   2. Peter will become a truck driver, <u>unless he decides to go back to school for further training</u>.

   a   3. She always picks up her mail <u>after she eats lunch</u>.

   b   4. <u>Because violence is regularly shown on television</u>, children accept it as an ordinary part of life.

   b   5. <u>Since comparison shopping is a necessary part of the buying process</u>, wise consumers look for differences in quality as well as price.

| **Exercise A-3** | *Directions: After reading each of the following sentences, decide whether it is a coordinate or a subordinate sentence. Mark C in the space provided if the sentence is coordinate, and underline both sets of subjects and predicates. Mark S if it is subordinate, and underline the more important idea.* |

___C___ 1. The <u>personnel office</u> eagerly <u>accepted</u> my application for a job, and <u>I expect</u> to receive an offer next week.

___C___ 2. <u>Computers have become</u> part of our daily lives, but their <u>role</u> in today's college classrooms <u>has</u> not yet <u>been fully explored</u>.

___S___ 3. As far as we can tell from historical evidence, <u>humankind has inhabited</u> this earth for several million years.

___S___ 4. Because sugar is Cuba's main export, <u>the Cuban economy depends</u> upon the worldwide demand for sugar.

___C___ 5. <u>We</u> never <u>learn</u> anything in a vacuum; <u>we</u> are always <u>having other experiences</u> before and after we <u>learn</u> new material.

Step 4: Understanding How Modifiers Change Meaning

After you have identified the key ideas, the next step in understanding a sentence is to see how the modifiers affect its meaning. **Modifiers** are words that change, describe, qualify, or limit the meaning of another word or sentence part. Most modifiers either add to or change the meaning of the key idea. Usually they answer such questions about the subject or predicate as *what, where, which, when, how,* or *why.* For example:

EXAMPLES

                  where   when

<u>Sam</u> <u>drove</u> his car to Toronto last week.

    when   how   which

Last night <u>I</u> <u>read</u> with interest a magazine article on sailing.

As you read a sentence, be sure to notice how the details change, limit, or add to the meaning of the key idea. Decide, for each of the following examples, how the underlined portion affects the meaning of the key idea.

EXAMPLES

Maria took her dog to the pond <u>yesterday</u>.

Recently, I selected <u>with great care</u> a wedding gift for my sister.

The older Cadillac <u>with the convertible top</u> belongs to my husband.

In the first example, the underlined detail explains *when* Maria took her dog to the pond. In the second example, the underlined words tell *how* the gift was selected. In the last example, the underlined phrase indicates *which* Cadillac.

Exercise A–4

Directions: After reading each of the following sentences, circle the subject and predicate and decide what the underlined words tell about the key idea. Write which, when, where, how, *or* why *in the space provided.*

1. You can relieve tension through exercise. _____ how _____

2. Many students in computer science courses can use the computer terminals only late at night. _____ which _____

3. Many shoppers clip coupons to reduce their grocery bills. _____ why _____

4. After class I am going to talk to my instructor. _____ when _____

5. The world's oil supply is concentrated in only a few places around the globe. _____ where _____

Step 5: Expressing the Ideas in Your Own Words

The best way to be sure you have understood an author's idea is to express it in your own words. Putting an author's thoughts into your own words is called **paraphrasing**. Paraphrasing can help you sort out what is important in a sentence, and it can also help you remember what you read. Here are some tips for paraphrasing.

1. Use your own words, not the author's wording. Pretend you are telling a friend what a sentence means.

2. Use synonyms. A **synonym** is a word that has the same general meaning as another word. The following pairs of words are synonyms:

   ruin—destroy   rich—affluent
   rough—harsh   repeat—reiterate

Now, look at the following sentence from the U.S. Constitution:

EXAMPLE

The Congress shall have power to regulate commerce with foreign nations, and among the several States and with the Indian tribes.

The sentence below paraphrases the original by substituting the underlined synonyms.

EXAMPLE   Congress is <u>allowed</u> to <u>control trade</u> with foreign <u>countries</u>, among states, and with Indian tribes.

When selecting synonyms use the following guidelines.

  3. Choose words close in meaning to the original.

EXAMPLE   Prehistoric people worshipped *animate* objects.

The words *living, alive,* and *vital* are synonyms for *animate,* but in the previous sentence, *living* is closest in meaning to *animate.*

  4. Split lengthy, complicated sentences into two or more shorter sentences.

EXAMPLES   **Lengthy Sentence**
Fads—temporary, highly imitated outbreaks of unconventional behavior—are particularly common in popular music, where the desire to be "different" continually fosters the emergence of new looks and sounds.

Split into Two Sentences
Fads are occurrences of nontraditional behavior. They are especially common in popular music because the need to set oneself apart from others encourages the development of new looks and sounds.

Exercise A–5   *Directions: Using the procedures suggested in this section, paraphrase each of the following sentences.* Answers may vary.

  1. There has been an increase in female sports participation since the early 1970s.

  Female participation in sports has increased since the 1970s.

  2. A distinction still exists between what are traditionally considered to be male and female sports.

  There is a difference between what are typically thought to be male and female sports.

  3. The right of citizens of the United States, who are 18 years of age or older, to vote shall not be denied or abridged by the United States or any state on account of age. (Amendment XXIV to the U.S. Constitution)

  The United States cannot deny the right to vote to anyone who is at least 18 years old.

4. In armed robberies, potential violence—violence that is rarely carried out—enables the robber to achieve his or her material goal, usually money.

   Potential violence is rarely carried out in armed robberies. However, it is this potential violence that allows the robber to attain his/her goal—generally money.

5. In trying to identify the causes of problem drinking, some researchers have stressed the role of genetic factors, while others have viewed it as an inability to adjust to the stress of life.

   According to some researchers, the cause of problem drinking lies in the part played by genetics. Other researchers perceive the cause of problem drinking as an inability to cope with stress.

Using Your Dictionary: A Review

The first step in using your dictionary is to become familiar with the kinds of information it provides. In the following sample entry, each kind of information is marked:

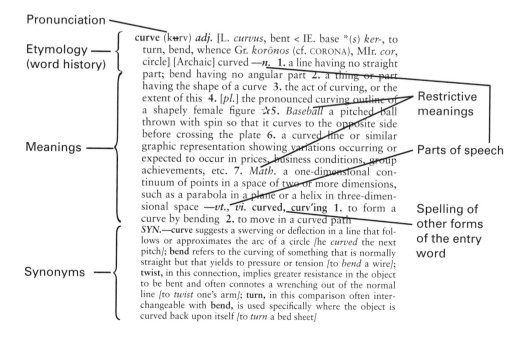

You can see that a dictionary entry provides much more than the definition of a word. Information about the word's pronunciation, part of speech, history, and special uses can also be found.

Exercise B-1

Directions: *Use the sample dictionary entry to complete the following exercises. Write your answer in the space provided.* Answers may vary.

1. Find three meanings for *curve* and write a sentence using each.

   a thing or part having the shape of a curve; a line having no straight part; the act of curving

   _____

   _____

   _____

2. Explain what *curve* means when used in baseball.

   a pitched ball thrown with a spin

3. Explain how the meaning of *curve* differs from the meaning of the word *bend*.

   Bend refers to twisting something that is normally straight.

Exercise B-2

Directions: *Find each of the following words in your dictionary. In the space provided, list all the different parts of speech it can be.*

1. that pronoun, adjective, adverb, conjunction

2. except preposition, conjunction, verb, noun

3. clear adjective, adverb, verb, noun/answers may vary

4. fancy noun, adjective, verb, interjection

5. record noun, verb, adjective

The dictionary provides a great deal of information about each word. The following is a brief review of the parts of a dictionary entry most often found confusing.

Abbreviations

All dictionaries provide a key to abbreviations used in the entry itself as well as some commonly used in other printed material. Most often this key appears on the inside front cover or on the first few pages of the dictionary.

Exercise B–3	*Directions: Find the meaning of each of the following symbols and abbreviations in a dictionary. You may need to consult a list of abbreviations at the front or back of your dictionary. Write your answer in the space provided.*

Answers will vary.

1. v.t. <u>transitive verb</u>

2. < <u>less than</u>

3. c. <u>circa; about; around the time of</u>

4. Obs. <u>obscure; obsolete</u>

5. Fr. <u>French; France</u>

6. pl. <u>plural</u>

Word Pronunciation

After each word entry, the pronunciation of the word is given in parentheses.

EXAMPLES

helmet (hĕl′mĭt)   connection (kə-nek′shən)

apologize (ə-pŏl′ə-jīz)   orchestra (ôr′kĭ-strə)

This part of the entry shows how to pronounce a word by spelling it the way it sounds. Different symbols are used to indicate certain sounds. Until you become familiar with this symbol system, you will need to refer to the pronunciation key. Most dictionaries include a pronunciation key at the bottom of every or every other page. Here is a sample key from the *American Heritage Dictionary*:

ă pat/ā pay/â care/ä father/b bib/ch church/d deed/ĕ pet/ē be/f fife/g gag/h hat/hw which/ĭ pit/i pie/îr pier/j judge/k kick/l lid, needle/m mum/n no, sudden/ng thing/ŏ not/ō toe/ô paw, for/oi noise/ou out/o͝o took/o͞o boot/p pop/r roar/s sauce/sh ship, dish/t tight/th thin, path/*th* this, bathe/ŭ cut/ûr urge/v valve/w with/y yes/z zebra, size/zh vision/ə about, item, edible, gallop, circus/

The key shows the sound the symbol stands for in a word you already know how to pronounce. For example, suppose you are trying to pronounce the word *helix* (hē′lĭks). The key shows that the letter *e* in the first part of the word sounds the same as the *e* in the word *be*. The *i* in *helix* is pronounced the same way as the *i* in *pit*. To pronounce a word correctly, you must also accent (or put stress on) the appropriate part of the word. In a dictionary respelling, an accent mark (′) usually follows the syllable, or part of the word, that is stressed most heavily.

EXAMPLES

audience	ō′de- əns
football	fŏŏt′bôl
literacy	lĭt′ər-ə-sē
juror	jŏŏr′ər
immediate	ĭ-mē′dē-ĭt

Some words have two accents—a primary stress and a secondary stress. The primary one is stressed more heavily and is printed in darker type than the secondary accent.

EXAMPLES

interstate	in′ter-sta-t′
homicide	hôm′i-sīd′

Try to pronounce each of the following dictionary respellings, using the pronunciation key:

dĭ-vûr′s-fī′ **[diversify]**   bŏŏsh′əl **[bushel]**

chăl′ənj **[challenge]**   bär′bĭ-kyŏŏ′ **[barbecue]**

Exercise B–4

Directions: Use the pronunciation key on previous page to sound out each of the following words. Write the word, spelled correctly, in the space provided.

1. kə-mĭt′ **commit** _____

2. kăp′chər **capture** _____

3. bə-röm′ĭ-tər **barometer** _____

4. skĕj′ŏŏl **schedule** _____

5. i-den′te-fĭ-kā′shən **identification** _____

6. ĭn-dĭf′ər-əns **indifference** _____

7. lûr′nĭd **learned** _____

8. lĭk′wĭd **liquid** _____

9. nŏŏ′səns **nuisance** _____

10. fär′mə-sē **pharmacy** _____

Etymology

Many dictionaries include information on each word's **etymology**—its origin and development. A word's etymology is its history, traced back as far as possible to its earliest use, often in another language. The sample dictionary entry on page 325 shows that the word "curve" was derived from the Latin word *curvus* and the Greek word *koronos*.

Exercise B–5

Directions: Find the origin of each of the following words in a dictionary. Write your answer in the space provided. **Answers will vary.**

1. ginger **from Middle English "gingivere," Old English "gingifer," Old French "gingivre," Medieval Latin "gingiver," Latin "zinziberi," Greek "ziggiberis," Prakit "singabera," and Sanskrit "srngaveram"**

2. tint **from Latin "tinctus" and Italian "tinto"**

3. calculate **from Latin "calculare" and Greek "khalix"**

4. fantastic **from Middle English "fantastik," Old French "fantastique," Latin "fantasticus," and Greek "phantastikos"**

5. authentic **from Middle English "autentik," Old French "autentique," Latin "authenticus," and Greek "authentikos"**

Source: American Heritage Dictionary

Restrictive Meanings

Many dictionaries include restrictive meanings of words. These are definitions that apply only when the word is being used with respect to a specific topic or field of study. The sample entry on page 325 gives two restrictive meanings for the word "curve"—one for baseball and another for math.

Exercise B–6

Directions: Locate the following words in a dictionary and find the meaning that applies to the field of study given in parentheses after each word. Write the definitions in the space provided.

1. trust (law) **a legal title to property held by one party for the benefit of another**

2. induction (logic) <u>reasoning from the particular to the general</u>

3. compound (chemistry) <u>a distinct substance composed of the atoms or ions of two</u>
<u>or more elements in definite proportions</u>

4. primary (government) <u>a preliminary election in which the registered voters</u>
<u>of a political party nominate candidates for office</u>

5. journal (accounting) <u>a book of original entry in a double-entry system, indicating</u>
<u>all transactions and the accounts in which they belong</u>

Multiple Meanings

Most words have more than one meaning. When you look up the meaning of a new word, you must choose the meaning that fits the way the word is used in the sentence context. The following sample entry for the word *green* contains many meanings for the word.

MEANINGS
GROUPED BY
PARTS OF SPEECH

11 Adjectives

8 Nouns

1 Verb

green (grēn) *adj.* [ME. *grene* < OE., akin to G. *grün*, Du. *groen*: for IE. base see GRASS] **1.** of the color that is characteristic of growing grass **2.** overspread with or characterized by green plants or foliage [a *green* field] **3.** keeping the green grass of summer; snowless; a mild [a *green* December] **4.** sickly or bilious, as from illness, fear, etc. **5.** *a)* flourishing; active [to keep someone's memory *green*] *b)* of the time of one's youth [the *green* years] **6.** not mature; unripe [*green* bananas] **7.** not trained; inexperienced **8.** easily led or deceived; simple; naive **9.** not dried, seasoned, or cured; unprocessed [*green* lumber] **10.** fresh; new **11.** [cf. GREEN-EYED] [Colloq.] jealous —*n.* **1.** the color of growing grass; any color between blue and yellow in the spectrum: green can be produced by blending blue and yellow pigments **2.** any green pigment or dye **3.** anything colored green, as clothing **4.** [*pl.*] green leaves, branches, sprigs, etc., used for ornamentation **5.** [*pl.*] green leafy plants or vegetables eaten cooked or raw, as spinach, turnip tops, lettuce, etc. **6.** an area of smooth turf set aside for special purposes [a village *green*, a bowling *green*] ☆**7.** [Slang] money, esp. paper money: chiefly in **long green, folding green 8.** *Golf a)* the plot of carefully tended turf immediately surrounding each of the holes to facilitate putting *b)* an entire golf course —*vt., vi.* to make or become green — **green with envy** very envious — **green'ish** *adj.* — **green'ly** *adv.* — **green'ness** *n.*

MANY
DIFFERENT
MEANINGS

Unripe fruit

Inexperienced
person

Type of
vegetable

Part of golf
course

Source: American Heritage Dictionary

The meanings are grouped by part of speech and are numbered consecutively in each group. Generally, the most common meanings of the word are listed first, with more specialized, less common meanings appearing toward the end of the entry. Now find the meaning that fits the use of the word *green* in the following sentence.

EXAMPLE   The local veterans' organization held its annual fund-raising picnic on the village green.

In this sentence, *green* refers to "an area of grass used for special purposes." Since this is a specialized meaning of the word, it appears toward the end of the entry.

Here are a few suggestions for choosing the correct meaning from among those listed in an entry:

1. **If you are familiar with the parts of speech, try to use these to locate the correct meaning.** For instance, if you are looking up the meaning of a word that names a person, place, or thing you can save time by reading only those entries given after *n.* (noun).

2. **For most types of college reading, you can skip definitions that give slang and colloquial (abbreviated colloq.) meanings.** Colloquial meanings refer to informal or spoken language.

3. **If you are not sure of the part of speech, read each meaning until you find a definition that seems correct.** Skip over restrictive meanings that are inappropriate.

4. **Test your choice by substituting the meaning in the sentence with which you are working.** Substitute the definition for the word and see whether it makes sense in the context (see Chapter 2).

Suppose you are looking up the word *oblique* to find its meaning in the following sentence:

My sister's **oblique** answers to my questions made me suspicious.

Oblique is used in the above sentence as an adjective. Looking at the entries listed after *adj.* (adjective), you can skip over the definition under the heading *Geometry*, as it wouldn't apply here: Definition 2 (*indirect, evasive*) best fits the way *oblique* is used in the sentence.

o•blique (ō-blēk′, ə; *Military* ō-blīk′, ə) *adj. Abbr.* obl. **1. a.** Having a slanting or sloping direction, course, or position; inclined. **b.** *Geometry.* Designating lines or planes that are neither parallel nor perpendicular. **2.** Indirect or evasive in execution, meaning, or expression; not straightforward. **3.** Devious, misleading, or dishonest; *oblique answers*. **4.** Not direct in descent; collateral.

5. *Botany.* Having sides of unequal length or form: *an oblique leaf.*
6. *Grammar.* Designating any noun case except the nominative or the vocative.
7. *Rhetoric.* **Indirect** (*see*).—*n.* **1.** An oblique thing, such as a line, direction, or muscle. **2.** *Nautical.* The act of changing course by less than 90 degrees.—*adv.* *Military.* At an angle of 45 degrees: *Right oblique, march!* [Middle English *oblike,* from *Latin obliquus.*]—**o•blique′ly** *adv.*—**o•blique′ness** *n.*

Exercise B-7

Directions: *The following words have two or more meanings. Look them up in your dictionary and write two sentences with different meanings for each word.* **Answers may vary.**

1. culture She is a woman of culture who values music, literature, and art.

   My uncle is very involved with the culture of roses.

2. perch The parrot spent most of its day on its perch.

   The small cabin was perched high in the mountains.

3. surge The small boat was capsized by the sudden surge.

   The music surged through the auditorium.

4. apron The blacksmith wore a leather apron.

   Park your car on the apron beside the garage.

5. irregular Your behavior is highly irregular.

   New England's coastline is an irregular one.

Exercise B-8

Directions: *Use a dictionary to help you find an appropriate meaning for the boldfaced word in each of the following sentences. Insert your answer in the space provided.*

1. The last contestant did not have a **ghost** of a chance.

   slight trace

2. The race car driver won the first **heat.**

   a round in a race

3. The police took all possible **measures** to protect the witness.

   courses of action; procedures

4. The orchestra played the first **movement** of the symphony.

   principal division within a musical symphony

5. The plane stalled on the **apron.**

    hard-surfaced area in front of an airplane hangar

Spelling

Every dictionary entry gives the correct spelling of a word. It also shows how the spelling changes when a word is made plural or endings (suffixes— see Chapter 3) are added, as in the following examples.

EXAMPLES

Word	Word + Ending
budget	budgetary
	budgeter
exhibit	exhibitor
	exhibition
fancy	fancily
	fanciness
	fancier

Entries may also include alternative spellings of words when there are two acceptable ways to spell the word. If you see the word *also* or *or* following the entry word, you will know that either is acceptable. Usually, the first spelling is the preferred one.

EXAMPLES   medieval *also* mediaeval

archaeology *or* archeology

Each entry shows how the word is divided into syllables, so you know how to hyphenate a word when it appears at the end of a line of print (hyphens are placed only between syllables).

EXAMPLE   liv-a-ble   mil-li-me-ter   ob-li-ga-tion

For verbs, each entry contains the verb's principal parts: past tense, past participle, present participle (if different from the past), and third person singular present tense.

EXAMPLES   **go**   went, gone, going, goes

feed   fed, feeding, feeds

<table>
<tr>
<td>

Exercise B-9

</td>
<td>

Directions: *Use a dictionary to answer the following questions. Write your answers in the space provided.*

</td>
</tr>
</table>

1. What is the plural form of *crisis?* <u>crises</u>

2. What is the alternative spelling of *judgment?* <u>judgement</u>

3. If you had to hyphenate *surprise* at the end of a line, where would you divide it? <u>sur-prise</u>

4. What is the past form of *burst?* <u>burst</u>

5. What is the adverb form of *criminal?* <u>criminally</u>

Usage Notes

Some collegiate dictionaries contain a usage note or synonym section of the definition for words that are close in meaning to others. For example, a usage note for the word *indifferent* may explain how it differs in meaning from *unconcerned, detached,* and *uninterested.*

<table>
<tr>
<td>

Exercise B-10

</td>
<td>

Directions: *Use a dictionary to explain the differences in meaning between the following pairs of words. If your dictionary does not list usage notes, then look up each word separately. Write your explanations in the space provided.*

</td>
</tr>
</table>

1. petite, diminutive <u>Diminutive means unusually small. Petite often applies to a woman's figure and means small and trim.</u>

2. careless, thoughtless <u>Careless means inattentive or unconcerned, and it can imply negligence. Thoughtless suggests a lack of consideration for others.</u>

3. odor, aroma <u>Odor is a neutral word meaning "smell." Aroma refers to a pleasant odor, often a spicy one.</u>

4. grin, smirk <u>A grin is a broad smile exposing the teeth and a natural expression of happiness. A smirk is an affected, bold smile expressing derision, smugness, or conceit.</u>

5. hurt, damage <u>Hurt refers to physical or mental distress or lessening the worth of something. Damage refers to an injury to one's reputation or status or that decreases the value of property.</u>

Idioms

An idiom is a phrase that has a meaning other than what the common meanings of the words in the phrase mean. For example, the phrase "wipe the slate clean" is not about slates. It means "to start over." Most idiomatic expressions are not used in academic writing because they are considered trite or overused.

Exercise B-11

Directions: Use a dictionary to help you explain the meanings of the following underlined idiomatic expressions. Write your explanation in the space provided.

1. One thousand dollars is nothing to <u>sneeze at</u>.

   look down upon; reject; make light of

2. The home team <u>kicked off</u> the season with an easy win.

   started; began

3. I intend to <u>turn over a new leaf</u> and work harder next semester.

   start fresh; improve; make a change for the better

4. The lake is two miles from here <u>as the crow flies</u>. (Hint: look under entry for "crow".)

   on a straight line; by the shortest route

5. The owner's incompetent nephew was <u>kicked upstairs</u> rather than fired.

   promoted to a better position that has less power; promoted to a higher but less desirable position

Other Aids

Many dictionaries (especially hardback editions) also contain numerous useful lists and tables. These are usually printed at the end of the dictionary. Frequently included are tables of weights and measures and of periodic elements in chemistry, biographical listings for famous people, a pronouncing gazetteer (a geographical dictionary), and lists of standard abbreviations, colleges, and signs and symbols.

Test-Taking Strategies: A Review

Taking exams demands sharp thinking and reasoning skills. This appendix is intended to show you how to approach all types of exams with an advantage and how to apply thinking and reasoning skills to objective exams.

Starting with an Advantage

One key to success on any type of examination is to approach it in a confident, organized, and systematic manner.

Bring the Necessary Materials

When going to any examination, be prepared to take along any materials you might be asked or allowed to use. Be sure you have a watch and an extra pen, and take several number 2 pencils in case you must make a drawing or diagram or fill in an electronically scored answer sheet. Take paper—you may need it for computing figures or writing essay answers. Take along anything you have been allowed to use throughout the semester, such as a pocket calculator, conversion chart, or dictionary. If you are not sure whether you may use them, ask the instructor.

Time Your Arrival Carefully

Arrive at the examination room a few minutes early, in time to get a seat and get organized before the instructor arrives. If you are late, you may miss instructions and feel rushed as you begin the exam. If you arrive too early (more than 15 minutes ahead of time), you risk anxiety induced by panic-stricken students who are questioning each other, trading last-minute memory tricks, and worrying about how difficult the exam will be.

Sit in the Front of the Room

The most practical place to sit in an exam is in the front. There, you often receive the test first and get a head start. Also, it is easier to concentrate and avoid distractions.

Listen Carefully to Your Instructor's Directions

Your instructor may give specific instructions that are not included in the exam's written directions. If these are detailed instructions jot them down on your exam paper or on scrap paper.

Preview the Exam

Before you start to answer any of the questions, quickly page through the exam, noticing the directions, the length, the type of questions, the general topics covered, the number of points the questions are worth, and where to put your answers. Previewing provides an overview of the whole exam and helps to reduce anxiety.

Plan Your Time

After previewing, you will know the numbers and types of questions included. The next step is to estimate how much time you should spend on each part of the exam, using the point distribution as your guide.

Avoid Reading Too Much into the Question

Most instructors word their questions so that what is expected is clear. Do not anticipate hidden meanings or trick questions.

General Suggestions for Objective Exams

Before we examine particular types of objective exams, here are a few general suggestions to follow in approaching all types of objective exams.

- **Read the directions.** Before answering any questions, read the directions. Often, an instructor will want the correct answer marked in a particular way (for example, underlined rather than circled). The directions may contain crucial information that you must be aware of in order to answer the questions correctly. In the items below, if you did not read the directions and assumed the test questions were of the usual type, you could lose a considerable number of points.

True/False Directions: Read each statement. If the statement is true, mark a T in the blank to the left of the item. If the statement is false, add and/or subtract words that will make the statement correct.

Multiple-Choice Directions: Circle all the choices that correctly complete the statement.

- **Leave nothing blank.** Before turning in your exam, check through it to be sure you have answered every question. If you have no idea about the correct answer to a question, guess. You might be right!

  Students frequently turn in tests with some items unanswered because they leave difficult questions blank, planning to return to them later. Then, in the rush to finish, they forget them. To avoid this problem, when you are uncertain, choose what looks like the best answer, and mark the question number with an X or checkmark so you can return to it; then, if you have time at the end of the exam, give it further thought. If you run out of time, you will have an answer marked.

- **Look for clues.** If you encounter a difficult question, choose what seems to be the best answer, mark the question with an X or checkmark so that you can return to it, and keep the item in mind as you go through the rest of the exam. Sometimes you will see some piece of information later in the exam that reminds you of a fact or idea.

- **Write your answers clearly.** If your instructor cannot be sure of the answer you wrote, he or she will mark it wrong. Answer with block letters on multiple-choice and matching tests to avoid confusion. Write or print responses to fill-in-the-blank tests legibly. Be sure that your answers to short-answer questions are not only written neatly but are to the point and express complete thoughts.

- **Check over your answers before you turn in the exam.** As mentioned earlier, reserve some time at the end of the exam for reviewing your answers. Check to be sure you didn't use the same matching-test answer twice. Be sure your multiple-choice answers are written in the correct blanks or marked in the correct place on the answer grid. One answer marked out of sequence could lead to a series of answers being in error. If there is a separate answer sheet, verify that your fill-in-the-blanks and short answers correspond with the correct question numbers.

- **Don't change answers without a good reason.** When reviewing your answers during an exam, don't make a change unless you have a reason for doing so. Very often your first impressions are correct. If clues from a later test item prompt your recall of information for a previous item, change your answer.

Techniques for Taking Multiple-Choice Tests

Multiple choice is the most frequently used type of exam and often the most difficult to answer. The following suggestions should improve your success in taking this type of exam.

- **Begin by reading each question as if it is a fill-in-the-blank or short-answer question.** Cover up the choices and try to answer the question from your knowledge of the subject. In this way, you will avoid confusion that might arise from complicated choices. After you have formed your answer, compare it to each of the choices, and select the one that comes closest to your answer.

- **Read all choices first, considering each.** Do not stop with second or third choices, even if you are certain that you have found the correct answer. Remember, on most multiple-choice tests your job is to pick the *best* answer, and the last choice may be a better answer than any of the first three.

- **Read combination choices.** Some multiple-choice tests include choices that are combinations of previously listed choices, as in the following item:

    The mesodermal tissue layer contains cells that will become
    a. skin, sensory organs, and nervous systems.
    b. skin, sensory organs, and blood vessels.
    c. bones and muscle.
    d. stomach, liver, and pancreas.
    e. a and c.
    f. b, c, and d.
    g. a, c, and d.

The addition of choices that are combinations of the previous choices tends to make items even more confusing. Treat each choice, when combined with the stem, as a true or false statement. As you consider each choice, mark it true or false. If you find more than one true statement, then select the choice that contains the letters of all the true statements you identified.

- **Use logic and common sense.** Even if you are unfamiliar with the subject matter, you can sometimes reason out the correct answer. The following test item is taken from a history exam on Japanese-American relations after World War II:

  > Prejudice and discrimination are
  >
  > a. harmful to our society because they waste our economic, political, and social resources.
  > b. helpful because they ensure us against attack from within.
  > c. harmful because they create negative images of the United States in foreign countries.
  > d. helpful because they keep the majority pure and united against minorities.

Through logic and common sense, it is possible to eliminate choices *b* and *d*. Prejudice and discrimination are seldom, if ever, regarded as positive, desirable, or helpful since they are inconsistent with democratic ideals. Having narrowed your answer to two choices, *a* or *c*, you can see that choice *a* offers a stronger, more substantial reason why prejudice and discrimination are harmful. The attitude of other countries toward the United States is not as serious as a waste of economic, political, and social resources.

- **Examine closely items that are very similar.** Often, when two similar choices are presented, one is likely to be correct. Carefully compare the two choices. First, try to express each in your own words, and then analyze how they differ. Often, this process will enable you to recognize the right answer.

- **Pay special attention to the level of qualifying words.** As noted for true/false tests, qualifying words are important. Since many statements, ideas, principles, and rules have exceptions, be careful in selecting items that contain such extreme qualifying words as *best, always, all, no, never, none, entirely,* and *completely,* all of which suggest that a condition exists without exception. Items containing words that provide for some level of exception, or qualification, are more likely to be correct. Here are a few examples of such words: *often, usually, less, seldom, few, more,* and *most.* Likewise, numerical answers that are about in the middle of a range of choices are probably correct. In the following example, notice the use of the italicized qualifying words:

  > In most societies
  >
  > a. values are *highly* consistent.
  > b. people *often* believe and act on values that are contradictory.

    c. *all* legitimate organizations support values of the majority.

    d. values of equality *never* exist alongside prejudice and discrimination.

In this question, items *c* and *d* contain the words *all* and *never,* suggesting that those statements are true without exception. Thus, if you did not know the answer to this question based on content, you could eliminate items *c* and *d* on the basis of the level of qualifiers.

- **Some multiple-choice questions require application of knowledge or information.** You may be asked to analyze a hypothetical situation or to use what you have learned to solve a problem. Here is an example taken from a psychology test:

> Carrie is uncomfortable in her new home in New Orleans. When she gets dressed up and leaves her home and goes to the supermarket to buy the week's groceries, she gets nervous and upset and thinks that something is going to happen to her. She feels the same way when walking her four-year-old son Jason in the park or playground.

> Carrie is suffering from
> a. shyness.
> b. a phobia.
> c. a personality disorder.
> d. hypertension.

In answering questions of this type, start by crossing out unnecessary information that can distract you. In the preceeding example, distracting information includes the woman's name, her son's name, where she lives, why she goes to the store, and so forth.

- **Jot down the essence.** If a question concerns steps in a process or order of events or any other information that is easily confused, ignore the choices and use the margin or scrap paper to jot down the information as you can recall it. Then select the choice that matches what you wrote.

- **Avoid the unfamiliar.** Avoid choosing answers that are unfamiliar or that you do not understand. A choice that looks complicated or uses difficult words is not necessarily correct. If you have studied carefully, a choice that is unfamiliar to you or contains unfamiliar terminology is probably incorrect.

- **Eliminate choices that are obviously false.** Treat each choice in a troublesome question like you would a statement on a true-false test.

- **Choose the longest or most inclusive answers.** As a last resort, when you do not know the answer and are unable to eliminate any of the choices as wrong, guess by picking the one that seems most complete and contains the most information. This is a good choice because instructors are usually careful to make the correct answer complete. Thus, the answer often becomes long or detailed.

- **Be careful of "all of the above" and "none of the above" questions.** This type of question can be particularly difficult, since it usually involves five choices and can lead to confusion. To make it easier, first try to eliminate "all of the above." If even *one* choice is incorrect "all of the above" will be incorrect. If you think that at least *one* of the choices is correct, you can eliminate "none of the above." If you think two choices are correct but you are unsure of the third one, you should choose "all of the above." When questions such as these occur only a few times in a test, "all" or "none" is probably the correct choice.

- **Make educated guesses.** In most instances, you can eliminate one or more of the choices as obviously wrong. Even if you can eliminate only one choice, you have increased your odds on a four-choice item from one in four to one in three. If you can eliminate two choices, you have increased your odds to one in two, or 50 percent. Don't hesitate to play the odds and make a guess—you may gain points.

Exercise C-1

Directions: The following multiple-choice items appeared on an exam in psychology. Study each item and use your reasoning skills to eliminate items that seem incorrect. Then, making an educated guess, circle the letter of the choice that best completes the statement.

1. Modern psychological researchers maintain that the mind as well as behavior can be scientifically examined primarily by

   a. observing behavior and making inferences about mental functioning.

   b. observing mental activity and making inferences about behavior.

   c. making inferences about behavior.

   d. direct observation of behavior.

2. Jane Goodall has studied the behavior of chimpanzees in their own habitat. She exemplifies a school of psychology that is concerned with

   a. theories.

   b. mental processes.

   c. the individual's potential for growth.

   d. naturalistic behavior.

3. If a psychologist were personally to witness the effects of a tornado upon the residents of a small town, what technique would he or she be using?

   a. experimentation   (c.) observation

   b. correlational research   d. none of the above

4. A case study is a(n)

   a. observation of an event.

   b. comparison of similar events.

   c. study of changes and their effects.

   (d.) intense investigation of a particular occurrence.

5. Events that we are aware of at a given time make up the

   a. unconscious.   (c.) consciousness.

   b. subconscious.   d. triconscious.

6. Unlocking a combination padlock

   a. always involves language skills.

   (b.) always involves motor skills.

   c. seldom involves concentration skills.

   d. seldom involves memory skills.

Achieving Success with Standardized Tests

At various times in college, you may be required to take standardized tests. These are commercially prepared; they are usually lengthy, timed tests that are used nationally or statewide to measure specific skills and abilities. Your score on these tests compares your performance to that of large numbers of other students throughout the country or state.

Preparing for the Test

Use the following suggestions for preparing for standardized tests:

- **Find out as much as possible about the test.** Meet with your advisor or check the career center to obtain brochures and application forms. Find out about its general content, length, and timing. Determine its format and the scoring procedures used. Know when and where the test is given.

- **Take a review course.** Find out if your college offers a preparatory workshop to help you prepare for the test.

- **Obtain a review book.** Review books are available to help you prepare for many standardized tests. Purchase a review book at your college bookstore, a large off-campus bookstore, or through the Internet. If you cannot purchase a review book, you may be able to borrow one from your college library or public library.
- **Begin your review early.** Start to study well ahead of the exam, so that you can fit the necessary review time into your already hectic schedule.
- **Start with a quick overview of the test.** Most review books contain a section that explains the type of questions on the test and offers test-taking strategies. If a brief review of the subject matter is offered, read through it.
- **Take practice tests.** To become most comfortable with the test, take numerous timed practice tests and score them. Make your practice tests as much like the actual test as possible. Work at a well-lighted desk or table in a quiet setting and time yourself carefully.
- **Review your answers.** Thoroughly review the questions you answered incorrectly. Read through the explanations given in your review book and try to see why the keyed answer is best.
- **Keep track of your scores.** Keep a record of both your total score and sub-test scores on practice tests. This will help you judge your progress and can give you insights into areas of weakness that require extra review.

Taking the Test

Use the following suggestions to get as many points as possible on a standardized test:

- **Arrive in the exam room prepared.** Get to the testing site early so you can choose a good seat and become comfortable with the surroundings. Wear a watch, bring two sharpened pencils with erasers (in case one breaks), and two pens (in case one runs out).
- **Get organized before the timing begins.** Line up your answer sheet and test booklet so you can move between them rapidly without losing your place. Carefully fill out your answer sheet.
- **Skim the instructions.** This can save you valuable time. If you have prepared yourself properly, you should be very familiar with the format of the test and the instructions. A quick reading of the directions will be all that is necessary to assure yourself that they have not changed.
- **Work quickly and steadily.** Most standardized tests are timed, so the pace you work at is a critical factor. You need to work at a fairly rapid rate, but not so fast as to make careless errors.

- **Don't plan on finishing the test.** Many of these tests are designed so that most people do not finish. So work on the easier questions first and make a mark next to the harder ones, so you can return to them if time permits.

- **Don't expect to get everything right.** Unlike classroom tests or exams, you are not expected to get most of the answers correct.

- **Find out if there is a penalty for guessing.** If there is none, then use the last 20 or 30 seconds to randomly fill in an answer for each item that you have not had time to do. The odds are that you will get one out of every five correct. If there is a guessing penalty, guess only if you can narrow the answer down to two choices. Otherwise, leave it blank.

- **Check your answer sheet periodically.** If you have skipped a question, make sure that later answers match their questions. If the test has several parts, check to see that you are marking answers in the correct answer grid.

- **Don't just stop if you finish early.** If you have time left over, use it. Redo marked questions you skipped. Review as many answers as you can. Check over your answer sheet for stray marks and darken your answer marks.

Additional Reading Selections

NAME _____   SECTION _____

DATE _____   SCORE _____

COMING INTO MY OWN
Ben Carson, M.D.

Ben Carson is a famous pediatric neurosurgeon. Read this selection to learn how he overcomes racial prejudice in the medical profession.

> ## Vocabulary Preview
>
> These are some of the difficult words in this essay. The definitions here will help you if you can't figure out the meanings from the sentence context or word parts.
>
> **orderly** (par. 1) an attendant who does routine, nonmedical work in a hospital
>
> **intern** (par. 2) a recent graduate of a medical school undergoing supervised practical training
>
> **respiratory** (par. 10) related to breathing
>
> **therapy** (par. 10) treatment of illness or disability
>
> **entrepreneurs** (par. 19) people who organize and take risks in operating a business

1   The nurse looked at me with disinterest as I walked toward her station. "Yes?" she asked, pausing with a pencil in her hand. "Who did you come to pick up?" From the tone of her voice I immediately knew that she thought I was an orderly. I was wearing my green scrubs, nothing to indicate I was a doctor.

2   "I didn't come to pick up anyone." I looked at her and smiled, realizing that the only black people she has seen on the floor had been orderlies. Why should she think anything else? "I'm the new intern."

3   "New intern? But you can't—I mean—I didn't mean to—" the nurse stuttered, trying to apologize without sounding prejudiced.

4   "That's OK," I said, letting her off the hook. It was a natural mistake. "I'm new, so why should you know who I am?"

5   The first time I went into the intensive care unit, I was wearing my whites (our monkey suits, as we interns called them), and a nurse signaled me. "You're here for Mr. Jordan?"

6   "No, ma'am, I'm not."

7   "You sure?" she asked as a frown covered her forehead. "He's the only one who's scheduled for respiratory therapy today."

8   By then I had come closer and she could read my name badge and the word *intern* under my name.

9   "Oh, I'm so very sorry," she said, and I could tell she was.

10   Although I didn't say it, I would like to have told her, "It's all right because I realize most people do things based on their past experiences. You've never encountered a black intern before, so you assumed I was the only kind of black male you'd seen wearing whites, a respiratory therapist." I smiled again and went on.

11   It was inevitable that a few white patients didn't want a black doctor and they protested to Dr. Long. One woman said, "I'm sorry, but I do not want a black physician in on my case."

12   Dr. Long had a standard answer, given in a calm but firm voice. "There's the door. You're welcome to walk through it. But if you stay here, Dr. Carson will handle your case."

13   At the time people were making these objections, I didn't know about them. Only much later did Dr. Long tell me as he laughed about the prejudices of some patients. But there was no humor in his voice when he defined his position. He was adamant about his stance, allowing no prejudice because of color or ethnic background.

14   Of course, I knew how some individuals felt. I would have had to be pretty insensitive not to know. The way they behaved, their coldness, even without saying anything, made their feelings clear. Each time, however, I was able to remind myself they were individuals speaking for themselves and not representative of all whites. No matter how strongly a patient felt, as soon as he voiced his objection he learned that Dr. Long would dismiss him on the spot if he said anything more. So far as I know, none of the patients ever left!

15   I honestly felt no great pressures. When I did encounter prejudice, I could hear Mother's voice in the back of my head saying things like, "Some people are ignorant and you have to educate them."

16   The only pressure I felt during my internship, and in the years since, has been a self-imposed obligation to act as a role model for black youngsters. These young folks need to know that the way to escape their often dismal

situations is contained within themselves. They can't expect other people to do it for them. Perhaps I can't do much, but I can provide one living example of someone who made it and who came from what we now call a disadvantaged background. Basically I'm no different than many of them.

17   As I think of black youth, I also want to say I believe that many of our pressing racial problems will be taken care of when we who are among the minorities will stand on our own feet and refuse to look to anybody else to save us from our situations. The culture in which we live stresses looking out for number one. Without adopting such a self-centered value system, we can demand the best of ourselves while we are extending our hands to help others.

18   I see glimmers of hope. For example, I noticed that when the Vietnamese came to the United States they often faced prejudice from everyone—white, black, and Hispanics. But they didn't beg for handouts and often took the lowest jobs offered. Even well-educated individuals didn't mind sweeping floors if it was a paying job.

19   Today many of these same Vietnamese are property owners and entrepreneurs. That's the message I try to get across to the young people. The same opportunities are there, but we can't start out as vice president of the company. Even if we landed such a position, it wouldn't do us any good anyway because we wouldn't know how to do our work. It's better to start where we can fit in and then work our way up.

— ∙ —

CHECKING YOUR COMPREHENSION

Directions: Select the letter of the choice that best answers each of the following statements and write it in the space provided. Record your score on page 408.

____d____   1. This reading demonstrates that
    a. most white patients do not want black doctors.
    b. female nurses are prejudiced against male doctors.
    c. orderlies and respiratory therapists are not treated with respect by other medical professionals.
    d. it is possible to overcome prejudice and a disadvantaged background to become a success.

_____c_____ 2. The writer's purpose in describing the conversations in paragraphs 1–9 was to

    a. expose medical professionals as racists.

    b. defend his own behavior toward nurses

    c. illustrate the prejudice he faced as a black, male intern.

    d. explain the bitterness he feels toward whites in general.

_____b_____ 3. During his internship, the writer dealt with the prejudice of some of his patients by

    a. refusing to treat those patients.

    b. reminding himself that they did not represent the attitudes of all whites.

    c. quitting his internship and becoming a writer.

    d. becoming prejudiced against all whites.

_____d_____ 4. Dr. Long handled the prejudices of some of the white patients by

    a. asking the writer to complete his internship elsewhere.

    b. agreeing to personally treat the patients who objected to a black doctor.

    c. encouraging the writer to find another profession.

    d. informing the patients that they could either leave or be treated by the black intern.

_____a_____ 5. The statement that best expresses the main idea of paragraph 17 is that

    a. people should look to themselves rather than others to improve their situations.

    b. adopting a self-centered value system is the only way to succeed in our culture.

    c. the racial problems in our society are primarily caused by misunderstanding.

    d. extending help to others is not as important as getting ahead.

_____c_____ 6. From the situation described in paragraphs 1–4, the writer suggests

    a. all nurses are disrespectful to orderlies.

    b. all orderlies are black males.

    c. black, male doctors are not typical in the hospital described.

    d. doctors should be required to wear identification.

_c_ 7. From the reference to the writer's mother, you can tell that she

    a. was prejudiced against whites.

    b. thought fighting prejudice was hopeless.

    c. believed that one could change people's attitudes toward blacks.

    d. had never experienced prejudice.

_a_ 8. From paragraphs 18–19 the writer seems to believe that

    a. minorities should help themselves and work to solve their own problems.

    b. immigrants are taking jobs away from blacks.

    c. blacks should be given special treatment because they must face prejudice.

    d. minorities are better off today than they were ten years ago.

_a_ 9. The writer supports his ideas primarily by

    a. describing his personal experience.

    b. reporting statistics.

    c. defining medical terms.

    d. citing facts.

_b_ 10. By stating in paragraph 2 that he looked at the nurse "and smiled," the writer indicates that he

    a. was being sarcastic.

    b. understood the nurse's error and forgave her.

    c. was surprised at being treated that way.

    d. did not understand the situation.

WORDS IN CONTEXT

Directions: Locate each word in the paragraph indicated and reread that paragraph. Then, based on the way the word is used, write a synonym or brief definition in the space provided. You may use a dictionary if necessary.

1. scrubs (par. 1) protective clothing worn by hospital personnel

2. adamant (par. 13) firm, stubborn, unyielding

3. stance (par. 13) position

4. encounter (par. 15) meet

VOCABULARY REVIEW

Directions: Complete each of the following sentences by inserting a word from the Vocabulary Preview on page 348 in the space provided.

1. A person who assists with nonmedical work in a hospital is an
   _____orderly_____.

2. People who organize and take risks for business are called
   _____entrepreneurs_____.

3. An _____intern_____ is a medical doctor who is working in a hospital
   for practical training.

4. After knee surgery, the patient needed several weeks of physical
   _____therapy_____.

5. The elderly patient suffered from pneumonia and related
   _____respiratory_____ problems.

DISCUSSION QUESTIONS

1. Describe situations in which you have experienced or observed some type of prejudice. How did you respond to the situation?

2. This article focuses on racial prejudice. What other types of prejudice exist?

3. Explain why you agree or disagree with the following statement made by Dr. Carson, "The way [for disadvantaged youth] to escape their dismal situation is contained within themselves."

4. Dr. Carson wants to serve as a role model for black youngsters. Are you a role model for anyone? Who has served as a role model for you?

NAME _____ SECTION _____

DATE _____ SCORE _____

LIVING LIFE TO THE FULLEST
Maya Angelou

Are you living life to its fullest? Read this selection to find out. Maya Angelou tells a story that will help you answer this question.

Vocabulary Preview

These are some of the difficult words in this essay. The definitions here will help you if you can't figure out the meanings from the sentence context or word parts.

sinewy (par. 1) lean and muscular

incurred (par. 1) brought on; met with

tautly (par. 2) tightly

meticulous (par. 3) extremely careful

maven (par. 6) expert

camaraderie (par. 14) friendship

founts (par. 14) sources

convivial (par. 14) agreeable; cheerful

scenarios (par. 16) plans; expected events

---

1   Aunt Tee was a Los Angeles member of our extended family. She was seventy-nine when I met her, sinewy, strong, and the color of old lemons. She wore her coarse, straight hair, which was slightly streaked with gray, in a long braided rope across the top of her head. With her high cheekbones, old gold skin, and almond eyes, she looked more like an Indian chief than an old black woman. (Aunt Tee described herself and any favored member of her race as Negroes. *Black* was saved for those who had incurred her disapproval.)

2   She had retired and lived alone in a neat ground-floor apartment. Wax flowers and china figurines sat on elaborately embroidered and heavily starched doilies. Sofas and chairs were tautly upholstered. The only thing at ease in Aunt Tee's apartment was Aunt Tee.

3   I used to visit her often and perch on her uncomfortable sofa just to hear her stories. She was proud that after working thirty years as a maid, she

spent the next thirty years as a live-in housekeeper, carrying the keys to rich houses and keeping meticulous accounts.

4   "Living in lets the white folks know Negroes are as neat and clean as they are, sometimes more so. And it gives the Negro maid a chance to see white folks ain't no smarter than Negroes. Just luckier. Sometimes."

5   Aunt Tee told me that once she was housekeeper for couple in Bel Air, California, lived with them in a fourteen-room ranch house. There was a day maid who cleaned, and a gardener who daily tended the lush gardens. Aunt Tee oversaw the workers. When she had begun the job, she had cooked and served a light breakfast, a good lunch, and a full three- or four-course dinner to her employers and their guests. Aunt Tee said she watched them grow older and leaner. After a few years they stopped entertaining and ate dinner hardly seeing each other at the table. Finally, they sat in a dry silence as they ate evening meals of soft scrambled eggs, melba toast, and weak tea. Aunt Tee said she saw them growing old but didn't see herself aging at all.

6   She became the social maven. She started "keeping company" (her phrase) with a chauffeur down the street. Her best friend and her friend's husband worked in service only a few blocks away.

7   On Saturdays Aunt Tee would cook a pot of pigs' feet, a pot of greens, fry chicken, make potato salad, and bake a banana pudding. Then, that evening, her friends—the chauffeur, the other housekeeper, and her husband—would come to Aunt Tee's commodious live-in quarters. There the four would eat and drink, play records and dance. As the evening wore on, they would settle down to a serious game of bid whist.

8   Naturally, during this revelry jokes were told, fingers snapped, feet were patted, and there was a great deal of laughter.

9   Aunt Tee said that what occurred during every Saturday party startled her and her friends the first time it happened. They had been playing cards, and Aunt Tee, who had just won the bid, held a handful of trumps. She felt a cool breeze on her back and sat upright and turned around. Her employers had cracked her door open and beckoned to her. Aunt Tee, a little peeved, laid down her cards and went to the door. The couple backed away and asked her to come into the hall, and there they both spoke and won Aunt Tee's sympathy forever.

10   "Theresa, we don't mean to disturb you . . ." the man whispered, "but you all seem to be having such a good time . . ."

11   The woman added, "We hear you and your friends laughing every Saturday night, and we'd just like to watch you. We don't want to bother you. We'll be quiet and just watch."

12   The man said, "If you'll just leave your door ajar, your friends don't need to know. We'll never make a sound." Aunt Tee said she saw no harm in agreeing, and she talked it over with her company. They said it was OK with them, but it was sad that the employers owned the gracious house, the swimming pool, three cars, and numberless palm trees, but had no joy. Aunt Tee told me that laughter and relaxation had left the house; she agreed it was sad.

13   That story has stayed with me for nearly thirty years, and when a tale remains fresh in my mind, it almost always contains a lesson which will benefit me.

14   My dears, I draw the picture of the wealthy couple standing in a darkened hallway, peering into a lighted room where black servants were lifting their voices in merriment and camaraderie, and I realize that living well is an art which can be developed. Of course, you will need the basic talents to build upon: They are a love of life and ability to take great pleasure from small offerings, an assurance that the world owes you nothing and that every gift is exactly that, a gift. That people who may differ from you in political stance, sexual persuasion, and racial inheritance can be founts of fun, and if you are lucky, they can become even convivial comrades.

15   Living life as art requires a readiness to forgive. I do not mean that you should suffer fools gladly, but rather remember your own shortcomings, and when you encounter another with flaws, don't be eager to righteously seal yourself away from the offender forever. Take a few breaths and imagine yourself having just committed the action which has set you at odds.

16   Because of the routines we follow, we often forget that life is an ongoing adventure. We leave our homes for work, acting and even believing that we will reach our destinations with no unusual event startling us out of our set expectations. The truth is we know nothing, not where our cars will fail or when our buses will stall, whether our places of employment will be there when we arrive, or whether, in fact, we ourselves will arrive whole and alive at

the end of our journeys. Life is pure adventure, and the sooner we realize that, the quicker we will be able to treat life as art: to bring all our energies to each encounter, to remain flexible enough to notice and admit when what we expected to happen did not happen. We need to remember that we are created creative and can invent new scenarios as frequently as they are needed.

17   Life seems to love the liver of it. Money and power can liberate only if they are used to do so. They can imprison and inhibit more finally than barred windows and iron chains.

━━ ▪ ━━

CHECKING YOUR COMPREHENSION

Directions: Select the letter of the choice that best answers each of the following statements and write it in the space provided. Record your score on page 408.

___c___   1. One main point of the reading is that living well
   a. requires money.
   b. depends on other people.
   c. involves taking pleasure in small things.
   d. depends on one's personality.

___b___   2. Aunt Tee worked for the couple in Bel Air as a
   a. chauffeur.   c. maid.
   b. housekeeper.   d. gardener.

___a___   3. The couple in Bel Air won Aunt Tee's sympathy forever when they
   a. asked if they could watch Aunt Tee and her friends.
   b. allowed Aunt Tee to live with them.
   c. allowed Aunt Tee to use the swimming pool.
   d. employed Aunt Tee for thirty years.

___b___   4. The couple from Bel Air changed over the years when they
   a. became richer.
   b. stopped entertaining and ate dinner in silence.
   c. became ill and needed nursing care.
   d. became more demanding and difficult to work for.

_____a_____ 5. The main idea of paragraph 16 is expressed in which of the following sentences?

    a. first   c. third

    b. second   d. last

_____d_____ 6. Which one of the following is *not* a basic talent for living well?

    a. the ability to love life

    b. awareness that the world owes you nothing

    c. recognition that people different from you can be a source or pleasure

    d. acquiring the financial means to enjoy life

_____a_____ 7. The pattern of organization used in this reading is

    a. chronological order.   c. comparison and contrast.

    b. cause and effect.   d. process.

_____d_____ 8. In paragraph 5 which of the following words or phrases is a transition?

    a. there was   c. once

    b. hardly seeing each other   d. finally

_____c_____ 9. The couple in Bel Air had many possessions, but had no

    a. will power.   c. joy.

    b. direction.   d. grace.

_____a_____ 10. Aunt Tee could best be described as

    a. wise and fun-loving.   c. nonjudgmental.

    b. assertive and focused.   d. opinionated.

WORDS IN CONTEXT

Directions: Locate each word in the paragraph indicated and reread that paragraph. Then, based on the way the word is used, write a synonym or brief definition in the space provided. You may use a dictionary if necessary.

1. revelry (par. 8) _cheerful and noisy party_

2. beckoned (par. 9) _got her attention by gesturing_

3. peering (par. 14) _looking into_

4. stance (par. 14) _position, viewpoint_

VOCABULARY REVIEW

Directions: Match the words in column A with their meanings in column B. Write the letter of your choice in the space provided.

	Column A	Column B
d	1. camaraderie	a. tightly
g	2. meticulous	b. expert
e	3. scenarios	c. sources
f	4. incurred	d. friendship
b	5. maven	e. plans
h	6. convivial	f. brought on; met with
i	7. sinewy	g. extremely careful
a	8. tautly	h. agreeable; cheerful
c	9. founts	i. lean and muscular

DISCUSSION QUESTIONS

1. Describe your "requirements for good living."

2. Choose a favorite relative or friend and explain his or her outlook on life. How does it differ from Aunt Tee's?

3. Maya Angelou says that "life is pure adventure." Do you agree with this? Why?

A GUARD'S FIRST NIGHT ON THE JOB
William Recktenwald

A prison is a separate society with its own set of rules and behaviors. This selection describes one evening in a prison from the viewpoint of a new guard.

> ## Vocabulary Preview
>
> These are some of the difficult words in this essay. The definitions here will help you if you can't figure out the meanings from the sentence context or word parts.
>
> **rookie** (par. 1) beginner or novice
>
> **cursory** (par. 4) hastily done with little attention to detail
>
> **tiers** (par. 5) groups of cells, rooms, or items arranged above or behind each other
>
> **apprehensive** (par. 16) worried, anxious, or concerned
>
> **ruckus** (par. 17) noisy confusion or disturbance
>
> **mace** (par. 22) chemical with the combined effect of tear gas and nerve gas used to stun its victims
>
> **equivalent** (par. 25) equal to

1   When I arrived for my first shift, 3 to 11 P.M., I had not had a minute of training except for a one-hour orientation lecture the previous day. I was a "fish," a rookie guard, and very much out of my depth.

2   A veteran officer welcomed the "fish" and told us: "Remember, these guys don't have anything to do all day, 24 hours a day, but think of ways to make you mad. No matter what happens, don't lose your cool. Don't lose you cool!"

3   I had been assigned to the segregation unit, containing 215 inmates who are the most trouble. It was an assignment nobody wanted.

4   To get there, I passed through seven sets of bars. My uniform was my only ticket through each of them. Even on my first day, I was not asked for any identification, searched, or sent through a metal detector. I could have been carrying weapons, drugs, or any other contraband. I couldn't believe this was

what's meant by a maximum-security institution. In the week I worked at Pontiac, I was subjected to only one check, and that one was cursory.

5   The segregation unit consists of five tiers, or galleries. Each is about 300 feet long and has 44 cells. The walkways are about 3½ feet wide, with the cells on one side and rail and cyclone fencing on the other. As I walked along one gallery, I noticed that my elbows could touch cell bars and fencing at the same time. That made me easy picking for anybody reaching out of a cell.

6   The first thing they told me was that a guard must never go out on a gallery by himself. You've got no weapons with which to defend yourself, not even a radio to summon help. All you've got is the man with whom you're working.

7   My partner that first night was Bill Hill, a soft-spoken six-year veteran who immediately told me to take the cigarettes out of my shirt pocket because the inmates would steal them. Same for my pen, he said—or "They'll grab it and stab you."

8   We were told to serve dinner on the third tier, and Hill quickly tried to fill me in on the facts of prison life. That's when I learned about cookies and the importance they have to the inmates.

9   "They're going to try and grab them, they're going to try to steal them any way they can," he said. "Remember, you only have enough cookies for the gallery, and if you let them get away, you'll have to explain to the guys at the end why there weren't any for them."

10   Hill then checked out the meal, groaning when he saw the drippy ravioli and stewed tomatoes. "We're going to be wearing this," he remarked, before deciding to simply discard the tomatoes. We served nothing to drink. In my first six days at Pontiac, I never saw an inmate served a beverage.

11   Hill instructed me to put on plastic gloves before we served the meal. In view of the trash and waste through which we'd be wheeling the food cart, I thought he was joking. He wasn't.

12   "Some inmates don't like white hands touching their food," he explained.

13   Everything went routinely as we served the first 20 cells, and I wasn't surprised when every inmate asked for extra cookies.

14   Suddenly, a huge arm shot through the bars of one cell and began swinging a metal rod at Hill. As he ducked away, the inmate snared the cookie box.

15   From the other side of the cart, I lunged to grab the cookies—and was grabbed in turn. A powerful hand from the cell behind me was pulling my arm. As I jerked away, objects began crashing about, and a metal can struck me in the back.

16   Until that moment I had been apprehensive. Now I was scared. The food cart virtually trapped me, blocking my retreat.

17   Whirling around, I noticed that mirrors were being held out of every cell so the inmates could watch the ruckus. I didn't realize the mirrors were plastic and became terrified that the inmates would start smashing them to cut me up.

18   The ordinary din of the cell house had turned into a deafening roar. For the length of the tier, arms stretched into the walkway, making grabbing motion. Some of the inmates swung brooms about.

19   "Let's get out of here—now!" Hill barked. Wheeling the food cart between us we made a hasty retreat.

20   Downstairs, we reported what had happened. My heart was thumping, my legs felt weak. Inside the plastic gloves, my hands were soaked with sweat. Yet the attack on us wasn't considered unusual by the other guards, especially in segregation. That was strictly routine, and we didn't even file a report.

21   What was more shocking was to be sent immediately back to the same tier to pass out medication. But as I passed the cells from which we'd been attacked, the men in them simply requested their medicine. It was as if what had happened minutes before was already ancient history. From another cell, however, an inmate began raging at us. "Get my medication," he said. "Get it now, or I'm going to kill you." I was learning that whatever you're handing out, everybody wants it, and those who don't get it frequently respond by threatening to kill or maim you. Another fact of prison life.

22   Passing cell No. 632, I saw that a prisoner I had helped take to the hospital before dinner was back in his cell. When we took him out, he had been disabled by mace and was very wobbly. Hill and I had been extremely gentle, handcuffing him carefully, then practically carrying him down the stairs. As we went by his cell this time, he tossed a cup of liquid on us.

23   Back downstairs, I learned I would be going back to that tier for a third time, to finish serving dinner. This time, we planned to slip in the other side

of tier so we wouldn't have to pass the trouble cells. The plates were already prepared.

24   "Just get in there and give them their food and get out," Hill said. I could see he was nervous, which made me even more so. "Don't stop for anything. If you get hit, just back off, 'cause if they snare you or hook you some way and get you against the bars, they'll hurt you real bad."

25   Everything went smoothly. Inmates in the three most troublesome cells were not getting dinner, so they hurled some garbage at us. But that's something else I had learned: Getting no worse than garbage thrown at you is the prison equivalent of everything going smoothly.

— ▪ —

CHECKING YOUR COMPREHENSION

Directions: Select the letter of the choice that best answers each of the following statements and write it in the space provided. Record your score on page 408.

___a___   1. What main point about prisons does this selection make?
  a. being a prison guard is dangerous.
  b. conditions in prisons are deplorable.
  c. prisoners are not treated fairly.
  d. prisoners do not always receive proper medication.

___c___   2. The guards wear gloves to serve food
  a. to protect their hands.
  b. to avoid contaminating the food.
  c. because prisoners do not like white hands touching their food.
  d. because prisoners are concerned about infection.

___d___   3. As described in the selection, the prisoners used mirrors to
  a. shave.
  b. flash and reflect light.
  c. reflect television images.
  d. watch activity outside of their cells.

   b   4. Which statement best describes the guard's attitude toward beginning his job as a prison guard?

      a. He looked forward to the job.

      b. He felt untrained and unprepared.

      c. He felt he might offend some prisoners.

      d. He thought the job would be easy.

   a   5. Which statement best summarizes the conditions in the prison?

      a. Violence seems to be routine among prisoners.

      b. Prisoners are abused by the guards.

      c. The food is inedible.

      d. An inadequate amount of food and beverage is served.

   d   6. The prisoner who had been treated gently on the way to the hospital, threw a cup of liquid at the guards. This incident suggests that

      a. prisoners do not want hospitalization.

      b. the prisoner was grateful for the gentle treatment.

      c. prisoners don't want the liquid.

      d. prisoners and guards must act as enemies regardless of special care taken.

   a   7. This selection originally appeared in a textbook entitled *Introduction to Criminology*. Why would the author of the textbook include this selection?

      a. to provide students with a perspective on day-to-day life in the prison system

      b. to encourage students to consider careers in criminal justice

      c. to warn students to be careful on field visits to prisons

      d. to argue for reforms in the prison system

   d   8. The guard disagreed with all of the following details of the prison except

      a. the lack of training of the guards.

      b. the looseness of security.

      c. the guard's lack of weapons or radios.

      d. the quality of the food served.

_____c_____ 9. Which pattern of organization is used throughout this reading?
   a. process
   b. comparison and contrast
   c. chronological order
   d. definition

_____a_____ 10. The author's partner, Bill Hill, could best be described as
   a. experienced and cautious.
   b. angry and hostile.
   c. disgruntled and unhappy.
   d. sympathetic and understanding.

WORDS IN CONTEXT

Directions: Locate each word in the paragraph indicated and reread that paragraph. Then, based on the way the word is used, write a synonym or brief definition in the space provided. You may use a dictionary if necessary.

1. contraband (par. 4) __illegal or forbidden goods__

2. din (par. 18) __noise__

3. maim (par. 21) __do permanent bodily injury__

VOCABULARY REVIEW

Directions: Complete each of the following sentences by inserting a word from the Vocabulary Preview on page 360 in the space provided.

1. A beginner on a professional hockey team is called a _____rookie_____.

2. An instructor who spent little time reading essay exams could be said to have read them in a _____cursory_____ manner.

3. One kilometer is _____equivalent_____ to .62 miles.

4. The students were _____apprehensive_____ about their final grades in chemistry.

5. The class of kindergarten children visiting the zoo created a _____ruckus_____.

6. The police officer used _____mace_____ to stop the man who was attacking her.

7. The lobby of the new hotel had several _____tiers_____.

DISCUSSION QUESTIONS

1. Why are the cookies so important to the prisoners? What might they represent or be used for?

2. Explain a job or situation for which you felt unprepared and describe how you handled it.

3. Do you think prisoners deserve better conditions than were described in this article? Why or why not?

SHE SAID YES! SHE SAID YES! SHE SAID YES!
Michael Kernan

This humorous essay taken from the *Smithsonian* magazine describes unusual marriage proposals.

Vocabulary Preview

These are some of the difficult words in this essay. The definitions here will help you if you can't figure out the meanings from the sentence context or word parts.

enlightenment (par. 2) awareness; use of reason

amorous (par. 3) having to do with love or courtship

besotted (par. 4) intoxicated, stupefied

insouciance (par. 4) carefree feeling

equinoxes (par. 5) the days of the year when night and day are equal in length

ingenuity (par. 6) cleverness

amplified (par. 13) made louder

---

1   Not so very long ago, according to the cartoons of my youth, a guy who wanted to get married would hit his girl with a club, grab her by the hair, and drag her into his cave.

2   But a time came when it was discovered that you should *ask* for a woman's hand. You asked her father, of course, and he put a price on her, whether in cattle, gold, or debentures. Eventually what passes for enlightenment set in. Nowadays you can ask the girl herself. Or she can ask you.

3   Today, many amorous couples jump the gun, so to speak, draining a certain significance from a proposal. Perhaps as a result, an odd thing has happened: the proposal has gone public.

4   This may be the influence of our advertising-besotted age and the possibility that we have to see something on TV in order to believe it. Or it may be that, beneath our hard insouciance, we are still romantics. In any case, Americans are popping the question on talk shows, on billboards and even on the concert stage. Love-struck males hire planes to fly banners over stadiums

with messages like "Ethel, Will You Marry Me?" We broadcast our marital message at supermarkets, in airports, and almost anywhere where there is a public to be impressed.

5 Things have gotten to such a pass that one interested party down in Texas has proposed the establishment of an official Proposal Day to occur twice a year at the equinoxes, thus symbolizing the equality of men and women. It is aimed at the people who keep putting it off and putting it off. And there are a lot of them: baby boom women now in their 30s and 40s are roughly three times less likely to marry than were women that age a generation ago.

6 Inevitably, a lot of ingenuity goes into proposals nowadays, even by those who don't make a public spectacle of themselves. Consider Neil Nathanson and Leslie Hamilton. They met in Palo Alto, California, where they had separate apartments in one of those wonderful old shingled houses. Neil was studying law at Stanford. Leslie had just got her degree in city planning.

7 They soon discovered that they loved doing crosswords. On Sunday mornings they would hang out together working on the *San Francisco Examiner* puzzle. One Sunday Leslie noticed that many of the puzzle answers struck close to home. "State or quarterback" turned out to be MONTANA, which is where she came from. "Instrument" was CELLO, which she plays. There were references to weddings and marriage, *and* when she came to "Astronaut Armstrong," which could only be NEIL, she did a double take.

8 "I was about halfway through the puzzle," she remembers, "when I figured out that a string of letters running across the middle of the puzzle said 'DEAR—WILL YOU MARRY ME NEIL.' The missing clue was 'Actress Caron.' I didn't know who that was, it could have been Lauren for all I knew, so I began on the Down clues. Sure enough, it was LESLIE."

9 She was stunned. She looked up, found him staring at her, and said, "Yes." What else?

10 It seems Neil had talked to Merl Reagle, the *Examiner* puzzle maker and a genius of sorts, and they had worked on the project for four months. Neil and Leslie have been married four years and now have a daughter. What did the other puzzle solvers think? For them it was just a neat crossword on the theme of weddings.

11 Oh, and they invited Reagle to the wedding, in Great Falls, Montana.

12   "I never did finish the puzzle," she says.

13   That proposal was relatively private, though attended by millions of readers. Sportscaster Ahmad Rashad proposed to *The Cosby Show* star Phylicia Ayers-Mien live on a pregame TV show. And not too long ago singer Anita Baker, during a Radio City Music Hall concert, handed the mike to a young man who had come up from the audience by prearrangement. In ringing, amplified tones he asked, "Mitzi, will you marry me?" The audience gave the couple a standing ovation.

14   But what if the girl says no?

15   Tony Ferrante of Richmond, Virginia, had this great idea: he would lure his friend, Kathryn Webber, to a mall at Christmastime and get her to sit on Santa's lap for a gag photograph. Then Santa would hand her the usual little gift, only the gift would turn out to be an engagement ring.

16   Unfortunately, Kathryn had just finished her college finals and was tired, hungry and cross. Tony finally persuaded her to see Santa, but the ring hadn't arrived yet. So Tony had to drag her around the mall for another half-hour while a friend fetched the ring. At last Kathryn was sweet-talked into sitting on Santa's lap a second time. Santa gave her a tiny box.

17   Tony had to tell her to open it. She was so shaken that she couldn't give him an answer; they had never discussed marriage before. He thought he was a goner. But finally, seven hours later at dinner, she took pity on him. "I don't think I ever answered your question," she said. "Yes, I will."

18   Romantic is as romantic does. Randi Reese was not the kind of girl that anyone could surprise, or so her parents told Mark Roger. When they attended a performance of *Grandma Sylvia's Funeral,* an Off Broadway play in which the audience takes part, Mark arranged for one of the actors to approach him in his seat and say these lines from the script: "Grandma wanted to will you her engagement ring as long as you have someone you love to give it to."

19   At this point Mark jumped up, turned to Randi next to him, and said, for all the audience to hear, "Yes, I do! I would like to give this ring to Randi Reese, if she would marry me."

20   Randi was surprised.

21   They invited all the cast members to the wedding.

22   Here's a classic: it seems this Yale law school student kept staring at a certain girl in a civil liberties course. She had Coke-bottle glasses, no makeup and out-of-control hair. When he saw her again in the law library and started gawking, she got up and approached him. "If you're going to keep looking at me and I'm going to keep looking at you, we ought to at least know each other."

23   They dated, became close, moved to Fayetteville, Arkansas, where he was to teach law at the University of Arkansas. Despite offers from law firms in Washington, D.C., New York and Chicago, she stayed in Fayetteville. "I loved him," she says. "I had to stay."

24   Then he ran for office and lost, though he later won a big one. She started teaching law at the university, too. They did some dreaming. There was a particular brick house she loved. But she needed time before making any commitments, so she went home to Illinois to think things over.

25   When she returned, he met her at the airport. "I bought that house you like," he said, "so you better marry me because I can't live in it by myself."

26   They were married in the house. She took off her glasses for the occasion.

. . . .

27   We take you now from Arkansas to the Steel Valley School District in western Pennsylvania. Michael Bujdos, then a first-grade teacher at Barrett

Elementary, called Jean Kabo, his high school sweetheart from Serra Catholic High in McKeesport. "Jean," he said, "I'm having some volunteers come in to read stories to the class. Would you like to help me out?"

28   Sure, she replied. When she got to the school, Michael said the kids had an art project they wanted to show her before she read the story. In the classroom, first-graders were lined up at the blackboard with their hands behind them. She thought something was going on, because the kids were awfully serious. But giggling. While she stood there, more than somewhat bemused, Michael told the children, "All right, boys and girls. Show the lady what we made in art class."

29   At that, the children proudly held up sheets of paper that spelled the words, "Will You Marry Mr. B?"

30   "I sort of looked at it," she said recently from their home in Munhall, Pennsylvania. "I was in shock. It was really funny. I didn't notice a colleague of his videotaping the whole thing" from the back of the room.

31   For a long moment everyone stood there, the kids watching her, mouths open, Michael holding his breath.

32   "And I said yes. And the kids loved it. And they were laughing and jumping up and down and shouting, 'She said yes! She said yes! She said yes!'"

━━ ∎ ━━

CHECKING YOUR COMPREHENSION

Directions: Select the letter of the choice that best answers each of the following statements and write it in the space provided. Record your score on page 408.

__b__   1. The main point of this reading is that
   a. most people have unusual stories about their marriage proposals.
   b. some people are making their marriage proposals in public rather than in private.
   c. although people often turn down public proposals, only the positive answers make the news.
   d. people usually say "yes" to a public proposal, even if they are reluctant to marry.

_____d_____ 2. The main idea of paragraph 2 is that

    a. a woman proposing to a man is common now.

    b. dowries for brides should be brought back.

    c. men need to ask women to marry them.

    d. ways of arranging a marriage have changed.

_____c_____ 3. The main point of paragraph 6 is that

    a. apartment houses are good places to meet your mate.

    b. private proposals are usually not very interesting.

    c. a creative proposal does not have to be a public one.

    d. a public proposal requires a crowd.

_____c_____ 4. The official Proposal Day in Texas was suggested to

    a. give women a chance to propose to men.

    b. make women and men equal under the law.

    c. encourage people to propose.

    d. set a world record for the most proposals.

_____d_____ 5. Mark Rodgers was able to propose at *Grandma Sylvia's Funeral* because

    a. he was a cast member in the play.

    b. her parents approved.

    c. Randi's parents knew the director of the play.

    d. the audience routinely participates in the play.

_____a_____ 6. Which of the following is a reason offered to explain why proposals have gone public?

    a. the influence of advertising and television

    b. the lack of religious convictions

    c. changing sex roles

    d. the emphasis on sex in our society

_____a_____ 7. According to the author, proposals are becoming more

    a. clever and creative.   c. lengthy and technical.

    b. personalized.   d. indifferent.

_____b_____ 8. The author explains his ideas primarily by

    a. giving facts and statistics.   c. giving reasons.

    b. presenting stories of various couples.   d. making comparisons.

<u>d</u> 9. The proposal by a first-grade teacher, Michael Bujdos, to his high school sweetheart is told using which pattern of organization?

    a. definition   c. comparison and contrast

    b. cause and effect   d. chronological order

<u>c</u> 10. The tone of this article could best be described as

    a. sad and depressing.   c. light and informative.

    b. factual and scholarly.   d. convincing and persuasive.

WORDS IN CONTEXT

Directions: Locate each word in the paragraph indicated and reread that paragraph. Then, based on the way the word is used, write a synonym or brief definition in the space provided. You may use a dictionary if necessary.

1. standing ovation (par. 13) __applause given with the audience standing__

2. lure (par. 15) __lead into, tempt, attract__

3. bemused (par. 28) __confused, bewildered__

VOCABULARY REVIEW

Directions: Match the words in column A with their meanings in column B. Write the letter of your choice in the space provided.

	Column A		Column B
g	1. amorous	a.	made louder
a	2. amplified	b.	days when night and day are equal in length
e	3. besotted	c.	cleverness
b	4. equinoxes	d.	awareness
c	5. ingenuity	e.	intoxicated
d	6. enlightenment	f.	carefree feeling
f	7. insouciance	g.	having to do with love

DISCUSSION QUESTIONS

1. Describe the most unusual proposal you have heard, seen, or experienced.

2. Are formal proposals important? Do you think they are becoming more popular among your friends or family?

3. A public proposal involves a degree of risk (what if the person says "no"?). Do you think only certain types of people would offer a public proposal or be accepting of one? Explain your answer.

4. Would you or have you ever considered a public proposal? Why or why not?

NAME _____ SECTION _____

DATE _____ SCORE _____

HISPANIC, USA: THE CONVEYOR-BELT LADIES
Rose del Castillo Guilbault

An important part of many jobs is getting along with coworkers as well as working with supervisors and customers. In this article a young woman describes her experiences working in a vegetable packing plant. Read the article to find out how she came to be respected by her older coworkers.

Vocabulary Preview

These are some of the difficult words in this essay. The definitions here will help you if you can't figure out the meanings from the sentence context or word parts.

tedious (par. 4) tiresome, dull

strenuous (par. 4) requiring great physical effort or energy

sorority (par. 5) an organization of women

irrevocably (par. 10) impossible to change

stigmatize (par. 10) to brand or label

gregarious (par. 12) sociable

dyspeptic (par. 12) having a bad disposition, grouchy

pragmatic (par.17) practical

melancholic (par. 18) sad, gloomy

fatalism (par. 19) the belief that events in life are determined by fate and cannot be changed

crescendo (par. 29) a steady increase in volume or force

anticlimactic (par. 30) an ordinary or commonplace event that concludes a series of important events

1   The conveyor-belt ladies were the migrant women, mostly from Texas, I worked with during the summers of my teenage years. I call them conveyor-belt ladies because our entire relationship took place while sorting tomatoes on a conveyor belt.

2   We were like a cast in a play where all the action occurs on one set. We'd return day after day to perform the same roles, only this stage was a vegetable-packing shed, and at the end of the season there was no applause. The

players could look forward only to the same uninspiring parts on a string of grim real-life stages.

3   The women and their families arrived in May for the carrot season, spent the summer in the tomato sheds and stayed through October for the bean harvest. After that, they emptied the town, some returning to their homes in Texas (cities like McAllen, Douglas, Brownsville), while others continued on the migrant trail, picking cotton in the San Joaquin Valley or grapefruits and oranges in the Imperial Valley.

4   Most of these women had started in the fields. The vegetable packing sheds were a step up, easier than the back-breaking, grueling work the field demanded. The work was more tedious than strenuous, paid better, provided fairly steady hours and clean bathrooms. Best of all, you weren't subjected to the elements.

5   The summer I was 16, my mother got jobs for both of us as tomato sorters. That's how I came to be included in the seasonal sorority of the conveyor belt.

6   The work consisted of standing and picking flawed tomatoes off the conveyor belt before they rolled off into the shipping boxes at the end of the line. These boxes were immediately loaded onto waiting delivery trucks, so it was crucial not to let imperfect tomatoes through.

7   The work could be slow or intense, depending on the quality of the tomatoes and how many there were. Work increased when the company's deliveries got backlogged or after rainy weather had delayed picking.

8   During those times, it was not unusual to work from 7 A.M. to midnight, playing catch-up. I never heard anyone complain about the overtime. Overtime meant desperately needed extra money.

9   I was not happy to be part of the agricultural workforce. I would have preferred working in a dress shop or baby-sitting, like my friends. But I had a dream that would cost a lot of money—college. And the fact was, this was the highest-paying work I could do.

10   But it wasn't so much the work that bothered me. I was embarrassed because only Mexicans worked at packing sheds. I had heard my schoolmates joke about the "ugly, fat Mexican women" at the sheds. They ridiculed the way they dressed and laughed at the "funny way" they talked. I feared

working with them would irrevocably stigmatize me, setting me further apart from my Anglo classmates.

11   At 16 I was more American than Mexican and, with adolescent arrogance, felt superior to these "uneducated" women. I might be one of them, I reasoned, but I was not like them.

12   But it was difficult not to like the women. They were a gregarious, entertaining group, easing the long, monotonous hours with bawdy humor, spicy gossip and inventive laments. They poked fun at all the male workers and did hysterical impersonations of a dyspeptic Anglo supervisor. Although he didn't speak Spanish (other than *"Mujeres, trabajo, trabajo!"*)[1], he seemed to sense he was being laughed at. That would account for the sudden rages when he would stamp his foot and forbid us to talk until break time.

13   "I bet he understands Spanish and just pretends so he can hear what we say," I whispered to Rosa.

14   *"Ay, no hija,*[2] it's all the buzzing in his ears that alerts him that these *viejas* (old women) are bad-mouthing him!" Rosa giggled.

15   But it would have been easier to tie the women's tongues in a knot than to keep them quiet. Eventually the ladies had their way and their fun, and the men learned to ignore them.

16   We were often shifted around, another strategy to keep us quiet. This gave me ample opportunity to get to know everyone, listen to their life stories and absorb the gossip.

17   Pretty Rosa described her romances and her impending wedding to a handsome field worker. Bertha, a heavy-set, dark-skinned woman, told me that Rosa's marriage would cause nothing but headaches because the man was younger and too handsome. Maria, large, moon-faced and placid, described the births of each of her nine children, warning me about the horrors of childbirth. Pragmatic Minnie, a tiny woman who always wore printed cotton dresses, scoffed at Maria's stupidity, telling me she wouldn't have so many kids if she had ignored that good-for-nothing priest and gotten her tubes tied!

---

[1] Women, work, work.
[2] Oh, no, little one.

18   In unexpected moments, they could turn melancholic: recounting the babies who died because their mothers couldn't afford medical care; the alcoholic, abusive husbands who were their "cross to bear"; the racism they experienced in Texas, where they were branded "dirty Mexicans" or "Mexican dogs" and not allowed in certain restaurants.

19   They spoke with the detached fatalism of people with limited choices and alternatives. Their lives were as raw and brutal as ghetto streets—something they accepted with an odd grace and resignation.

20   I was appalled and deeply affected by these confidences. The injustices they endured enraged me; their personal struggles overwhelmed me. I knew I could do little but sympathize.

21   My mother, no stranger to suffering, suggested I was too impressionable when I emotionally told her the women's stories. "That's nothing," she'd say lightly. "If they were in Mexico, life would be even harder. At least there's opportunities here, you can work."

22   My icy arrogance quickly thawed, that first summer, as my respect for the conveyor-belt ladies grew.

23   I worked in the packing shed for several summers. The last season also turned out to be the last time I lived at home. It was the end of a chapter in my life, but I didn't know it then. I had just finished junior college and was transferring to the university. I was already over-educated for seasonal work, but if you counted the overtime, no other jobs came close to paying so well, so I went back one last time.

24   The ladies treated me with warmth and respect. I was a college student, deserving of special treatment.

25   Aguedia, the crew chief, moved me to softer and better-paying jobs within the plant. I went from the conveyor belt to shoving boxes down a chute and finally to weighing boxes of tomatoes on a scale—the highest-paying position for a woman.

26   When the union's dues collector showed up, the women hid me in the bathroom. They had decided it was unfair for me to have to join the union and pay dues, since I worked only during the summer.

27   "Where's the student?" the union rep would ask, opening the door to a barrage of complaints about the union's unfairness.

28   Maria (of the nine children) tried to feed me all summer, bringing extra tortillas, which were delicious. I accepted them guiltily, always wondering if I was taking food away from her children. Others would bring rental contracts or other documents for me to explain and translate.

29   The last day of work was splendidly beautiful, warm and sunny. If this had been a movie, these last scenes would have been shot in soft focus, with a crescendo of music in the background.

30   But real life is anticlimactic. As it was, nothing unusual happened. The conveyor belt's loud humming was turned off, silenced for the season. The women sighed as they removed their aprons. Some of them just walked off, calling *"Hasta la proxima!"* Until next time!

31   But most of the conveyor-belt ladies shook my hand, gave me a blessing or a big hug.

32   "Make us proud!" they said.

33   I hope I have.

— ▪ —

CHECKING YOUR COMPREHENSION

Directions: Select the letter of the choice that best answers each of the following statements and write it in the space provided. Record your score on page 408.

___c___ 1. This article focuses primarily on
        a. working conditions in vegetable-packing sheds.
        b. the life history of migrant workers.
        c. the author's experiences with the women with whom she worked.
        d. how migrant workers are treated unfairly.

___a___ 2. Through her experiences with the women workers, the author learns
        a. to understand and respect the women.
        b. how to avoid problems with the union.
        c. to avoid getting personally involved.
        d. how to get the best paying job.

_____d_____ 3. Why did the author choose to take a job at the packing shed?

a. She wanted to get to know the women.

b. It counted as community service.

c. She could not get hired elsewhere.

d. It was the highest paying job.

_____a_____ 4. Why was the author at first unhappy about working at the packing shed?

a. She thought her Anglo friends would make fun of her.

b. She thought the work would be tiring.

c. She disliked the poor working condition.

d. She thought the women would treat her poorly.

_____b_____ 5. Why did the ladies hide the author when the union's dues collector arrived?

a. They knew she was hired illegally.

b. They thought it was unfair for her to pay dues when she worked only in the summer.

c. They thought the collector would fire her.

d. They knew the collector was dishonest.

_____a_____ 6. The events in this article are arranged

a. chronologically.

b. according to the place in which they occurred.

c. according to jobs held.

d. from most to least important.

_____c_____ 7. Why did the author initially feel superior to the women with whom she worked?

a. They dressed differently than she did.

b. They gossiped.

c. She thought of them as uneducated.

d. They spoke Spanish.

_____d_____ 8. Which statement best describes the women's attitude toward education?

a. They thought it was a waste of time.

b. They thought only men should go to college.

c. They intended to get high school equivalency diplomas.

d. They respected and valued education.

_b_   9. Why did the author's attitude change toward her coworkers?

   a. She became part of their families.

   b. She was touched by their humor and kindness.

   c. She had to do so in order to keep her job.

   d. She decided they were not lazy, after all.

_b_   10. Which statement best summarizes the author's last day at the packing shed?

   a. The women expressed their appreciation.

   b. Nothing unusual happened.

   c. The women offered her advice for the future.

   d. Many tearful good-byes were said.

WORDS IN CONTEXT

Directions: Locate each word in the paragraph indicated and reread that paragraph. Then, based on the way the word is used, write a synonym or brief definition in the space provided. You may use a dictionary if necessary.

1. uninspiring (par. 2) __not interesting, not stimulating__

2. grueling (par. 4) __physically demanding__

3. impending (par. 17) __about to happen__

4. scoffed (par. 17) __made fun of__

5. recounting (par. 18) __telling a story about__

VOCABULARY REVIEW

Directions: Match the words in column A with their meanings in column B. Write the letter of your choice in the space provided. (This exercise continues on the next page.)

	Column A		Column B
_d_	1. gregarious	a.	label
_e_	2. dyspeptic	b.	unable to change
_a_	3. stigmatize	c.	practical
_k_	4. sorority	d.	sociable
_c_	5. pragmatic	e.	grouchy

i	6. tedious	f.	hard physical work
g	7. melancholic	g.	gloomy
b	8. irrevocably	h.	belief that life is controlled by fate
f	9. strenuous	i.	tiresome
h	10. fatalism	j.	steady increase in volume
l	11. anticlimactic	k.	group of women
j	12. crescendo	l.	commonplace event

DISCUSSION QUESTIONS

1. Describe a situation or event that changed your attitude toward a person or group.

2. What, if anything, have you learned from coworkers in a particular job?

3. The ladies treated the author specially because she was a college student. How do people treat college students today? Compare your treatment with that of the author.

NAME _____ SECTION _____

DATE _____ SCORE _____

A DAY ON WHEELS
Cheryl A. Davis

What should or shouldn't you say to a person who is disabled? This article describes some examples of rude behavior and the author's reactions to them.

Vocabulary Preview

These are some of the difficult words in this essay. The definitions here will help you if you can't figure out the meanings from the sentence context or word parts.

meditation (par. 4) deep thought

gratuitous (par. 5) uncalled for

persistent (par. 5) unrelenting

unsolicited overture (par. 7) unasked-for response

apropos (par. 12) relevant

comme il faut (par. 16) as it should be, appropriate

dubious (par. 17) doubtful

mediating (par. 25) settling, conciliating

mortified (par. 27) shamed, humiliated

flagellated (par. 28) punished

adroit (par. 28) clever

paraplegic (par. 29) without use of the legs

haughtier (par. 31) more contemptuous

civilities (par. 39) niceties, pleasantries

schizophrenia (par. 41) a mental illness

conciliatory (par. 45) soothing, friendly

---

1   "Man, if I was you, I'd shoot myself," said the man on the subway platform. No one else was standing near him. I realized he was talking to me.

2   "Luckily, you're not," I said, gliding gracefully away.

3   For me, this was not an unusual encounter; indeed, it was a typical episode in my continuing true-life sitcom, "Day on Wheels."

4   A train ride can be an occasion for silent meditation in the midst of mechanical commotion. Unfortunately, I rarely get to meditate.

5   I attract attention. I pretend to ignore them, the eyes that scrutinize me and then quickly glance away. I try to avoid the gratuitous chats with loosely wrapped passengers. Usually, I fail. They may be loosely wrapped, but they're a persistent lot.

6   I use a wheelchair; I am not "confined" to one. Actually, I get around well. I drive a van equipped with a wheelchair-lift to the train station. I use a powered wheelchair with high-amperage batteries to get to work. A manual chair, light enough to carry, enables me to visit the "walkies" who live upstairs and to ride in the Volkswagens.

7   My life has been rich and varied, but my fellow passengers assume that, as a disabled person, I must be horribly deprived and so lonely that I will appreciate any unsolicited overture.

8   "Do you work?" a woman on the train asked me recently.

9   I said I did.

10   "It's nice that you have something to keep you busy, isn't it?"

11   Since we are thought of as poor invalids in need of chatting up, people are not apt to think too hard about what they are saying to us. It seems odd, since they also worry about the "right" way to talk to disabled people.

12   "How do you take a bath?" another woman asked me, apropos of nothing.

13   One day, an elderly man was staring at me as I read the newspaper.

14   "Would you like to read the sports section?" I asked him.

15   "How many miles can that thing go before you need new batteries?" he responded.

16   When I was a little girl, I once saw a woman whose teeth looked strange. "Mommy, that lady has funny teeth," I said. My mother explained that it was not *comme il faut* to offer up personal observations about other people's appearances. I thought everyone's mommy taught that, but I was wrong.

17   For many years, I was in what some of us call "the phyz-diz-biz"—developing housing and educational programs for disabled people. I was active in the disability-rights movement. I went to "special" schools offering the dubious blessing of a segregated education. As a result, I have known several thousand disabled people, at one time or another, across the United States.

18   For those whose disablement is still recent, the gratuitous remarks and unsolicited contributions can be exceptionally hurtful. It takes time to learn how to protect yourself. To learn how to do it gracefully can take a lifetime.

19   Many of us take the position that the people who bother us are to be pitied for their ignorance. We take it upon ourselves to "educate" them. We forgive them their trespasses and answer their questions patiently and try to straighten them out.

20   Others prefer to ignore the rude remarks and questions altogether. I tried that, but it didn't work. There was one woman on the train who tipped the scales for me.

21   "You're much too pretty to be in a wheelchair," she said.

22   I stared straight ahead, utterly frozen in unanticipated rage.

23   Undaunted, she grabbed my left arm below the elbow to get my attention.

24   "I said, 'You're much too pretty to be in a wheelchair.'"

25   In a fury, I lost control. Between my brain and my mouth, the mediating force of acquired tact had vanished.

26   "What do you think?" I snapped. "That God holds a beauty contest and if you come in first, you don't have to be in one?"

27   She turned away and, a moment later, was chatting with an old woman beside her as if nothing had been said at all. But I was mortified, and I moved to the other end of the train car.

28   For that one lapse, I flagellated myself all afternoon. When I got home, I telephoned one of my more socially adroit disabled friends for advice.

29   Nick is a therapist, a Ph.D. from Stanford, and paraplegic. "How do you deal with the other bozos on the bus?" I asked him.

30   "I just say, 'Grow up,'" Nick answered.

31   That was a bit haughtier than I could pull off, I told him.

32   "Well, look," he said, "if those words don't do it, find something else. The main thing is to get them to stop bothering you, right?"

33   "Yes, but—"

34   "But what?"

35   "Nick, if I'm *too* rude, they won't learn a thing. They'll just tell themselves I'm maladjusted."

36   "Then tell them their behavior is inappropriate."

37   "Inappropriate. That's marvelous!" I decided to try it next time.

38   "Next time" arrived last week. I didn't see the man coming. I was on the train platform, and he approached me from behind and tapped me on the shoulder.

39   "What's your disability?" he asked, discarding civilities.

40   I turned and looked at him. "That is not an appropriate question to ask a stranger," I said quietly.

41   "Well, *I* have schizophrenia," he said proudly.

42   "I didn't ask you."

43   "I feel rejected," he said.

44   "Well, then don't say things like that to people you don't know."

45   The train came and we got on together. I offered him a conciliatory remark, and he quieted down. Clearly he was not the best person for my new approach, but I think I'm headed in the right direction.

━ ▪ ━

CHECKING YOUR COMPREHENSION

Directions: Select the letter of the choice that best answers each of the following statements and write it in the space provided. Record your score on page 408.

___d___ 1. The main point of this selection is that people often
   a. try to assist disabled people.
   b. say whatever they think.
   c. are curious about disabilities.
   d. say rude and embarrassing things to disabled people.

___a___ 2. The author's fellow passengers assume that a disabled person is
   a. lonely and unhappy.   c. undisciplined and carefree.
   b. mentally disturbed.   d. impatient and unkind.

___c___ 3. The author's mother had taught her that
   a. it is inappropriate to speak to strangers.
   b. one cannot trust strangers.
   c. it is wrong to comment about how people look.
   d. one should not stare at odd-looking people.

_____a_____ 4. What happened when the author tried to ignore a stranger's rude remark?

a. The stranger repeated her comment.

b. The stranger became angry.

c. The stranger ignored her.

d. The stranger was embarrassed.

_____c_____ 5. How did the author feel after she angrily snapped at the woman who told her she was too pretty to be in a wheelchair?

a. proud of herself   c. hurt and ashamed

b. pleased   d. amused

_____d_____ 6. Which statement best summarizes the author's position on dealing with the rude comments of strangers?

a. She is undecided about what to do.

b. She feels honesty is the best approach.

c. She realizes she needs counseling.

d. She has tried various approaches, and feels she is making progress.

_____a_____ 7. What is the author's purpose in writing the article?

a. To encourage people to be more sensitive when talking to disabled people.

b. To encourage other disabled people to ignore rude comments.

c. To make herself feel good.

d. To destroy negative images of disabled people.

_____c_____ 8. Which one of the following words or phrases has a negative connotation (shade of meaning)?

a. high-amperage   c. bozos on the bus

b. rich   d. disability-rights movement

_____a_____ 9. The tone of this selection can best be described as

a. realistic and blunt.   c. scholarly and serious.

b. light and amusing.   d. distant and withdrawn.

_a_ 10. Which statement best expresses the author's attitude toward nondisabled people who speak to her?

   a. They are thoughtless and insensitive.

   b. They are self-interested.

   c. They have no interest in disabled people.

   d. They make hasty decisions.

WORDS IN CONTEXT

Directions: Locate each word in the paragraph indicated and reread that paragraph. Then, based on the way the work is used, write a synonym or brief definition in the space provided. You may use a dictionary if necessary.

1. commotion (par. 4) __confusion__

2. scrutinize (par. 5) __look at closely__

3. high-amperage (par. 6) __high-powered__

4. undaunted (par. 23) __without hesitation, not discouraged__

VOCABULARY REVIEW

Directions: Complete each of the following sentences by inserting a word from the Vocabulary Preview on page 383 in the space provided.

1. Apologies are very _____apropos_____ since they smooth things over.

2. She was _____mortified_____ when her wig blew off.

3. The child's _____gratuitous_____ comments interrupted serious adult conversation.

4. Because the attorney was very _____adroit/persistent_____ , the firm decided to hire her.

5. _____Civilities_____ are often exchanged when people run into old friends.

6. The contestant on the game show looked _____dubious_____ as he gave his answer, but to his surprise, he learned it was correct.

7. Since the conversation was about museums, the comment about house-plants was not _____comme il faut_____ .

8. The child kept asking her father for candy; because she was so ___**persistent**___, he finally gave her some.

9. The ___**paraplegic**___ used an electric wheelchair.

10. The symptoms of ___**schizophrenia**___ include hallucination, illogical patterns of thinking, and delusions.

11. The parents used a ___**conciliatory**___ tone to talk with their angry daughter.

12. Jason regarded my comments on his new hairstyle and tattoos as an ___**unsolicited gesture**___.

13. Before the funeral service began, the family members sat quietly in deep ___**meditation**___.

14. Their child's comments acted as a ___**mediating**___ force for the divorced couple.

15. The angry mob ___**flagellated**___ the thief.

16. Janet was ___**haughtier**___ than her sister, although both women acted scornfully toward others on the staff.

DISCUSSION QUESTIONS

1. Describe a situation in which someone asked you an annoying, rude, or ignorant question about yourself. Explain how you responded.

2. Why do you think people ask the kind of questions the author mentions? What kind of response do you think these people deserve?

3. What other biases or stereotypes do disabled people face?

PEACEMAKER: AN INTERVIEW WITH LUIS RODRIGUEZ

Anita Merina

This reading is an interview with Luis Rodriguez, a well-known writer who used to be a gang member. He explains why young people join gangs, what they hope to find in a gang, and how they find life outside of a gang.

Vocabulary Preview

These are some of the difficult words in this essay. The definitions here will help you if you can't figure out the meanings from the sentence context or word parts.

alien (par. 3) foreign; enemy

unstructured (par. 3) unorganized; unplanned

potential (par. 7) capability; possible talent

activist (par. 7) working for a particular cause

articulate (par. 8) express or describe clearly

shallow (par. 10) not deeply thoughtful

summits (par. 12) meetings of leaders

clout (par. 13) power; influence

dimension (par. 14) features; viewpoint

---

1   By the age of 12, Luis Rodriguez was a veteran of gang warfare in East Los Angeles. For years, he felt trapped by the drugs and violence that destroyed friends and family.

2   His route out of "la vida loca," this crazy life? Writing—first poetry, then an autobiography. His latest work is a children's book, *America Is Her Name*, due out this spring. Rodriguez, now based in Chicago, spoke recently with *NEA Today* staff writer Anita Merina.

3   **Why do you say that it's tougher than ever to lure kids away from gangs and violence?** Gangs aren't alien powers. They begin as unstructured groupings, but they attract children who want the same things as any young person: respect. A sense of belonging. Protection. The same things that those who join the YMCA, Little League, or the Boy Scouts want.

4   Gangs flourish when there's a lack of recreation, decent education, or employment. I've talked to enough gang members and low-level dope dealers to know that they would quit today if they had a productive, livable-wage job and adults who care about them.

5   When I was growing up, even though there were gangs, there were also jobs available. Today's kids don't know where the world is going. They don't have anything meaningful to hang on to.

6   **Tell us about your school experiences.** My first day of school said a lot about my school life to come. I was taken to a teacher who didn't know what to do with me. I didn't know much English, but I understood much of what she was saying. I knew I wasn't wanted.

7   Later, even though my classmates and I were often tough on my teachers, there were still those who believed in us and our potential. We formed activist groups for Mexican-American students, and we learned to speak out for ourselves. As I discovered the power of words and learning, I began to turn away from gang life.

8   **Why do you work in schools now?** I've been on the streets, in gangs. I've done it all, the drugs and violence. Yet I was able to transcend all of this through the arts and poetry. Through my workshops with kids, I hope to help

Luis Rodriguez

students find their own voice to articulate their experiences, their pain. Words can give you the power to transcend even the strongest pain.

9   **What do you tell the teachers you work with?** I tell them these kids are worth fighting for. Too many people in power believe they aren't worth the effort. That's why my work is so important. These kids can be extraordinary in the right environment and with the right commitment.

10   **What can educators do?** I've visited schools where teachers and staff aren't following the old traditional ways of setting up classrooms: doing everything themselves, filling the room with shallow decorations like the rows of Presidents or animals. Instead, they're engaging young people with their own creativity.

11   At two schools in Atlanta, both with violent histories, the staff began using computers to get the children to tell their own stories. The kids seemed to change and became much more excited about learning.

12   **What are some of you success stories?** My son Romiro is the best example, even though he's still in a gang. I wrote my autobiography, *Always Running,* to warn him of the dangers of gang life. He's become a poet and has spoken across the country. He's also cofounded Youth Struggling for Survival, which has organized gang peace summits and peace retreats. The group also works with Video Machete, which teaches young people about editing and filmmaking. All this after he was told he was never going to amount anything.

13   **Why's he still involved with a gang?** He feels he has more clout convincing gang members to get involved in other activities. He's showing many of his gang members that there's an alternative to violence.

14   **Why did you decide to write a children's book?** I found few books for children that had the dimension I wanted for my own children. There were few stories about Mexican-American children or children of color.

15   Drawing on the experiences of so many children I met during visits to schools, I've written *America Is Her Name*. It's about a young Mexican girl who barely speaks in class. But slowly she begins to discover her voice through poetry.

16   So many silent children—particularly immigrant children—have stories that remain untold. It's time to give them their public voice.

━━ ▪ ━━

CHECKING YOUR COMPREHENSION

Directions: Select the letter of the choice that best answers each of the following statements and write it in the space provided. Record your score on page 408.

___a___ 1. The main point Rodriguez makes about gangs is that
   a. gangs offer kids respect and belonging.
   b. gangs promote structured violence.
   c. gangs deny individuality.
   d. gangs provide recreation.

___d___ 2. What can educators do to prevent students from joining gangs?
   a. Point out the short- and long-term dangers of gang membership.
   b. Discuss gang membership openly with students.
   c. Serve as positive role models.
   d. Involve students and encourage their own creativity.

___c___ 3. The author decided to write a children's book because
   a. he wanted to encourage others to write.
   b. he felt it would improve his reputation.
   c. there were not many stories about Mexican American children.
   d. the main character resembles Rodriguez's daughter.

___d___ 4. The author's son, Romiro, is still in a gang because
   a. he is afraid to leave the gang.
   b. upon joining he agreed to lifetime membership.
   c. he still wants to benefit from its protection.
   d. he thinks he can change the gang culture from within.

___c___ 5. The staff at two Atlanta schools encouraged student self-expression using
   a. former gang members.   c. computers.
   b. videotape.   d. hidden cameras.

___a___ 6. Rodriguez considers his son, Romiro, a success because he has
   a. become a poet and national speaker.
   b. written his autobiography.
   c. become a teacher.
   d. plans to write a children's book.

<u>d</u>   7. On his first day at school as a child, Rodriguez could understand very little English, but he knew he wasn't wanted. Which one of the following statements is the most reasonable explanation?

     a. He used a fellow student as an interpreter.

     b. He asked the teacher to speak in Spanish.

     c. He used a Spanish-American dictionary.

     d. He could tell by the teacher's tone of voice, gestures, or facial expressions.

<u>a</u>   8. The questions in bold print that the interviewer asked Rodriguez function as

     a. topic sentences.   c. details.

     b. context clues.   d. patterns or organization.

<u>b</u>   9. Rodriguez would be most likely to support which of the following activities?

     a. A national Mexican-American awareness day.

     b. A seminar in schools to encourage minority writers to tell their stories.

     c. A political campaign for an Mexican-American president.

     d. A drug awareness program.

<u>a</u>   10. Why does Rodriguez feel qualified to write about and discuss gangs?

     a. He is a former gang member.

     b. His daughter was killed by a gang member.

     c. He studied gang culture in college.

     d. He made a film about gang warfare.

WORDS IN CONTEXT

Directions: Locate each word in the paragraph indicated and reread that paragraph. Then, based on the way the word is used write a synonym or brief definition in the space provided. You may use a dictionary if necessary.

1. flourish (par. 4) <u>grow, thrive</u>

2. transcend (par. 8) <u>rise above, go beyond</u>

3. alternative (par. 13) <u>other choice, substitute</u>

VOCABULARY REVIEW

Directions: Match the words in column A with their meanings in column B. Write the letter of your choice in the space provided.

	Column A		Column B
h	1. summits	a.	feature; viewpoint
f	2. unstructured	b.	not deeply thoughtful
g	3. clout	c.	foreign; enemy
b	4. shallow	d.	working for a particular cause
a	5. dimension	e.	capability; possible talent
d	6. activist	f.	unorganized; unplanned
e	7. potential	g.	power; influence
i	8. articulate	h.	meetings of leaders
c	9. alien	i.	express or describe clearly

DISCUSSION QUESTIONS

1. What else can educators do to help steer kids away from gangs?

2. Describe your experiences or observations about why kids join gangs.

3. Are there any positive effects of gang membership? If so, describe them.

BLUE HIGHWAYS
William Least Heat Moon

Have you ever felt as if you needed to be alone, completely away from everything and everyone you know? This selection is taken from the first few pages of a book titled *Blue Highways*. It is the story of a man, part Sioux, who tries to sort out his life by leaving everything behind and going on the road.

Vocabulary Preview

These are some of the difficult words in this essay. The definitions here will help you if you can't figure out the meanings from the sentence context or word parts.

askew (par. 1) out of order; disorganized

remote (par. 1) far away

jeopardy (par. 3) great danger or peril

undulating (par. 5) moving in a wavy manner; weaving

cartographer (par. 7) mapmaker

contaminated (par. 13) impure; infected; polluted

perfidious (par. 13) not trustworthy; disloyal

delusion (par. 15) false belief; misleading or deceiving idea

futility (pars. 15, 16) sense of hopelessness or uselessness

1   Beware thoughts that come in the night. They aren't turned properly; they come in askew, free of sense and restriction, deriving from the most remote of sources. Take the idea of February 17, a day of canceled expectations, the day I learned my job teaching English was finished because of declining enrollment at the college, the day I called my wife from whom I'd been separated for nine months to give her the news, the day she let slip about her "friend"—Rick or Dick or Chick. Something like that.

2   That morning, before all the news started hitting the fan, Eddie Short Leaf, who worked a bottomland section of the Missouri River and plowed snow off campus sidewalks, told me if the deep cold didn't break soon the trees would freeze straight through and explode. Indeed.

3   That night, as I lay wondering whether I would get sleep or explosion, I got the idea instead. A man who couldn't make things go right could at least go. He could quit trying to get out of the way of life. Chuck routing. Live the real jeopardy of circumstance. It was a question of dignity.

4   The result: on March 19, the last night of winter, I again lay awake in the tangled bed, this time doubting the madness of just walking out on things, doubting the whole plan that would begin at daybreak—to set out on a long (equivalent to half the circumference of the earth), circular trip over the back roads of the United States. Following a circle would give a purpose—to come around again—where taking a straight line would not. And I was going to do it by living out of the back end of a truck. But how to begin a beginning?

5   A strange sound interrupted my tossing. I went to the window, the cold air against my eyes. At first I saw only starlight. Then they were there. Up in the March blackness, two entwined skeins of snow and blue geese honking north, an undulating W-shaped configuration across the deep sky, white bellies glowing eerily with the reflected light from town, necks stretched northward. Then another flock pulled by who knows what out of the south to breed and remake itself. A new season. Answer: begin by following spring as they did— darkly, with neck stuck out.

6   The vernal equinox[1] came on gray and quiet, a curiously still morning not winter and not spring, as if the cycle paused. Because things go their own way, my daybreak departure turned to a morning departure, then to an after-noon departure. Finally, I climbed into the van, rolled down the window, looked a last time at the rented apartment. From a dead elm sparrow hawks used each year came a high *whee* as the nestlings squealed for more grub. I started the engine. When I returned a season from now—if I did return— those squabs would be gone from the nest.

7   Accompanied only by a small, gray spider crawling the dashboard (kill a spider and it will rain), I drove into the street, around the corner through the intersection, over the bridge, onto the highway. I was heading toward those little towns that get on the map—if they get on at all—only because some

---

[1] The day in spring when night and day are of equal length.

cartographer has a blank space to fill: Remote, Oregon; Simplicity, Virginia; New Freedom, Pennsylvania; New Hope, Tennessee; Why, Arizona; Whynot, Mississippi; Igo, California (just down the road from Ono), here I come.

8   A pledge: I give this chapter to myself. When done with it, I will shut up about *that* topic.

9   Call me Least Heat Moon. My father calls himself Heat Moon, my elder brother Little Heat Moon. I, coming last, am therefore Least. It has been a long lesson of a name to learn.

10   To the Siouan peoples, the Moon of Heat is the seventh month, a time also known as the Blood Moon—I think because of its dusky midsummer color.

11   I have other names: Buck, once a slur—never mind the predominant Anglo features. Also Bill Trogdon. The Christian names come from a grandfather eight generations back, one William Trogdon, an immigrant Lancashireman living in North Carolina, who was killed by the Tories for providing food to rebel patriots and thereby got his name in volume four of *Makers of America*. Yet to the red way of thinking, a man who makes peace with the new by destroying the old is not to be honored. So I hear.

12   One summer when Heat Moon and I were walking the ancestral grounds of the Osage near the river of that name in western Missouri, we talked about bloodlines. He said, "Each of the people from anywhere, when you see in them far enough, you find red blood and a red heart. There's a hope."

13   Nevertheless, a mixed-blood—let his heart be where it may—is a contaminated man who will be trusted by neither red nor white. The attitude goes back to a long history of "perfidious" half breeds, men who, by their nature, had to choose against one of their bloodlines. As for me, I will choose for heart, for spirit, but never will I choose for blood.

14   One last word about bloodline. My wife, a woman of striking mixed-blood features, came from the Cherokee. Our battles, my Cherokee and I, we called the "Indian wars."

15   For these reasons I named my truck Ghost Dancing, a heavy-handed symbol alluding to ceremonies of the 1890s in which the Plains Indians, wearing cloth shirts they believed rendered them indestructible, danced for the return of warriors, bison, and the fervor of the old life that would sweep away the new. Ghost dances, desperate resurrection rituals, were the dying

rattles of a people show last defense was delusion—about all that remained to them in their futility.

16   A final detail: on the morning of my departure, I had seen thirty-eight Blood Moons, an age that carries its own madness and futility. With a nearly desperate sense of isolation and a growing suspicion that I lived in an alien land, I took to the open road in search of places where change did not mean ruin and where time and men and deeds connected.

— • —

CHECKING YOUR COMPREHENSION

Directions: Select the letter of the choice that best answers each of the following statements and write it in the space provided. Record your score on page 408.

___b___   1. The main point of the selection is
   a. thoughts that occur in the middle of the night are often dangerous.
   b. the author is taking a road trip in search for some meaning in his life.
   c. when things go wrong, it pays to take a big risk.
   d. at the beginning of a trip you often see signs from nature.

___d___   2. The main idea of paragraph 13 is that
   a. mixed-blood people cannot be trusted by anyone.
   b. mixed-blood people no longer face the same conflict they once did.
   c. because the author is not a mixed-blood person, he does not have difficult choices to make.
   d. mixed-blood people usually have to choose between their racial identities.

___a___   3. The main idea of paragraph 5 is that the geese
   a. are a symbol of how to take risks.
   b. usually fly north on the first night of the spring.
   c. are beautiful flying at night.
   d. will show the author the direction he should drive the next day.

_a_   4. The author names his truck Ghost Dancing because

      a. the name reminds him of an Indian ceremony of resurrection.

      b. his truck seat is covered with a cloth shirt like those worn in a Indian dance.

      c. his truck is old and will probably break down on his trip.

      d. the name suggests he will never return from his trip.

_c_   5. The author

      a. is a Cherokee.

      b. is the oldest son in the family.

      c. is 38 years old.

      d. misses his dead father.

_b_   6. This essay takes place in

      a. California at Christmas.

      b. Missouri at the end of winter.

      c. Osage country in the summer.

      d. North Carolina during the month of the Blood Heat.

_d_   7. Which paragraph best summarized the author's feelings about his journey?

      a. paragraph 7   c. paragraph 12

      b. paragraph 9   d. paragraph 16

_b_   8. February 17 was a bad day for the author because on that date he

      a. lost his wife.   c. decided to divorce his wife.

      b. lost his job.   d. decided to change his name.

_d_   9. In paragraph 6, which of the following words serves as a transition?

      a. from   c. came

      b. if   d. finally

_b_   10. Which phrase best describes the author's state of mind as he departs on his journey?

      a. playful and carefree   c. bored and angry

      b. unhappy but hopeful   d. indifferent

WORDS IN CONTEXT

Directions: Locate each word in the paragraph indicated and reread that paragraph. Then, based on the way the word is used, write a synonym or brief definition in the space provided. You may use a dictionary if necessary.

1. skeins (par. 5) _flock or group of birds in flight_

2. configuration (par. 5) _pattern, arrangement_

3. alluding (par. 15) _referring to_

VOCABULARY REVIEW

Directions: Match the words in column A with their meanings in column B. Write the letter of your choice in the space provided.

	Column A	Column B
b	1. cartographer	a. false belief
i	2. futility	b. mapmaker
e	3. perfidious	c. weaving
c	4. undulating	d. far away
f	5. contaminated	e. not trustworthy
d	6. remote	f. infected
a	7. delusion	g. out of order
h	8. jeopardy	h. great danger
g	9. askew	i. sense of hopelessness

DISCUSSION QUESTIONS

1. Least Heat Moon says "chuck routine." Have you ever wanted to chuck routine or done so?

2. Speculate about the outcome of Least Heat Moon's road trip. (To find out if you are right, obtain a copy of the book!)

3. Discuss the meaning of the statement in paragraph 13, "I will choose for heart, for spirit, but never will I chose for blood."

4. Least Heat Moon chooses a trip when faced with seemingly unsurmountable problems. Would you find an escape to a different place helpful if you were upset or faced with problems? If not, discuss what strategies might help.

NAME _____ SECTION _____

DATE _____ SCORE _____

LEGIBLE CLOTHING
Joseph A. DeVito

What do the clothes you wear reveal about you? In this article, taken from a book titled *Human Communication*, the author discusses the messages that clothing sends about the wearer.

Vocabulary Preview

These are some of the difficult words in this essay. The definitions here will help you if you can't figure out the meanings from the sentence context or word parts.

status (par. 1) social standing or position

paraphrase (par. 3) explain in other words

affiliation (par. 4) association or connection with a group

trophy (par. 4) prize or memento

metaphorical (par. 4) one thing representing another

satirizing (par. 4) making fun of

insignia (par. 5) a distinguishing sign

1   Legible clothing is anything that you wear which contains some verbal message; such clothing can literally be read. In some instances it says status; it tells others that you are, for example, rich or stylish or youthful. The Gucci or Louis Vuitton logos on your luggage communicate your status and financial position. In a similar way your sweatshirt saying Bulls or Pirates communicates your interest in sports and perhaps your favorite team.

2   John Molloy, in *Molloy's Live for Success*, advises you to avoid legible clothing except the kind that says rich. Legible clothing, argues Molloy, communicates lower status and lack of power. Humorist Fran Lebowitz says that legible clothes "are an unpleasant indication of the general state of things. I mean, be realistic. If people don't want to listen to you, what makes you think they want to hear from your sweater?"

3   Yet legible clothing is being bought and worn in record numbers. Many designers and manufacturers have their names integrated into the design of

the clothing: DKNY, Calvin Klein, L.L. Bean, and Levi's are just a few examples. At the same time that you are paying extra to buy the brand name, you also provide free advertising for the designer and manufacturer. To paraphrase Vidal Sassoon, "As long as you look good, so does the advertiser. And, when you look bad, the advertiser looks bad." Imitators—the cheap knock-offs you see on the street—are resisted by the original manufacturers not only because these impact on their own sales. In fact, the impact is probably minimal since the person who would pay $6,000 for a Rolex would not buy a $10 imitation on the street. Rather, such knock-offs are resisted because they are perceived to be worn by the wrong people—people who would destroy the image the manufacturer wishes to communicate.

4   T-shirts and sweatshirts are especially popular as message senders. In one study, the types of t-shirt messages were classified into four main categories. The order in which these are presented reflects the shirts the subjects (600 male and female college students) considered their favorites. Thirty-three percent, for example, considered affiliation message shirts their favorites while 17 percent considered those with personal messages their favorites. The order from most favorite down, was:

1. Affiliation messages—for example, a club or school name. It communicates that you are a part of a larger group.
2. Trophy—for example, a shirt from a high-status event such as a concert or perhaps a ski lodge. This is a way of saying that the wearer was in the right place.
3. Metaphorical expressions—for example, pictures of rock groups or famous athletes.
4. Personal message—for example, beliefs, philosophies and causes as well as satirizing current events.

5   Another important dimension of clothing, currently being debated in educational and legal circles, is the use of gang clothing. Some argue that gang clothing and gang colors contribute to violence in the schools and should therefore be prohibited. Others argue that gang clothing—or any clothing—is covered by the first amendment to the Constitution. Consider a specific case. In Harvard, Illinois, you can be arrested for wearing a Star of David in public—not because it's a religious symbol, but because certain gangs use

it as a gang symbol. In 1993, Harvard passed a law that makes it illegal "for any person within the city to knowingly use, display or wear color, emblems, or insignia" that would communicate their membership in (or sympathy for) gangs.

6   Consider your own use of legible clothing. Do you wear legible clothing? What messages do you wish to communicate? Are you successful in communicating the message you want? Do labels influence your perceptions of others? How do you feel about the law in Harvard, Illinois? Would you support such a law in your own community?

━━ ▪ ━━

CHECKING YOUR COMPREHENSION

Directions: Select the letter of your choice that best answers each of the following statements and write it in the space provided. Record your score on page 408.

__c__   1. The main point of the reading is that legible clothing
  a. is only worn by members of the lower class.
  b. has negative effect on sales of higher-priced clothing.
  c. says something about the wearer.
  d. is often banned in high schools.

__d__   2. The main idea of paragraph 4 is that
  a. many people wear personal messages on shirts.
  b. college students are the most likely group to wear legible clothing.
  c. sport sweatshirts indicate your favorite team.
  d. messages on shirts fit into four categories.

__b__   3. Which of the following statements best summarizes the main point of paragraph 5?
  a. Legible clothing is a form of free speech protected by the U.S. Constitution.
  b. The role of gang-related clothing is being discussed by both lawyers and teachers.
  c. The Star of David has become a gang symbol in Illinois.
  d. Gang violence in schools is increasing.

_____a_____ 4. According to the passage, manufacturers are mainly against name brand knock-offs because

    a. knock-offs destroy the image the manufacturer wants to communicate.

    b. the profits of the manufacturers are effectively cut in half by knock-offs.

    c. knock-offs do not provide free advertising for the manufacturers.

    d. the brand name products generally cost more than the knock-offs.

_____d_____ 5. According to the passage, which of the following examples of t-shirt message is an example of an affiliation message?

    a. Rolling Stones Spring 1995 tour

    b. a Michael Jordan picture

    c. "Life, liberty, and the pursuit of chocolate"

    d. Howard University

_____b_____ 6. A trophy message often refers to

    a. a favorite person.   c. personal beliefs.

    b. an event or place.   d. favorite possessions.

_____a_____ 7. The author's purpose is to:

    a. explain what legible clothing is

    b. explain why T-shirts are popular

    c. show how fashions change

    d. describe gang clothing

_____a_____ 8. In paragraph 4, which of the following words or phrases is a transition?

    a. for example   c. the order

    b. especially   d. this is

_____c_____ 9. The dictionary defines "legible" as "able to be read." As used in the selection, "legible" includes all of the following except

    a. pictures on clothing.

    b. words and numbers on shirts.

    c. shape of a shirt.

    d. logos and labels on clothing.

_____c_____ 10. The main purpose of the questions in the last paragraph of this selection is most likely to

  a. review the main point.

  b. emphasize technical vocabulary.

  c. make you think about yourself.

  d. solve problems.

WORDS IN CONTEXT

Directions: Locate each word in the paragraph indicated and reread that paragraph. Then based on the way the word is used, write a synonym or brief definition in the space provided. You may use a dictionary if necessary.

1. logos (par. 1) **name, symbol, or trademark**

2. integrated (par. 3) **made part of**

3. knock-offs (par. 3) **imitations**

4. dimension (par. 5) **aspect, element**

VOCABULARY REVIEW

Directions: Match the words in column A with their meanings in column B. Write the letter of your choice in the space provided.

Column A

_____d_____ 1. satirizing

_____f_____ 2. paraphrase

_____a_____ 3. insignia

_____g_____ 4. status

_____c_____ 5. metaphorical

_____e_____ 6. trophy

_____b_____ 7. affiliation

Column B

a. distinguishing sign

b. connection with a group

c. one thing representing another

d. making fun of

e. memento

f. explain in other words

g. social standing

DISCUSSION QUESTIONS

1. What types of legible clothing are worn on your campus? Rank the four types of messages from most to least commonly seen on your campus.

2. Why do you or don't you wear legible clothing?

3. Would you purchase a knock-off item? Why or why not?

4. If you lived in Harvard, Illinois, would you feel your rights have been violated by the law regarding the use of gang clothing?

Additional Reading Selections

RECORDING YOUR PROGRESS

Reading	Test	Number Right	Score
1 Coming into My Own	Checking Your Comprehension	_____ × 10 =	_____ %
2 Living Life to the Fullest	Checking Your Comprehension	_____ × 10 =	_____ %
3 A Guard's First Night on the Job	Checking Your Comprehension	_____ × 10 =	_____ %
4 She Said Yes! She Said Yes! She Said Yes!	Checking Your Comprehension	_____ × 10 =	_____ %
5 Hispanic, USA: The Conveyor-Belt Ladies	Checking Your Comprehension	_____ × 10 =	_____ %
6 A Day on Wheels	Checking Your Comprehension	_____ × 10 =	_____ %
7 Peacemaker: An Interview with Luis Rodriguez	Checking Your Comprehension	_____ × 10 =	_____ %
8 Blue Highways	Checking Your Comprehension	_____ × 10 =	_____ %
9 Legible Clothing	Checking Your Comprehension	_____ × 10 =	_____ %

EVALUATING YOUR PROGRESS

Based on your test performance, rate how well you have mastered your comprehension skills by checking one of the boxes below or by writing your own evaluation.

☐ **Need More Improvement**
Tip: Try using the Reading Road Trip CD-ROM for extra practice with comprehension questions.

☐ **Need More Practice**
Tip: Try using the Reading Road Trip CD-ROM that accompanies this textbook to brush up on your comprehension skills, or visit this textbook's Website at **http://ablongman.com/mcwhorter.**

☐ **Good**
Tip: To maintain your skills, log on to the Website that accompanies this textbook at **http://ablongman.com/mcwhorter** for a quick review.

☐ **Excellent**

YOUR EVALUATION: _____

_____

_____

Limited Answer Key

Chapter 1: Reading Actively

Exercise 1-1 (p. 3)

1. NH	6. NH
2. NH	7. H
3. NH	8. H
4. H	9. H
5. H	10. NH

Exercise 1-2 (p. 6)

1. T	4. T
2. T	5. T
3. F	

Exercise 1-3 (p. 7)

1. c	4. b
2. a	5. c
3. d	

Exercise 1-4 (p. 8)

1. e	4. d
2. a	5. b
3. c	

Exercise 1-5 (p. 9)

1. b	4. a
2. c	5. b
3. c	

What Have You Learned? (p. 10)

1. F	4. T
2. T	5. T
3. F	6. F

Chapter 2: Building Vocabulary: Using Context Clues

Exercise 2-1 (p. 33)

1. d	6. b
2. d	7. b
3. d	8. c
4. b	9. d
5. b	10. c

Exercise 2-2 (p. 35)

1. c	6. b
2. a	7. c
3. b	8. c
4. b	9. c
5. b	10. c

Exercise 2-3 (p. 37)

1. a	6. b
2. d	7. c
3. b	8. a
4. a	9. a
5. c	10. c

Exercise 2-4 (p. 38)

1. c	6. b
2. b	7. b
3. c	8. a
4. b	9. c
5. b	10. a

What Have You Learned? (p. 40)

1. context
2. Context clues
3. synonym
4. definitions
5. inference

Chapter 3: Building Vocabulary: Using Word Parts

Exercise 3-1 (p. 60)

1. f	6. b
2. d	7. j
3. i	8. c
4. a	9. g
5. h	10. e

Exercise 3-2 (p. 61)

1. bi (lingual)
2. im(perfect)
3. ir(reversible)
4. mis(informed)

5. dis(continued)
6. sub(standard)
7. retro(active)
8. inter(mediaries)
9. re(plicate)
10. dis(colored)

Exercise 3-3 (p. 63)

1. i
2. h
3. j
4. a
5. d
6. b
7. e
8. c
9. f
10. g

Exercise 3-4 (p. 64)

1. verdict
2. scriptures
3. visualize
4. spectators
5. prescribed
6. apathetic
7. synchronized
8. graphic
9. extraterrestrial
10. deduce

Exercise 3-5 (p. 66)

1. conversation
2. assistant
3. qualifications
4. internship
5. eaten
6. audible
7. sincerity
8. permission
9. instructive
10. remembrance
11. mortality
12. presidential
13. feminist
14. hazardous
15. destiny
16. differences
17. friendship
18. comfortable
19. popularity
20. apologetic

What Have You Learned? (p. 69)

1. F
2. T
3. F
4. T
5. T
6. F

Chapter 4: Locating Main Ideas

Exercise 4-1 (p. 88)

1. b
2. c
3. a
4. c
5. b
6. d
7. c
8. c
9. a
10. b

Exercise 4-2 (p. 89)

1. b
2. c
3. b
4. c
5. c

Exercise 4-3 (p. 90)

1. b
2. c
3. a
4. d
5. c

Exercise 4-4 (p. 94)

1. Overall, studies have shown pizza to be highly nutritious.
2. Perhaps the most common method for defending or justifying something that has been said and may be perceived negatively is "the excuse."
3. But within that field, it's also a good idea to maintain a high degree of visibility.
4. Dirty words are often used by teenagers in telling off-color stories and this can be considered part of their sex education.
5. In this respect it is best to go home before making a selection.
6. The 1950s were to most Americans a time of great security.
7. The more you know about your audience, the more you can target your speech to their needs, values, and interests, and the more interesting your speech will be.
8. The words "effortless exercise" are a contradiction in terms.
9. Burger King Corporation offers both a service and a product to its customers. Burger King, then, is marketing a positive experience, as promised by its advertising and promotional efforts and delivered by its product.
10. Thus, there are significant cultural differences in the way people are taught to view themselves.

What Have You Learned? (p. 97)

1. a
2. c
3. c
4. a
5. b

Chapter 5: Identifying Supporting Details

Exercise 5-1 (p. 119)

A. *Key detail:* information about tastes
   Key detail: through memory
   Minor details: humans use fragrances
   Minor details: smell of chicken roasting
   Minor details: woman wearing one brand
                    of perfume
                    fragrance of a brand of shaving
                    cream
B. 1. First   2. also   3. third   4. finally

Exercise 5-2 (p. 120)

1. K a. Voice changes in boys begin to occur at
       age 13 or 14.
   K b. Facial proportions may change during
       adolescence.
   K c. Adolescents, especially boys, gain several
       inches in height.
   K e. Primary sex characteristics begin to
       develop for both boys and girls.
2. K a. By the time an infant is six months old,
       he or she can make twelve different
       speech sounds.
   K c. During the first year, the number of
       vowel sounds a child can produce is
       greater than the number of consonant
       sounds he or she can make.
   K d. Between six and twelve months, the
       number of consonant sounds a child
       can produce continues to increase.
3. K a. By becoming involved with the actors and
       their problems, members of the audience
       temporarily forget about their personal
       cares and concerns and are able to relax.
   K c. Almost everyone who attends a play
       expects to be entertained.
   K e. There is a smaller audience that looks to
       theater for intellectual stimulation.
4. K b. Licorice blends with tobacco and
       provides added mildness.
   K c. Licorice provides a unique flavor and
       sweetens many types of tobacco.
   K e. Licorice helps tobacco retain the correct
       amount of moisture during storage.
5. K a. The automobile industry is a good
       example of an oligopoly, even though
       it gives the appearance of being highly
       competitive.

K b. The breakfast cereal, soap, and cigarette
     industries, although basic to our economy,
     operate as oligopolies.
K e. In the oil industry there are only a few
     producers, so each producer has a fairly
     large share of the sales.

Exercise 5-3 (p. 122)

1. first
2. Individuals continually meet new people of
   opposite sex.
   Living longer can lead to marital discontent.
   Many functions of marriage are fulfilled by
   other institutions.
3. first, second, third
4. living longer
5. minor detail

Exercise 5-4 (p. 124)

1. Later
2. on the other hand
3. Next
4. For example
5. In addition
6. because
7. however
8. Similarly
9. For example
10. because

Exercise 5-5 (p. 125)

1. e   6. h
2. g   7. c
3. j   8. d
4. a   9. b
5. i   10. f

What Have You Learned? (p. 126)

1. main idea
2. key details
3. Transitions
4. *finally*
5. on the other hand

Chapter 6: Understanding Implied Main Ideas

Exercise 6-1 (p. 144)

1. b   4. a
2. b   5. c
3. c

Exercise 6-2 (p. 145)
1. c
2. a
3. c
4. b
5. a

Exercise 6-3 (p. 146)
1. the flu
2. dying
3. in an accident
4. a power outage
5. closed

Exercise 6-4 (p. 147)
1. The two people are involved in an automobile accident.
2. The two people are arguing: The woman is accusing the man of some wrongdoing; the man is not accepting blame.

Exercise 6-5 (p. 150)
1. Topic: Divorce
   Details: one in seven marriages
   one in three marriages
   highest of any major industrialized nation (almost one divorce for every two marriages)
   Implied main idea: divorce rate has increased
2. Topic: Immigration
   Details: population
   rural/urban
   middle
   mortality
   Implied main idea: Immigration

What Have You Learned? (p. 152)
1. implied
2. general/specific
3. important
4. details
5. in your own words

Chapter 7: Keeping Track of Information

Exercise 7-1 (p. 176)
1. money
2. Example 2
3. too much highlighting; wouldn't save time when studying
4. a. anyone on a small income
   b. wealthy people

Exercise 7-2 (p. 178)
Answers may vary.

Exercise 7-3 (p. 181)
I. A.
   3. Two or more children
   B. Households of today
   1. Single parent
   2. No children
   3. Only one person
II. A. Americans stay single longer
   C. Gap between male and female life expectancies
III. B.
   1. More income per person
   2. Need smaller houses, cars, food packages
   3. Spend more on entertainment and fads
   4. Spend more on travel

Exercise 7-4 (p. 185)
Suggestions for Overcoming Procrastination
Clear your desk
Give yourself 5 minutes to start
Divide task into manageable parts
Start somewhere
Recognize when you need more information

   1. a. First   b. Second   c. Next   d. Then
      e. Finally

Exercise 7-5 (p. 185)
Answers for examples may vary.

Exercise 7-6 (p. 187)
A. 1. F
   2. T
   3. T
B. 4. c
   5. a

What Have You Learned? (p. 189)
1. T
2. F
3. T
4. F
5. F
6. T
7. F

Chapter 8: Recognizing the Basic Patterns of Organization

Exercise 8-1 (p. 214)
1. for instance
2. a. low grade on biology lab report
   b. car "dies"

c. argument with a close friend
d. checking account overdrawn
3. first
4. a. new job or career
    b. marriage
    c. divorce
    d. birth of a child
    e. death of someone close
    f. beginning college
5. second
6. for example
7. a. hot kitchen
    b. noisy machine shop
    c. coworkers who don't do their share
8. first
9. for example
10. ask yourself how you can finish a task

Exercise 8-2 (p. 217)

1. partnership
2. used in small businesses; two or more owners; partners establish conditions, contribution of partners, division of profits, authority, duties, and liability (answers may vary)
3. stress
4. yes
5. for example; in addition
6. Term: Small Business Administration
7. a. assists people getting into business
    b. helps them stay in business
    c. helps small firms win federal contracts
    d. acts as a strong advocate for small business
8. no
9. assimilation and accommodation
10. through examples/stories about Harry (answers may vary)

Exercise 8-3 (p. 221)

1. 2   4. 3
    1   2
    4   4
    3   1
2. 3   5. 4
    2   1
    4   3
    1   2
3. 2
    3
    1
    4

Exercise 8-4 (p. 224)

1. b
2. a
3. c
4. First/also/In addition/Last but not least
5. A. The number of such companies has risen
        2. 75 percent had codes in 1970
    B.
        1. They increase public confidence
        3. They improve internal operations
        4. They prescribe a response to unethical behavior

What Have You Learned? (p. 226)

1. patterns of organization
2. definition
3. chronological order
4. listing
5. for instance
6. distinguishing features
7. process
8. next

Chapter 9: Recognizing Comparison/ Contrast and Cause/Effect Patterns

Exercise 9-1 (p. 250)

1. Answers will vary.

Exercise 9-2 (p. 252)

they are very much **alike**
and they are **both** good
They also have **in common**
Another **similarity**
her two brothers are the **same**

Exercise 9-3 (p. 253)

A. that they are very **different**
    system is **unlike**
    In New York, **on the other hand** or **however**
    Another **contrast**
    In New York, **however or on the other hand**
    a major **difference**
    Despite their northern
B. 1. First of all   2. Another   3. Finally

Exercise 9-4 (p. 255)

1. b
2. d
3. *Similarities*
    1. both small

2. both involve face-to-face
   contacts/friendly
3. both important

Answers may vary. Examples are given.

Differences
1. primary are personal and intimate;
   secondary are impersonal
2. secondary more formal
3. secondary come together for specific purpose
4. more time spent in secondary groups
5. primary groups are person-oriented;
   secondary are goal-oriented

Exercise 9-5 (p. 257)
1. mental illness
2. a. physical changes
   b. chemical imbalances
   c. environment/childhood experiences/stress
   d. combination of causes

Answers may vary.

Exercise 9-6 (p. 258)
A. several serious **effects**
   several hours **because of**
   Consequently, those who
   Another **result**, which
   was the main **reason** for
B. 1. car accident
   2. a. two people died
      b. traffic was delayed
      c. people missed the fireworks
      d. speed limit was lowered
   3. yes
   4. a. First b. In addition c. Another d. After

What Have You Learned? (p. 259)
1. cause/effect
2. comparison/contrast
3. topic sentence
4. cause/effect
5. comparison/contrast

Chapter 10: Understanding Inference and the Writer's Purpose

Exercise 10-1 (p. 284)
1. T	6. T
2. F	7. T
3. F	8. T
4. T	9. T
5. F	10. F

Exercise 10-2 (p. 286)
1. c	4. b
2. a	5. d
3. b	

Exercise 10-3 (p. 288)
1. c	4. a
2. d	5. d
3. b	

Exercise 10-4 (p. 290)
1. b	4. d
2. c	5. b
3. a	

Exercise 10-5 (p. 293)
1. request
2. overlook
3. tease
4. glance
5. display
6. gown
7. showy
8. awkward
9. artificial
10. take
11. limousine
12. large
13. dine
14. inquire
15. keepsake

What Have You Learned? (p. 294)
1. c	4. f
2. e	5. d
3. b	6. a

Student Resource Guide A: Understanding Sentences: A Review

Exercise A-1 (p. 317)
1. parents; travel
2. children; learn
3. William Faulkner; wrote
4. Psychologists; are interested
5. patients; may refuse
6. use; is increasing
7. method; is based
8. elements; exist
9. attention; may be defined
10. instructions; are written

Exercise A-2 (p. 320)

1. d   4. b
2. c   5. b
3. a

Exercise A-3 (p. 321)

1. C. personnel office/accepted/I expect
2. C. Computers have become/role/has/not yet been fully explored
3. S. Humankind has inhabited this earth for several million years.
4. S. the Cuban economy depends upon the worldwide demand for sugar.
5. C. We/learn/we are/having other experiences

Exercise A-4 (p. 322)

1. how
2. which
3. why
4. when
5. where

Exercise A-5 (p. 323)

1. Female participation in sports has increased since the 1970s.
2. There is a difference between what are typically thought to be male and female sports.
3. The United States cannot deny the right to vote to anyone who is at least 18 years old.
4. Potential violence is rarely carried out in armed robberies. However, it is this potential violence that allows the robber to attain his/her goal—generally money.
5. According to some researchers, the cause of problem drinking lies in the part played by genetics. Other researchers perceive the cause of problem drinking as an inability to cope with stress.

Student Resource Guide B: Using Your Dictionary: A Review

Exercise B-1 (p. 326)

1. a thing or part having the shape of a curve; a line having no straight part; the act of curving
2. a pitched ball thrown with a spin
3. Bend refers to twisting something that is normally straight.

Exercise B-2 (p. 326)

1. pronoun, adjective, adverb, conjunction
2. preposition, conjunction, verb, noun
3. adjective, adverb, verb, noun/answers may vary
4. noun, adjective, verb, interjection
5. noun, verb, adjective

Exercise B-3 (p. 327)

1. transitive verb
2. less than
3. circa; about; around the time of
4. obscure; obsolete
5. French; France
6. plural

Exercise B-4 (p. 328)

1. commit
2. capture
3. barometer
4. schedule
5. identification
6. indifference
7. learned
8. liquid
9. nuisance
10. pharmacy

Exercise B-5 (p. 329)

1. from Middle English "gingivere," Old English "gingifer," Old French "gingivre," Medieval Latin "gingiver," Latin "zinziberi," Greek "ziggiberis," Prakit "singabera," and Sanskrit "srngaveram"
2. from Latin "tinctus" and Italian "tinto"
3. from Latin "calculare" and Greek "khalix"
4. from Middle English "fantstik," Old French "fantastique," Latin "fantasticus," and Greek "phantastikos"
5. from Middle English "autentik," Old French "autentique, " Latin "authenticus," and Greek "authentikos"

Exercise B-6 (p. 329)

1. a legal title to property held by one party for the benefit of another
2. reasoning from the particular to the general
3. a distinct substance composed of the atoms or ions of two or more elements in definite proportions

4. a preliminary election in which the registered voters of a political party nominate candidates for office
5. a book of original entry in a double-entry system, indicating all transactions and the accounts in which they belong

Exercise B-7 (p. 332)
Answers may vary.

Exercise B-8 (p. 332)
1. slight trace
2. a round in a race
3. courses of action; procedures
4. principal division within a musical symphony
5. hard-surfaced area in front of an airplane hangar

Exercise B-9 (p. 334)
1. crises
2. judgement
3. sur-prise
4. burst
5. criminally

Exercise B-10 (p. 334)
1. Diminutive means unusually small. Petite often applies to a woman's figure and means small and trim.
2. Careless means inattentive or unconcerned, and it can imply negligence. Thoughtless suggests a lack of consideration for others.
3. Odor is a neutral word meaning "smell." Aroma refers to a pleasant odor, often a spicy one.
4. A grin is a broad smile exposing the teeth and a natural expression of happiness. A smirk is an affected, bold smile expressing derision, smugness, or conceit.
5. Hurt refers to physical or mental distress or lessening the worth of something. Damage relates to an injury to one's reputation or status or that decreases the value of property.

Exercise B-11 (p. 335)
1. look down upon; reject; make light of
2. started; began
3. start fresh; improve; make a change for the better
4. on a straight line; by the shortest route

5. promoted to a better position that has less power; promoted to a higher but less desirable position

Student Resource Guide C: Test-Taking Strategies: A Review

Exercise C-1 (p. 343)
1. a
2. d
3. c
4. d
5. c
6. b

Additional Reading Selections
Reading Selection 1
Checking Your Comprehension (p. 350)
1. d
2. c
3. b
4. d
5. a
6. c
7. c
8. a
9. a
10. b

Words in Context (p. 352)
1. protective clothing worn by hospital personnel
2. firm, stubborn, unyielding
3. position
4. meet

Vocabulary Review (p. 353)
1. orderly
2. entrepreneurs
3. intern
4. therapy
5. respiratory

Reading Selection 2
Checking Your Comprehension (p. 357)
1. c
2. b
3. a
4. b
5. a
6. d
7. a
8. d
9. c
10. a

Words in Context (p. 358)
1. cheerful and noisy party
2. got her attention by gesturing
3. looking into
4. position, viewpoint

Vocabulary Review (p. 359)

1. d
2. g
3. e
4. f
5. b
6. h
7. i
8. a
9. c

Reading Selection 3

Checking Your Comprehension (p. 363)

1. a
2. c
3. d
4. b
5. a
6. d
7. a
8. d
9. c
10. a

Words in Context (p. 365)

1. illegal or forbidden goods
2. noise
3. do permanent bodily injury

Vocabulary Review (p. 365)

1. rookie
2. cursory
3. equivalent
4. apprehensive
5. ruckus
6. mace
7. tiers

Reading Selection 4

Checking Your Comprehension (p. 371)

1. b
2. d
3. c
4. c
5. d
6. a
7. a
8. b
9. d
10. c

Words in Context (p. 373)

1. applause given with the audience standing
2. lead into, tempt, attract
3. confused, bewildered

Vocabulary Review (p. 373)

1. g
2. a
3. e
4. b
5. c
6. d
7. f

Reading Selection 5

Checking Your Comprehension (p. 379)

1. c
2. a
3. d
4. a
5. b
6. a
7. c
8. d
9. b
10. b

Words in Context (p. 381)

1. not interesting, not stimulating
2. physically demanding
3. about to happen
4. made fun of
5. telling a story about

Vocabulary Review (p. 381)

1. d
2. e
3. a
4. k
5. c
6. i
7. g
8. b
9. f
10. h
11. l
12. j

Reading Selection 6

Checking Your Comprehension (p. 386)

1. d
2. a
3. c
4. a
5. c
6. d
7. a
8. c
9. a
10. a

Words in Context (p. 388)

1. confusion
2. look at closely
3. high-powered
4. without hesitation, not discouraged

Vocabulary Review (p. 388)

1. apropos
2. mortified
3. gratuitous
4. adroit/persistent
5. Civilities
6. dubious
7. comme il faut
8. persistent
9. paraplegic
10. schizophrenia

11. conciliatory
12. unsolicited gesture
13. mediation
14. mediating
15. flagellated
16. haughtier

Reading Selection 7

Checking Your Comprehension (p. 393)

1. a	6. a
2. d	7. d
3. c	8. a
4. d	9. b
5. c	10. a

Words in Context (p. 394)

1. grow, thrive
2. rise above, go beyond
3. other choice, substitute

Vocabulary Review (p. 395)

1. h	6. d
2. f	7. e
3. g	8. i
4. b	9. c
5. a	

Reading Selection 8

Checking Your Comprehension (p. 399)

1. b	6. b
2. d	7. d
3. a	8. b
4. a	9. d
5. c	10. b

Words in Context (p. 401)

1. flock or group of birds in flight
2. pattern, arrangement
3. referring to

Vocabulary Review (p. 401)

1. b	6. d
2. i	7. a
3. e	8. h
4. c	9. g
5. f	

Reading Selection 9

Checking Your Comprehension (p. 404)

1. c	6. b
2. d	7. a
3. b	8. a
4. a	9. c
5. d	10. c

Words in Context (p. 406)

1. name, symbol, or trademark
2. made part of
3. imitation
4. aspect, element

Vocabulary Review (p. 406)

1. d	5. c
2. f	6. e
3. a	7. b
4. g	

Credits

Photo Credits

Page xxii (left): Michael Krasowitz/FPG International LLC; **xxii (right):** Jeff Greenberg/Photo Researchers, Inc.; **19:** Karl Hentz/Imagebank; **30:** Patrik Giardino/Corbis Images; **50:** Jon Freilich/AP/Wide World Photos; **56:** Stephen Frisch/Stock, Boston, Inc.; **78:** Joseph Van Os/Imagebank; **86:** PhotoFest; **108:** Universal Press Syndicate; **116:** Romilly Lockyer/Imagebank; **135:** Billy E. Barnes/Stock, Boston Inc.; **142:** © The New Yorker Collection 1999 Arnie Levin from cartoonBank.com. All Rights Reserved; **146:** Index Stock Imagery; **147:** Bob Daemmrich/The Image Works; **166:** Jeff Isaac Greenberg/Photo Researchers, Inc.; **210 (top):** Bonnie Kamin/PhotoEdit; **210 (bottom):** Leslie Barbara/FPG, International LLC; **239:** Morton Beebe, S.F./Corbis Images; **248:** Novastock/Photo Researchers, Inc.; **274:** Jerry Wachter/Photo Researchers, Inc.; **280:** Paul Schutzer/Time Pix; **303:** Reuters New Media Inc./Corbis Images.

Text Credits

Chapter 1

Joseph A. DeVito, *Human Communication*, Seventh Edition. Copyright © 1997 by Addison-Wesley Longman Educational Publishers.

Michael R. Solomon, Elnora W. Stuart, *Marketing*, Second Edition, pp. 161–162. Copyright © 2000 by Prentice-Hall.

Joseph A. DeVito, *Messages: Building Interpersonal Communication Skills*, Fourth Edition, p. 100. Copyright © 1999 by Addison-Wesley Longman Publishers, Inc.

DeVry Institute, "Survival of the Fittest," from *Directions*, Winter/Spring 1997. Reprinted by permission of DeVry, Inc.

Chapter 2

Alex Thio, *Sociology*, Fifth Edition, p. 235. Copyright © 1998 by Addison-Wesley Longman Publishers, Inc.

Seaborn "Beck" Weathers, "A Night Out in the Death Zone," *Everest: Mountain Without Mercy*, edited by Broughton Coburn, Tim Cahill (Introduction), David Breashears. Copyright © 1997 by the National Geographic Society.

Chapter 3

Dan Greenburg, "The Dolphin Affair," *Modern Maturity*, May/June 1998. Copyright © 1998 by Dan Greenburg.

Chapter 4

Excerpts from Curtis O. Byer, Louis W. Shainberg (Contributor), *Living Well: Health in Your Hands*, pp. 256 and 289. Copyright © 1995 by Addison-Wesley Longman Publishers, Inc.

K. Warner Schaie and James Geiwitz, *Adult Development and Aging*, pp. 371–372. Copyright © 1972 by Little, Brown, & Company.

Richard George, *The New Consumer Survival Kit*, p. 212. Copyright © 1978 by Little, Brown, & Company.

Warren Kendall Agee, Phillip H. Ault, Edwin Emery, *Introduction to Mass Communication*, Twelfth Edition, p. 153. Copyright © 1997 by Addison-Wesley Longman Publishers, Inc.

David Hicks and Margaret Gwynne, *Cultural Anthropology* Second Edition, p. 270. Copyright © 1996 by HarperCollins Publishers.

Joseph A. DeVito, *Human Communication*, Seventh Edition, pp. 78, 180. Copyright © 1997 by Addison-Wesley Longman Educational Publishers.

Bob Weinstein, *Jobs for the 21st Century*, p. 118. Copyright © 1983 by Macmillan.

Joyce Brothers, "What Dirty Words Really Mean," *Good Housekeeping*, May 1973.

Jean L. Weirich, *Personal Financial Management*, p. 155. Copyright © 1983 by Little, Brown, & Company.

Excerpts from John Dorfman, *Well Being: An Introduction of Health*, pp. 27, 263. Copyright © 1980 by Scott Foresman and Company.

Edward S. Fox, Edward W. Wheatley, *Modern Marketing*. Copyright © 1978 by Scott Foresman, p. 142.

Roger LeRoy Miller, *Economics Today*, Eighth Edition, p. 84. Copyright © 1984 by HarperCollins Publishers.

Christopher M. Anson, Robert A. Schwegler, *Longman Handbook for Readers and Writers*, p. 78. Copyright © 1999 by Addison-Wesley Longman Publishers, Inc.

Joseph A. DeVito, *The Elements of Public Speaking*, Seventh Edition, p. 164. Copyright © 2000 by Addison-Wesley Longman Publishers, Inc.

Spencer A. Rathus, *Human Sexuality*, Fourth Edition, pp. 189, 221. Copyright © 2000 by Prentice-Hall Publishers.

Wendy G. Lehnert, *Light on the Internet*, pp. 53, 55. Copyright © 1999 by Addison-Wesley Longman Publishers, Inc.

Deborah Tannen, Ph.D., "Don't Ask" from *You Just Don't Understand* by Deborah Tannen, Ph.D. Copyright © 1990 by William Morrow and Company.

Chapter 5

Margaret Anderson Gwynne, David B. Hicks, *Cultural Anthropology*, Second Edition, p. 258. Copyright © 1996 by HarperCollins Publishers.

Richard George, *The New Consumer Survival Kit*, p. 114. Copyright © 1978 by Little, Brown, & Company.

James M. Henslin, *Essentials of Psychology*, Second Edition, p. 239. Copyright © 1997 Prentice-Hall Publishers.

Ricky W. Griffin and Ronald J. Ebert, *Business*, Fifth Edition, p. 43. Copyright © 1999 by Prentice-Hall Publishers.

Richard Koone, "How to Ace a Job Interview," *Training and Development*, Volume 51, Number 3, Copyright © 1997.

Chapter 6

Excerpts from Michael R. Solomon, *Consumer Behavior, Buying, Having, and Being*, Fourth Edition, pp. 48, 49–50. Copyright © 1999 by Prentice-Hall Publishers.

James William Coleman, Donald R. Cressey, *Social Problems*, Sixth Edition, p. 130. Copyright © 1996 by Addison-Wesley Longman Publishers, Inc.

Nora Newcombe, *Child Development*, p. 354. Copyright © 1996 by Addison-Wesley Longman Publishers, Inc.

Frans Gerritsen, *Theory and Practice of Color*, p. 9. Copyright © 1975 by Van Nostrand Publishers.

From Jack Schutlz and Ian Baldwin, "Trees Talk to One Another," *Science Digest*, p. 47, January 1984. Copyright © 1984 by *Science Digest*.

From John Naisbitt, *Megatrends*, p. 23. Copyright © 1982 by Warner Books.

Wendy G. Lehnert, *Internet 101: A Beginner's Guide to the Internet and World Wide Web*, p. 95. Copyright © 1999 by Addison-Wesley Longman Publishers, Inc.

Roger LeRoy Miller, *Economics Today*, Eighth Edition, pp. 185, 513. Copyright © 1984 by HarperCollins Publishers.

Patsy Neal, "My Grandmother, the Bag Lady" by Patsy Neal. Patsy Neal is Wellness Coordinator at Mission St. Joseph's Health System in Asheville, North Carolina. Neal has written 7 books. She has also won four Freedom Foundation Awards for essays, and was a three-time All-American basketball player. Neal was captain of the US Team in the 1964 World Basketball Tournament in Peru, South America, and was inducted into the AAU Women's Basketball Hall of Fame in 1993.

Kim McLarin, "Primary Colors." National Creative Management, Inc., copyright © 1998 by Kim McLarin.

Chapter 7

Excerpts from Curtis O. Byer, Louis W. Shainberg, *Living Well: Health in Your Hands*, pp. 78–79. Copyright © 1995 by Addison-Wesley Longman Publishers, Inc.

Thomas C. Kinnear, Kenneth L. Bernhardt, Kathleen A. Krentler, *Principles of Marketing*, Fourth Edition, pp. 39–40, 132. Copyright © 1995 by HarperCollins Publishers.

Alex Thio, *Sociology*, Fifth Edition, p. 534. Copyright © 1998 by Addison-Wesley Longman Publishers, Inc.

Neil A. Campbell, et al., *Biology*, Third Edition, p. 430. Copyright © Addison-Wesley Longman Publishers, Inc.

Bruce E. Gronbeck, et al., *Principles of Speech Communication*, Twelfth Edition, p. 302. Copyright © 1995 HarperCollins Publishers.

Laura Uba, Karen Huang, *Psychology*, p. 148. Copyright © 1999 by Addison-Wesley Longman Publishers, Inc.

"Don't Be Blinded by Road Rage." Copyright © Allstate Insurance Company.

Excerpts from Michael R. Solomon, *Consumer Behavior, Buying, Having, and Being*, Fourth Edition, pp. 252–253. Copyright © 1999 by Prentice-Hall Publishers.

Excerpts from Rebecca Donatelle, *Health: The Basics*, Fourth Edition, pp. 99, 213. Copyright © 2001 Allyn and Bacon Publishers.

From: "School's Out for 98? But This is Only April?" from *USA Today*, April 16, 1998. Copyright © 1998 by *USA Today*.

Chapter 8

Sydney B. Newell, *Chemistry: An Introduction*, p. 11. Copyright © 1980 by Little, Brown, & Company.

Laura Uba, Karen Huang, *Psychology*, p. 483. Copyright © 1999 by Addison-Wesley Longman Publishers, Inc.

Excerpts from Pickle and Abrahamson, *Introduction to Business*, pp. 40, 119. Copyright © 1987 by Scott Foresman and Company.

Carole Wade and Carol Tavris, *Psychology*, Fifth Edition, p. 499. Copyright © Addison-Wesley Longman Publishers, Inc.

Adapted from William M. Kephart, Davor Jedlicka, *The Family, Society, and the Individual*, pp. 332–333. Copyright © 1991 by HarperCollins Publishers.

Richard Weaver, *Understanding Personal Communication*, p. 123. Copyright © 1987 by Scott Foresman and Company.

Robert A. Wallace, *Biology*, Seventh Edition, p. 572. Copyright © 1998 Addison Wesley-Longman Publishers, Inc.

James M. Henslin, *Essentials of Psychology*, Second Edition, p. 272. Copyright © 1997 Prentice-Hall Publishers.

John V. Thill, Courtland L. Bovee, *Excellence in Business Communication*, Fourth Edition, p. 79. Copyright © 1999 by Addison-Wesley Longman Publishers, Inc.

Joseph A. DeVito, *The Elements of Public Speaking*, Seventh Edition, p. 164. Copyright © 2000 by Addison-Wesley Longman Publishers, Inc.

Ricky W. Griffin, Ronald J. Ebert, *Business*, Fifth Edition, p. 83. Copyright © 1999 Addison-Wesley Longman Publishers, Inc.

Excerpts from World Book, Volume 13, pp. 474b, 795, 796. Copyright © 1985 World Book, Inc.

Adapted from Paul G. Hewitt, *Conceptual Physics*, Eighth Edition, p. 96. Copyright © Addison-Wesley Longman Publishers, Inc.

Adapted from Coah, et al., *Tourism: The Business of Travel*, Chapter 9. Copyright © by Prentice-Hall.

Diane Cyr, "How to Mange Your Doctor." Copyright © 1998 by Diane Cyr.

Chapter 9

Adapted from Paul G. Hewitt, *Conceptual Physics*, Eighth Edition, p. 96. Copyright © Addison-Wesley Longman Publishers, Inc.

Excerpts from J. Ross Eshleman, Barbara G. Cashion, *Sociology: An Introduction*, Second Edition, pp. 88 and 583. Copyright © 1985 by Little, Brown, & Company.

Joseph A. DeVito, *Messages: Building Interpersonal Communciations Skills*, Third Edition, p. 153. Copyright © 1997 Addison Wesley Longman Publishers, Inc.

John D. Daniels, Lee H. Radebaugh, *International Business Environments and Operations*, Eighth Edition, p. 679. Copyright © 1998 by Addison-Wesely, Longman Publishers, Inc.

Thomas C. Kinnear, Kenneth L. Bernhardt, Kathleen A. Krentler, *Principles of Marketing*, Fourth Edition, p. 218. Copyright © 1995 by HarperCollins Publishers.

Rich Weiss, "Acupuncture" from *Health*. Copyright © 1995 by *Health*.

Carole Wade and Carol Tavris, *Psychology*, Fifth Edition, p. 494. Copyright © Addison-Wesley Longman Publishers, Inc.

Robert A. Wallace, *Biology*, Seventh Edition, p. 572. Copyright © 1998 Addison Wesley-Longman Publishers, Inc.

Chapter 10

From *Paul Harvey's The Rest of the Story* by Paul Arandt, p. 116. Edited and compiled by Lynne Harvey. Copyright © 1977 by Doubleday.

Richard Weaver, *Understanding Personal Communication*, p. 291. Copyright © 1987 by Scott Foresman and Company.

From *Know Your Rights* by Lewis Katz, p. 54. Copyright © 1993 by Banks Baldwin Law.

From *Legends, Lies, and Cherished Myths of American History* by Richard Shenkman, pp. 37, 38. Copyright © 1988 by William Morrow.

From "The Father and His Daughter" from *Further Fables of Our Time* by James Thurber, pp. 51–53. Copyright © 1984 by Simon and Schuster.

Robert A. Wallace, *Biology: The World of Life*, p. 271. Copyright © 1986 by Scott Foresman and Company.

From *Seasons of Shame: The New Violence in Sports* by Robert C. Yeager, p. 6. Copyright © 1979 by McGraw-Hill.

From *The Rainmaker's Dog* by Cynthia Dresser, p. 110–111. Copyright © 1999 by Cambridge University Press.

From Dorothy Conniff "What's Best for the Child?" from *The Progressive*, November. Copyright © 1988 by *The Progressive*.

From McMiller "Stiff Laws Nab Deadbeats" from *USA Today*, August 16, 1995. Copyright © 1995 by *USA Today*.

From Roger Swardson "Greeting from the Electronic Plantation" from *City Pages*, October 21, 1992. Copyright © 1992 by *City Pages*.

Adapted from Mary Bricker-Jenkins, *The Strengths in Social Work Practice*, Second Edition. Copyright © 1997 Addison-Wesley Longman Publishers, Inc.

Student Resource Guide B

Dictionary Entry for Curve, Pronunciation Key, from American Heritage Dictionary of the English Language, Third Edition, 1996. Copyright © 1996 by Houghton Mifflin.

Dictionary Entry for Green, from Webster's New Worlds Dictionary, Second Edition, 1986. Copyright © 1986 by Simon and Schuster.

Dictionary Entry for Oblique, from American Heritage Dictionary of the English Language, New College Edition, 1980. Copyright © 1980 by Houghton Mifflin.

Additional Readings

Excerpt from: *Gifted Hands: The Ben Carson Story* by Ben Carson with Cecil Murphey, p. 115–117. Copyright © 1990 by HarperCollins Publishers.

Excerpt from: *Wouldn't Take Nothing for My Journey Now* by Maya Angelou. Copyright © 1993 by Maya Angelou.

From "She Said Yes! She Said Yes! She Said Yes!" by Michael Kernan from the *Smithsonian*, February 1997. Copyright © 1997 by the *Smithsonian*.

From "Hispanic USA: The Conveyor-Belt Ladies" by Rose del Castillo Guilbault as appeared in the *San Francisco Chronicle*, April 15, 1990.

From "A Day on Wheels" by Cheryl A. Davis as appeared in *The Progressive*, 1987.

From "Peacemaker" by Anita Merina, *NEA Today*, February 1996, Vol. 14, No. 6.

From William Least Heat Moon, *Blue Highways: A Journey into America*. Copyright © 1982 by Little, Brown, & Company.

Excerpts from Joseph A. DeVito, *Human Communication*, Seventh Edition. Copyright © 1997 by Addison-Wesley Longman Publishers, Inc.

Index